CIMA

Paper F3

Financial Strategy

Study Text

CIMA PUBLISHING

WORKING TOGETHER FOR YOU

ELSEVIER

KAPLAN PUBLISHING

CIMA Publishing is an imprint of Elsevier
The Boulevard, Langford Lane, Kidlington, Oxford, OX5 1GB, UK
225 Wyman Street, Waltham, MA 02451, USA
Kaplan Publishing UK, Unit 2 The Business Centre, Molly Millars Lane, Wokingham, Berkshire RG41 2QZ

British Library Cataloguing in Publication Data
A catalogue record for this book is available from the British Library

ISBN 978 0 85732 463 4

Printed and bound in Great Britain

11 12 11 10 9 8 7 6 5 4 3 2 1

Contents

chapter

Intro

Paper Introduction

How to Use the Materials

These Official CIMA learning materials brought to you by Elsevier/CIMA Publishing and Kaplan Publishing have been carefully designed to make your learning experience as easy as possible and to give you the best chances of success in your *'Financial Strategy'* exam.

The product range contains a number of features to help you in the study process. They include:

- a detailed explanation of all syllabus areas;
- extensive 'practical' materials;
- generous question practice, together with full solutions;
- an exam preparation section, including a suggested approach on how to tacke the pre-seen information, both before and during the exam.

This Study Text has been designed with the needs of home-study and distance-learning candidates in mind. Such students require very full coverage of the syllabus topics, and also the facility to undertake extensive question practice. However, the Study Text is also ideal for fully taught courses.

This main body of the text is divided into a number of chapters, each of which is organised on the following pattern:

- *Detailed learning outcomes* expected after your studies of the chapter are complete. You should assimilate these before beginning detailed work on the chapter, so that you can appreciate where your studies are leading.
- *Step-by-step topic coverage*. This is the heart of each chapter, containing detailed explanatory text supported where appropriate by worked examples and exercises. You should work carefully through this section, ensuring that you understand the material being explained and can tackle the examples and exercises successfully. Remember that in many cases knowledge is cumulative: if you fail to digest earlier material thoroughly, you may struggle to understand later chapters.

- *Activities*. Some chapters are illustrated by more practical elements, such as comments and questions designed to stimulate discussion.
- *Question practice*. The test of how well you have learned the material is your ability to tackle exam style questions. Make a serious attempt at producing your own answers, but at this stage do not be too concerned about attempting the questions in exam conditions. In particular, it is more important to absorb the material thoroughly by completing a full solution than to observe the time limits that would apply in the actual exam.
- *Solutions*. Avoid the temptation merely to 'audit' the solutions provided. It is an illusion to think that this provides the same benefits as you would gain from a serious attempt of your own. However, if you are struggling to get started on a question you should read the introductory guidance provided at the beginning of the solution, where provided, and then make your own attempt before referring back to the full solution.

Having worked through the chapters you are ready to begin your final preparations for the examination. The final two chapters of this Study Text provide you with the guidance you need. They include the following features:

- How to use the pre-seen information and prepare for the exam.
- Guidance on how to tackle the exam itself.
- An exam standard set of pre-seen information, with detailed analysis and example requirements and answers.
- Revision questions. These are exam standard and should be tacked in exam conditions, especially as regards the time allocation.
- Solutions to the revision questions.
- A sample paper that you can attempt under exam conditions, along with the relevant answers.

You should plan to attempt the sample paper just before the date of the real exam. By this stage your revision should be complete and you should be able to attempt the sample paper within the time constraints of the real exam.

If you work conscientiously through the official CIMA Study Text according to the guidelines above you will be giving yourself an excellent chance of exam success. Good luck with your studies!

Icon Explanations

Definition – these sections explain important areas of knowledge which must be understood and reproduced in an exam environment.

Key Point – identifies topics which are key to success and are often examined.

Supplementary reading – identifies a more detailed explanation of key terms, these sections will help to provide a deeper understanding of core areas. Reference to this text is vital when self studying.

Test Your Understanding – following key points and definitions are exercises which give the opportunity to assess the understanding of these core areas.

Illustration – to help develop an understanding of particular topics. The illustrative exercises are useful in preparing for the Test your understanding exercises.

Exclamation Mark – this symbol signifies a topic which can be more difficult to understand, when reviewing these areas care should be taken.

Study technique

Passing exams is partly a matter of intellectual ability, but however accomplished you are in that respect you can improve your chances significantly by the use of appropriate study and revision techniques. In this section we briefly outline some tips for effective study during the earlier stages of your approach to the exam. Later in the text we mention some techniques that you will find useful at the revision stage.

Planning

To begin with, formal planning is essential to get the best return from the time you spend studying. Estimate how much time in total you are going to need for each subject you are studying.

Remember that you need to allow time for revision as well as for initial study of the material. You may find it helpful to read "Pass First Time!" second edition by David R. Harris ISBN 978-1-85617-798-6. This book will provide you with proven study techniques. Chapter by chapter it covers the building blocks of successful learning and examination techniques. This is the ultimate guide to passing your CIMA exams, written by a past CIMA examiner and shows you how to earn all the marks you deserve, and explains how to avoid the most common pitfalls. You may also find "The E Word: Kaplan's Guide to Passing Exams" by Stuart Pedley-Smith ISBN: 978-0-85732-205-0 helpful. Stuart Pedley-Smith is a senior lecturer at Kaplan Financial and a qualified accountant specialising in financial management. His natural curiosity and wider interests have led him to look beyond the technical content of financial management to the processes and journey that we call education. He has become fascinated by the whole process of learning and the exam skills and techniques that contribute towards success in the classroom. This book is for anyone who has to sit an exam and wants to give themselves a better chance of passing. It is easy to read, written in a common sense style and full of anecdotes, facts, and practical tips. It also contains synopses of interviews with people involved in the learning and examining process.

With your study material before you, decide which chapters you are going to study in each week, and which weeks you will devote to revision and final question practice.

Prepare a written schedule summarising the above and stick to it!

It is essential to know your syllabus. As your studies progress you will become more familiar with how long it takes to cover topics in sufficient depth. Your timetable may need to be adapted to allocate enough time for the whole syllabus.

Students are advised to refer to the notice of examinable legislation published regularly in CIMA's magazine (Financial Management), the students e-newsletter (Velocity) and on the CIMA website, to ensure they are up-to-date.

Tips for effective studying

(1) Aim to find a quiet and undisturbed location for your study, and plan as far as possible to use the same period of time each day. Getting into a routine helps to avoid wasting time. Make sure that you have all the materials you need before you begin so as to minimise interruptions.

(2) Store all your materials in one place, so that you do not waste time searching for items around your accommodation. If you have to pack everything away after each study period, keep them in a box, or even a suitcase, which will not be disturbed until the next time.

(3) Limit distractions. To make the most effective use of your study periods you should be able to apply total concentration, so turn off all entertainment equipment, set your phones to message mode, and put up your 'do not disturb' sign.

(4) Your timetable will tell you which topic to study. However, before diving in and becoming engrossed in the finer points, make sure you have an overall picture of all the areas that need to be covered by the end of that session. After an hour, allow yourself a short break and move away from your Study Text. With experience, you will learn to assess the pace you need to work at.

(5) Work carefully through a chapter, making notes as you go. When you have covered a suitable amount of material, vary the pattern by attempting a practice question. When you have finished your attempt, make notes of any mistakes you made, or any areas that you failed to cover or covered more briefly.

(6) Make notes as you study, and discover the techniques that work best for you. Your notes may be in the form of lists, bullet points, diagrams, summaries, 'mind maps', or the written word, but remember that you will need to refer back to them at a later date, so they must be intelligible. If you are on a taught course, make sure you highlight any issues you would like to follow up with your lecturer.

(7) Organise your notes. Make sure that all your notes, calculations etc can be effectively filed and easily retrieved later.

Structure of subjects and learning outcomes

Each subject within the syllabus is divided into a number of broad syllabus topics. The topics contain one or more lead learning outcomes, related component learning outcomes and indicative knowledge content.

A learning outcome has two main purposes:

(a) To define the skill or ability that a well prepared candidate should be able to exhibit in the examination

(b) To demonstrate the approach likely to be taken in examination questions

The learning outcomes are part of a hierarchy of learning objectives. The verbs used at the beginning of each learning outcome relate to a specific learning objective e.g.

"Evaluate the proposed strategy to expand into the North American market."

The verb **'evaluate'** indicates a level five learning objective.

These verbs are outlined in the first chapter of the text.

PAPER F3
FINANCIAL STRATEGY

Syllabus overview

Paper F3 deals with the key elements in designing and managing the organisation's financial strategy, in the context of contributing to achieving the organisation's objectives and within its external constraints, such as the general regulatory and investment environment. The features and implications of the full range of major financing instruments are covered. A broad range of types of investment decision is also covered and it is recognised throughout that such decisions need to take account of broader strategic issues as well the financial analysis.

Syllabus structure

The syllabus comprises the following topics and study weightings:

A	Formulation of Financial Strategy	25%
B	Financing Decisions	30%
C	Investment Decisions and Project Control	45%

Assessment strategy

There will be a written examination paper of three hours, plus 20 minutes of pre-examination question paper reading time. The examination paper will have the following sections:

Section A – 50 marks
A maximum of four compulsory questions, totalling fifty marks, all relating to a pre-seen case study and further new un-seen case material provided within the examination.

(***Note:*** The pre-seen case study is common to all three of the strategic level papers at each examination sitting i.e. Paper E3, P3 and F3).

Section B – 50 marks
Two questions, from a choice of three, each worth twenty five marks. Short scenarios will be given, to which some or all questions relate.

F3 – A. FORMULATION OF FINANCIAL STRATEGY (25%)

Learning outcomes **On completion of their studies students should be able to:**		**Indicative syllabus content**
Lead	**Component**	
1. discuss potential strategic financial objectives, and the relationships among and constraints on the elements of financial strategy.	(a) discuss the potential strategic financial objectives of an organisation; (b) discuss the interrelationships between decisions concerning investment, financing and dividends; (c) discuss the impact of internal and external constraints on financial strategy, including the impact of regulation on business combinations.	• The financial and non-financial objectives of different organisations (e.g. value for money, maximising shareholder wealth, providing a surplus). • The three key decisions of financial management (investment, financing and dividend) and their links. • Benefits of matching characteristics of investment and financing in the longer term, (e.g. in cross-border investment) and in short-term hedging strategies. • Considerations in the formulation of dividend policy and dividend decisions, including meeting the cash needs of the business. • External constraints on financial strategy (e.g. funding, regulatory bodies, investor relations, strategy, and economic factors). • Developing financial strategy in the context of regulatory requirements (e.g. price and service controls exercised by industry regulators) and international operations. • The implications of regulation for business combinations. (***Note:*** Detailed knowledge of the City Code and EU competition rules will not be tested).

Learning outcomes **On completion of their studies students should be able to:**		**Indicative syllabus content**
Lead	**Component**	
2. evaluate the financial strategies and objectives of an organisation and the extent of their attainment.	(a) identify an organisation's objectives in financial terms; (b) evaluate the attainment of an organisation's financial objectives; (c) evaluate current and forecast performance taking account of potential variations in economic and business factors; (d) evaluate alternative financial strategies for an organisation taking account of external assessment of the organisation by financiers and other stakeholders, including likely changes to such assessment in the light of developments in reporting.	• The financial objectives of an organisation and economic forces affecting its financial plans (e.g. interest, inflation and exchange rates). • Assessing attainment of financial objectives. • Use of financial analysis in the external assessment of a company (e.g. in assessing creditworthiness and compliance with financing covenants). • Modelling and forecasting cash flows and financial statements based on expected values for economic variables (e.g. interest rates) and business variables (e.g. volume and margins) over a number of years. • Analysis of sensitivity to changes in expected values in the above models and forecasts. • Assessing the implications for shareholder value of alternative financial strategies, including dividend policy. (***Note:*** Modigliani and Miller's theory of dividend irrelevancy will be tested in broad terms. The mathematical proof of the model will not be required, but some understanding of the graphical method is expected). • The lender's assessment of creditworthiness. • Current and emerging issues in financial reporting (e.g. proposals to amend or introduce new accounting standards) and in other forms of external reporting (e.g. environmental accounting).

F3 – B. FINANCING DECISIONS (30%)

Learning outcomes On completion of their studies students should be able to:		**Indicative syllabus content**
Lead	**Component**	
1. evaluate the financing requirements of an organisation and strategies for meeting those requirements.	(a) analyse the short and long-term financing requirements of an organisation; (b) evaluate alternative methods of meeting financing requirements, taking account of the implications for the organisation's financial statements, its tax position and financial stakeholders; (c) evaluate the weighted average cost of capital of an organisation; (d) recommend methods of funding specific investments, taking account of basic tax considerations and risk exposures (to interest and currency exchange rate fluctuations); (e) recommend optimal strategies for the management of working capital and satisfaction of longer term financing requirements.	• Identifying financing requirements (both in respect of domestic and international operations) and the impacts of different types of finance on models and forecasts of performance and position. • Working capital management strategies. (***Note:*** No detailed testing of cash and stock management models will be set since these are covered at a lower level within the syllabus). • Types and features of domestic and international long-term finance: share capital (ordinary and preference shares, warrants), long-term debt (bank borrowing and forms of securitised debt, e.g. convertibles) and finance leases, and methods of issuing securities. • The operation of stock exchanges (e.g. how share prices are determined, what causes share prices to rise or fall, and the efficient market hypothesis). (***Note:*** No detailed knowledge of any specific country's stock exchange will be tested). • The impact of changing capital structure on the market value of a company. (***Note:*** An understanding of Modigliani and Miller's theory of gearing, with and without taxes, will be expected, but proof of their theory will not be examined). • The capital asset pricing model (CAPM): calculation of the cost of equity using the dividend growth model (knowledge of methods of calculating and estimating dividend growth will be expected), the ability to gear and un-gear betas and comparison to the arbitrage pricing model. • The ideas of diversifiable risk (unsystematic risk) and systematic risk. (***Note:*** Use of the two-asset portfolio formula will not be tested). • The cost of redeemable and irredeemable debt, including the tax shield on debt. • The weighted average cost of capital (WACC): calculation, interpretation and uses. • The lease or buy decision (with both operating and finance leases).

Learning outcomes On completion of their studies students should be able to:		Indicative syllabus content
Lead	**Component**	
		• Criteria for selecting sources of finance, including finance for international investments. • The effect of financing decisions on balance sheet structure and on ratios of interest to investors and other financiers (gearing, earnings per share, price-earnings ratio, dividend yield, dividend cover gearing, interest cover).
2. discuss the treasury function.	(a) discuss the role and management of the treasury function.	• The role of the treasury function in terms of setting corporate objectives, liquidity management, funding management, and currency management. • The advantages and disadvantages of establishing treasury departments as profit centres or cost centres, and their control.

F3 – C. INVESTMENT DECISIONS AND PROJECT CONTROL (45%)

Learning outcomes **On completion of their studies students should be able to:**		**Indicative syllabus content**
Lead	**Component**	
1. evaluate investment choices.	(a) analyse relevant costs, benefits and risks of an investment project; (b) evaluate investment projects (domestic and international), including their financial and strategic implications, taking account of potential variations in business and economic factors; (c) evaluate potential investments in organisations of different types and intangible assets; (d) recommend investment choice in the presence of capital rationing and/or real options.	• Identification of a project's relevant costs (e.g. infrastructure, marketing and human resource development needs), benefits (including incremental effects on other activities as well as direct cash flows) and risks (i.e. financial and non-financial, including reputation risk arising from ethical considerations and risks of legal change or uncertainty). • Linking investments with customer requirements and product/service design. • Linking investment in IS/IT with strategic, operational and control needs (particularly where risks and benefits are difficult to quantify). • Calculation of a project's net present value and internal rate of return, including techniques for dealing with cash flows denominated in a foreign currency and use of the weighted average cost of capital. • The modified internal rate of return based on a project's "terminal value" (reflecting an assumed reinvestment rate). • The effects of taxation (including foreign direct and withholding taxes), potential changes in economic factors (inflation, interest and exchange rates) and potential restrictions on remittances on these calculations. • Recognising risk using the certainty equivalent method (when given a risk free rate and certainty equivalent values). • Adjusted present value. (***Note:*** The two step method may be tested for debt introduced permanently and debt in place for the duration of the project). • Valuation bases for assets (e.g. historic cost, replacement cost and realisable value), earnings (e.g. price/earnings multiples and earnings yield) and cash flows (e.g. discounted cash flow, dividend yield and the dividend growth model). • The strengths and weaknesses of each valuation method and when each is most suitable, e.g. by reference to type of investee organisation (service, capital intensive etc). • Forms of intangible asset (including intellectual property rights, brands etc). and methods of valuation.

Learning outcomes On completion of their studies students should be able to:		Indicative syllabus content
Lead	**Component**	
		• Application of the efficient market hypothesis to business valuations. • Selection of an appropriate cost of capital for use in valuation. • Capital investment real options (i.e. to make follow-on investment, abandon or wait). • Single period capital rationing for divisible and non-divisible projects. (***Note:*** Multi-period rationing will not be tested).
2. evaluate opportunities for merger, acquisition and divestment.	(a) evaluate the financial and strategic implications of proposals for mergers and acquisitions, including their terms, post-transaction values and processes, and exit strategies; (b) evaluate the financial and strategic implications of demergers and divestments.	• Recognition of the interests of different stakeholder groups in mergers, acquisitions and company valuations. • The reasons for merger or acquisitions (e.g. synergistic benefits). • Forms of consideration and terms for acquisitions (e.g. cash, shares, convertibles and earn-out arrangements), and their financial effects. • The post-merger or post-acquisition integration process (e.g. management transfer and merger of systems). • The function/role of management buy-outs and venture capitalists. • Types of exit strategy and their implications. • The reasons for (e.g. strategic change, opportunity cost of investment) and mechanisms of demerger or divestment.
3. evaluate procedures for investment projects.	(a) evaluate procedures for the implementation and control of investment projects.	• Project implementation and control in the conceptual stage, the development stage, the construction stage and initial manufacturing/operating stage. • Post completion audit of investment projects.

MATHS TABLES AND FORMULAE

Present value table

Present value of 1.00 unit of currency, that is $(1 + r)^{-n}$ where r = interest rate; n = number of periods until payment or receipt.

Periods	Interest rates (*r*)									
(*n*)	1%	2%	3%	4%	5%	6%	7%	8%	9%	10%
1	0.990	0.980	0.971	0.962	0.952	0.943	0.935	0.926	0.917	0.909
2	0.980	0.961	0.943	0.925	0.907	0.890	0.873	0.857	0.842	0.826
3	0.971	0.942	0.915	0.889	0.864	0.840	0.816	0.794	0.772	0.751
4	0.961	0.924	0.888	0.855	0.823	0.792	0.763	0.735	0.708	0.683
5	0.951	0.906	0.863	0.822	0.784	0.747	0.713	0.681	0.650	0.621
6	0.942	0.888	0.837	0.790	0.746	0.705	0.666	0.630	0.596	0.564
7	0.933	0.871	0.813	0.760	0.711	0.665	0.623	0.583	0.547	0.513
8	0.923	0.853	0.789	0.731	0.677	0.627	0.582	0.540	0.502	0.467
9	0.914	0.837	0.766	0.703	0.645	0.592	0.544	0.500	0.460	0.424
10	0.905	0.820	0.744	0.676	0.614	0.558	0.508	0.463	0.422	0.386
11	0.896	0.804	0.722	0.650	0.585	0.527	0.475	0.429	0.388	0.350
12	0.887	0.788	0.701	0.625	0.557	0.497	0.444	0.397	0.356	0.319
13	0.879	0.773	0.681	0.601	0.530	0.469	0.415	0.368	0.326	0.290
14	0.870	0.758	0.661	0.577	0.505	0.442	0.388	0.340	0.299	0.263
15	0.861	0.743	0.642	0.555	0.481	0.417	0.362	0.315	0.275	0.239
16	0.853	0.728	0.623	0.534	0.458	0.394	0.339	0.292	0.252	0.218
17	0.844	0.714	0.605	0.513	0.436	0.371	0.317	0.270	0.231	0.198
18	0.836	0.700	0.587	0.494	0.416	0.350	0.296	0.250	0.212	0.180
19	0.828	0.686	0.570	0.475	0.396	0.331	0.277	0.232	0.194	0.164
20	0.820	0.673	0.554	0.456	0.377	0.312	0.258	0.215	0.178	0.149

Periods	Interest rates (*r*)									
(*n*)	11%	12%	13%	14%	15%	16%	17%	18%	19%	20%
1	0.901	0.893	0.885	0.877	0.870	0.862	0.855	0.847	0.840	0.833
2	0.812	0.797	0.783	0.769	0.756	0.743	0.731	0.718	0.706	0.694
3	0.731	0.712	0.693	0.675	0.658	0.641	0.624	0.609	0.593	0.579
4	0.659	0.636	0.613	0.592	0.572	0.552	0.534	0.516	0.499	0.482
5	0.593	0.567	0.543	0.519	0.497	0.476	0.456	0.437	0.419	0.402
6	0.535	0.507	0.480	0.456	0.432	0.410	0.390	0.370	0.352	0.335
7	0.482	0.452	0.425	0.400	0.376	0.354	0.333	0.314	0.296	0.279
8	0.434	0.404	0.376	0.351	0.327	0.305	0.285	0.266	0.249	0.233
9	0.391	0.361	0.333	0.308	0.284	0.263	0.243	0.225	0.209	0.194
10	0.352	0.322	0.295	0.270	0.247	0.227	0.208	0.191	0.176	0.162
11	0.317	0.287	0.261	0.237	0.215	0.195	0.178	0.162	0.148	0.135
12	0.286	0.257	0.231	0.208	0.187	0.168	0.152	0.137	0.124	0.112
13	0.258	0.229	0.204	0.182	0.163	0.145	0.130	0.116	0.104	0.093
14	0.232	0.205	0.181	0.160	0.141	0.125	0.111	0.099	0.088	0.078
15	0.209	0.183	0.160	0.140	0.123	0.108	0.095	0.084	0.079	0.065
16	0.188	0.163	0.141	0.123	0.107	0.093	0.081	0.071	0.062	0.054
17	0.170	0.146	0.125	0.108	0.093	0.080	0.069	0.060	0.052	0.045
18	0.153	0.130	0.111	0.095	0.081	0.069	0.059	0.051	0.044	0.038
19	0.138	0.116	0.098	0.083	0.070	0.060	0.051	0.043	0.037	0.031
20	0.124	0.104	0.087	0.073	0.061	0.051	0.043	0.037	0.031	0.026

Cumulative present value of 1.00 unit of currency per annum

Receivable or Payable at the end of each year for *n* years $\left[\frac{1-(1+r)^{-n}}{r}\right]$

Periods	Interest rates (*r*)									
(*n*)	1%	2%	3%	4%	5%	6%	7%	8%	9%	10%
1	0.990	0.980	0.971	0.962	0.952	0.943	0.935	0.926	0.917	0.909
2	1.970	1.942	1.913	1.886	1.859	1.833	1.808	1.783	1.759	1.736
3	2.941	2.884	2.829	2.775	2.723	2.673	2.624	2.577	2.531	2.487
4	3.902	3.808	3.717	3.630	3.546	3.465	3.387	3.312	3.240	3.170
5	4.853	4.713	4.580	4.452	4.329	4.212	4.100	3.993	3.890	3.791
6	5.795	5.601	5.417	5.242	5.076	4.917	4.767	4.623	4.486	4.355
7	6.728	6.472	6.230	6.002	5.786	5.582	5.389	5.206	5.033	4.868
8	7.652	7.325	7.020	6.733	6.463	6.210	5.971	5.747	5.535	5.335
9	8.566	8.162	7.786	7.435	7.108	6.802	6.515	6.247	5.995	5.759
10	9.471	8.983	8.530	8.111	7.722	7.360	7.024	6.710	6.418	6.145
11	10.368	9.787	9.253	8.760	8.306	7.887	7.499	7.139	6.805	6.495
12	11.255	10.575	9.954	9.385	8.863	8.384	7.943	7.536	7.161	6.814
13	12.134	11.348	10.635	9.986	9.394	8.853	8.358	7.904	7.487	7.103
14	13.004	12.106	11.296	10.563	9.899	9.295	8.745	8.244	7.786	7.367
15	13.865	12.849	11.938	11.118	10.380	9.712	9.108	8.559	8.061	7.606
16	14.718	13.578	12.561	11.652	10.838	10.106	9.447	8.851	8.313	7.824
17	15.562	14.292	13.166	12.166	11.274	10.477	9.763	9.122	8.544	8.022
18	16.398	14.992	13.754	12.659	11.690	10.828	10.059	9.372	8.756	8.201
19	17.226	15.679	14.324	13.134	12.085	11.158	10.336	9.604	8.950	8.365
20	18.046	16.351	14.878	13.590	12.462	11.470	10.594	9.818	9.129	8.514

Periods	Interest rates (*r*)									
(*n*)	11%	12%	13%	14%	15%	16%	17%	18%	19%	20%
1	0.901	0.893	0.885	0.877	0.870	0.862	0.855	0.847	0.840	0.833
2	1.713	1.690	1.668	1.647	1.626	1.605	1.585	1.566	1.547	1.528
3	2.444	2.402	2.361	2.322	2.283	2.246	2.210	2.174	2.140	2.106
4	3.102	3.037	2.974	2.914	2.855	2.798	2.743	2.690	2.639	2.589
5	3.696	3.605	3.517	3.433	3.352	3.274	3.199	3.127	3.058	2.991
6	4.231	4.111	3.998	3.889	3.784	3.685	3.589	3.498	3.410	3.326
7	4.712	4.564	4.423	4.288	4.160	4.039	3.922	3.812	3.706	3.605
8	5.146	4.968	4.799	4.639	4.487	4.344	4.207	4.078	3.954	3.837
9	5.537	5.328	5.132	4.946	4.772	4.607	4.451	4.303	4.163	4.031
10	5.889	5.650	5.426	5.216	5.019	4.833	4.659	4.494	4.339	4.192
11	6.207	5.938	5.687	5.453	5.234	5.029	4.836	4.656	4.486	4.327
12	6.492	6.194	5.918	5.660	5.421	5.197	4.988	7.793	4.611	4.439
13	6.750	6.424	6.122	5.842	5.583	5.342	5.118	4.910	4.715	4.533
14	6.982	6.628	6.302	6.002	5.724	5.468	5.229	5.008	4.802	4.611
15	7.191	6.811	6.462	6.142	5.847	5.575	5.324	5.092	4.876	4.675
16	7.379	6.974	6.604	6.265	5.954	5.668	5.405	5.162	4.938	4.730
17	7.549	7.120	6.729	6.373	6.047	5.749	5.475	5.222	4.990	4.775
18	7.702	7.250	6.840	6.467	6.128	5.818	5.534	5.273	5.033	4.812
19	7.839	7.366	6.938	6.550	6.198	5.877	5.584	5.316	5.070	4.843
20	7.963	7.469	7.025	6.623	6.259	5.929	5.628	5.353	5.101	4.870

FORMULAE

Valuation models

(i) Irredeemable preference shares, paying a constant annual dividend, d, in perpetuity, where P_0 is the ex-div value:

$$P_0 = \frac{d}{k_{pref}}$$

(ii) Ordinary (equity) shares, paying a constant annual dividend, d, in perpetuity, where P_0 is the ex-div value:

$$P_0 = \frac{d}{k_e}$$

(iii) Ordinary (equity) shares, paying an annual dividend, d, growing in perpetuity at a constant rate, g, where P_0 is the ex-div value:

$$P_0 = \frac{d_1}{k_e - g} \quad \text{or} \quad P_0 = \frac{d_0[1+g]}{k_e - g}$$

(iv) Irredeemable bonds, paying annual after-tax interest, $i\,[1 - t]$, in perpetuity, where P_0 is the ex-interest value:

$$P_0 = \frac{i[1-t]}{k_{dnet}}$$

or, without tax:

$$P_0 = \frac{i}{k_d}$$

(v) Total value of the geared entity, V_g (based on MM):

$$V_g = V_u + TB$$

(vi) Future value of S, of a sum X, invested for n periods, compounded at r% interest:

$$S = X[1 + r]^n$$

(vii) Present value of 1·00 payable or receivable in n years, discounted at r% per annum:

$$PV = \frac{1}{[1+r]^n}$$

(viii) Present value of an annuity of 1·00 per annum, receivable or payable for n years, commencing in one year, discounted at r% per annum:

$$PV = \frac{1}{r}\left[1 - \frac{1}{[1+r]^n}\right]$$

(ix) Present value of 1·00 per annum, payable or receivable in perpetuity, commencing in one year, discounted at r% per annum:

$$PV = \frac{1}{r}$$

(x) Present value of 1·00 per annum, receivable or payable, commencing in one year, growing in perpetuity at a constant rate of g% per annum, discounted at r% per annum:

$$PV = \frac{1}{r - g}$$

Cost of capital

(i) Cost of irredeemable preference shares, paying an annual dividend, d, in perpetuity, and having a current ex-div price P_0:

$$k_{pref} = \frac{d}{P_0}$$

(ii) Cost of irredeemable bonds, paying annual net interest, $i[1 - t]$, and having a current ex-interest price P_0:

$$k_{d\ net} = \frac{i[1-t]}{P_0}$$

(iii) Cost of ordinary (equity) shares, paying an annual dividend, d, in perpetuity, and having a current ex-div price P_0:

$$k_e = \frac{d}{P_0}$$

(iv) Cost of ordinary (equity) shares, having a current ex-div price, P_0, having just paid a dividend, d_0, with the dividend growing in perpetuity by a constant g% per annum:

$$k_e = \frac{d_1}{P_0} + g \quad \text{or} \quad k_e = \frac{d_0[1+g]}{P_0} + g$$

(v) Cost of ordinary (equity) shares, using the CAPM:

$$k_e = R_f + [R_m - R_f]ß$$

(vi) Cost of ordinary (equity) share capital in a geared entity :

$$k_{eg} = k_{eu} + [k_{eu} - k_d]\frac{V_D[1-t]}{V_E}$$

(vii) Weighted average cost of capital, k_0 or WACC

$$WACC = k_e\left[\frac{V_E}{V_E + V_D}\right] + k_d[1-t]\left[\frac{V_D}{V_E + V_D}\right]$$

(viii) Adjusted cost of capital (MM formula):

$$K_{adj} = k_{eu}[1 - tL] \quad \text{or} \quad r^* = r[1 - T^*L]$$

(ix) Ungear $ß$:

$$ß_u = ß_g\left[\frac{V_E}{V_E + V_D[1-t]}\right] + ß_d\left[\frac{V_D[1-t]}{V_E + V_D[1-t]}\right]$$

(x) Regear $ß$:

$$ß_g = ß_u + [ß_u - ß_d]\frac{V_D[1-t]}{V_E}$$

(xi) Adjusted discount rate to use in international capital budgeting (International Fisher effect)

$$\frac{1 + \text{annual discount rate B\$}}{1 + \text{annual discount rate A\$}} = \frac{\text{Future spot rate A\$/B\$ in 12 months' time}}{\text{Spot rate A\$/B\$}}$$

where A\$/B\$ is the number of B\$ to each A\$

Other formulae

(i) Expectations theory:

$$\text{Future spot rate A\$/B\$} = \text{Spot rate A\$/B\$} \times \frac{1+\text{nominal country B interest rate}}{1+\text{nominal country A interest rate}}$$

where:

A$/B$ is the number of B$ to each A$, and
A$ is the currency of country A and B$ is the currency of country B

(ii) Purchasing power parity (law of one price):

$$\text{Future spot rate A\$B\$} = \text{Spot rate A\$/B\$} \times \frac{1+\text{country B inflation rate}}{1+\text{country A inflation rate}}$$

(iii) Link between nominal (money) and real interest rates:

$$[1 + \text{nominal (money) rate}] = [1 + \text{real interest rate}][1 + \text{inflation rate}]$$

(iv) Equivalent annual cost:

$$\text{Equivalent annual cost} = \frac{PV \text{ of costs over } n \text{ years}}{n \text{ year annuity factor}}$$

(v) Theoretical ex-rights price:

$$\text{TERP} = \frac{1}{N+1}[(N \times \text{cum rights price}) + \text{issue price}]$$

(vi) Value of a right:

$$\frac{\text{Theoretical ex rights price} - \text{issue price}}{N}$$

where N = number of rights required to buy one share.

chapter

1

CIMA Verb Hierarchy – strategic level exams

Chapter learning objectives

CIMA VERB HIERARCHY

CIMA place great importance on the choice of verbs in exam question requirements. It is thus critical that you answer the question according to the definition of the verb used.

1 CIMA verb hierarchy – strategic level

In strategic level exams you will mainly meet verbs from levels 3, 4 and 5. Examiners have commented on many occasions that they ask a level 5 verb and get a level 2 response. It is vital that the higher level verbs are understood and responded to. Very occasionally you will also see level 1 and 2 verbs but these should not account for more than 5–10% of the marks in total.

Level 3 – APPLICATION

How you are expected to apply your knowledge

VERBS USED	DEFINITION
Apply	Put to practical use.
Calculate	Ascertain or reckon mathematically.
Demonstrate	Prove with certainty or exhibit by practical means.
Prepare	Make or get ready for use.
Reconcile	Make or prove consistent/compatible.
Solve	Find an answer to.
Tabulate	Arrange in a table.

Level 4 – ANALYSIS

How you are expected to analyse the detail of what you have learned.

VERBS USED	DEFINITION
Analyse	Examine in detail the structure of.
Categorise	Place into a defined class or division.
Compare and contrast	Show the similarities and/or differences between.
Construct	Build up or compile.
Discuss	Examine in detail by argument.
Interpret	Translate into intelligible or familiar terms.
Prioritise	Place in order of priority or sequence for action.
Produce	Create or bring into existence.

Level 5 – EVALUATION

How you are expected to use your learning to evaluate, make decisions or recommendations.

VERBS USED	DEFINITION
Advise	Counsel, inform or notify.
Evaluate	Appraise or assess the value of.
Recommend	Propose a course of action.

2 Further guidance on strategic level verbs that cause confusion

Verbs that cause students most confusion at this level are as follows:

Level 3 verbs

- **The verb "to apply"**

  Given that all level 3 verbs involve application, the verb "apply" is rare in the real exam. One of the other more specific verbs is used instead.

- **The verb "to reconcile"**

  This is a numerical requirement and usually involves starting with one of the figures, adjusting it and ending up with the other.

  For example, in a bank reconciliation you start with the recorded cash at bank figure, adjust it for unpresented cheques, etc, and (hopefully!) end up with the stated balance in the cash "T account".

- **The verb "to demonstrate"**

  The verb "to demonstrate" can be used in two main ways.

  Firstly it could mean to prove that a given statement is true or consistent with circumstances given. For example, the Finance Director may have stated in the question that the company will not exceed its overdraft limit in the next six months. The requirement then asks you to demonstrate that the Director is wrong. You could do this by preparing a cash flow forecast for the next six months.

  Secondly you could be asked to demonstrate **how** a stated model, framework, technique or theory **could be used** in the particular scenario to achieve a specific result – for example, how a probability matrix could be used to make a production decision. Ensure in such questions that you do not merely describe the model but use it to generate the desired outcome.

Level 4 verbs

- **The verb "to analyse"**

  To analyse something is to examine it in detail in order to discover its meaning or essential features. This will usually involve breaking the scenario down and looking at the fine detail, possibly with additional calculations, and then stepping back to see the bigger picture to identify any themes to support conclusions.

For example, if asked to analyse a set of financial statements, then the end result will be a set of statements about the performance of the business with supporting evidence. This could involve the following:

(1) You could break down your analysis into areas of profitability, liquidity, gearing and so on.

(2) Under each heading look at key figures in the financial statements, identifying trends (e.g. sales growth) and calculating supporting ratios (e.g. margins).

(3) Try to explain what the figures mean and why they have occurred (e.g. why has the operating margin fallen?)

(4) Start considering the bigger picture – are the ratios presenting a consistent message or do they contradict each other? Can you identify common causes?

(5) Finally you would then seek to pull all this information together and interpret it to make some higher level comments about overall performance.

The main error students make is that they fail to draw out any themes and conclusions and simply present the marker with a collection of uninterpreted, unexplained facts and figures.

- **The verb "to discuss"**

To discuss something is very similar to analysing it, except that discussion usually involves two or more different viewpoints or arguments as the context, rather than a set of figures, say. To discuss viewpoints will involve looking at their underlying arguments, examining them critically, trying to assess whether one argument is more persuasive than the other and then seeking to reach a conclusion.

For example, if asked to discuss whether a particular technique could be used by a company, you would examine the arguments for and against, making reference to the specific circumstances in the question, and seek to conclude.

- **The verb "to prioritise"**

To prioritise is to place objects in an order. The key issue here is to decide upon the criteria to use to perform the ordering. For example, prioritising the external threats facing a firm could be done by considering the scale of financial consequences, immediacy, implications for the underlying business model and so on.

The main mistake students make is that they fail to justify their prioritisation – why is this the most important issue?

Level 5 verbs

- **The verb "to evaluate"**

To evaluate something is to assess it with a view to placing a value on it. In many respects "evaluate" should be seen as a higher level version of "analyse" and "discuss" and could include qualitative and quantitative factors within your criteria. Your resulting arguments will need to be prioritised and weighed against each other to form a conclusion.

For example, suppose you are asked to evaluate a proposed strategy in paper E3. At its simplest your answer could contain a series of arguments for and against the strategy. Each argument should be discussed to assess its importance. The arguments can then be weighed up against each other to form a conclusion. You are thus evaluating the factors within each argument and then evaluating the arguments against each other.

With such questions many students struggle to generate enough points or arguments. Part of the solution is to produce mental checklists when studying the paper concerned. These give criteria to use for valuing the matter at hand. With the above example on strategy evaluation, criteria could include any of the following:

- Are there any useful calculations – e.g. NPV, impact on profit?
- Does the strategy resolve any major threats faced by the firm?
- Does the strategy capitalise on the firm's strengths or do weaknesses need resolving first?
- Does the strategy enhance the firm's competitive strategy?
- Does the strategy lead to a better "fit" with the environment?
- What are the risks and are they acceptable?
- What are the implications for different stakeholders and would it be acceptable to them?
- What are the resource implications – how feasible is the strategy?

Use of such a checklist will ensure you have enough points to pass.

In some questions you may have to do more preliminary work before you can evaluate. For example, if asked to evaluate a firm's approach to change management you would start by identifying what type of approach they are taking (referencing to different models of change management) before you can evaluate it.

- **The differences between the verbs "to evaluate", "to advise" and "to recommend"**

All three level 5 verbs involve a mixture of identifying relevant issues, analysing them, evaluating them and then finishing with some form of conclusion. Some writers see this as a three step approach:

(1) **What?** Identify relevant issues.

(2) **So what?** Why are the issues relevant? How significant are they?

(3) **What now?** What response is required by the firm being considered?

The difference between the level 5 verbs lies in where the main emphasis is in these three steps. With "advise" and "recommend" the examiner will be looking for more detail in step 3. Recommendations in particular could involve formulating a plan of action that includes both short and longer term aspects.

chapter

2

An Introduction to Financial Strategy

Chapter learning objectives

Lead	Component
A1: Discuss potential strategic financial objectives, and the relationships among and constraints on the elements of financial strategy.	(a) discuss the potential strategic objectives of an organisation. (b) discuss the interrelationships between decisions concerning investment, financing and dividends. (c) discuss the impact of internal and external constraints on financial strategy, including the impact of regulation on business combinations.

Indicative syllabus content

- The financial and non-financial objectives of different organisations (e.g. value for money, maximising shareholder wealth, providing a surplus).
- The three key decisions of financial management (investment, financing and dividend) and their links.
- Benefits of matching characteristics of investment and financing in the longer term, (e.g. in cross-border investment) and in short-term hedging strategies.
- Considerations in the formulation of dividend policy and dividend decisions, including meeting the cash needs of the business.
- External constraints on financial strategy (e.g. funding, regulatory bodies, investor relations, strategy, and economic factors).
- Developing financial strategy in the context of regulatory requirements (e.g. price and service controls exercised by industry regulators) and international operations.

1 Overview of Chapter

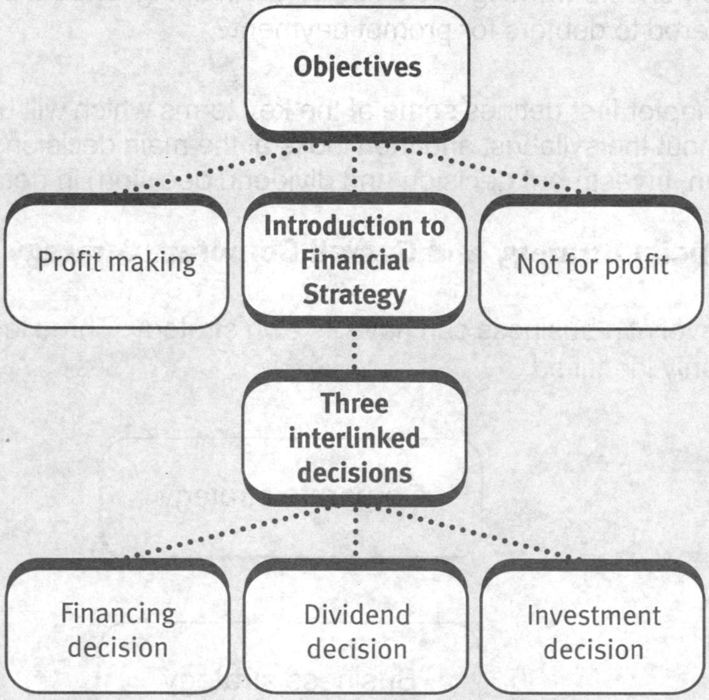

Definitions of key terms

Strategy: A course of action, including the specification of resources required, to achieve a specific objective. (CIMA Official Terminology, 2005)

Financial strategy is the aspect of strategy which falls within the scope of financial management, which will include decisions on investment, financing and dividends.

Strategic financial management: The identification of the possible strategies capable of maximising an entity's net present value, the allocation of scarce capital resources among the competing opportunities and the implementation and monitoring of the chosen strategy so as to achieve stated objectives. (CIMA Official Terminology, 2005)

2 The Importance of Financial Strategy to the Organisation

An organisation's financial managers must plan their courses of action to achieve the organisation's financial objectives. Decisions that they must take include:

- From which sources should funds be raised?
- Should proposed investments be undertaken?

- How large a dividend should be paid?
- How should working capital be controlled, e.g. should discounts be offered to debtors for prompt payment?

This Chapter first defines some of the key terms which will be used throughout the syllabus, and then looks at the main decisions (financing decision, investment decision and dividend decision) in detail.

3 Financial Strategy and Overall Corporate Strategy

Each level of a business can have its own strategy. Three levels are commonly identified:

Corporate strategy – This concerns the decisions to be made by senior management such as the particular business that the company is in, and whether new markets should be entered or current markets withdrawn from.

Business strategy – This concerns the decisions to be made by the separate strategic business units within the group. Each unit will try to maximise its competitive positions within its chosen market.

Operational strategy – This concerns how the different functional areas within a strategic business unit plan their operations to satisfy the corporate and business strategies being followed. We are of course most interested in the decisions facing the finance functions.

Financial strategy will be important at each level in this hierarchy. For example, investment decisions and financing decisions may be important at all the levels (although a large number of companies manage financing centrally). Dividend decisions will be made at the corporate level only.

4 Objectives

Financial objectives of profit seeking organisations

Decisions to be made depend on the ultimate objectives of an organisation.

Academic studies have shown that organisations often have many, **sometimes conflicting,** objectives.

It is generally accepted that the primary strategic objective of a commercial company is the long-term goal of the **maximisation of the wealth of the shareholders**.

However, an organisation has many other stakeholders with both long- and short-term goals, such as:

- Equity investors (ordinary shareholders)
- The community at large
- Company employees
- Company managers/directors
- Customers
- Suppliers
- Finance providers
- The government

Definition of stakeholders

Stakeholders: Those persons and entities that have an interest in the strategy of an entity. Stakeholders normally include shareholders, customers, staff and the local community. (CIMA Official Terminology, 2005)

Examples of stakeholder objectives

Equity investors (ordinary shareholders) – Within any economic system, the equity investors provide the risk finance. There is a very strong argument for maximising the wealth of equity investors. In order to attract funds, the company has to compete with other risk-free investment opportunities, e.g. government securities. The shareholders require returns from the company in terms of dividends and increases in share prices.

The community at large – The goals of the community will be broad but will include such aspects as legal and social responsibilities, pollution control and employee welfare.

Company employees – Returns = wages or salaries. However, maximising the returns to employees does assume that risk finance can be raised purely on the basis of satisficing the returns to finance providers. The employees' other interests also include job security and good conditions of employment.

Company managers/directors – Such senior employees are in an ideal position to follow their own aims at the expense of other stakeholders. Their goals will be both long-term (defending against takeovers, sales maximisation) and short-term (profit margins leading to increased bonuses).

Customers – Satisfaction of customer needs will be achieved through the provision of value for money products and services.

Suppliers – Suppliers to the organisation will have short-term goals such as prompt payment terms alongside long-term requirements including contracts and regular business. The importance of the needs of suppliers will depend upon both their relative size and the number of suppliers.

Finance providers – Providers of loan finance (banks, loan creditors) will primarily be interested in the ability of the firm to repay the finance including interest. As a result it will be the firm's ability to generate cash both long and short term that will be the basis of the goals of these providers.

The government – The government will have political and financial interests in the firm. Politically it will wish to increase exports and decrease imports whilst monitoring companies via the Competition Commission. Financially it requires long-term profits to maximise taxation income.

Objectives and economic forces

When setting the company's financial strategy the financial manager is often constrained by both internal and external factors.

For example, significant expansion and an increase in dividends may not be feasible if the entity has a lack of skilled staff, and may become uneconomic if interest rates are set to rise (thus increasing the amount payable to banks and other debt finance providers).

Internal and external constraints on financial strategy

Internal constraints on financial strategy

Two of the main internal constraints on financial strategy are financing and gearing (if there are covenants in debt agreements).

The main argument in favour of gearing is that introducing borrowings into the capital structure attracts tax relief on interest payments. The argument against borrowing is that it introduces financial risk into the entity. Financial managers have to formulate a policy that balances the effects of these opposing features.

Other internal constraints on financial strategy include:

- the need to maintain good investor relations and provide a satisfactory return on investment;
- a shortage of key skills;
- limited production capacity.

External constraints on financial strategy

Major external constraints include:

- Limited access to sources of finance
- Government influence (see below)
- Regulatory bodies (see below)
- Major economic influences, such as interest rates, growth in GDP, inflation rates and exchange rates. The effects of interest rate and inflation changes on the economy are covered below.
- Accounting concepts. (Note: Detailed knowledge of accounting procedures will not be examined in this paper.)

Government influence

Governments often play a large part in influencing business activity. Some examples of the way in which governments can have an influence are as follows:

- Employment policy. Governments play a major role in attempting to stimulate employment. They can do this by funding vocational training programmes and funding employment programmes.
- Regional policy. Governments may make funds available to support regions of high unemployment and social deprivation.

- Inflation policy. Governments may use interest rates to control inflation. Increasing interest rates makes it more expensive for profit-making entities to borrow. It also makes borrowing more expensive for consumers, who then have less to spend. This will help to push prices down.
- Taxation policy. The government raises taxes on the profits generated by profit-making entities and on shareholders' dividends.
- International policy. Governments can promote trade, encourage experts or discourage imports.
- Legislation. Laws set out how people can and should behave towards one another, and particularly, how business should be conducted.

Developing financial strategy in the context of regulatory requirements

The financial manager must have a proper understanding of those aspects of legislation which impact upon entities. Such legislation will include the Companies Acts, health and safety regulations, laws relating to consumer protection and consumer rights, laws relating to contract and agency, employment law and laws relating to protection of the environment and promoting competition.

Listed companies also have to comply with Stock Exchange regulations, and entities which operate in some high profile industries will also find regulatory bodies monitoring their performance. For example, in the UK, Oftel (telecommunications), Ofcom (media) and Ofwat (water) have been set up by the government to monitor and regulate their respective industries.

Regulatory bodies

A clear set of objectives is required for each regulatory body. These objectives may be classified under three headings:

(1) The protection of customers from monopoly power.

(2) The promotion of social and macroeconomic objectives.

(3) The promotion of competition.

(1) Monopoly power

Where market participants are judged to possess significant market power, and where there is no other protection for customers, controls on prices and on quality of service may be considered.

(2) Social objectives

Government objectives may include the availability and affordability of services in particular areas and to particular groups such as customers in remote rural areas.

(3) Competition

Where a market is not competitive, or is in the early stages of becoming so, there is a need for regulators whose role is to try to balance the interests of the various stakeholders.

Important issues for regulation are the prevention of 'cross-subsidy', that is the transferring or offloading of portions of overhead costs from lower- to higher-margin products, the limitation of non-price barriers affecting the entry of new competitors, and assuring reasonable quality of product in relation to price. Non-price barriers could include trade restrictions, or restricted access to supplies or distribution channels.

The effect of interest rate and inflation changes

The effects of interest rate changes

Changes in interest rates affect the economy in many ways. The following consequences are the main effects of an increase in interest rates:

Spending falls – expenditure by consumers, both individual and business, will be reduced. This occurs because the higher interest rates raise the cost of credit and deter spending. If we take incomes as fairly stable in the short term, higher interest payments on credit cards/mortgages, etc., leave less income for spending on consumer goods and services. This fall in spending means less aggregate demand in the economy and thus unemployment results.

Asset values fall – the market value of financial assets will drop, because of the inverse relationship (between bonds and the rate of interest) explained earlier. This, in turn, will reduce many people's wealth. It is likely that they will react to maintain the value of their total wealth and so may save, thereby further reducing expenditure in the economy. This phenomenon seems to fit the UK recession of the early 1990s when the house-price slump deepened the economic gloom. For many consumers today a house, rather than bonds, is their main asset.

Foreign funds are attracted into the country – a rise in interest rates will encourage overseas financial speculators to deposit money in the country's banking institutions because the rate of return has increased relative to that in other countries. Such funds could be made available as loans to firms in that country by the banking sector.

The exchange rate rises – the inflow of foreign funds raises demand for the domestic currency and so pushes up the exchange rate. This has the benefit of lowering import prices and thereby bearing down on domestic inflation. However, it makes exports more expensive and possibly harder to sell. The longer-term effect on the balance of payments could be beneficial or harmful depending on the elasticity of demand and supply for traded goods.

Inflation falls – higher interest rates affect the rate of inflation in three ways. First, less demand in the economy may encourage producers to lower prices in order to sell. This could be achieved by squeezing profit margins and/or wage levels. Second, new borrowing is deferred by the high interest rates and so demand will fall. Third, the higher exchange rate will raise export prices and thereby threaten sales which in turn pressurises producers to cut costs, particularly wages. If workers are laid off then again total demand is reduced and inflation is likely to fall.

The effects of inflation

Inflation is defined simply as 'rising prices' and shows the cost of living in general terms.

If the rate of inflation is low, then the effects may be beneficial to an economy. Business people are encouraged by fairly stable prices and the prospect of higher profits. However, there is some argument about whether getting inflation below 3% to, say, zero, is worth the economic pain (of, say, higher unemployment). There is agreement, though, that inflation above 5% is harmful – worse still if it is accelerating. The main arguments are that such inflation:

Distorts consumer behaviour – people may bring forward purchases because they fear higher prices later. This can cause hoarding and so destabilise markets, creating unnecessary shortages.

Redistributes income – people on fixed incomes or those lacking bargaining power will become relatively worse off, as their purchasing power falls. This is unfair.

Affects wage bargainers – trades unionists on behalf of labour may submit higher claims at times of high inflation, particularly if previously they had underestimated the future rise in prices. If employers accept such claims this may precipitate a wage–price spiral which exacerbates the inflation problem.

Undermines business confidence – wide fluctuations in the inflation rate make it difficult for entrepreneurs to predict the economic future and accurately calculate prices and investment returns. This uncertainty handicaps planning and production.

Weakens the country's competitive position – if inflation in a country exceeds that in a competitor country, then it makes exports less attractive (assuming unchanged exchange rates) and imports more competitive. This could mean fewer sales of that country's goods at home and abroad and thus a bigger trade deficit. For example the decline of Britain's manufacturing industry can be partly attributed to the growth of cheap imports when they were experiencing high inflation in the period 1978–1983.

Redistributes wealth – if the rate of interest is below the rate of inflation, then borrowers are gaining at the expense of lenders. The real value of savings is being eroded. This wealth is being redistributed from savers to borrowers and from payables to receivables. As the government is the largest borrower, via the national debt, it gains most during inflationary times.

Stakeholder conflicts

Faced with a broad range of stakeholders, managers are likely to find they cannot simultaneously maximise the wealth of their shareholders and keep all the other stakeholders content.

In practice, the main strategic objective may be interpreted as achieving the maximum profit possible, consistent with balancing the needs of the various stakeholders in the entity.

Such a policy may imply achieving a satisfactory return for shareholders, whilst (for example) establishing competitive terms and conditions of service for the employees, and avoiding polluting the environment.

Conflicts of objectives between managers and shareholders

Agency theory

A possible conflict can arise when ownership is separated from the day-to-day management of an entity. In larger entities, the ordinary shares are likely to be diversely held, and so the actions of shareholders are likely to be restricted in practical terms. The responsibility of running the entity will be with the board of directors, who may only own a small percentage of the shares in issue.

The managers of an entity are essentially agents for the shareholders, being tasked with running the entity in the shareholders' best interests. The shareholders, however, have little opportunity to assess whether the managers are acting in the shareholders' best interests.

Agency theory: Hypothesis that attempts to explain elements of organisational behaviour through an understanding of the relationships between principals (such as shareholders) and agents (such as company managers and accountants). A conflict may exist between the actions undertaken by agents in furtherance of their own self-interest, and those required to promote the interests of the principals. (CIMA Official Terminology, 2005)

Investor relations

Where ownership is separated from the day-to-day management of an entity, managers may be motivated to behave in ways that are not optimal to the shareholders of the entity:

- Shareholders can spread their risk by investing in a number of entities. Managers have personal and financial capital invested in the entity and so may be averse to investing in a risky investment.
- Shareholder wealth will be maximised by investing in projects with positive net present values. Managers may be more interested in short-term payback than net present value as the investment criterion, in order to help further their own promotion prospects.
- Managers of entities that are subject to a takeover bid often put up a defence to repel the predator. While arguing this action is in the shareholders' best interests, shareholders of acquired entities often receive large gains in the value of their shares. The managers of the acquired entity often lose their jobs or status.
- Managers may be motivated to award themselves and staff better terms and conditions of service. This will incur costs and reduce profits. If equity investors are losing too much as a consequence, they may sell their shares and the market value of the entity will fall.

Goal congruence

Goal congruence: In a control system, the state which leads the individuals or groups to take actions which are in their self-interest and also in the best interest of the entity. (CIMA Official Terminology, 2005)

It is evident that an important element within profit-making entities is the extent to which all members of the management team and their staff work together to achieve the strategic objectives of that entity. An aspect of agency theory aims to demonstrate that while various kinds of contract exist, formal and informal (such as job descriptions, departmental responsibilities and office and factory rules), these can only be effective in helping to make an entity successful if there is general acceptance of them in practice, and a concerted effort by all concerned to strive in the same direction, that is, to achieve genuine goal congruence.

Performance and progress indicators (PIs)

In order to achieve the overall objective companies should set specific targets, financial and non-financial, in order to both communicate direction and measure performance, for example:

Financial

Profitability – e.g.annual 10% improvement in earnings, or earnings per share.

Cash generation – e.g. annual 10% improvement in operating cashflow.

Non-financial

Market share – e.g. four products out of six are dominant in the market.

Customer satisfaction – e.g. complaints to reduce from 5% to 2%.

These targets can be used to direct managers' attention towards key stakeholder requirements, to ensure that the organisation balances the needs of its different stakeholders and minimises the conflict between the different stakeholder groups.

More on financial and non financial objectives

Traditionally, managers have focused on financial measures of performance and progress. Increasingly, entities in both the private and public sectors are using non-financial indicators to assess success across a range of criteria, which need to be chosen to help an entity meet its objectives.

We discuss a number of common financial and non-financial indicators below.

Financial performance indicators

Return to investors. The return from ownership of shares in a profit-making entity can be measured by the formula:

$$\text{Annual return to investors} = \frac{(P_1 - P_0) + \text{Dividend}}{P_0}$$

This is the capital appreciation on the shares (the difference between P_1 and P_0 – the share price at the end and the start of the year respectively), plus dividends received during the year.

Cash generation. Poor liquidity is a greater threat to the survival of an entity than is poor profitability. Unless the entity is prepared to fund growth with high levels of borrowings, cash generation is vital to ensure investment in future profitable ventures. In the private sector the alternative to cash via retained earnings is borrowing. In the public sector this choice has not been available in the past, and all growth has been funded by government. However, in the face of government-imposed cash limits, local authorities and other public-sector entities are beginning to raise debt on the capital markets, and are therefore beginning to be faced with the same choices as profit-making entities.

Value added. This is primarily a measure of performance. It is usually defined as revenues less the cost of purchased materials and services. It represents the value added to an entity's products by its own efforts. A problem here is comparability with other industries – or even with other entities in the same industry. It is less common in the public sector, although the situation is changing and many public sector entities – for example those in the health service – are now publishing information on their own value added.

Profitability. Profitability may be defined as the rate at which profits are generated. It is often expressed as profit per unit of input (e.g. investment). However, profitability limits an entity's focus to one output measure – profit. It overlooks quality, and this limitation must be kept in mind when using profitability as a measure of success. Profitability as a measure of decision-making has been criticised because:

- it fails to provide a systematic explanation as to why one business sector has more favourable prospects than another;
- it does not provide enough insight into the dynamics and balance of an entity's individual business units, and the balance between them;
- it is remote from the actions that create value, and cannot therefore be managed directly in any but the smallest entities;
- the input to the measure may vary substantially between entities.

Nevertheless, it is a well-known and accepted measure which, once the input has been defined, is readily understood. Provided the input is consistent across entities and time periods, it also provides a useful comparative measure. Although the concept of profit in its true sense is absent from most of the public sector, profitability may be used to relate inputs to outputs if a different measure of output is used – for example: surplus after all costs, to capital investment.

Return on assets (RoA). This is an accounting measure, calculated by dividing annual profits by the average net book value of assets. It is therefore subject to the distortions inevitable when profit, rather than cash flows, is used to determine performance. Distorting factors for interpretation and comparison purposes include depreciation policy, inventory revaluations, write-off of intangibles such as goodwill, etc. A further defect is that RoA ignores the time value of money, although this may be of minor concern when inflation is very low.

RoA may not adequately reflect how efficiently assets were utilised: in a commercial context, taking account of profits but not the assets used in their making, for whatever reason, would overstate an entity's performance. In the public sector, the concept of profit is absent, but it is still not unrealistic to expect entities to use donated assets with maximum efficiency. If depreciation on such assets were to be charged against income, this would depress the amount of surplus income over expenditure. Other points which may affect interpretation of RoA in the public sector are:

- difficulty in determining value;
- there may be no resale value;
- are for use by community at large;
- charge for depreciation may have the effect of 'double taxation' on the taxpayer.

Non-financial performance indicators

Market share. A performance indicator that could conceivably be included in the list of financial measures, market share is often seen as an objective for an entity in its own right. However, it must be judged in the context of other measures such as profitability and shareholder value. Market share, unlike many other measures, can take quality into account – it must be assumed that if customers do not get the quality they want or expect, then the entity will lose market share.

Gaining market share must be seen as a long-term goal of entities to ensure outlets for their products and services, and to minimise competition. However, market share can be acquired only within limits if a monopoly situation is to be avoided.

It is a measure that is becoming increasingly relevant to the public sector – for example universities and health provision. Health providers must now 'sell' their services to trusts established to 'buy' from them. Those providers which are seen to fail their customers will lose market share as the trusts will buy from elsewhere (within certain limits).

Customer satisfaction. This can be linked to market share. If customers are not satisfied they will take their business elsewhere and the entity will lose market share and go into liquidation. Measuring customer satisfaction is difficult to do formally, as the inputs and outputs are not readily defined or measurable. Surveys and questionnaires may be used but these methods have known flaws, mainly as a result of respondent bias. It can of course be measured indirectly by the level of sales and increase in market share.

Competitive position. The performance of an entity must be compared with that of its competitors to establish a strategic perspective. A number of models and frameworks have been suggested by organisational theorists as to how competitive position may be determined and improved. A manager needing to make decisions must know by whom, by how much, and why he is gaining ground or being beaten by competitors. Conventional measures, such as accounting data, are useful but no one measure is sufficient. Instead, an array of measures is needed to establish competitive position. The most difficult problem to overcome in using competitive position as a success factor is in collecting and acquiring data from competitors.

The public sector is increasingly in competition with other providers of a similar service both in the private and public sectors. For example hospitals now have to compete for the funds of health trusts. Their advantage is that it is easier to gain access to data from such competitors than it is in the private sector.

Risk exposure. Risk can be measured according to finance theory. Some risks – for example exchange-rate risk and interest-rate risk – can be managed by the use of hedging mechanisms. Shareholders and entities can therefore choose how much risk they wish to be exposed to for a given level of return. However, risk can take many forms, and the theory does not deal with risk exposure to matters such as recruitment of senior personnel or competitor activity.

Public sector entities tend to be risk-averse because of the political repercussions of failure and the fact that taxpayers, unlike shareholders, do not have the option to invest their money in less (or more) risky ventures.

Objectives of not-for-profit organisations

Organisations such as charities and trade unions are not run to make profits but to benefit prescribed groups of people. For example, the primary objective of a charity is to pursue whatever charitable objectives it was set up for.

Since the services provided are limited primarily by the funds available, secondary objectives are to raise the maximum possible funds each year (net of fund-raising expenses), and to use the funds efficiently to maximise the benefit generated.

Financial objectives in the public sector

Financial objectives in public corporations

This category of organisation includes such bodies as nationalised industries and local government organisations. They represent a significant part of many countries' economies and sound financial management is essential if their affairs are to be conducted efficiently. The major problem here lies in obtaining a measurable objective.

For a stock market listed company we can take the maximisation of shareholder wealth as a working objective and know that the achievement of this objective can be monitored with reference to share price and dividend payments. For a public corporation the situation is more complex.

The entity's mission statement will lay out its key objectives. However, generally such organisations are run in the interests of society as a whole and therefore we should seek to attain the position where the gap between the benefits they provide to society and the costs of their operation is the widest (in positive terms).

The cost is relatively easily measured in accounting terms. However, many of the benefits are intangible. For example, the benefits of such bodies as the National Health Service or Local Education Authorities are almost impossible to quantify.

Such government organisations tend to use a low discount rate in investment appraisals (to take account of "time preference") and have complex methods of quantifying non-financial benefits in a standard NPV analysis.

Economists have tried to evaluate many public sector investments through the use of cost benefit analysis, with varying degrees of success. Problems are usually encountered in evaluating all the benefits. Value for money audits can be conducted in the public sector but these concentrate on monetary costs rather than benefits.

Note: A value for money audit is defined as an"investigation into whether proper arrangements have been made for securing economy, efficiency and effectiveness in the use of resources." (CIMA Official Terminology 2005)

Regulation

It is worth remembering that organisations that have had a public sector history or are themselves natural monopolies are often regulated in order to ensure the public are not the victims of the monopoly power these companies enjoy. This regulation can take many forms but can include the capping of the selling process, the taxing of super profits or simply a limit on the profits these organisations are allowed to make.

Performance and progress indicators – Public sector

Public sector entities are often appraised according to the "value for money" (VFM) that they generate.

Value for money may be defined as "performance of an activity in such a way as to simultaneously achieve economy, efficiency and effectiveness." (CIMA Official Terminology 2005)

This means maximising benefits for the lowest cost and has three constituent elements:

Economy is a measure of inputs to achieve a certain service or level of service.

Effectiveness is a measure of outputs, i.e. services/facilities.

Efficiency is the optimum of economy and effectiveness, i.e. the measure of outputs over inputs.

More detail on VFM

Measurement of VFM

In practice, value for money is difficult to measure, and it is a relative rather than an absolute measure. There will often be different views of what the objectives of a not-for-profit entity should be, and therefore, whether appropriate objectives have been achieved. What value does one put on curing an illness, or saving a life? Should the success of a hospital be measured by shorter waiting lists? These are societal matters, the discomfort being one of the reasons they are placed firmly in the public sector, rather than being left to the ‘survival of the fittest’ philosophy associated with the competitive markets.

A public sector college will measure the number of students, the number of courses, the ratio of lecturers to students, and so on. It will also seek its customers' assessments of the standard of, for example its lecturing and catering, and compare them with preset targets. In the language of strategic financial management, these are answers to the question 'How well did we do what we chose to do?'. You should also be aware, by now, of the dangers of concentrating on what can be measured. Note, for example that it is possible to measure crime detection, but it is not possible to measure crime prevention; it is possible to measure the extent to which the sick are cured, but not the extent to which sickness is prevented. People can be rewarded on the basis of measurables, but it should come as no surprise if they then skimp on the immeasurables: you get what you measure. Measuring performance is only a part of monitoring progress.

5 The Key Decisions of Financial Management

Three key decisions of financial management that can be identified are:

- Investment – what projects should be undertaken by the organisation?
- Finance – how should the necessary funds be raised?
- Dividends – how much cash should be allocated each year to be paid as a return to shareholders?

These three areas are very closely interlinked.

Investment decision

Financial managers have responsibility for the allocation of financial resources to achieve the organisation's objectives. An important part of their job is to understand the short, medium and long-term capital requirements for investment in fixed assets and working capital that fits with the overall strategy.

Whilst financial managers are unlikely to be solely responsible for the final choice of capital investment projects to be undertaken, they will be actively involved in the evaluation of possible investment opportunities.

More detail on the investment decision

When considering whether a project is worthwhile, a company must consider its implications. Any potential investment is likely to affect:

- **The liquidity of the company** – All projects involve cash flows in and out. The size and timing of such flows should be considered when appraising projects. If an aim of investment appraisal is to satisfy shareholders then it is important to remember that, if a company has no cash, it cannot pay a dividend.
- **The reported profit and earnings** – All projects will change the revenues, expenses and asset values shown in the financial accounts. If shareholders are concerned about such statistics as earnings per share, then the effect of investments on reported figures must be part of the investment appraisal.
- **The variability of cash flows and earnings** – Investors are concerned about the variability of returns from their investments. The greater the variability, the greater the risk, and therefore the greater the return they will require. Thus, when appraising potential projects, managers should consider not only the likely size and direction of cash flows and profits but also whether they are likely to add to or reduce the variability of such flows.

Finance decision

For both fixed asset and working capital investment, the financial manager must decide on the most appropriate type and source of funding.

This will include such considerations as:

- the extent to which requirements can be funded internally, from the organisation's operations. This will involve considerations of dividend policy and tax implications;
- if new, externally provided, finance is required, whether it should be in the form of equity or debt finance. This may affect the level of gearing (the ratio of debt to equity finance) which can have implications for returns required by the providers of capital;
- the extent to which working capital should be financed by long-term finance or short-term credit.

More detail on the financing decision

Financing decisions relate to acquiring the optimum finance to meet financial objectives and seeing that non-current assets and working capital are effectively managed.

The financial manager must possess a good knowledge of the sources of available funds and their respective costs, and should ensure that the entity has a sound capital structure, that is, a proper balance between equity capital and borrowings. Such managers also need to have a very clear understanding of the difference between profit and cash flow, bearing in mind that profit is of little avail unless the entity is adequately supported by cash to pay for assets and sustain the working capital cycle.

Financing decisions also call for a good knowledge of evaluation of risk: excessive borrowing carries high risk for an entity's equity because of the priority rights of the lenders.

A major area for risk-related decisions is in establishing foreign subsidiaries, where an entity is vulnerable to currency fluctuations. Foreign debt is often appropriate to create a hedge of the change in value of the net investment in the subsidiary as a result of currency movements.

Benefits of matching characteristics of investment and financing

The matching approach to financing is where the profile of the of the entity's financing matches the profile of the assets being funded.

This principle can be applied to the matching of maturities.

For example, using long-term finance to fund both non-current assets and permanent current assets, and financing fluctuating current assets by short-term borrowings.

Another area where the matching principle can be applied is in relation to funding a foreign subsidiary.

A matching foreign currency borrowing can be used to hedge of the net investment in the subsidiary against currency movements.

Hedge: Transaction to reduce or eliminate an exposure to risk. (CIMA Official Terminology, 2005)

Dividend decision

When deciding on the type of investment and level of finance needed, the financial manager must have regard for the potential effects on the risk and level of dividends payable to shareholders. If the shareholders are not happy with their return, they will be reluctant to invest further, which in turn will affect the funding available for future investment.

The dividend decision thus has two elements:

- the amount to be paid out, and
- the amount to be retained to support the growth of the entity (note that this is also a financing decision).

The level and regular growth of dividends represent a significant factor in determining a profit-making entity's market value, that is, the value placed on its shares by the stock market.

Links between the three key decisions

It is clear from the discussions above that the three areas are closely interrelated.

Investment decisions cannot be taken without consideration of where and how the funds are to be raised to finance them. The type of finance available will, in turn, depend to some extent on the nature of the project – its size, duration, risk, capital asset backing, etc.

Dividends represent the payment of returns on the investment back to the shareholders, the level and risk of which will depend upon the project itself, and how it was financed.

Debt finance, for example, can be cheap (particularly where interest is tax deductible) but requires an interest payment to be made out of project earnings, which can increase the risk of the shareholders' dividends.

6 Dividend Policy

One long-standing question in corporate finance is: Is shareholders' wealth affected by a company's dividend policy?

Notice that the question is not asking whether *dividends* matter – of course they do (as we know from the dividend valuation model) – what the question asks is whether the chosen *policy* matters. Examples of such policies may include:

(i) paying a constant annual dividend;

(ii) paying out a constant proportion of annual earnings;

(iii) increasing dividends in line with the annual rate of inflation, etc;

(iv) paying out what's left after financing all future investment – the residual policy.

Four aspects to consider in relation to the payment of dividends are:

(1) Modigliani and Miller's (M & M) dividend irrelevancy argument.

(2) The clientele effect.

(3) The bird-in-the-hand argument.

(4) The signalling effect or information content of dividends.

Dividend irrelevancy

M & M's dividend irrelevancy theory says that the pattern of dividend payout should be irrelevant. As long as companies continue to invest in positive NPV projects, the wealth of the shareholders should increase whether or not the company makes a dividend payment this year.

M & M's Dividend Irrelevancy Theory

M & M's argument here is built up as follows:

(i) The return on a share is determined by the share's (systematic) risk.

(ii) The return itself is delivered to shareholders in two parts: one part is the dividend paid and the other is the capital gain/loss in the share price.

(iii) The dividend decision that a company makes is a decision as to how the return is delivered: how much of the annual earnings should be paid out as dividends and how much of the annual earnings should be retained and re-invested within the company – and so flow through to shareholders in the form of a capital gain on the share price.

(iv) As the dividend decision does not affect the *risk* of the shares, it does not affect their *return*. All the dividend decision therefore does is to determine *how* the return is to be split up between dividends and capital gains.

(v) Do shareholders mind how their returns are split between dividends and capital gains? The answer according to M & M is: no, they do not *if* we assume:

(a) There are no taxes (really, there are no differences between the taxation on dividends and on capital gains).

(b) Shares can be bought and sold free of any transaction costs (such as stock-brokers' commission).

M & M argue that shareholders can 'manufacture' a dividend policy irrespective of the company policy. For instance, if a person is holding shares for income but the company withholds a dividend, the shareholder can sell some of the shares to replace the lost income.

The assumptions that M & M make play a key role. Obviously, if dividends were taxed and capital gains were tax free, shareholders *would* mind how their return was delivered - they would strongly prefer it to be delivered in the form of capital gains rather than dividends.

Similarly, investors who were holding shares for the income they generated *would* mind how their return was delivered if they had to incur transaction costs when realising their capital gains so as to turn them into income – such investors would strongly prefer if the return were delivered in the form of dividends, rather than capital gains.

However, given their assumptions hold good, M & M could claim that shareholders are indifferent between dividends and capital gains and so the dividend decision / the dividend policy that the company pursues is irrelevant.

Clientele effect

This analysis argues that, in the real world, there are differential tax treatments of dividends and capital gains, and there are transaction costs on share dealings.

As a result, shareholders *are* concerned as to how their return is delivered to them by the company. Thus companies should follow a *consistent* dividend policy so as to ensure that they gather to them a clientele of shareholders who like that particular policy.

Thus the argument here is that the *actual* dividend policy that a company follows is unimportant but, having decided on a particular policy, it should then keep to it.

The bird-in-the-hand argument

This analysis puts forward a very simple argument. Some investors may find capital gains more tax-efficient than dividends, and some investors will avoid transaction costs if their returns are delivered in the form of capital gains rather than dividends; despite all this, investors generally have a strong preference for dividends.

The reason given is that a dividend is *certain* and investors prefer a certain dividend *now*, to the promise of uncertain *future* dividends (arising out of retaining and re-investing earnings).

The signalling effect

This theory holds that investors read 'signals' into the company's dividend decision and that these signals say as much about the company's *future* financial performance as they say about its *past* financial performance.

Thus management will not necessarily reduce the dividend per share just because last year's performance was poor, if they believe that *next* year's performance will be good.

If this theory is correct, and investors do indeed read signals into the dividend decision, then the dividend decision becomes important: it becomes important for the company *not* to give the *wrong* signal.

More details on signalling

It is widely believed that there are two very strong dividend signals:

(1) a *reduction in the dividend* per share signals that the company is in financial difficulties;

(2) a *failure to pay out any dividend* at all signals that the company is very close to receivership.

Thus a company must take great care when settings dividend levels and ensure that the market is kept fully informed of future prospects.

These ideas are very widely held in practice and this view is supported by Lintner who discovered that dividend growth lagged two to three years behind earnings growth. This evidence can be interpreted to mean that managers are reluctant to increase the dividend per share until they are *confident* that they will be able to maintain that new level of dividends in the future (and will not be subsequently obliged to reduce the dividend per share).

How to reconcile these differing views of dividend policy in the real world

Given these contrasting views, how are managers to decide on the dividend policy that they should pursue?

The answer is that, in the real world, like so much else in corporate finance, managers have to make a *judgement* after taking many varying factors into account.

In this process they will consider:

(1) What dividends are our shareholders expecting (i.e. the clientele effect)?

(2) What dividend did we pay last time (i.e. we must not pay less than that because of the signal that it might give)?

However they will also take into account a range of other factors, such as:

(3) Is it legal to pay out a dividend?

(4) Is the cash available to pay out a dividend?

(5) Do we have a minimum gearing ratio imposed on the company as a financial covenant in a debt agreement?

(6) What is the tax impact for shareholders of paying dividends?

(7) What investment opportunities does the company face?

(8) How difficult/expensive is it to raise external finance?

(9) What has been the rate of inflation (and so what dividend increase is needed to maintain the purchasing power of last year's dividends)?

(10) What has been the capital gain/loss in the share price over the last year?

Scrip / bonus dividends and share repurchase

Scrip dividends

A scrip dividend (or bonus / scrip issue) is where shareholders are offered bonus shares free of charge as an alternative to a cash dividend.

They are useful where the company wishes to retain cash in the business or where shareholders wish to reinvest dividends in the company but avoid brokerage costs of buying shares. There may also be tax advantages of receiving shares rather than cash in some jurisdictions.

A recent issue by Santander bank in February 2011 was set up in a similar manner to a rights issue except that the rights were issued without charge.

Shareholders were given rights to receive additional Santander shares and three options for their allotment of rights:

(1) Sell the rights off market to Santander and receive a fixed cash amount.

(2) Sell the rights on market and receive cash.

(3) Hold the rights and receive new Santander shares, 1 share for every 65 rights held.

If all shareholders opt for bonus shares, the scrip issue has the effect of capitalising reserves. Reserves reduce and share capital increases.

The disadvantage to shareholders is that, unlike reserves, share capital is non-distributable in the future. In addition, both share price and earnings per share are likely to fall due to the greater number of shares in issue, although the overall value of each shareholder's shares and share in future earnings should, theoretically, remain unchanged.

However, it has the important advantage to the issuer of retaining cash in the business while still achieving a distribution of reserves.

Share repurchase

A share repurchase can be used to return surplus cash to shareholders.

It tends to be used when the company has no positive NPV projects to invest the cash in, so it returns the cash to shareholders so that they can make better use of it rather than it sitting idle (in cash investments) in the company.

Alternatively, a share repurchase can be used to privatise a company, by buying back a listed company's shares from a wide pool of investors. However, this is rare.

Share repurchase v one-off large dividend

As an alternative to a share repurchase, a company may decide to use a one-off large dividend to return surplus cash to shareholders.

If all shareholders agree to the repurchase, both a share repurchase and a one-off large dividend have the same impact on the cash, and the gearing of the company (they reduce the value of equity, so increase the gearing and hence financial risk and cost of equity). Although the impact on shareholder value is the same for any individual shareholder, the impact on the price per share will differ. A dividend results in a lower share price as the number of shares remains the same, but a share repurchase is unlikely to affect the individual share price but only the number of shares in issue.

The one-off dividend has the advantage of certainty of ultimate payout. However, a share repurchase has the following advantages:

- investors can choose whether or not to sell their shares back (they may prefer to keep the shares if they feel that future returns will be high)
- it avoids the risk of a false dividend signal – after a one-off large dividend, the shareholders may be disappointed when the higher level of dividend is not maintained in the future.

7 Exam style questions

Test your understanding 1 – Stakeholders

Quotation 1

'The directors of all businesses must consider the wishes of all potential stakeholders for whose support they are competing – not just owners but employees, suppliers, customers, lenders, regulators and the community in which their business operates.'

Quotation 2

'Stakeholder theory is incompatible with business and its objectives and should be firmly resisted.'

Required:

Discuss the opposing arguments in the two quotations given above, and explain how these views might be reconciled.

Test your understanding 2 – Public v private sector objectives

Public sector organisations do not have the requirement to produce 'profit' in the same sense as the private sector. However, they are expected to work within budgets and recognise aspects of financial management familiar to the private sector.

The following are four examples of differences between the public and private sector:

(1) A company that operates a chain of private hospitals uses a discount rate of 16% to evaluate its investment decisions and generally expects an accounting rate of return of 25%. A government-funded hospital trust is required to achieve a return of only 6% on assets.

(2) Private sector companies are moving towards a more flexible approach to budgeting. Organisations in the public sector are moving in the opposite direction i.e. towards a more rigid approach to budgeting, enforced by the Treasury (up to three years).

(3) Public sector pay is subject to government controls and has for many years failed to keep pace with inflation. Market forces determine wages and salaries in the private sector.

Required:

Discuss the causes and consequences of the three scenarios outlined above, using examples to illustrate your answer where appropriate.

Note: Overseas candidates may use examples of organisations in their own country.

Test your understanding 3 – Dividend policy and financing

DIVS plc is a large international company with widespread interests in advertising, media and various consultancy activities associated with sales promotion and marketing. In recent years the company's earnings and dividend payments, in real terms, have grown on average by 15% and 12% per year respectively. The company is likely to have substantial cash surpluses in the coming year, but a number of investment opportunities are being considered for the subsequent two years. The senior managers of the company are reviewing their likely funding requirements for the next two to three years and the possible consequences for dividend policy.

At present the company has a debt : equity ratio of 1 : 5, measured in market value terms. It does not want to increase this ratio at the present time but might need to borrow to pay a maintained dividend in the future.

The senior managers of the company are discussing a range of issues concerning financial strategy in general and dividend policy in particular.

Required:

Assume you are an independent financial advisor to the board of DIVS plc. Write a report to the board which discusses the following issues:

(i) **The re-purchase of some of the company's shares in the coming year using the forecast surplus cash, the aim being to reduce the amount of cash needed to pay dividends in subsequent years. Other implications of share repurchase for the company's financial strategy should also be considered.**

(ii) **The advisability of borrowing money to pay dividends in years 2 and 3.**

(iii) **The likely effect on the company's cost of equity if the company decides on share repurchase and / or further borrowing.**

(25 marks)

Test your understanding answers

Test your understanding 1 – Stakeholders

A sensible starting point is to list the various stakeholders and show how their interests may conflict, before reconciling the two statements.

A firm is a collection of contributors, all of whom have a stake in its ongoing success and survival. In a narrow sense, their respective interests are bound to conflict if pushed to the limit.

- Owners – want maximum dividends and share price.
- Lenders – want maximum security for their investment.
- Managers – want maximum pay and other forms of remuneration.
- Other employees – want maximum pay for minimum effort plus optimal health and safety standards.
- Customers – want maximum quality at minimum price plus maximum credit.
- Suppliers – want minimum settlement delay.
- Government – wants maximum tax take.
- Society – wants maximum environmental safeguards, contributions to charity and local community projects.

If pushed to the limit, most of these aims are likely to bankrupt the business. If shareholders' aims are pursued neglecting all else, it requires screwing down wages and conditions to minimal levels, racking up prices to take maximum advantage of short-term opportunities, never paying suppliers until threatened with legal action, and so on.

Such behaviour is not just anti-social, it is anti-survival. It will attract critical attention from the government and other bodies, resulting in penalties, fines and ongoing scrutiny which will damage the firm's reputation and market position irretrievably.

The SWM aim is not a short-term profit maximising aim. It aims to create sustainable and permanent value for owners. It is thoroughly consistent with treating customers and employees well and building up an image as a respected contributor to society.

It is thus easy to reconcile the two statements – firms that treat their stakeholders badly are unlikely to survive into the long term. To 'consider the wishes of all potential stakeholders' does not require *maximising* everyone's particular interests but striking a balance between them to the ultimate and ongoing benefit of all. This is simply good business.

Test your understanding 2 – Public v private sector objectives

(1) **Rates of return**

The private sector company has a higher required rate of return, and uses more measures of financial success than the public sector entity.

Causes

The private sector entity has a primary objective to increase shareholder wealth, so it has to measure financial performance carefully.

Its required rate of return is higher because the investors in the private entity perceive risk to be high. Public sector entities face lower risk since they are supported by governments.

The cost of finance for the public sector entity (provided by the government) will be lower, since the government can usually borrow money very cheaply. This means that the required return can be lower.

Consequences

The public sector entity will be more inclined to undertake relatively low return projects which the private sector entity will reject. Therefore, "unprofitable" treatments will still be undertaken in the public sector.

The private sector entity will perform a narrow range of treatments very efficiently. The public sector entity will offer a much broader range of treatments.

The lower required return in the public sector will give less incentive to reduce costs, so the public sector entity may be less efficient than the private sector.

(2) **Budgets**

Private sector entities have more flexible budgeting procedures than public sector entities.

Causes

Public sector entities tend to be larger, and have more bureaucratic structures. Hence, public sector budgeting can be a much more complex process.

The public sector is expected to look further into the future (3 years) whereas a private sector budget may only last for 1 year.

Private sector entities have a flexible approach to financing (effectively any project can be undertaken if the finance can be found). Public sector entities are allocated finance by government and therefore have an objective to work within this imposed constraint. Flexibility is therefore less important in a public sector entity.

The government likes to be able to compare performance of different public sector entities, so often a standard, rigid method of budgeting is proposed to enable comparisons to be made easily.

Consequences

Private sector entities find it easier to adapt quickly to real world factors which impact them.

Private sector entities tend to have a more flexible, "can-do" culture.

Public sector budgets tend to contain more budgetary slack, because the budget has often been set well in advance and then not amended to reflect new factors which come to light.

(3) **Pay**

Public sector pay lags behind that in the private sector.

Causes

Public sector job security tends to be better, so pay is not the only attraction of holding a public sector job.

Also, public sector pensions tend to be government funded, final salary schemes. In the private sector, final salary schemes are becoming less prevalent as firms struggle to afford them.

The government often tries to control inflation by keeping public sector pay rises under control. A low pay rise for public sector workers can be used as a signal of financial prudence.

Public sector staff are paid relatively little as a bonus or incentive payment. Most of the pay tends to be a basic salary determined by a very detailed pay scale.

Consequences

Public sector morale and motivation is often lower than in the private sector.

Good quality staff are often attracted to private sector roles where the staff are better rewarded.

The lack of bonuses in the public sector sometimes stifles creativity and discourages the use of initiative.

Test your understanding 3 – Dividend policy and financing

Report

To: Board of Directors, DIVS plc

From: Independent financial advisor

Date: XX/XX/XX

Re: Dividend policy and other financing issues

You are currently considering the current and future position of the company as regards dividend payments and financing over the next two to three years, in the light of your current cash surplus and the investment opportunities available to you from next year.

This report addresses the following issues:

- the implications of share re-purchase to reduce future dividend payments;
- borrowing funds to finance dividends;
- the possible effects on cost of equity if either or both of the above actions are taken.

(i) *Share re-purchase*

You are likely to have substantial cash surpluses in the coming year. Your first decision is to decide how much to distribute, bearing in mind both your investment financing requirements in the future and the possible reactions of shareholders and other market players. In the current climate, it is expected that 'spare' cash, in excess of that required for specific profitable investment opportunities, should be returned to the shareholders to do with as they wish.

You have some investment opportunities open to you in the near future. Whether or not you have to retain some of the current surplus cash to fund these will depend upon the extent to which you expect there to be spare funds generated in the next two or three years.

Once the amount to be distributed (if any) has been decided upon, you then need to decide whether to return it to all the shareholders as a dividend, or to some of them in the form of a share re-purchase. The latter option will result in only a small number of shareholders – likely to be the large institutional investors – receiving cash, although their proportionate holding, and therefore entitlement to future dividends, will be reduced. Other shareholders will have to sell shares, incurring transaction costs, to 'manufacture' dividends should they need them.

It should be noted that a share re-purchase is administratively more complex in that it requires prior approval from a general meeting of shareholders (assuming the Articles of Association provide that it can happen at all). It is also no longer possible for institutions to reclaim tax on the distribution in the UK.

The two types of distribution will also affect share prices differently. When a dividend is declared, the value of the shares falls from cum-div to ex-div, the shareholders having had some of their capital investment realised as cash.

In theory, if the share re-purchase is made at current market price, a share re-purchase should leave the individual share price unchanged – there has been a reduction in total market value in proportion to the total number of shares in issue.

It should also be noted that a share re-purchase would result in a higher future EPS figure than if a normal dividend had been paid. However this should not affect the market's perception of the health of the company, as it is purely a result of the same earnings being spread over a smaller number of shares.

Overall, it would appear that there is no particularly strong argument for a share re-purchase in preference to a dividend payment to all shareholders. Whilst you may see this as a means of reducing future dividend payments, it is likely that the remaining shareholders, who would be holding a greater proportion of shares than previously, would expect a higher dividend per share. If this expectation is not met, share prices may be affected adversely.

(ii) *Borrowing to pay dividends*

If it is decided to distribute an amount in the current year that cannot be maintained (with planned growth) in future years out of operational cash flows, then additional funds will need to be borrowed.

This will raise the company's gearing level above the current 1:5 debt:equity ratio, with two consequences. First, the company will be funded by a greater proportion of cheap finance, particularly as debt interest is tax deductible. Second, shareholders may perceive a greater risk as being attached to their dividends, as more of the earnings are attributed to fixed interest payments. It is a question of finding the optimum balance between these two effects.

(iii) Effect on cost of equity

The probable effect of increasing the gearing level will be, as discussed in (ii) above, to increase the required return by (cost of) equity. Borrowing will directly affect the gearing level, by increasing the debt element.

The payment of a dividend or a share repurchase will also increase the gearing level, by lowering the value of the equity (as discussed in (i) above, a dividend results in a lower share price with the number of shares being maintained; a share repurchase results in a maintained share price with a lower number of shares).

Thus both actions may result in a higher cost of equity.

Overall recommendations

It is advised that any surplus cash over and above the needs of all positive NPV investments should be paid out in the form of a dividend. This 'residual' dividend policy may lead to fluctuating dividends, however, and institutional investors generally prefer a steady dividend pattern; you will need to keep a careful eye on your share price to ensure it is not being adversely affected in the long term.

Should you need to borrow in the future, you should find this to your advantage, as your current gearing level is quite low, and the benefits of cheaper debt should outweigh any increase in cost of equity.

chapter

3

Performance Measurement in Financial Strategy

Chapter learning objectives

Lead	Component
A2: Evaluate the strategic financial strategies and objectives of an organisation and the extent of their attainment.	(a) identify an organisation's objectives in financial terms. (b) evaluate the attainment of an organisation's financial objectives. (c) evaluate current and forecast performance taking account of potential variations in economic and business factors. (d) evaluate alternative financial strategies for an organisation, taking account of assessment of the organisation by financiers and other stakeholders, including likely changes to such assessment in the light of developments in reporting.

Indicative syllabus content

- The financial objectives of an organisation and economic forces affecting its financial plans (e.g. interest, inflation and exchange rates).
- Assessing attainment of financial objectives.
- Use of financial analysis in the external assessment of a company (e.g. in assessing creditworthiness and compliance with financing covenants).
- Modelling and forecasting cash flows and financial statements based on expected values for economic variables (e.g. interest rates) and business variables (e.g. volume and margins) over a number of years.
- Analysis of sensitivity to changes in expected values in the above models and forecasts.
- Assessing the implications for shareholder value of alternative financial strategies, including dividend policy. (Note: Modigliani and Miller's theory of dividend irrelevancy will be tested in broad terms.The mathematical proof of the model will not be required, but some understanding of the graphical method is expected).
- The lender's assessment of creditworthiness.
- Current and emerging issues in financial reporting (e.g. proposals to amend or introduce new accounting standards) and in other forms of external reporting (e.g. environmental accounting).

1 Overview of Chapter

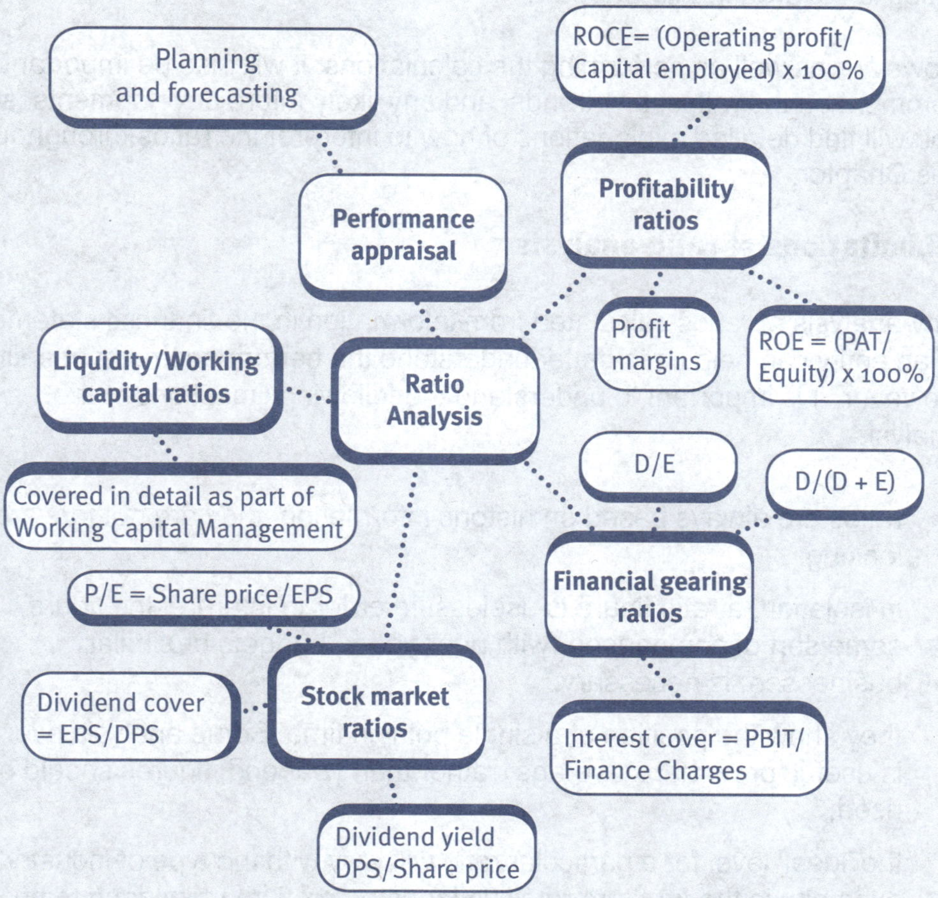

Performance evaluation

Investors (both shareholders and lenders) will often appraise the performance of an organisation, to assess whether the organisation represents a good investment. If it is shown that the organisation's performance is declining, the shareholders may decide to sell their shares, and the lenders might change their assessment of the organisation's creditworthiness.

In an exam question, you might also be asked to use ratio analysis to assess whether an entity has met its objectives.

To appraise performance, it is necessary to first calculate ratios under the following headings:

- profitability ratios,
- liquidity ratios (essentially the working capital ratios covered in the later Chapter 'Short Term Finance – Working Capital Management'),
- gearing ratios,
- stock market ratios.

With the exception of the liquidity ratios covered in the later Chapter 'Short Term Finance – Working Capital Management', the calculation of these ratios is covered in this Chapter.

However, as well as performing the calculations, it will also be important to comment on the ratios, any trends, and any likely future developments, so you will find detailed explanations of how to interpret the ratios throughout this Chapter.

2 Limitations of ratio analysis

Any analysis of ratios calculated from information in the financial statements of an entity can help us to better understand the performance of that entity. However, it is important to understand the following limitations of the analysis:

- ratios are always based on historic information, they are not forward looking;
- in isolation, a ratio figure is useless. In order to interpret the figure, some sort of comparison (with prior years, budgets or similar businesses) is necessary;
- they show the position at a single point in time. Some analysis over time is useful, or perhaps average, rather than year end, figures should be used;
- the 'ideal' level for a particular ratio will vary with the type of industry. For example, in the furniture retailing industry, profit margins tend to be much higher than in the food retailing industry;
- different accounting policies might distort some ratios, making it difficult to compare different businesses;
- the basic ratio figures need to be interpreted carefully. For example, an entity with high levels of receivables will appear to have good liquidity ratios, when in fact it may be struggling to collect overdue debts.

3 Profitability Ratios

Several profit figures (gross profit, operating profit, net profit) can be identified in a typical income statement.

Each may be used to evaluate the profitability of the business.

Rationale for analysing profitability

Profitability and revenue

When analysing the performance of an entity, a useful starting point is the examination of revenue. Revenue is important in both absolute and relative terms.

Increases or decreases in revenue may be attributable to changes in selling prices or sales volumes or a combination of the two factors.

Problems can arise in making a valid interpretation of movements in revenue. For example:

- Accounting policies on revenue recognition may vary between businesses. There may be inconsistencies between accounting periods, especially where the business derives some or all of its revenue from long-term contracts.
- Inflation may account for some of the increase in price.
- A detailed breakdown of revenue for the business may not be available. To some extent, IAS 14 Segment reporting stipulates revenue details for different segments of the entity.

Understanding the reasons for movements in revenue may help to explain movements in costs such as cost of sales, advertising, selling and distribution costs and telephone charges.

If revenue increases, then a similar increase in these revenue-related costs could be expected. Conversely, an increase in, say, marketing and advertising expenditure might help to explain an increase in revenue.

Definitions of different profit figures

Profit figures in the income statement

Gross profit = Sales – Cost of Sales

Operating profit = profit from the trading activities of an entity i.e. sales – operating costs, but before finance costs (interest) and tax

Net profit = Profit after deduction of the finance costs (interest) and tax

EBITDA

EBITDA is an acronym for earnings before interest, tax, depreciation and amortization. In recent years many large entities have adopted EBITDA as a key measure of financial performance. Sceptics suggest that they do this in order to publicise a higher measure of earnings than profit from operations (this type of measurement is sometimes cynically referred to as EBB – earnings before the bad bits).

However, it does make some sense to measure EBITDA, provided that the user fully understands what is included and what is left out. Depreciation and amortization are accounting adjustments, not representing cash flows, that are determined by management. It can therefore be argued that excluding these items in assessing earnings eliminates a major area where management bias can operate. Unfortunately, EBITDA is consequently often misunderstood as being a measurement of cash flow, which of course it is not. Even though two categories of non-cash adjustment are eliminated, financial statements are prepared on an accruals basis. EBITDA makes no adjustments in respect of accruals or working capital movements, and so is emphatically not a cash flow measurement.

Profit margin calculations

Gross profit margin

$$\text{Gross profit margin} = \frac{\text{Gross profit}}{\text{Revenue}} \times 100$$

Generally, a high profit margin is perceived to be indicative of good performance.

This ratio might be expected to be more or less constant from one year to the next within an entity. Even if there is an increase in direct costs, an efficient entity could be expected to pass on the increases in the form of increased sales prices. However, this may not be the case in practice.

The gross profit margin requires a detailed breakdown in order to gain an understanding of variations. Ideally, the analyst requires information relating to opening and closing inventories, purchases, direct wages and overheads. Further information as to the following items would be required in order to evaluate gross profit margin fully:

- breakdown by product, geographical area or other segment;
- inventory valuation policies;
- overhead allocation methods;
- purchasing details such as bulk discounts, purchasing errors, wastage or theft;
- selling prices of different products over the period.

Obviously, much of this information is not available from an entity's annual report. Some businesses do not even report gross profits.

Operating profit margin

$$\text{Operating profit margin} = \frac{\text{Operating profit}}{\text{Revenue}} \times 100$$

The operating profit margin is trading or operating profit in relation to revenue, expressed as a percentage.

Further analysis might include measuring operating costs as a percentage of revenue, and comparing to benchmarks, budgets, previous years or industry averages. For example:

$$\frac{\text{Admin. costs}}{\text{Revenue}} \times 100$$

$$\frac{\text{Advertising costs}}{\text{Revenue}} \times 100$$

Net profit margin

Net profit margin expresses the relationship between net profit and sales.

$$\text{Net profit margin} = \frac{\text{Net profit}}{\text{Revenue}} \times 100$$

Where comparing net profit year on year, it is important to allow for any exceptional charges or credits. Also, it would be sensible to take into account any large adjustments in respect of under- or over-provided tax provisions.

There are two measures critical to any analysis of profitability:

(1) **Return on Capital Employed (ROCE)**

(2) **Return on Equity (ROE)**

Return on capital employed (ROCE)

Return on capital employed (ROCE) is a measurement that is frequently used in the analysis of financial statements.

It shows the overall performance of the entity, expressed as a percentage return on the total investment. It measures management's efficiency in generating profits from the resources available.

ROCE is expressed as a percentage, and is calculated as follows:

$$\text{ROCE} = \frac{\text{Operating profit}}{\text{Capital employed}} \times 100$$

where Capital employed = The total funds invested in the business, i.e. shareholders' funds + long term debt, or total assets less current liabilities.

Return on equity (ROE)

ROE gives an indication as to how well the company has performed in relation to its shareholders, the most important stakeholder.

ROE is expressed as a percentage, and is calculated as follows:

$$\text{ROE} = \frac{\text{Net profit}}{\text{Equity}} \times 100$$

where Equity = The book value of shareholders' funds

It is useful to compare the ROE to the ROCE to measure the amount of the return underlying the business that pertains to the shareholder. Note, however, that they are not directly comparable, ROE being based on net profit and ROCE based on operating profit.

Activity ratios

A further, related, set of ratios can be calculated that indicate the efficiency of usage of the entity's assets in producing revenue and profits.

Asset turnover

$$\text{Asset turnover} = \frac{\text{Revenue}}{\text{Capital employed}}$$

This calculation is usually expressed as a simple ratio, rather than as a percentage. It shows how much revenue is produced per $ of investment in capital employed. The overall ratio can be further broken down to show revenue in relation to other categories of asset. For example, a useful ratio in certain contexts is:

$$\frac{\text{Revenue}}{\text{Non-current assets}}$$

This ratio shows the productivity of non-current assets in generating sales. It should be noted that this ratio is not always useful or informative. Where an entity is using assets that are nearing the end of their useful lives, having been subject to annual depreciation charges over a relatively long period, the ratio is likely to be rather high. Similarly, where an entity uses the historical cost convention, unmodified by revaluation, asset values are also likely to be relatively low, an effect which is more intrusive as the assets age. Also, in labour-intensive entities, where the non-current asset base is low, the ratio tends to lack significance.

Inventory turnover

Conventionally, inventory turnover is expressed in terms of cost of sales, rather than of revenue. If cost of sales is not available, perhaps because the entity does not have a policy of disclosing gross profit, revenue could be used. Provided it is used consistently when making comparisons, the ratio will have some information content.

However, where the information is available, cost of sales is to be preferred. The inventory turnover ratio indicates the liquidity of inventories. The higher the ratio, the more quickly inventory is being sold:

$$\text{Inventory turnover} = \frac{\text{Cost of sales}}{\text{Average inventory}}$$

Application of this formula gives a figure which shows the number of times, on average, that inventory has turned over during the year. If only a closing figure is available for inventory, then that can be used. However, the result must be treated with some caution, as the closing figure may be unrepresentative.

Return on capital employed – further analysis

When trying to analyse ROCE, it can be useful to break it down as follows into two component ratios:

ROCE = Operating profit margin × Asset turnover

The relationship becomes clear when we put the ratio calculations into the formula:

$$\frac{\text{Operating profit}}{\text{Capital employed}} \times 100 = \frac{\text{Operating profit}}{\text{Revenue}} \times 100 \times \frac{\text{Revenue}}{\text{Capital employed}}$$

Analysing the component ratios may throw some light on the cause of a change in ROCE.

For example, a fall in ROCE could be caused by:

- generating lower sales from the company's capital (lower asset turnover), and / or
- generating a lower profit margin on the sales which have been achieved (lower operating profit margin).

Example 1

A company is considering two funding options for a new project. The new project may be funded by GBP10m of equity or debt. Below are the forecast financial statements reflecting both methods of funding.

Balance sheet extract

	Equity	*Debt*
	GBPm	GBPm
Long term liabilities (10% debentures)	0.0	10.0
Capital		
Share capital (50 pence)	11.0	3.5
Share premium	4.0	1.5
Reserves	5.0	5.0
	20.0	10.0

Income Statement extract

	GBPm
Revenue	100.0
Gross profit	20.0
Less expenses (excluding finance charges)	(15.0)
Operating profit	5.0

Corporation tax is charged at 30%.

Required:

(a) **Calculate the operating profit margin and the asset turnover.**

(b) **Calculate Return on Capital Employed and Return on Equity, and compare the financial performance of the company under the two funding methods.**

(c) **What is the impact on the company's performance of financing by debt rather than equity?**

Interpretation of profitability ratios

In general terms, high levels of profitability are desirable.

An entity with high profit margins and a high ROCE is usually perceived to be performing well. Similarly, if the ratios grow over time, this is usually perceived to be positive.

The ideal value for the profitability ratios will vary from industry to industry, so be sure to compare the figures to previous years and to other similar businesses if possible.

4 Financial Gearing

Definition of gearing

CIMA's Official Terminology provides the following definition of gearing:

> the relationship between an entity's borrowings, which includes both prior charge capital and long-term debt, and its shareholders' funds (ordinary share capital plus reserves).

Rationale for analysing gearing

Analysis of capital structure

The gearing ratio is an important measure of risk. It is important to analyse, particularly for users such as shareholders and creditors, the ability to satisfy debts falling due after one year. There are two elements to consider: repayment of capital and payment of interest.

The assessment of an entity's gearing risk can be identified from two areas. The balance sheet shows the current liquidity and capital structure of the entity, that is the short-term liquidity and the level of fixed prior charge capital. The income statement shows the profitability of the entity generally, indicating its ability to generate cash, some of which may be available to repay debt.

The capital structure of the entity provides information about the relative risk that is accepted by shareholders and creditors. As long-term debt increases relative to share-holders' funds then more risk is assumed by long-term creditors and so they would require higher rewards, thereby decreasing resources available for the shareholders. As risk increases, creditors require higher interest in order to compensate for the higher risk.

However, the use of debt by management in their capital structure can assist in increasing profits available to shareholders. Cash received into the business from lenders will be used to generate revenue and profits. As interest costs are fixed, any profits generated in excess of the interest costs will accrue to the shareholders. There is, however, a negative side to the use of debt in the business. If the cash from the debt does not raise sufficient profits then the fixed interest cost must be paid first and so profits available to shareholders are decreased, and may be extinguished completely.

Gearing is the mix of debt to equity within a firm's permanent capital. There are two particularly useful measures:

(1) Capital gearing – a statement of financial position (balance sheet) measure.

(2) Interest cover – an income statement measure.

Capital gearing – a measure of capital structure

There are two key measures of capital gearing:

$$\text{Capital gearing} = \frac{\text{Debt}}{\text{Equity}} \times 100$$

$$\frac{\text{Debt}}{\text{Debt + Equity}} \times 100$$

The calculation of capital gearing can be done in a number of different ways. In an exam, make sure that you show your workings, and use the same formula consistently.

What do debt and equity contain?

Debt

All permanent capital charging a fixed charge (interest) may be considered to be debt. This includes debentures and loans naturally. It may include bank overdraft if significant and considered part of the permanent financing. Similarly, cash and cash equivalents should be deducted when calculating debt in gearing calculations if the cash is regarded as a 'permanent' cash buffer.

Equity

All ordinary share capital and share premium together with reserves (they relate to the ordinary shareholders).

A note on preference shares:

Preference shares should be treated in the following way - if they are irredeemable, treat as equity and, if redeemable, treat as debt.

Market value and book value of equity and debt

Wherever possible, market values should be used in preference to book values for the capital gearing ratio.

When using market values, care must be taken when calculating the market value of equity:

When equity is valued using book values it must include any reserves and retained profits that are attributable to the ordinary shareholders that is:

Book value of equity = ordinary share capital + reserves

When market values are used, reserves must be excluded since they are considered to be already incorporated into the market price of the shares, that is:

Market value of equity = Number of shares × Share price

Interest cover

The interest cover ratio indicates the number of times profits will cover the interest charge; the higher the ratio, the better.

$$\text{Interest cover} = \frac{\text{Profit before interest and tax}}{\text{Interest payable}}$$

The interest cover ratio is used by lenders to determine the vulnerability of interest payments to a drop in profit.

As an alternative to the formula shown here, investors often use EBITDA rather than profit before interest and tax in the formula, because EBITDA is a better approximation to the cash generated by the business (and available to pay interest with).

The debt ratio

Debt ratio

Another useful ratio is the ratio of long-term debt to total assets, which is calculated as follows:

$$\text{Debt ratio} = \frac{\text{Total long term debt}}{\text{Total assets}}$$

This can provide very useful information for creditors as it measures the availability of assets in the business in relation to the total debt.

Example 2

Balance sheet (statement of financial position) for X Co

	USDm
Non-current assets (total)	23.0
Current assets (total)	15.0
TOTAL ASSETS	**38.0**
Equity and Liabilities	
Ordinary share capital	10.0
Ordinary share premium	4.0
Preference share capital (irredeemable)	1.5
Reserves	1.5
Non-current liabilities	
Debenture 10%	8.0
Current liabilities	
Trade creditors	8.0
Bank overdraft	5.0
TOTAL EQUITY & LIABILITIES	**38.0**

X Co Income Statement Extract

	USDm
Operating profit (PBIT)	4.0
Finance Charges	(1.0)
Profit before tax (PBT)	3.0
Tax @ 30%	(0.9)
Net profit	2.1

Required:

(a) **Calculate the interest cover and the capital gearing ratio for X Co.**

(b) **Comment on the results of your calculations in part (a).**

Operating and financial leverage

The use of borrowings introduces financial risk to the balance sheet. This financial risk means that the earnings available to the ordinary shareholders become more volatile if the interest charges on borrowings are fixed.

This effect on earnings is similar to the effect of leverage, which considers the relationship between fixed and variable charges and their effect on profits.

Leverage may be calculated using the following two ratios:

$$\text{Operating leverage} = \frac{\text{Contribution}}{\text{Profit before interest and tax}}$$

$$\text{Financial leverage} = \frac{\text{Profit before interest and tax}}{\text{Profit before tax}}$$

Their use is best explained by means of an example:

	Year 1	Year 2	% change
	$000	$000	
Revenue	1,000	1,100	10
Variable costs	(400)	(440)	
Fixed costs	(200)	(200)	
Operating profit	400	460	15
Interest payments	(50)	(50)	
Profit before tax	350	410	17.1

For year 1, **operating leverage** = 600 / 400 = 1.5

Operating leverage indicates by how much fixed costs could increase without the company making an operating loss. Operating leverage is sometimes referred to as operating gearing. The figure of 1.5 also indicates that a 10% increase in sales would result in a 15% increase in operating profits (10 × 1.5).

For year 1, **financial leverage** = 400 / 350 = 1.14

Financial leverage indicates by how much interest payments could increase without the company making a pre-tax loss.

By multiplying the two leverage measures together, it can be shown that a 10% increase in sales would result in a 17.1% increase in profit before tax, that is,

Total leverage = (1.5 ×1.14) = 1.71, giving an increase in profit before tax of 17.1% (10 × 1.71).

These projected increases are illustrated in the income statement figures for year 2 above, which assume an increase in sales of 10%.

Interpretation of gearing ratios

Statement of financial position

A high proportion of debt finance in the entity's capital structure is seen as being risky by the entity's shareholders (which causes them to demand higher returns on their equity – see 'Capital Structure' Chapter for more details).

However, it is difficult to give any practical guidance as to what a 'safe' level of gearing might be. Compare the gearing ratio to prior years and budgets, and to the gearing ratio of similar entities, to assess whether it looks too high.

Also, consider in particular the level of non-current assets on the balance sheet which could be used for security. A high level of non-current assets (much higher than the current value of debt finance) indicates that potentially the entity should be able to raise more debt finance quite easily.

Income statement

An interest cover ratio less than 1 indicates that the entity is having trouble servicing its debt finance. The higher the ratio is above 1, the easier it should be for the entity to continue paying its interest, so the less risky the entity appears to be.

However, note that a lack of cash, rather than a lack of profit, is usually the reason why a company fails to meet its interest obligations. This is why analysts often substitute EBITDA (or even cashflow) into the formula instead of profit, to give a more useful measure of cover.

5 Stock Market Ratios

Investors will wish to assess the performance of the shares they have invested in (against competing entities in the same sector, against the market as a whole, and over time).

There are a number of ratios which will be of specific interest to investors (both debt investors and equity investors).

Market price per share

The market price per share used throughout the following ratio formulae is the ex-dividend market price.

Ex-dividend means that in buying a share today, the investor will not participate in the forthcoming dividend payment.

Sometimes in an examination, the market price may be quoted cum-dividend which means with dividend rights attached. Here the investor will participate in the forthcoming dividend if purchasing the share today. Arguably the investor will be willing to pay a higher price for the share, knowing that a dividend payment is forthcoming in the near future.

The relationship between the cum-dividend price and the ex-dividend price is then:

Ex dividend market price = Cum dividend market price – Forthcoming dividend per share

Earnings per share (EPS)

Before we can calculate any ratios we need to calculate a key measure of return, the Earnings per share (EPS).

$$\text{EPS} = \frac{\text{Earnings}}{\text{Number of ordinary shares in issue}}$$

where Earnings = Profit distributable to ordinary shareholders, i.e. after interest, tax and any preference dividend.

More details on EPS

An important point to remember is that EPS is a historical figure and can be manipulated by changes in accounting policies, mergers or acquisitions, etc.

Market analysts and company executives occasionally appear obsessed about EPS as a performance measure, an obsession which many think is quite disproportionate to its true value.

It is future earnings which should concern investors, a figure far more difficult to estimate.

P/E ratio

The P/E ratio is a measure of growth; it compares the market value (a measure of future earnings) to the current earnings.

$$\text{P/E ratio} = \frac{\text{Current share price}}{\text{EPS}}$$

or, alternatively, Total market capitalisation / Total earnings.

The higher the P/E ratio, the greater the market expectation of future earnings growth. This may also be described as market potential.

Earnings yield

The P/E ratio is the reciprocal (in maths, a number or quantity divided into 1) of the earnings yield.

$$\text{Earnings yield} = \frac{\text{EPS}}{\text{Current share price}}$$

or, alternatively, Total earnings / Total market capitalisation.

The market price will incorporate expectations of all buyers and sellers of the entity's shares, and so this is an indication of the future earning power of the entity.

Dividend-payout rate

The cash effect of payment of dividends is measured by the dividend-payout rate.

$$\text{Payout rate} = \frac{\text{Dividend per share}}{\text{EPS}}$$

or, alternatively, Total dividend / Total earnings.

The relationship between the above investors' ratios is usually that an entity with a high P/E ratio has a low dividend payout ratio as the high growth entity needs to retain more resources in the entity. A more stable entity would have a relatively low P/E ratio and higher dividend-payout ratio.

When analysing financial statements from an investor's point of view it is important to identify the objectives of the investor. Does the investor require high capital growth and high risk, or a lower risk, fixed dividend payment and low capital growth?

Dividend yield

This is the relationship of the dividend paid to the current market value of a share.

$$\text{Dividend yield} = \frac{\text{Dividend per share}}{\text{Current share price}}$$

or, alternatively, Total dividend / Total market capitalisation.

However, the dividend represents only part of the overall return from a share.

The other part of the return is the capital gain from an increase in the value of the share. The capital gain from a share may well be far more significant than the dividend.

Dividend cover

Dividend cover measures the ability of the entity to maintain the existing level of dividend and is used in conjunction with the dividend yield.

$$\text{Dividend cover} = \frac{\text{Earnings per share}}{\text{Dividend per share}}$$

or, alternatively, Total earnings / Total dividend.

The higher the dividend cover the more likely it is that the dividend yield can be maintained.

Dividend cover also gives an indication of the level of profits being retained by the entity for reinvestment by considering how many times this year's dividend is covered by this year's earnings.

Example 3

Lilydale Co has 5m ordinary shares in issue. Its results for the year are:

	USD000
Profit before tax	750
Tax	(150)
Profit after tax (PAT)	600
Ordinary dividend – proposed	(150)
Retained profit	450

The market price per share is currently 83 cents cum-dividend.

Required:

Calculate the following ratios:

(a) **Price/earnings ratio**

(b) **Dividend payout rate**

(c) **Dividend yield, and**

(d) **Dividend cover.**

6 The use of published accounts for ratio analysis

When external stakeholders, such as potential investors and lenders, try to assess the performance of an entity, the most readily available source of information is the published accounts of the entity.

In trying to interpret the ratios calculated from the published accounts figures, it is important to understand the limitations of the published figures.

Limitations of published accounts figures for ratio analysis

- Published accounts are historic records, not forward looking. However, the Operating and Financial Review (OFR), which companies are encouraged to present as part of their published accounts, will contain the directors' view of the company's prospects.

- The income statement is prepared using the accruals concept, so it is difficult to relate the figures to the entity's cash position. However the inclusion of the cash flow statement in the published accounts helps to give an impression of the cash position.
- The published accounts have historically contained only financial information. In recent years entities have been encouraged to report on wider issues (such as environmental and social issues), so users of the accounts are able to see a fuller view of the entity's performance.

More on recent developments in financial reporting

Extending the scope of external reports

According to the IASB's Framework, the objective of financial statements is to 'provide information about the financial position, performance and changes in financial position of an entity that is useful to a wide range of users in making economic decisions'.

To help users make decisions, it may be helpful to provide information relating to the future as well as the historic information that financial statements provide.

However, the inclusion of forecasts is unlikely to be acceptable to the management team.

- What if forecasts aren't achieved?
- What if forecasts are deliberately pessimistic?
- Forecasts may provide too much information to competitors.
- Preparing forecast information may be costly.

There has also been increasing pressure for entities to provide more information in their annual reports beyond just the financial statements since non-financial information can also be important to users' decisions.

Entities have also begun to accept over recent years that they have responsibilities to stakeholders other than just shareholders, for example:

- customers and suppliers
- local communities
- society as a whole and the environment.

Operating and Financial Review

The UK's ASB provided guidelines to companies in 1993 (updated in 2003) on including an 'Operating and Financial Review' (OFR) within their annual reports. At this time providing an OFR was voluntary. In May 2005, the ASB issued a reporting standard requiring quoted companies within the UK to prepare an OFR. This requirement was withdrawn at the beginning of 2006 and again companies are encouraged to produce an OFR as best practice.

The standard requires that the OFR should reflect the directors' view of the business and have a 'forward-looking orientation'. While the OFR should focus on matters that are relevant to shareholders, the information will also be useful to other users.

Advantages of preparing an OFR may include:

- Helps companies appear transparent and willing to communicate
- May enhance a company's reputation to produce such documents voluntarily
- Can be used to explain the background behind certain numbers in the financial statements, especially if they may otherwise be perceived in a negative light.

Disadvantages of preparing an OFR may include:

- Costly and time-consuming since it is likely to require significant time of senior management
- Lack of requirements in terms of content will reduce the comparability of reports across entities
- Companies may be selective and biased in the information they choose to discuss which will reduce its reliability for users.

International financial reporting

As more and more companies operate globally, there has been an increasing need for accounting practices to become more harmonised.

Advantages	Disadvantages
• Increased efficiency and decreased costs for global companies	• Costs for non-global companies
• Increase comparability	• Changing attitudes and traditions
• Increased competition in world markets	

The EU issue directives which member states are required to adopt within their national legislation.

One of these directives requires EU listed entities to prepare consolidated financial statements in accordance with International Accounting Standards from 1 January 2005.

The UK's ASB are also in the process of harmonising UK accounting standards with International Standards.

The lender's assessment of creditworthiness

When an entity is seeking to raise loan finance, the lender will carry out an assessment of the entity.

Analysis of financial statements and business plan

The lender will analyse the financial statements of the borrower, paying particular attention to the liquidity and gearing ratios. The credit rating of the company and of the company's bonds is also an important factor. Entities with sub-investment grade ratings are unlikely to be able to issue bonds in the capital markets.

In order to apply for the finance from a bank, the borrower will have to put together a business plan which explains:

- the purpose of the loan;
- the amount of the loan;
- the duration of the loan;
- if there are assets available to offer as security for the loan;
- how the borrower is proposing to repay the loan – cash flow forecasts will generally be presented;
- the level of borrowings currently outstanding.

A full prospectus with detailed financial information is required for a public bond issue.

The bank or other potential investors will use the detailed financial information provided, together with the credit ratings and their own analysis of the financial strength of the company, to assess the creditworthiness of the borrower.

Use of ratio analysis

The analysis undertaken by the lender will use many of the ratios that we have covered so far in this Chapter.

For example, the interest cover ratio will be particularly important, since it gives an idea of how likely it is that the firm will continue to be able to meet its interest payments even if profits fall.

Lenders might be even more interested in calculating interest cover with regard to EBITDA or cash (rather than profits) to give a more practical measure of cover.

Other ratios such as the stock market ratios (P/E ratio in particular) will also give the lender a feel for how the rest of the market views the firm. If the firm has a high P/E ratio, its growth prospects are good, so lending to such a firm would be perceived as low risk.

Independent credit rating agencies

In order to help with the assessment, credit ratings issued by an independent credit rating agency (such as Moody's, Fitch or Standard and Poor's) will often be also be referred to. For public issues of bonds, the company will obtain a specific rating for that issue from a rating agency before the issue itself.

These large credit rating agencies monitor the performance of all major businesses and rate them according to how likely it is that they will be able to afford to repay any debts.

The rating agency will focus on:

- Plans and forecasts of the company
- The strength and trends in the industry in which the company operates and the company's competitive position within that industry.
- Country risks – the political and regulatory risks
- The quality of the management team, including experience and track record
- Corporate attitude to risk taking
- Financial position – including capital structure and current debt profile
- Financial ratios
- Any parental support such as guarantees.

The link between creditworthiness and interest rate

An entity rated 'AAA' (the best rating) by Standard and Poor's is a very low risk investment.

Consequently, a lender would generally set a relatively low interest rate on a loan to an 'AAA' entity. By contrast, a lower rated entity would generally have to pay higher rates of interest.

This is because risk and return are always linked: if an investor is likely to face high risks, he demands a high return to compensate him for this risk.

NEW

7 Forecasting – Profits, Cash Flows and the Balance Sheet

Planning

All businesses need to plan. They need to identify exactly what their business will look like financially should they choose to go ahead with a particular strategy.

Objective of planning – to allow an organisation to influence its own future by thinking and acting in advance.

A very popular exam requirement is to calculate a forecast income statement, balance sheet and / or cash flow.

Guidance for forecasting financial statements

Forecasting cash flows

Cash flow forecasts are vital to the management of cash.

They show, over periods varying between a single day, a week, a month, a year or even longer, the expected inflows and outflows of cash through the company. They help to show cash surpluses and cash shortages.

Management can therefore use cash budgets to plan ahead to meet those eventualities; arranging borrowing when a deficit is forecast, or buying short-term investments during times of excess cash.

Remember that there will be differences between the cash flow forecast for a period and the forecast income statement for that period. This is because the cash budget is concerned with cash payments and cash receipts, while the income statement is concerned with income earned and expenses consumed in a period.

Areas where the two statements may show different amounts include:

- the cash budget will record budgeted cash receipts from customers, while the income statement will show forecast revenue for the period;
- the cash budget will record budgeted cash payments to suppliers, while the income statement will show forecast cost of sales, which will reflect opening inventory, plus purchases, less closing inventory;
- the cash budget shows the budgeted cash payments for expenses such as wages, electricity and rates. The income statement will record the expenditure expected to be consumed in the period, reflecting any accounts or prepayments;
- the cash budget will reflect the cost of purchasing a non-current asset at the expected date of purchase and the proceeds at the date of sale. The income statement will record a depreciation charge for the consumption of the asset and a profit or loss on disposal.

Forecasting financial statements

Forecasting financial statements can be constructed for several years starting from a base year, but will require a number of assumptions to be made. Here we consider the three main financial statements and provide guidance for forecasting each of them.

Forecast income statements

Forecasting an income statement calls for some estimate to be made of the future amount of each item in the entity's income statement.

Remember that cash flows are not the same as income. The key issues are likely to be as follows:

- Revenue – usually assumed to be a percentage change on the previous year.
- Cost of sales – usually assumed to be a percentage change on the previous year.
- Gross profit – revenue minus cost of sales.
- Operating expenses – usually assumed to be a percentage change on the previous year. However, deal with depreciation separately if information is available.
- Depreciation – remember the depreciation charge for the year will need to reflect assets purchased or disposed of in the year.
- Interest payable – the amount of interest payable will change if new loans are taken out in the year, or if existing loans are redeemed in the year.
- Taxation – taxation payable is based on the taxable profit for the year rather than the accounting profit. To arrive at the taxable profit it will be necessary to add depreciation back to the accounting profit before tax and deduct tax allowable depreciation (see Example below). Other adjustments may be required as specified in a question.
- Dividends – usually assumed to be a percentage change on the previous year. However, it may also be assumed that the dividend payout ratio (dividend/profit after tax) will be maintained.

Forecast balance sheet (statement of financial position)

Forecasting a balance sheet calls for some estimate to be made of the future amount of each item in the entity's balance sheet. Usually the cash balance or bank overdraft may be used as the balancing figure, although this can usually be reconciled with sufficient time. The key issues are likely to be as follows:

- Intangible assets – consider any additions or write-downs to their existing balance sheet value.
- Tangible non-current assets – the balance sheet values will need to be adjusted for any purchases or disposals in the year. The carrying value will also need to be adjusted for in-year depreciation charges.
- Inventories – possibly based on a percentage of the cost of sales.

- Receivables – possibly based on a percentage of revenue.
- Cash or overdraft – usually the balancing figure.
- Trade payables – possibly based on a percentage of the cost of sales.
- Taxation – the amount payable should be based on a percentage of the taxable profit for the year.
- Dividends payable – usually an estimate based on the profit after tax for the year.
- Non-current liabilities – the main item under this heading will be long-term loans. The amount will change if new loans are taken out in the year, existing loans are redeemed, or the redemption date is within 12 months resulting in a reclassification of the loan as a current liability.
- Share capital – the amount will remain constant unless new shares are to be issued. In such a case the share capital will increase by the nominal amount issued, while the premium must be added to the share premium account.
- Accumulated profits – remember to add retained profits for the year to the balance of accumulated profit brought forward from previous years.

Cash flow forecasts

There are many ways of computing cash flow forecasts. Formats are not usually prescribed in the examination, so the aim is to identify the cash inflows and cash outflows for the year as quickly as possible. Here we will adopt the IAS7 Cash Flow Forecast format. The key issues are likely to be as follows:

Net cash flow from operations

- Inventories – show the change in value from one balance sheet date to the next.
- Receivables – show the change in value from one balance sheet date to the next.
- Trade payables – show the change in value from one balance sheet date to the next.
- Gross profit before depreciation – this should be taken directly from the income statement for the year.
- Operating expenses – this should be taken directly from the income statement for the year, but must exclude any depreciation charges.

Returns on investments and servicing of finance

- Interest paid – the amount paid in the year, which might not be the same as the amount payable shown in the income statement.
- Dividends paid – the amount paid in the year, which might not be the same as the amount payable shown in the income statement. Typically the amount will be equal to the previous year's proposed dividend plus the interim dividend paid in the current year.
- Taxation paid – the amount paid in the year, which might not be the same as the amount payable shown in the income statement. Typically this will be the payment of the taxation liability for the previous year.

Investing activities

- Non-current assets – include purchase cost of any assets procured in the year. Include sale proceeds of any assets disposed of in the year.

Financing activities

- Share capital – include proceeds of any new share issues within the year, remembering to include the value of any share premium.
- Non-current liabilities – include proceeds from issuing new loans within the year. Include cash payment for any loans redeemed within the year.

In an examination you may be required to model annual cash-flow forecasts and other financial statements using expected changes in values, based on data for a base year.

Forecasting income statement and balance sheet values

This is a very simple process. For example, if sales are currently USD10m and growth is forecast to be 5%, future sales can be forecast as:

Year 1: USD10m x 1.05	USD10.5m
Year 2: USD10m x $(1.05)^2$	USD11.025m

Tax adjustments

This is the main source of difficulty in many questions. The tax should not be charged directly on the accounting profits. Instead, the firm's depreciation should be added back and then the capital allowances deducted to give taxable profit, to which the tax rate can be applied.

Example 4 – Tax adjustments

Fallow Co's depreciation on its plant and machinery next year will be EUR 2m on a straight line basis. For tax purposes, tax depreciation allowances can be claimed at a rate of 25% p.a. (reducing balance basis). The current book value, and tax written down value, of the plant is EUR 10m. The expected accounting profit for the coming year is EUR 8m. Corporation tax is 30%.

Required:

Calculate the expected tax charge for next year.

Illustration 1 – Exam style forecasting question

GSD Ltd is a private UK company owned by the two families that started the business in 20X0. The company produces organic food products for distribution in the domestic UK market using food products from UK farms. The company is experiencing a period of rapid growth, with revenue expected to rise by 15% in each of the following five years.

The company is hoping to retain a profit margin (profit before interest and taxes divided by revenue) of 30% throughout the next five years. The ratio of working capital to revenue is expected to remain constant, where working capital is inventories plus trade receivables less trade payables.

Interest is paid on the overdraft and bank loan at 6% per annum. Interest on the bank loan and overdraft is calculated on the balance outstanding at the beginning of the year. Corporation tax is paid one year in arrears at a rate of 30%, with a 100% tax allowance for capital expenditure in the year in which it is incurred. In arriving at operating profit, depreciation is charged at 25% on a reducing balance basis based on year-end balances.

Extracts from the management accounts of GSD Ltd on 31 December 20X4 are as follows: (N.B. the currency of GSD is the British Pound – GBP, or £)

Balance sheet as at 31 December 20X4

	£m
Property, plant and equipment	15
Working capital	9
	24
Share capital (50p ordinary)	10
Retained earnings	4
Long-term borrowings (bank loan)	8
Short-term borrowings (overdraft)	1
Current tax payable	1
	24

Income statement for the year ended 31 December 20X4

Revenue	£45.0m
Profit before interest and taxes	£13.5m
Dividend paid in 20X4	50p a share

Capital expenditure plans are for expenditure on property, plant and equipment of £10m in 20X5, £10m in 20X6 and £7m in each of years 20X7 to 20X9. No disposals of property, plant and equipment are expected in this period.

Shareholders expect a year-on-year increase in dividends of 5%. Any funds deficit in the year will be funded by overdraft and any surplus funds used to reduce the overdraft. However, with the increased demands on the funds of the business to finance growth, the directors are concerned that they may exceed the overdraft limit of £1.5m. They may, therefore, need to negotiate an increase in the bank loan, although the bank has indicated that it would not accept gearing higher than 70% based on book values where gearing is defined as long- and short-term borrowings (including overdraft) divided by equity. The shareholders have indicated that they do not wish to inject any additional capital into the business.

Required:

Construct the balance sheet, income statement and a cash flow analysis of the company for each of the years 20X5 and 20X6 and advise the company on the extent of any additional funding requirement in that period. In your answer, round figures to the nearest £1,000.

Solution:

	20X4	*20X5*	*20X6*
Income statements	£k	£k	£k
Revenue (15% increase pa)	45,000	51,750	59,513
Profit before interest and tax (30% of revenue)	13,500	15,525	17,854
Interest on bank loan (6% × £8m)		(500)	(500)
Interest on overdraft (6% × opening balance, see below)		(60)	(158)
Profit before tax		14,965	17,196
Tax (W1)		(3,365)	(4,315)
Profit after tax		11,600	12,881

Cash flow analysis	*20X5* £k	*20X6* £k
Profit before interest and tax	15,525	17,854
Add back depreciation (W2)	6,250	7,188
Deduct increase in working capital (W3)	(1,350)	(1,553)
Cash flow from operations	20,425	23,489
Interest paid on bank loan (6% × £8m)	(500)	(500)
Interest paid on overdraft (6% × opening balance)	(60)	(158)
Dividends paid (5% increase pa)	(10,500)	(11,025)
Tax paid (W1)	(1,000)	(3,365)
Capital expenditure	(10,000)	(10,000)
Net cash flow for the year	(1,635)	(1,559)
Cash b/f	(1,000)	(2,635)
Cash c/f	(2,635)	(4,194)

Balance sheets	*20X5* £k	*20X6* £k
Property, plant and equipment (W2)	18,750	21,562
Working capital (20% × revenue)	10,350	11,903
	29,100	33,465
Share capital	10,000	10,000
Retained earnings (W4)	5,100	6,956
	15,100	16,956
Long-term borrowings (bank loan)	8,000	8,000
Short-term borrowings (overdraft, from cash flow analysis)	2,635	4,194
Current tax payable	3,365	4,315
	29,100	33,465

Workings

		20X5	20X6
(W1) *Tax expense*		£k	£k
Profit before interest and tax		15,525	17,854
Add back depreciation (W2)		6,250	7,188
Deduct capital allowances		(10,000)	(10,000)
Interest on bank loan		(500)	(500)
Interest on overdraft (6% × opening balance)		(60)	(158)
Taxable profit		11,215	14,384
Tax expense at 30%		3,365	4,315

	20X5	20X6
(W2) *Property, plant and equipment*	£k	£k
Balance b/f	15,000	18,750
Capital expenditure	10,000	10,000
Net total	25,000	28,750
Depreciation at 25%	(6,250)	(7,188)
Balance c/f	18,750	21,562

		20X5	20X6
(W3) *Movements in working capital*	£k	£k	£k
Working capital b/f	9,000		
Working capital c/f (9/45 × 51,750)	10,350		
Increase in year		1,350	
Working capital b/f	10,350		
Working capital c/f (9/45 × 59,513)	11,903		
Increase in year			1,553

(W4) *Retained earnings*	*20X5* £k	*20X6* £k
Balance b/f	4,000	5,100
Profit for the year	11,600	12,881
Dividends	(10,500)	(11,025)
Balance c/f	5,100	6,956

Advice to the company

The overdraft limit is £1.5m, whereas the above forecasts show a forecast overdraft of approximately £2.7m at the end of 20X5 and £4.2m at the end of 20X6, if the long-term bank loan is kept constant. This is not acceptable, so the company must approach the bank and seek to increase the bank loan by the excess £4.2m – £1.5m = £2.7m. Forecast total borrowings at 31 December 20X6 are £12.2m.

Forecast equity at 31 December 20X6 is £16.9m.

The forecast gearing ratio at 31 December 20X6 is $\frac{12.2}{16.9} \times 100\% = 72\%$,

which is above the bank's limit. Some amendments to the company's plans are necessary, as discussed in the next Example.

Example 5 – Exam style forecasting question – continued

Following on from the forecasting Illustration above (regarding GSD Ltd).

Required:

Discuss the interrelationships between financing, investment and dividend strategies with reference to the liquidity requirements of GSD Ltd. Include in your discussion how each could be adapted to meet the company's liquidity requirements in the years 20X5 and 20X6 and provide a recommendation.

8 Exam style questions

Test your understanding 1 – Ratio analysis

The directors of ABC, a conglomerate listed on a stock exchange, are appraising one of their wholly-owned subsidiaries, XYZ, with a view to disinvestment. The subsidiary is primarily involved in the manufacture and distribution of car care products.

Financial data for XYZ are shown in the table below.

Required:

(a) **Calculate five ratios for each of the two years 20X1 and 20X2 which you consider to be appropriate for the evaluation of the subsidiary's gearing, profitability and liquidity over the two-year period. Your selection of ratios should ensure measurement of the company's performance in all three areas.**

(10 marks)

(b) **Prepare a report for the management of ABC. This report should discuss the following:**

(i) **the performance of the subsidiary during the past two years, using the ratios calculated in part (a) to guide your comments;**

(ii) **the limitations of the type of historical analysis you have just provided;**

(iii) **suggestions for the parent company's future course of action in respect of the subsidiary, including comment on an appropriate procedure for valuing the company;**

(iv) **other, non-financial information which would be useful to the directors of ABC before they make any decision.**

(15 marks)

(Total: 25 marks)

Summary accounts for XYZ

Balance sheet (statement of financial position) at 31 December

	20X2	*20X1*
	$000	$000
Non-current assets (plant & equip)	2,650	2,255
Other long-term assets (Note 1)	750	675
Cash and marketable securities	195	162
Receivables	765	476
Inventory and work-in-progress	1,250	893
Other current assets	150	91
Total assets	5,760	4,552
Shareholders' funds	2,520	1,726
Long-term debt	2,250	1,976
Other long-term liabilities (Note 2)	275	206
Current liabilities	715	644
Total equity & liabilities	5,760	4,552

Extracts from the income statements for the years ended 31 December

	20X2	*20X1*
	$000	$000
Turnover	6,575	5,918
Cost of goods sold	5,918	5,444
Other expenses	658	592
Other income	23	20
Earnings before finance charges and tax	22	(98)
Finance Charges	395	339
Tax on ordinary activities (Note 3)	(120)	(149)
Net loss	(253)	(288)

Notes:

(1) Other long-term assets are motor vehicles and office equipment.
(2) Other long-term liabilities are finance leases.
(3) The tax shown in the 20X1 profit and loss extract will be recovered in 20X2.

Other financial information

	$000
Depreciation 20X2	175
Net realisable value of inventory	1,091
Net realisable value of plant and equipment	3,907
Inventory and work-in-progress at 1 January 20X1	850
Receivables at 1 January 20X1	435

Test your understanding 2 – Forecasting and ratio analysis

STR is a well-established marketing consultancy in a country with a low interest rate. STR is a successful business which has experienced rapid growth in recent years. There are 20 million $1 ordinary shares in issue. These ordinary shares are quoted on a recognised stock exchange and 40% are owned by the founders of the business. Dividends were 40 cents per share in 20X3 and grew by 5% per annum between 20X3 and 20X6. This pattern is expected to continue beyond 20X6. Dividends are paid in the year in which they are declared.

Extracts from the financial statements for the past three years are as follows:

	20X4	20X5	20X6
	$million	$million	$million
Profit before tax	21.6	24.4	26.7
Tax expense	7.7	2.6	4.3
Net cash generated after deducting interest, tax and net capital expenditure, but excluding ordinary dividends	19.2	(7.1)	18.8

Additional information:

- The opening cash balance in 20X4 for cash and cash equivalents was $6 million;
- The opening book value of equity in 20X4 was $60 million;

- Long-term borrowings remained at $50 million throughout the three years and the annual gross interest cost on the borrowings was $1 million;
- There were a number of disposals of non-current assets in 20X4 and an exceptionally high level of capital expenditure in 20X5.

The directors have noticed the build-up of cash and cash equivalents. They are concerned that this might not be in the best interest of the shareholders and could have an adverse effect on the share price. Various proposals have been made to reduce the level of cash and cash equivalents.

Required:

(a) **Calculate the following financial information for STR for each of the years 20X4 to 20X6:**

– **Closing cash balance;**

– **Closing book value of equity.**

(3 marks)

(b) **Analyse and discuss the financial performance of the entity from the viewpoint of both the lenders and shareholders, referring to the information calculated in part (a) above and making appropriate additional calculations. Up to 6 marks are available for calculations.**

(10 marks)

(c)

(i) **Discuss the comparative advantages and disadvantages of a share repurchase versus a one-off dividend payment.**

(7 marks)

(ii) **Advise the directors of STR on alternative financial strategies that they could consider that would reduce the level of surplus cash.**

(5 marks)

(Total for part (c) = 12 marks)

(Total: 25 marks)

Test your understanding 3 – Objectives / performance appraisal

(a) You are a newly appointed Finance Manager of an Educational Institution that is mainly government-funded, having moved from a similar post in a service entity in the private sector. The objective, or mission statement, of this Institution is shown in its publicity material as:

'To achieve recognized standards of excellence in the provision of teaching and research.'

The only financial performance measure evaluated by the government is that the Institution has to remain within cash limits. The cash allocation each year is determined by a range of non-financial measures such as the number of research publications the Institution's staff have achieved and official ratings for teaching quality.

However, almost 20% of total cash generated by the Institution is now from the provision of courses and seminars to private sector entities, using either its own or its customers' facilities. These customers are largely unconcerned about research ratings and teaching quality as they relate more to academic awards such as degrees.

The Head of the Institution aims to increase the percentage of income coming from the private sector to 50% over the next 5 years. She has asked you to advise on how the management team can evaluate progress towards achieving this aim as well as meeting the objective set by the government for the activities it funds.

Required:

Discuss the main issues that an institution such as this has to consider when setting objectives. Advise on whether a financial objective, or objectives, could or should be determined; and whether such objective(s) should be made public.

(9 marks)

(b) The following is a list of financial and non-financial performance measures that were in use in your previous profit-making entity:

Financial	*Non financial*
Value added	Customer satisfaction
Profitability	Competitive position
Return on investment	Market share

Required:

Choose two of each type of measure, explain their purpose and advise on how they could be used by the Educational Institution over the next 5 years to assess how it is meeting the Head of the Institution's aims.

(16 marks)

Note: A report format is not required in answering this question.

(Total 25 marks)

Test your understanding answers

Example 1

(a) Asset turnover = 100m/20m = 5.0 times

Operating profit margin = 5m/100m × 100 = 5%

	Equity finance	Debt finance
(b) Return on capital employed =	5m/20m × 100	= 5m/20m × 100
=	25%	= 25%

Working

	GBPm	GBPm
Operating profit	5.0	5.0
Interest	0.0	(1.0)
	5.0	4.0
Tax (@30%)	(1.5)	(1.2)
Net profit	3.5	2.8

Return on equity = 3.5m/20m × 100 = 2.8m/10m × 100

= 17.5% = 28%

The financial performance of the two funding options is exactly the same for ROCE. This should not be a surprise given that ROCE is an indication of performance before financing, or underlying performance.

(c) When considering the ROE we see that the geared option achieves a higher return than the equity option. This is because the debt (10%) is costing less than the return on capital (25%). The excess return on that part funded by debt passes to the shareholder enhancing their return.

The only differences between ROCE and ROE will be due to taxation and gearing.

Example 2

(a) **Capital gearing ratio**

Debt	=	5m + 8m	= USD13m
Equity	=	10m + 4m + 1.5m + 1.5m	= USD17m
Either	=	13m/17m × 100	= 76.5%
Or	=	13m/(13m + 17m) × 100	= 43.3%

Interest cover = 4m/1m = 4 times

(b) The capital gearing figure looks to be a high percentage, but without further analysis of trends and industry average figures, it is difficult to conclude whether the gearing is too high or whether it is at an acceptable level based on this value alone.

The interest cover measure attempts to equate the earning of profits with ability to pay interest as it falls due. There will be some correlation between the two; however, it is very risky to equate profits earned to cash flow.

However, a value of 4 indicates that the entity was easily able to meet its interest obligations in the most recent accounting period, and that the interest payments are not particularly vulnerable to a drop in profits.

Example 3

$$\text{EPS} = \frac{\text{Profit distributable to ordinary shareholders}}{\text{Number of ordinary shares in issue}}$$

= 600,000 / 5m = USD 0.12

$$\text{DPS (dividend per share)} = \frac{\text{Ordinary dividend}}{\text{Number of shares}}$$

= 150,000 / 5m = USD 0.03

Share price (ex dividend) = 0.83 - 0.03 = USD 0.80

(a) Price/earnings ratio = 0.80 / 0.12 = 6.7

(b) Dividend payout rate = 0.03 / 0.12 = 25%

(c) Dividend yield = 0.03 / 0.80 = 3.75%

(d) Dividend cover = 0.12 / 0.03 = 4

Example 4 – Tax adjustments

		EUR m
Forecast accounting profit		8.00
Add: Accounting depreciation		2.00
		10.00
Less: Tax depreciation allowances	25% × 10m	(2.50)
Taxable profit		7.50
Forecast tax	30% × 7.50m	2.25m

Example 5 – Exam style forecasting question – continued

Introduction

GSD Ltd has a problem in that its current rapid growth plan leads to forecast borrowings at 31 December 20X6 that are above what the bank is willing to finance. The company must therefore consider its financing, investment and dividend strategies which could individually or together solve the problem.

The £2.7m additional funding requirement forecast for the end of 20X6 could be met by obtaining new finance, deferring its investment plans (i.e. the planned capital expenditure) or by reducing the level of dividends paid. Consider each of these options in turn.

Obtaining new finance

It is unfortunate that the shareholders have indicated that they are unwilling to inject additional capital into the business. They must know that the company is growing rapidly and that large amounts of capital expenditure are necessary, and they appear happy to receive large dividends from the profits that are being generated. They should be approached again and reminded that there will not be any dividends in the future if the company collapses through lack of finance. The shareholders should be invited to play their part in financing the growth of the company by being willing to subscribe for new shares.

If the shareholders are adamant that they will not inject additional capital, then it is back to the bank to discuss matters with them. Perhaps they can be persuaded to adjust the gearing limit to, say, 75%. The company has forecast net cash outflows in 20X5 and 20X6, but a forecast net cash inflow in 20X7, as proved below.

Cash flow forecast for 20X7

	£m
Profit before interest and tax (17,854 × 1.15)	20,532
Add back depreciation (25% × (21,562 + 7,000))	7,140
Deduct increase in working cap (13,688 – 11,903)	(1,785)
Cash flow from operations	25,887
Interest paid (6% × 12,194)	(732)
Dividends paid	(11,576)
Tax paid	(4,315)
Capital expenditure	(7,000)
Net cash flow for the year	2,264

Thus the bank can be assured that the maximum debt position is at the end of 20X6, with positive cash flows thereafter easing the situation. Given this, the bank is likely to accept the adjusted gearing limit that is being requested of them.

Deferring capital expenditure

It would probably be possible in theory to scale back the plans for capital expenditure over the next few years, but this would presumably reduce the company's growth rate, and allow competitors in to satisfy demand that GSD cannot satisfy. This may have serious long-term implications.

A more attractive idea is to look at alternative methods of paying for the capital expenditure. At present the company appears to be buying the new assets for cash and paying immediately. It is this that is having a particularly adverse effect on the forecast cash flows. If another method of paying can be arranged, such as paying over a number of years in instalments or acquiring the assets by hire purchase or leasing, then there will not be the same up-front negative cash impact.

Reducing the dividend

GSD is a private company, so there is no need to consider the impact on the share price of cutting the dividend. Whether it is an acceptable option depends on the attitudes of the individual shareholders. If they personally have large regular cash outgoings that they have been satisfying from the dividend income from GSD, then they will not want the dividend level to be cut. If this is not the case, they may be willing to see a reduction in dividend in the short term, while the company is growing so fast and requiring funds for capital expenditure.

Recommendation

A new share issue or a temporary reduction in dividend would avoid the problem in 20X6, although the shareholders would have to be willing to go along with these suggestions. If they are not willing, then the bank should be approached to increase the bank loan, and methods of delaying payments for the capital expenditure should be investigated.

It seems probable that some solution can be found to the impending liquidity problem. In strategic terms it would not be a good idea to scale back the growth plans, since this would enable competitors to grab market share which it would be difficult to seize back in the future.

Test your understanding 1 – Ratio analysis

Key answer tips

Part (a) – There are many other alternative ratios which could have been calculated (other than those below), as long as between them the five ratios cover the efficiency, profitability and liquidity of the company. It would also be possible to calculate different figures for each ratio, depending on whether the 'other financial information' was used, whether year-end or average balance sheet figures were used, etc. What is important is that you show clearly how you have derived each of your chosen ratios, and that you do not overrun the time allowed for this part of the question.

(a) The following ratios can be calculated from the figures in the summary accounts:

Profitability ratios

		20X2	**20X1**
Return on Capital Employed =	Operating profit / Capital employed	22 / 2,520+2,250	(98) / 1,726+1,976
		= 0.0046	= (0.0265)
Operating profit margin	Operating profit / Sales	22 / 6,575	(98) / 5,918
		= 0.33%	= (1.66%)

Gearing ratios

$$\text{At 31 Dec 20X2, gearing} = \frac{2{,}250 - 195}{2{,}250 + 2{,}250} = 43\%$$

$$\text{At 31 Dec 20X1, gearing} = \frac{1{,}976 - 162}{1{,}726 + 1{,}976} = 49\%$$

Liquidity ratios (covered in detail in the later Chapter 'Short Term Finance – Working Capital Management')

Current ratio =	Current assets / Current liabilities	2360 / 715	1622 / 644
		3.3 : 1	2.5 : 1
Quick ratio	Current assets less inventory / Current liabilities	2360 -1250 / 715	1622 - 893 / 644
		= 1.6 : 1	= 1.1 : 1

(b)

Report

To: The Management of ABC

From: The Management Accountant

Date: X-X-20XX

Subject: Proposed disinvestment of XYZ

Introduction

This report has been prepared to appraise the financial performance of our wholly-owned subsidiary XYZ, with a view to recommending whether the company should be divested. The analysis has used XYZ's summary accounts for 20X1 and 20X2.

Analysis of recent performance

The period 20X1 to 20X2 saw turnover increase by 11% while cost of sales increased by 9%, resulting in an improvement in underlying profitability. However, over the same period receivables rose by 61% and inventory by 40% in cost terms, both large increases requiring explanation. The increase in receivables days may imply that the credit control function needs strengthening to chase up overdue debts. The increase in inventory levels may imply that the company is finding it harder to sell its products.

The increase in working capital referred to above has been financed by an increase in long-term debt ($274,000) and increased shareholders' funds ($794,000). Since the company reported a loss in 20X1 but shareholders' funds have risen, it is clear that a new capital injection has been made. Since XYZ is a wholly-owned subsidiary of ABC, it appears likely that ABC has bought new shares in XYZ during 20X2. The cash subscribed appears to be 794,000 + 253,000 = $1.047m. Given that ABC has subscribed an extra $1m share capital in XYZ in the year just ended, it seems premature to be considering selling the company so soon after this investment. The company's liquidity ratios have improved from 20X1 to 20X2, reflecting the new injection of funds identified above. Current liabilities are now comfortably covered by quickly realisable current assets. Gearing has fallen over the period as a result of the new equity injection exceeding the increase in net borrowings.

$$\text{At 31 Dec 20X2, gearing} = \frac{2{,}250 - 195}{2{,}250 + 2{,}250} = 43\%$$

$$\text{At 31 Dec 20X1, gearing} = \frac{1{,}976 - 162}{1{,}726 + 1{,}976} = 49\%$$

The company was struggling to pay its finance charge in 20X1 out of available profits; although the profitability situation has improved slightly in 20X2, finance charges payable still exceeds available profits so that a net loss is reported.

Limitations of historical analysis

The analysis above has been carried out on the summary accounts of XYZ for 20X1 and 20X2 which were presumably drawn up under the historical cost convention. In a period of changing prices such accounts can become misleading, for instance with the depreciation charge being calculated on the out-of-date historical cost of the fixed assets. Capital gearing ratios such as calculated above do not give the true picture; it would be more helpful if the summary accounts could be restated under a current cost basis.

There is the further conflict that a decision is to be made about the future based on an analysis of the past. The summary accounts give a historical record of what has happened over the last two years, but give no evidence of the company's likely future prospects. The decision as to whether XYZ should be divested should be taken on the basis of future opportunities and threats to which the company will be exposed.

A final weakness of analysis from accounts is that conventional accounting statements do not recognise a number of important assets that a company might have – a trained workforce, a new product about to be launched on to the market which has been fully researched, other sorts of inherent goodwill. It is impossible to look at the full picture of a company's situation while these assets have been ignored.

Future course of action

Given that ABC has subscribed an extra $1m of share capital of XYZ within the past 12 months, it seems premature to be considering divesting the company. It is perhaps more reasonable to allow the newly invested funds to settle down and reap the benefits for which, presumably, the investment was made. However, if ABC insists on divestment, there is a choice between closing the business (and selling the assets piecemeal) or selling the business as a going concern. If the assets are to be sold piecemeal, their relevant values are their net realisable values, e.g. inventory $1.091m and plant and equipment $3.907m. An aggregate total of the net assets valued at net realisable value would be the minimum acceptable offer.

In the more likely situation of selling the business as a going concern, the value of the business forgone if sold would be the aggregate of the forecast cash flows arising to ABC from XYZ, discounted at ABC's cost of capital. Such a computation requires many estimates to be made, including future growth of XYZ's business and of the car care products business sector as a whole. It may only be possible to identify a range of possible values, but even if it contains a degree of estimation the exercise will still be valuable.

Other valuable non-financial information

Several valuable items of non-financial information have already been identified above which would be useful to the directors of ABC before they make any decision:

(i) the financial results of XYZ on a current cost basis, i.e. after the effects of price changes have been eliminated;

(ii) whether the company has significant intangible assets not currently recognised in the accounts;

(iii) the future prospects for the company and its place in its business sector if it is retained within the ABC group;

(iv) whether a prospective purchaser of the company has already been identified;

(v) the effect on the morale of the remaining workforce if the company is closed or sold.

Please let me know if I can be of any further assistance.

Signed: The management accountant

Test your understanding 2 – Forecasting and ratio analysis

Key answer tips

In part (a) ensure that your workings are clearly set out. In part (b) it is vital that you discuss any ratios calculated rather than simply presenting the examiner with a set of numbers. Part (c) is bookwork and a good reminder that you need to be familiar with all aspects of the syllabus.

(a) **Cash balances**

	20X4	*20X5*	*20X6*
	$m	$m	$m
Net cash flow before dividends	19.2	(7.1)	18.8
Dividends (W1)	(8.4)	(8.8)	(9.3)
Net cash flow	10.8	(15.9)	9.5
Cash b/f	6	16.8	0.9
Cash c/f	16.8	0.9	10.4

Book value of equity

	20X4	*20X5*	*20X6*
	$m	$m	$m
Profit before interest and tax (bal)	22.6	25.4	27.7
Interest	(1.0)	(1.0)	(1.0)
Profit before tax	21.6	24.4	26.7
Tax expense	(7.7)	(2.6)	(4.3)
Profit after tax	13.9	21.8	22.4
Dividends (W1)	(8.4)	(8.8)	(9.3)
Retained profit	5.5	13.0	13.1
Book value of equity b/f	60	65.5	78.5
Book value of equity c/f	65.5	78.5	91.6

(W1) *Dividends*

20X4: dividend = 20 million × $0.40 × 1.05 = $8.4 million

20X5: dividend = $8.4 million × 1.05 = $8.82 million

20X6: dividend = $8.82 million × 1.05 = $9.261 million

(b) **Additional calculations**

	20X4	20X5	20X6
Interest cover	22.6×	25.4×	27.7×
Dividend cover	1.65×	2.48×	2.41×
Earnings per share (cents)	69.5	109	112

Gearing = debt net of cash / (debt + equity)

	20X4	20X5	20X6
Debt	50	50	50
Cash	16.8	0.9	10.4
Debt net of cash	33.2	49.1	39.6
Equity	65.5	78.5	91.6
Debt (net) + equity	98.7	127.6	131.2
Gearing	33.6%	38.5%	30.2%

Return on equity

	20X4	20X5	20X6
Profit after tax	13.9	21.8	22.4
Equity	65.5	78.5	91.6
Return on equity	21.2%	27.8%	24.5%

Return on capital employed, using net debt + equity

	20X4	20X5	20X6
Profit before interest and tax (bal)	22.6	25.4	27.7
Debt (net) + equity	98.7	127.6	131.2
Return on capital	22.9%	19.9%	21.1%

Comments

The financial performance from the shareholders' point of view has generally been encouraging:

- Both earnings per share and the book value of equity have been increasing.
- Dividends have increased.
- Return on equity has consistently been above 20%.
- Financial gearing has fallen in 20X6 and dividend cover is now over two, indicating lower risk attached to the dividends.

The only area of worry, however, is that return on equity fell from 20X5 to 20X6.

The financial performance from the lenders' point of view has been less convincing. On a positive note:

- Interest cover is very high and rising, suggesting a low default risk.
- Gearing fell in 20X6, again suggesting less risk for lenders.

However,

- STR had poor cash flow in 20X5. Lenders may wish to see more detailed analysis of cash flow to determine if any underlying problems persist.

(c)

(i) The relative advantages of a share repurchase verses a one-off dividend are as follows:

Share repurchase	*One-off dividend*
• A repurchase may be more tax efficient than a dividend for some shareholders.	• A dividend may be more tax advantageous for some shareholders.
• A reduction in the number of shares should boost EPS.	• All shareholders are treated fairly.
• Increased gearing as equity is reduced. This is only an advantage if STR is moved closer to its optimal gearing level.	• The amount of cash paid is more certain – with a repurchase it will not be known in advance how many shareholders will choose to sell.
• Does not create an expectation of higher future dividends. On the contrary, less cash will be needed for future dividends due to fewer shares.	

(ii) Alternative strategies for reducing a cash surplus include the following:

- increase the growth rate of dividends
- long-term equity investments – e.g. acquire other firms and/or buy stakes in rivals, customers, etc
- reduce debt by repaying loans
- increase capital expenditure
- increase investment in research and development – e.g. to enter new markets.

Test your understanding 3 – Objectives / performance appraisal

(a) The main issues to consider are:

- Who are the main stakeholders?
- Where is the financing coming from, and in what proportions?
- Are there other, higher level objectives that will supersede those set by the Institution, for example political aims/goals by the government?
- Does the objective need to be measurable?
- How can one objective meet all the competing aims of the stakeholders?
- Will information on the Educational Institution's performance be publicly available?

Setting a financial objective has the main advantage of being measurable. If it is made public, it can also be compared with other, similar, institutions if they also set and make public their objective and their subsequent performance. One objective will probably be insufficient, especially as the Institution has two main markets with very different requirements, costs and revenue structures.

The disadvantages of setting and making public an organisation's objectives are:

- The Educational Institution may not be allowed freedom to choose its own policies, for example on charging fees or selection of state-funded students.
- Political decisions may not affect all publicly funded institutions in the same way or to the same extent.
- Cost allocation between state-funded business and private-sector business may be difficult and politically sensitive.

(b) **Examiner's Note**

The question asks for comments on two performance indicators from each list, four criteria in all. In this answer comments are provided for all six criteria. Candidates may only receive marks for a maximum of two indicators from each list (i.e. no compensation between the lists.)

Introduction

Traditionally, financial measures have been the focus of management attention. Increasingly companies are using non-financial indicators to assess success across a range of criteria, which need to be chosen to help a company meet its objectives. However, an indicator, which is appropriate for one group of stakeholders in an organisation, may not be suitable for another group. Also, indicators that are suitable for short-term performance assessment may be unsuitable, or not optimum, for the long term.

The objective, or mission statement, of this institution is entirely qualitative (and subjective) and makes no concession to financial considerations or constraints.

Financial performance measures

Value added

This is primarily a measure of performance. It is usually defined as sales value less the cost of purchased materials and services. It represents the value added to a company's products by its own efforts. A problem here is comparability with other industries or even other companies in the same industry.

It is less common in the public sector, although the situation is changing and many public sector organisations are now publishing information on their own value added, for example, in the health service.

In respect of teaching, value added could be measured by the percentage of students who leave with a qualification. In post-graduate or executive education, it could be the increase in salary or improved jobs/job prospects obtained by graduates on obtaining their qualification. This may not precisely measure the qualitative aspects of the Institution's objectives, but could provide a close approximation.

In respect of research, the measure is much easier to apply and interpret. Research output can be measured by the number of staff publications in various categories of journal.

Profitability

Profitability may be defined as the rate at which profits are generated. It is often expressed as profit per unit of input (e.g. investment). However, profitability limits an organisation's focus to one output measure – profit. It overlooks quality and this limitation needs to be kept in mind when using it as a measure of success. Profitability as a measure of decision-making has been criticised because

- it fails to provide a systematic explanation as to why one business sector has more favourable prospects than another;
- it does not provide enough insight into the dynamics and balance of an enterprise's individual business units and the balance between them;
- it is remote from the actions that actually create value and cannot therefore be managed directly in all but the smallest of organisations;
- the input to the measure may vary substantially between organisations.

However, it is a well-known and accepted measure that, once the input has been defined, is readily understood. Provided the input is consistent across organisations and time periods it also provides a useful comparative measure. Although the concept of profit in its true sense is absent from most of the public sector, profitability may be used to relate inputs to outputs if a different measure of output is used, for example surplus after all costs to capital investment.

In the case of the educational institution, a problem may be determining the value of the initial investment, which may have been purchased by the government many years ago and appear to have cost nothing. A notional value could be attached to these assets for the purpose. Profits would be fees and other income less costs of salaries and other expenses. Notional rents or depreciation would also have to be estimated.

This measure would have little relevance to the Institution's only stated objective and its calculation is fraught with uncertainties and unknowns. This would be a measure that the organisation might wish to introduce some time in the future, but first it needs to estimate the value of its assets and the true nature of its costs.

Return on investment (ROI)

This is an accounting measure, which is calculated by dividing annual profits by the average net book value of assets. It is, therefore, subject to the distortions inevitable when profit rather than cash flows are used to determine performance. Distorting factors for interpretation and comparison purposes include depreciation policy, stock revaluations, write off of intangibles such as goodwill. A further defect is that ROI ignores the time value of money, although this may be of less concern when inflation rates, and therefore money discount rates, are very low.

Return on assets may not adequately reflect how efficiently assets were utilised; in a commercial context taking account of profits, but not the assets used in their making, for whatever reason, would overstate a company's performance. In the public sector, the concept of profit is absent, but it is still not unrealistic to expect organisations to use donated assets with maximum efficiency. If depreciation on such assets were to be charged against income, this would depress the amount of surplus income over expenditure. Other points which may affect interpretation of ROI in any public sector organisation, including educational institutions are: difficulty in determining value; assets may have no re-sale value; they are, or were originally intended, for use by the community at large and any charge for depreciation may have the effect of 'double taxation' on the taxpayer.

As with profitability, the relevance of this measure at the present time and to the stated objective is limited. First of all, it needs to estimate the value of its assets and the true nature of its costs.

Non-financial performance measures

Customer satisfaction

This measure can be linked to market share. If customers are not satisfied, they will take their business elsewhere and the company will lose market share or go into liquidation. Measuring customer satisfaction is difficult to do formally, as the inputs and outputs are not readily defined or measurable. Surveys and questionnaires may be used, but these methods have known flaws, mainly as a result of respondent bias. It can, of course, be measured indirectly by the level of sales and increase in market share.

In the United Kingdom, the Citizens' Charter was designed to help 'customers' of public services gain satisfaction and redress if they do not, for example refunds on late trains. There are many criteria for determining customer satisfaction in an educational institution, if we assume the 'customer' is the student. For example:

- Evaluations by students at the end of modules or entire programmes. There are problems of bias with this type of measure, but this is true of all surveys.
- Quality audits by government agencies and other regulatory bodies.
- Internal peer reviews.

However, the customer could also be the employer or sponsor of the graduating student. Surveys of satisfaction from this type of customer are less likely to be biased.

This type of measure will already be in place and possibly to a greater extent than in many private-sector institutions. If the Institution wishes to increase its proportion of private funding, then it needs to focus on developing its surveys of employers and likely providers of research funding.

Competitive position

The performance of a business needs to be compared with that of its competitors to establish a strategic perspective. A number of models and frameworks have been suggested by organisational theorists as to how a competitive position may be determined and improved. A manager needing to make decisions must know by whom, by how much and why he is gaining ground or being beaten by competitors. Conventional measures such as accounting data are useful, but no one measure is sufficient. Instead, an array of measures is needed to establish competitive position. The most difficult problem to overcome in using competitive position as a success factor is in collecting and acquiring data from competitors.

The public sector is increasingly in competition with other providers of a similar service, both in the private and public sector. For example, universities must now compete for government funding on the basis of research output as well as meeting a range of targets for student recruitment. Their advantage is that it is easier to gain access to data from such competitors than is possible in the private sector, as all this information is ultimately in the public domain. Less publicly available is data on the amount of privately-funded teaching obtained by public-sector educational institutions.

This measure will also be already extensively used by the Institution, certainly in respect of its competitive position for students worldwide. Where it might need to develop its measures and improve its measurement data is in respect of privately-funded or sponsored students or courses.

Market share

Market share, a performance indicator that could conceivably be included under the financial heading as well as non-financial, is often seen as an objective for a company in its own right. However, it must be judged in the context of other measures such as profitability and shareholder value. Market share, unlike many other measures, can take quality into account as, it must be assumed, if customers do not get the quality they want or expect the company will lose market share.

Gaining market share must be seen as a long-term goal of companies to ensure outlets for their products and services and to minimise competition. However, market share can only be acquired within limits if a monopoly situation is to be avoided.

It is a measure that is becoming increasingly relevant to the public sector, for example universities and the health service. In educational institutions, the market share within the home country can be measured quite easily by reference to student numbers, in total and by programme/course. It is more difficult to compare market share worldwide. However, this measure of market share is on volume not value. Some institutions have high value programmes, such as MBAs, that distort this simple volume measure.

This institution needs to determine its mix of programmes and courses and set targets aimed at specific markets, for example to achieve x per cent of the market share of home-based MBA students by 2xxx. Such a target by itself will not be a guide to the quality of teaching and would need to be combined with other measures, such as customer satisfaction.

chapter

4

Long Term Finance

Chapter learning objectives

Lead	Component
B1: Evaluate the financing requirements of an organisation and strategies for meeting those requirements.	(a) analyse the short- and long-term financing requirements of an organisation. (b) evaluate alternative methods of meeting financing requirements, taking account of the implications for the organisation's financial statements, its tax position and financial stakeholders; (d) recommend methods of funding specific investments.

Indicative syllabus content

- Identifying financing requirements (both in respect of domestic and international operations) and the impacts of different types of finance on models and forecasts of performance and position.
- Types and features of domestic and international long-term finance: share capital (ordinary and preference shares, warrants), long-term debt (bank borrowing and forms of securitised debt, e.g. convertibles) and finance leases, and methods of issuing securities.
- The operation of stock exchanges (e.g. how share prices are determined, what causes share prices to rise or fall, and the efficient market hypothesis). (Note: No detailed knowledge of any specific country's stock exchange will be tested).
- The lease or buy decision (with both operating and finance leases).
- Criteria for selecting sources of finance, including finance for international investments.
- The effect of financing decisions on balance sheet structure and on ratios of interest to investors and other financiers (gearing, earnings per share, price-earnings ratio, dividend yield, dividend cover gearing, interest cover).

1 Overview of Chapter

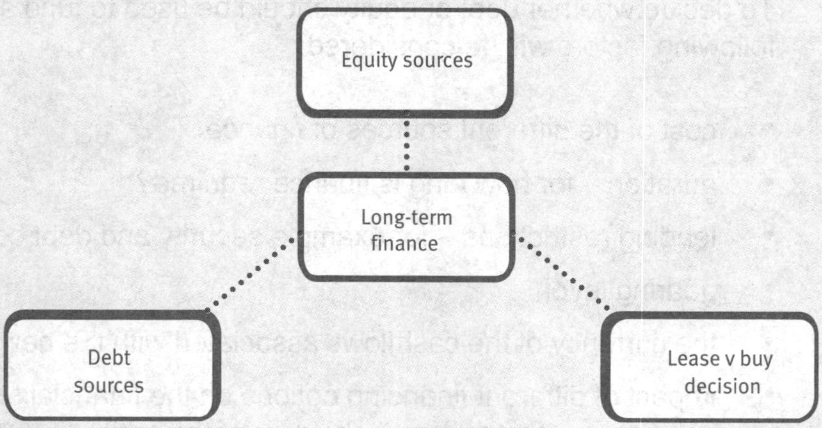

Sources of finance

If a company has a large cash surplus, it may be able to afford to undertake new investment projects without having to resort to external sources of finance.

However, if external funds are required, the company might raise finance from the following sources:

(1) The capital markets:
- new share issues, for example by companies acquiring a stock market listing for the first time;
- rights issues;
- issues of marketable debt.

A company must be quoted / listed on a recognised stock exchange in order to be able to raise finance from the capital markets.

(2) Bank borrowings – long-term loans or short-term loans, including bank facilities such as revolving credit facilities (RCFs) and money market lines.

(3) Venture capital funds.

This is high risk finance provided by specialist organisations. The main problem is that the providers of venture capital funding tend to demand significant equity participation in a company and will also want to influence the policy of the company.

(4) Government and similar sources.

In general, finance can be raised from Equity or Debt sources.

Criteria for selecting sources of finance

To decide whether debt or equity should be used to fund a new project, the following factors will be considered:

- cost of the different sources of finance
- duration – for how long is finance required?
- lending restrictions – for example security and debt covenants
- gearing level
- the currency of the cashflows associated with the new project
- impact of different financing options on the financial statements, tax position and financial stakeholders of the entity
- availability – availability of finance depends on the creditworthiness of the borrower and also the willingness of lenders to extend credit (for bank borrowings) or liquidity of the capital markets (for equity and bonds).

In an exam, you will need to discuss these general factors and apply them to the specific circumstances of the entity in the question, in order to identify the preferred choice of finance in a particular situation.

More details on financing criteria

Cost

Each source of finance has a different cost. With debt capital, a company must pay interest on the debt, and to raise new debt finance it must pay a current rate of interest to persuade investors to provide capital. The cost of interest is an allowable expense for tax purposes, so the cost of debt capital to a company is the interest cost less the tax relief on the interest. This fact, and the fact that the providers of debt finance have lower risk than the providers of equity finance tend to make debt finance cheaper than equity.

The cost of equity capital is the return that ordinary shareholders expect on their investment, in the form of current dividends and expectations of dividend and share price growth in the future. Although a company does not have a legal obligation to pay dividends to its shareholders, it must provide a satisfactory return to support the share price. Without the prospect of good returns, investors will not subscribe for new equity when the company needs to raise new capital.

It is important here to appreciate that debt finance tends to be cheaper than equity. This is because providers of debt take less risks than providers of equity and therefore earn less return. Interest on debt finance is also normally corporation tax deductible, returns to equity are not. The period of the finance will also affect the cost as long-term finance tends to be more expensive than short-term finance.

Duration

Equity capital is long-term 'permanent' capital. Most debt capital, on the other hand, is obtained for a fixed term. The length of borrowing can range from very short term (overdraft facility) to long-term. Bank loans are generally for no longer than the medium term (say, five to seven years) whereas debt finance raised by issuing bonds can be for a much longer term.

When a company is deciding whether to obtain long-term or short-term capital, it should apply the rule: 'Long-term assets should be financed by long-term funds'. Short-term assets, such as inventories and receivables, should normally be financed by a mixture of short-term and long-term funds.

Thus we would expect to see working capital financed partly by short-term facilities such as trade payables and a bank overdraft, whilst non-current assets should be funded by long-term sources of finance. This rule might be broken to gain access to cheap short-term funds, particularly short-term trade payables (which have no obvious cost) but the risks involved should be appreciated.

Lending restrictions

Security is often required for debt finance. This could be derived from existing assets or new assets to be acquired. Assets such as land and buildings hold their value better and are easier for a lender to sell than, say, plant and machinery.

Debt covenants are clauses written into existing debt agreements which protect the lender's interests by requiring the borrower to satisfy certain criteria.

Examples of debt covenants are:

- the interest cover must not fall below 5, and
- the ratio of non-current liabilities to equity must not increase beyond 0.75:1.

The lender will be reassured that the risk associated with the borrower will not change dramatically as long as such covenants are not breached.

Gearing

Gearing is the ratio of debt to equity finance. A high gearing ratio can be very risky. Although high gearing involves the use of cheap debt finance, high levels of debt also create an obligation to meet interest payments and debt principal repayment schedules. If these are not met the company could end up in liquidation. A company should try to achieve a satisfactory balance between equity finance and medium- and long-term debt for its long-term funding, to benefit from the lower cost of debt finance without exposing itself to the risks arising from excessive debt obligations.

The issue of gearing is dealt with in more detail in the later 'Capital Structure' Chapter.

The currency of the cashflows associated with the new project

If the cashflows from the investment project are expected to be denominated in a foreign currency, the entity may decide to raise finance denominated in the same foreign currency, to reduce the risk of exchange rate movements by matching the receipts from the project with the servicing costs of the finance.

International investment projects and the financing options associated with them are covered more fully in the later Chapter on 'International Investment Appraisal'.

The impact of different financing options on the financial statements, tax position and financial stakeholders of the entity

In the earlier Chapter on 'Performance Measurement in Financial Strategy' we saw that investors (both debt holders and shareholders) will use ratio analysis to assess the performance of the business. It is therefore important that management consider the impact of any new financing on the financial statements of the business. For example, raising debt finance will affect the Return on Equity of the business, as well as the interest cover and gearing ratios.

Also, raising debt finance will give rise to interest payments which are tax deductible, so impacting the tax position of the business.

The existing financial stakeholders of the business (debt holders and shareholders) will be constantly monitoring the business's performance, so it will be important for management to clearly explain the rationale for any new financing method which impacts the financial statements or the tax position.

Availability

Not all companies have access to all sources of finance. Small companies traditionally have problems in raising both equity and long-term debt finance. Remember that many firms do not have an unlimited choice of funding arrangements.

In the earlier Chapter on 'Performance Measurement in Financial Strategy', it was noted that the availability of debt finance is enhanced if an entity has a good credit rating.

The more creditworthy a borrower is assessed as being, the more likely it is that funds will be relatively easy to raise.

2 Equity Finance

Equity is another name for shares or ownership rights in a business.

Capital markets

Capital markets (or stock markets) must fulfil both primary and secondary functions.

Primary function:

The primary function of a stock market is to enable companies to raise new finance (either equity or debt). Through the stock market, a company can communicate with a large pool of potential investors, so it is much easier for a company to raise finance in this way, rather than contacting investors individually.

Note that in the UK, a company must be a plc before it is allowed to raise finance from the public on the stock market.

Secondary function:

The secondary function of a stock market is to enable investors to sell their investments to other investors. A listed company's shares are therefore more marketable than an unlisted company's, which means that they tend to be more attractive to investors.

Listed v private companies

Private limited company (Ltd in UK terminology)

A private company limited by shares, usually called a private limited company, has shareholders with limited liability and its shares may not be offered to the general public, unlike those of a public limited company (see details below).

"Limited by shares" means that the company has shareholders, and that the liability of the shareholders to creditors of the company is limited to the capital originally invested, i.e. the nominal value of the shares and any premium paid in return for the issue of the shares by the company. A shareholder's personal assets are thereby protected in the event of the company's insolvency, but money invested in the company will be lost.

A limited company may be "private" or "public". A private limited company's disclosure requirements are lighter, but for this reason its shares may not be offered to the general public (and therefore cannot be traded on a public stock exchange). This is the major distinguishing feature between a private limited company and a public limited company. Most companies, particularly small companies, are private.

Public limited company (plc in UK terminology)

A public limited company is a limited liability company that may sell shares to the public. It can be either an unlisted company, or a listed company on the stock exchange.

A stock exchange listing

When an entity obtains a listing (or quotation) for its shares on a stock exchange this is referred to as a flotation or an Initial Public Offering (IPO).

Advantages of a listing

- Once listed, the market will provide a more accurate valuation of the entity than had been previously possible.
- Realisation of paper profits.
- Raise profile of entity, which may have an impact on revenues, credibility with suppliers and long-term providers of finance.
- Raise capital for future investment.
- Makes employee share schemes more accessible.

Disadvantages of a listing

- Costly for a small entity (flotation, underwriting costs, etc.)
- Making enough shares available to allow a market.
- Reporting requirements are more onerous.
- Stock exchange rules for obtaining a quotation can be stringent.

UK capital markets

There are two important capital markets in the UK:

- the full Stock Exchange – a market for larger companies. Entry costs are high and scrutiny is very high for companies listed on the "full list", but the profile of a Stock Exchange listed company's shares is very high, so the shares are extremely marketable.
- the Alternative Investment Market (AIM) - a market for smaller companies, with lower associated costs and less stringent entry criteria.

Methods of issuing new shares

The three most commonly used methods of issuing shares are:

- (A) IPO (initial public offering), or flotation
- (B) placing
- (C) rights issue

If a company already has a listing on a stock market then the company will either raise new funds by means of a rights issue, or by means of a placing.

An IPO is more suitable when a company seeks a listing on the stock exchange for the first time.

These three methods will now be covered in turn below.

A **An IPO (or flotation)**

Shares are offered for sale to investors, through an issuing house. The offer could be made at a fixed price set by the company, or in a tender offer investors are invited to tender for new shares issued at their own suggested price. All shares are subsequently sold at the best price at which they would be taken up.

B **Placing**

Shares are placed directly with certain investors (normally institutions) on a pre-arranged basis.

More details on IPOs and placings

IPO

These offers may be of completely new shares or they may derive from the transfer to the public of shares already held privately. An issuing house, normally a merchant bank, acquires the shares and then offers them to the public at a fixed price.

The offers are usually made in the form of a prospectus detailed in newspapers, sometimes in an abbreviated form. Buying new issues through the prospectus in the newspaper avoids dealing charges.

Other examples of such issues include:

- government privatisations; and
- privately held shares transferred to the public.

It is easier for prospective purchasers to form a judgement about such entities where there is some track record, rather than with offers for a completely new entity.

Some investors apply for new issues in the hope of selling immediately and reaping a quick profit. For this to succeed the number of shares purchased must be sufficiently high to cover selling charges. For oversubscribed issues, the allocation may be scaled down and the applicant may receive only a small number of shares. The strategy of selling immediately is called stagging (and investors who do it are called stags).

There have been some notable successes for stags, particularly in some of the privatisation issues, but there have also been cases where the initial dealing price has been substantially below the offer price.

A tender offer is an alternative to a fixed price offer. Under a tender offer, subscribers tender for the shares at, or above, a minimum fixed price. The shares are allotted at the highest price at which they will all be taken up. This is known as the strike price.

Placing

In this type of issue the shares are not offered to the public, but the issuing house will arrange for the shares to be issued to its institutional clients.

This method is very popular, being cheaper and quicker to arrange than most other methods. However, it does not normally lead to a very active market for the shares after flotation.

Advisors to an IPO

Investment banks usually take the lead role in an IPO and will advise on:

- the appointment of other specialists (e.g. lawyers);
- stock exchange requirements;
- forms of any new capital to be made available;
- the number of shares to be issued and the issue price;
- arrangements for underwriting;
- publishing the offer.

Stockbrokers provide advice on the various methods of obtaining a listing. They may work with investment banks on identifying institutional investors, but usually they are involved with smaller issues and placings.

Institutional investors have little direct involvement other than as investors, agreeing to buy a certain number of shares. They may also be used by the entity and its advisors to provide an indication of the likely take up and acceptable offer price for the shares. Once the shares are in issue institutional investors have a major influence on the evaluation and the market for the shares.

C **Rights issue**

A rights issue is where new shares are offered for sale to existing shareholders, in proportion to the size of their shareholding.

The right to buy new shares ahead of outside investors is known as the 'pre-emption rights' of shareholders. Note that the purpose of pre-emption rights is to ensure that shareholders have an opportunity to prevent their stake being diluted by new issues. Pre-emption rights are protected by law, and can only be waived with the consent of shareholders.

Rights issues are far cheaper to organise than a public share issue, but may be more expensive than a placing.

An issue price must be set which is:

- low enough to secure acceptance of shareholders; but
- not too low, so as to avoid excessive dilution of the earnings per share.

More details on rights issues

Definition

A rights issue may be defined as:
Raising of new capital by giving existing shareholders the right to subscribe to new shares in proportion to their current holdings. These shares are usually issued at a discount to market price. (CIMA, Official Terminology, 2005)

Explanation

In a rights issue, the entity sets out to raise additional funds from its existing shareholders.

It does this by giving them the opportunity to purchase additional shares. These shares are normally offered at a price lower than the current share price quoted, otherwise shareholders will not be prepared to buy, since they could have purchased more shares at the existing price anyway. The entity cannot offer an unlimited supply at this lower price, otherwise the market price would fall to this value. Accordingly the offer they make to the existing shareholders is limited. For example they may offer one new share for every four held.

Selection of an issue price

In theory, there is no upper limit to an issue price but in practice it would never be set higher than the prevailing market price (MPS) of the shares, otherwise shareholders will not be prepared to buy as they could have purchased more shares at the existing market price anyway. Indeed, the issue price is normally set at a discount on MPS. This discount is usually in the region of 20%. In theory, there is no lower limit to an issue price but in practice it can never be lower than the nominal value of the shares. Subject to these practical limitations, any price may be selected within these values. However, as the issue price selected is reduced, the quantity of shares that has to be issued to raise a required sum will be increased.

Underwriting

Underwriting avoids the possibility that the entity will not sell all of the shares it is issuing, and so receive less funds than it expects. Underwriters are normally financial institutions such as merchant banks. In return for a fee, they agree to buy any shares that are not subscribed for in the issue. Underwriters receive their fee whether or not they are required to take up any unsubscribed shares.

The underwriting costs could potentially be avoided through a deep-discounted rights issue. In such an issue, the issue price is set at a large discount to the current market price so reducing the possibility of shareholders not taking up their rights.

Selection of an issue quantity

It is normal for the issue price to be selected first and then the quantity of shares to be issued becomes a passive decision. The effect of the additional shares on earnings per share, dividend per share and dividend cover should be considered. The selected additional issue quantity will then be related to the existing share quantity for the issue terms to be calculated. The proportion is normally stated in its simplest form, for example, 1 for 4, meaning that shareholders may subscribe to purchase one new share for every four they currently hold

Terms of a rights issue

The issue price for a rights issue can be set by the company.

For example, if Lauchlan Co wanted to raise $2m for a new investment project, it could issue 1m shares at $2 each, or 500,000 shares at $4 each, or 250,000 shares at $8 each, etc.

To decide on the final terms of the issue, the current share price needs to be considered.

Assume that in this example, Lauchlan Co currently has 2m $1 ordinary shares in issue, with a current market price of $5 per share.

Issuing new shares at anything greater than the existing share price of $5 per share would not help to encourage investors to take up their rights. In order to attract investors, a discount on current market value is usually offered.

However, note that if the new shares were issued at (say) $2 each, this would require 1m new shares to be issued, and so many new shares would have a big impact on the company's earnings per share.

In this case, it would seem sensible to balance the various requirements by offering the new shares to investors at $4 per share. This is sufficiently below current market price to give an incentive to the shareholders to take up their rights, while at the same time only requiring 500,000 new shares to be issued, so restricting the impact on earnings per share.

If the new shares were offered to existing shareholders at $4 per share, 500,000 new shares would need to be issued. Given that there are 2m shares currently in issue, the new issue would be announced as a "1 for 4 rights issue at $4 per share". (2m / 500,000 = 4)

Market price after issue

- After the announcement of a rights issue there is a tendency for share prices to fall.
- The temporary fall is due to uncertainty about:
  - consequences of the issue;
  - future profits; and
  - future dividends.
- After the actual issue the market price will normally fall again because:
  - there are more shares in issue (adverse affect on earnings per share); and
  - new shares were issued at market price discount.

'Cum rights'

When rights issue is announced, all existing shareholders have the right to subscribe for new shares, and so there are rights ('cum rights') attached to the shares, and the shares are traded 'cum rights'.

'Ex rights'

On the first day of dealings in the newly issued shares, the rights no longer exist and the old shares are now traded 'ex rights' (without rights attached).

Theoretical prices/values

(a) Theoretical 'ex rights' price is the theoretical price that the class of shares will trade at on the first trading day after issue. It is calculated as follows:

$$\frac{(N \times \text{cum rights price}) + \text{Issue price}}{N+1}$$

(b) Theoretical 'value of rights' per share is calculated as:

(Theoretical ex rights price – issue price)/N

where N= no of rights required to buy 1 share

Rights issue illustration

TERP

Using the figures for Lauchlan Co (in the section "Terms of a rights issue" above), where:

Cum rights price = $5

Issue price = $4

N = 4

Therefore, TERP = [(4 × $5) + $4] / 5 = $4.80

Value of the rights

Also, the value of the rights = (4.80 - 4) = $0.80 per new share, or 0.80 / 4 = $0.20 per old share.

Example 1

(a) Plover Co has 1 million GBP1 ordinary shares quoted at GBP4.50 ex div. It is considering a 1 for 5 rights issue at GBP4.20 per share.

Required:

Calculate the theoretical ex rights share price.

(b) Assume that Plover Co intends to use the funds raised to finance a project with an NPV of GBP300,000.

Note: The NPV method has been covered earlier in the CIMA syllabus. A reminder of the method is covered in the later Chapter 'Investment appraisal – basic techniques'.

Required:

Calculate the theoretical ex rights share price if the project is undertaken.

Yield adjusted ex-rights price

The calculations of theoretical ex-rights price above assume that the additional funds raised will generate a return at the same rate as existing funds. If an entity expects (and the market agrees) that the new funds will earn a different return than is currently being earned on the existing capital then a 'yield-adjusted' TERP should be calculated.

Yield adjusted TERP

$= [\text{Cum rights price} \times N/(N+1)] + [(\text{Issue price}/N+1) \times (Y_n/Y_0)]$

where

Y_o = Yield on 'old' capital

Y_n = Yield on 'new' capital

Using the figures for Lauchlan Co (in the section "Terms of a rights issue" above), where:

Cum rights price = $5

Issue price = $4

and the rights issue was a 1 for 4 issue,

and also assuming:

- the rate of return (yield) on the new funds = 15%
- the rate of return on the existing funds = 12%

The yield-adjusted ex-rights price becomes:

Yield adjusted TERP = $(5 \times 4 / 5) + [(4 /5) \times (15/12)] = \$5$

Alternatively, this is 1 new share at $4 × (15/12), plus 4 old shares at $5 each i.e. $25 in total, or $5 per share.

Notice that if the new funds are expected to earn a return above the rate generated by existing funds, there will be less dilution of the market price than suggested by the original TERP calculation.

Note: If you are given the NPV of the new project which the rights issue has funded (as in Example 1 above), the yield adjusted TERP is calculated as

(Original company market capitalisation + NPV of project + rights issue proceeds) / New total number of shares

Courses of action open to a shareholder

Possible actions for a shareholder are:

- do nothing. (Shareholders may be protected from the consequences of inaction by the company selling the rights on behalf of inactive shareholders);
- renounce the rights and sell them on the market;
- exercise the rights (that is buy all the shares at the rights price);
- renounce part of the rights and take up the remainder.

Illustration of actions open to a shareholder

A shareholder receiving notification of a rights issue from an entity has a number of options available.

Consider the position of a shareholder in Lauchlan Co (from the above example in the "Terms of a rights issue" section.

If the shareholder owns 1,200 shares (worth $5 each), in the 1 for 4 rights issue he will be offered 300 new shares at $4 each.

Option 1 – Do nothing.

In this situation, the market value of the investment could be expected to fall by $240 from $6,000 to $5,760 (1,200 shares at $4.80).

The company would normally reserve the right to sell any ‘unaccepted’ shares for the best price available in the market. After having deducted any expenses and, of course, $4 per share, the balance would be sent to the shareholder. This cash balance could fully or partially compensate the shareholder for the reduction in market value. The shareholder’s percentage share of the entity would reduce.

Option 2 – Sell the rights.

In this situation, the shareholder decides to sell the right to buy the shares at $4 each to another investor. A rational investor would not be expected to pay more than 80 cents per share (TERP - $4) for such a right. The existing shareholder might receive $240 (300 at 80 cents) less any dealing costs incurred. The shareholder's percentage share of the entity would be reduced.

Option 3 – Fully subscribe for the new shares.

In this situation, the shareholder will have to increase the value of the shareholding by paying the entity $1,200 for the 300 new shares. The shareholder will then own 1,500 shares which, using TERP, will be valued at $7,200. The shareholder's percentage share of the entity will be maintained.

Option 4 – Sell some rights to buy some new shares.

In this situation, the shareholder may be unable or unwilling to invest more funds in the entity. Since the rights can normally be sold in the market, the shareholder could sell sufficient of the rights to purchase the balance. In the Lauchlan Co example, each block of 5 rights sold at 80 cents raises sufficient cash to purchase one new share at $4. The shareholder could sell 250 at 80 cents to raise $200 which would be sufficient to purchase 50 at $4. The value of the investment will be maintained at $6,000 but the shareholder's percentage share of the entity will be reduced.

Implications of a rights issue

(a) From the viewpoint of the shareholders:

- they have the option of buying shares at preferential price;
- they have the option of withdrawing cash by selling their rights;
- they are able to maintain their existing relative voting position (by exercising the rights).

(b) From the viewpoint of the company:

- it is simple and cheap to implement;
- it is usually successful ('fully subscribed');
- it often provides favourable publicity.

Example 2 – more on TERPs

Molson Co has a paid-up ordinary share capital of EUR2,000,000 represented by 4 m shares of 50 cents each.

Earnings after tax in the most recent year were EUR750,000 of which EUR250,000 was distributed as dividend. The current price/earnings ratio of these shares, as reported in the financial press, is 8.

The entity is planning a major investment that will cost EUR2,025,000 and is expected to produce a positive NPV of EUR402,400.

The necessary finance is to be raised by a rights issue to the existing shareholders at a price 25% below the current market price of the entity's shares.

Required:

(a) **Calculate:**

- (i) **the current market price of the shares already in issue;**
- (ii) **the price at which the rights issue will be made;**
- (iii) **the number of new shares that will be issued;**
- (iv) **the price at which the shares of the entity should theoretically be quoted on completion of the rights issue (i.e. the 'ex-rights price'), ignoring incidental costs and assuming that the market accepts the entity's forecast of project NPV.**

(b) It has been said that, provided the required amount of money is raised and that the market is made aware of the earning power of the new investment, the financial position of existing shareholders should be the same whether or not they decide to subscribe for the rights they are offered.

Required:

Illustrate and comment on this statement.

Preference shares

Preference shares are a form of equity that pays a fixed dividend, which is paid in preference to (before) ordinary shares, hence the name.

They are not tax efficient, any return being paid out of post-tax income.

Preference shares are not very popular, since they offer the worst of both worlds i.e.

- not tax efficient;
- no opportunity for capital gain (fixed return).

3 Debt Finance

This is the loan of funds to a business without conferring ownership rights. The key features of debt financing arise from this 'arm's length relationship' are:

- It is paid out of pre-tax profits as an expense of the business.
- It carries a risk of default if interest and principal payments are not met.

Security – charges

The lender of funds will normally require some form of security against which the funds are advanced. This means that, in the event of default, the lender will be able to take assets in exchange of the amounts owing. There are two types of 'charge' or security that may be offered/required:

(1) **Fixed charge** – The debt is secured against a specific asset, normally land or buildings. This form of security is preferred because, in the event of liquidation, it puts the lender at the 'front of the queue' of creditors.

(2) **Floating charge** – The debt is secured against the general assets of the business. This form of security is not as strong; again it confers a measure of security on liquidation as a 'preferred creditor', meaning the lender is higher in the list of creditors than otherwise.

Covenants

A further means of limiting the risk to the lender is to restrict the actions of the directors through the means of covenants. These are specific requirements or limitations laid down as a condition of taking on debt financing. They may include:

(1) **Dividend restrictions** – Limitations on the level of dividends a company is permitted to pay. This is designed to prevent excessive dividend payments which may seriously weaken the company's future cash flows and thereby place the lender at greater risk.

(2) **Financial ratios** – Specified levels below which certain ratios may not fall, e.g. debt to net assets ratio, current ratio.

(3) **Financial reports** – Regular accounts and financial reports to be provided to the lender to monitor progress.

(4) **Issue of further debt** – The amount and type of debt that can be issued may be restricted. Subordinated bonds (i.e. bonds ranking below the existing unsecured bonds) can usually still be issued.

Types of debt finance

Debt may be raised from two general sources – banks or capital markets.

Bank finance

For companies that are unlisted, and for many listed companies, the first port of call for borrowing money would be the banks.

These could be the high street banks or, more likely for larger companies, merchant banks.

Terms and conditions are negotiable dependent on the term of the loan, the amount borrowed, and the credit rating of the company wishing to make the borrowing.

Capital markets

As an alternative to borrowing funds from a bank the company, if listed on the stock exchange, may issue long term debt to investors in the capital markets.

Examples of long term debt finance – terminology

Bank finance

Money market borrowings

The money market consists of financial institutions and dealers in money or credit who wish to either borrow or lend.

The money market is used by participants as a means for borrowing and lending in the short term, from several days to just under a year. This contrasts with the capital market for longer-term funding, for example bonds and equity.

The core of the money market consists of interbank lending--banks borrowing from, and lending to, each other. However, large profit-making entities will also borrow and lend on the money market.

Revolving credit facilities (RCFs)

Under a RCF the borrower may use or withdraw funds up to a pre-approved credit limit. The amount of available credit decreases and increases as funds are borrowed and then repaid.

The borrower makes payments based only on the amount they've actually used or withdrawn, plus interest and the borrower may repay the borrowing over time or in full at any time.

RCFs are very flexible debt financing options, and they enable a company to minimise interest payments because the amount of funds borrowed fluctuates over time and is never more than the company needs.

Often the RCF will be offered by a single bank, or in the case of a large amount of finance required, a syndicate (group) of banks may offer the RCF to reduce the risk to any one lender.

Capital markets

Bonds

A bond is a debt security, in which the issuer owes the holders a debt and, depending on the terms of the bond, is obliged to pay interest (the coupon) and/or to repay the principal at a later date. i.e. a bond is a formal contract to repay borrowed money with interest at fixed intervals.

Thus a bond is like a loan: the issuer is the borrower (debtor), the holder is the lender (creditor), and the coupon is the interest. Bonds provide the borrower with external funds to finance long-term investments.

Bonds and shares are both securities which can be traded in the capital markets, but the major difference between the two is that shareholders have an equity stake in the company (i.e., they are owners), whereas bondholders have a creditor stake in the company (i.e., they are lenders). Another difference is that bonds usually have a defined term, or maturity, after which the bond is redeemed, whereas shares may be outstanding indefinitely.

Commercial paper

Large profit-making entities may issue unsecured short-term loan notes in the capital market, referred to as commercial paper.

These loan notes will generally mature within 9 months, typically between a week and 3 months. The notes can be traded at any time before their maturity date.

International debt finance

Large companies can borrow money in foreign currencies as well as their own domestic currency from banks at home or abroad.

The main reason for wanting to borrow in a foreign currency is to fund a foreign investment project or foreign subsidiary.

The foreign currency borrowing provides a hedge of the value of the project or subsidiary to protect against changes in value due to currency movements. The foreign currency borrowing can be serviced from cash flows arising from the foreign currency investment.

More detail on foreign currency borrowings

The choice of currency for debt finance

In the developed countries of the world, companies can choose which currency they prefer for both bank debt and bonds. The later Chapter on 'International Investment Appraisal' explains the key issues to consider when making the choice of which currency to use.

In most developing countries, companies will need to raise bonds in an international currency such as US dollars.

Eurobond markets

Eurobonds are bonds issued on the international bond markets.

They can be denominated in any major international currency (i.e. not necessarily denominated in euro). Eurocurrency bonds may be listed on the domestic currency stock exchange but cannot be traded through that exchange. They are usually bearer instruments and pay interest annually, gross of tax.

This is in contrast to domestic bonds which are both listed and traded on the local stock exchange. They are usually registered bonds, that is, registered to a named holder, and pay interest semi-annually (twice a year), net of tax.

The eurobond market is a self-regulated off-shore market. Self-regulation is promoted by the International Capital Market Association (ICMA) who set rules for members to follow in areas such as processing transactions and payment of commission.

The yield on debt

A common exam question requirement is to calculate the "yield" to the lender of debt finance.

An investor who purchases a traded debt instrument (e.g. debenture, bond) receives a return, known as a "yield", in the form of the annual interest (or "coupon") payments and, if the debt is redeemable, the final redemption payment. This return is also known as the "yield to maturity" (YTM), or "redemption yield" on the bond, and it is defined as:

YTM = effective average annual percentage return to the investor, relative to the current market value of the bond

If the bond is irredeemable, the calculation is very simple. However, the calculations are more complex if the bond is redeemable, or if it is denominated in a foreign currency.

Yield on irredeemable debt

For irredeemable debt,

YTM = (annual interest received / current market value of debt) × 100%

Example 3

Knife plc, a UK listed company, has some 5% coupon, GBP100 nominal value, irredeemable bonds in issue, which have a current market value of GBP95.

Required:

Calculate the yield to maturity for these bonds.

Yield on redeemable debt

For redeemable debt,

YTM = the internal rate of return (IRR) of the bond price, the annual interest received, and the final redemption amount.

Note: the IRR (Internal Rate of Return) was covered earlier in the CIMA syllabus. A reminder of the method is covered in the later Chapter 'Investment Appraisal – basic techniques'.

This ensures that the yield calculation incorporates a return in the form of the final redemption amount as well as the annual interest amounts.

Example 4

Knife plc also has some 7% coupon, GBP 100 nominal value bonds in issue, which are redeemable at a 10% premium in 5 years. The current market value of the bonds is GBP 98.

Required:

Calculate the yield to maturity for these bonds.

Yield to maturity for foreign currency bonds

The calculation of yield to maturity (YTM) is complicated further when we look at foreign currency loans. As above, let's start by considering the impact on irredeemable bonds, then move on to look at redeemables.

Irredeemable foreign currency bonds

Assume that Knife plc now issues some USD 100 irredeemable bonds at par, with a coupon rate of 5%. If the exchange rate between the USD and GBP is expected to stay constant, the YTM calculation is exactly the same as it was before. However, a problem arises when the exchange rate is expected to change.

For example, if the USD is expected to strengthen by 3% per annum against the GBP, paying the interest in USD each year will effectively cost Knife plc 3% more per annum as time goes by, on top of the 5% coupon rate payable.

Thus, the YTM on the irredeemable USD bonds would be

$[(1.05 \times 1.03) - 1] = 8.15\%$ per annum.

Redeemable foreign currency bonds

Now, let's calculate the YTM if Knife plc issues some USD 100, 5% coupon bonds at par, redeemable in 5 years at USD 110, and the USD is expected to strengthen by 3% per annum against the GBP. Assume that the current (spot) exchange rate is GBP/USD 1.5000 (that is, GBP 1 = USD 1.5000).

Following the example above on redeemable bonds, we know that the YTM is the IRR of the current market value, the interest payments and the redemption amount. The complication in this case is that the cashflows will first need to be converted into GBP (Knife plc's home currency), using exchange rates which change each year, as follows:

		USD	Ex rate (GBP1 = USD...)	GBP
t_0	Current MV	(100)	1.5000	(66.67)
t_1	Interest	5	1.5000/1.03=1.4563	3.43
t_2	Interest	5	1.4563/1.03=1.4139	3.54
t_3	Interest	5	1.4139/1.03=1.3727	3.64
t_4	Interest	5	1.3727/1.03=1.3327	3.75
t_5	Interest and redemption	115	1.3327/1.03=1.2939	88.88

Hence, the IRR (the YTM) can be calculated as follows:

	GBP	DF 8%	PV	DF 10%	PV
t_0	(66.67)	1	(66.67)	1	(66.67)
t_1	3.43	0.926	3.18	0.909	3.12
t_2	3.54	0.857	3.03	0.826	2.92
t_3	3.64	0.794	2.89	0.751	2.73
t_4	3.75	0.735	2.76	0.683	2.56
t_5	88.88	0.681	60.53	0.621	55.19
			5.72		(0.15)

Hence IRR = 8% + [2% × 5.72/(5.72 + 0.15)] = 9.95%

4 Other Sources of Finance

Retained earnings / existing cash balances

There is a common misconception that a company with a large amount of retained earnings in its balance sheet (statement of financial position) can fund its new investment projects using these retained earnings. This is not the case.

A company can only use internal sources of finance to fund new projects if it has enough cash in hand.

The level of retained earnings reflects the amount of profit accumulated over the company's life. It is not the same as cash.

Sale and leaseback

This means selling good quality fixed assets such as high street buildings and leasing them back over many years (25+). Funds are released without any loss of use of assets.

Any potential capital gain on assets is forgone.

Sale and leaseback is a popular means of funding for retail organisations with substantial high street property e.g. Tesco, Marks and Spencer.

Grants

These are often related to technology, job creation or regional policy. They are of particular importance to small and medium-sized businesses (i.e. unlisted). Their key advantage is that they do not need to be paid back.

Grants can be provided by local governments, national governments, and other larger bodies such as the European Union.

Debt with warrants attached

A warrant is an option to buy shares at a specified point in the future for a specified (exercise) price. Warrants are often issued with a bond as a sweetener to encourage investors to purchase the bonds.

The warrant offers a potential capital gain where the share price may rise above the exercise price.

The holder has the option to buy the share on the exercise date but can also choose to sell the warrant before that date.

Convertible debt

This is similar in effect to attaching a warrant to a debt instrument except that the warrant cannot be detached and traded separately. The convertible debt is where the debt itself can be converted into shares at a predetermined price at a date or range of dates in the future.

This has the effect of giving the debt holder a potential capital gain over and above the return from the debt interest. If the value of the shares is greater than that of the debt on the exercise date, then conversion will be made by the investor. If, however, the share value is lower than the debt value, the investor may retain the debt to maturity.

Venture capital

This is finance provided to young, unquoted profit-making entities to help them to expand. It is usually provided in the form of equity finance, but may be a mix of equity and debt.

Venture capitalists generally accept low levels of dividends and expect to make most of their returns as capital gains on exit. A typical exit route is an IPO or flotation, which enables the venture capitalist to sell his stake in the entity on the stock market.

Venture capital is covered in more detail in the later Chapter on 'Financial and Strategic Implications of Mergers and Acquisitions'.

Business angels

Business angels are similar to venture capitalists. Venture capitalists are rarely interested in investing in very small businesses, on the grounds that monitoring progress is uneconomic.

Business angels are wealthy investors who provide equity finance to small businesses.

Government assistance

Governments will often have a number of schemes, aimed at providing assistance to:

- small- and medium-sized profit-making entities;
- entities wanting to expand or relocate in particular regions;
- promote innovation and technology;
- projects that will create new jobs or protect existing ones.

You do not need to have knowledge of any specific scheme, but relevant discussion of methods of government assistance in your own country will earn credit in the examination.

5 The Lease v Buy Decision

If a new project requires the use of an asset, such as a machine, a business often has the choice of whether to buy the asset outright, or whether to lease it.

Terminology

(a) **Lease**

An agreement whereby the lessor conveys to the lessee, in return for a payment or series of payments, the right to use an asset for an agreed period of time. (CIMA Official Terminology, 2005)

(b) **Finance lease**

A lease agreement that transfers substantially all the risks and rewards incidental to ownership of an asset from the lessor to the lessee. (CIMA Official Terminology, 2005)

(c) **Operating lease**

A lease agreement other than a finance lease. (CIMA Official Terminology, 2005)

Reasons for leasing

- It is a readily available form of finance, especially for plant and equipment or motor vehicles. It is therefore very convenient for companies to enter into such arrangements.
- It removes the need for a significant capital outlay at the beginning of a project's life i.e. it avoids the need to find the capital at the outset.
- It may be cheaper in financial terms than conventional debt financing i.e. the effective interest rate on leasing may be less than the interest payable on a loan.

More details on operating and finance leases

Leasing is a method of financing that enables one entity (the lessee) to obtain the use of an asset, while legal ownership of the asset remains with another entity (the lessor). The lease agreement does not give the lessee the right to ownership at the end of the lease term.

Finance leases

Finance leases are essentially term loans. These have to be shown in the lessee's accounts as assets and liabilities and the depreciation and financing charged against profits.

The term of the lease normally extends over the full useful life of the asset. The lessor therefore receives lease payments that will fully cover the cost of the asset. The agreement will usually not be cancellable and will not provide for any maintenance of the asset. The lessee effectively holds all the risks of asset ownership without being the legal owner. The leasing entity is not normally involved in dealing with the assets themselves, being a bank or finance entity. The asset is selected by the firm that will use it, who negotiates price, delivery, etc. The leasing entity simply buys the asset and arranges a lease contract with the lessee. At the end of the lease period there will usually be an agreement where the sale proceeds from the asset are shared between the lessor and lessee, or if the lessee desires it can carry on using the asset for payment of a nominal amount each year, called a peppercorn rent.

Sale and leaseback

Entities can use what is known as a sale and leaseback arrangement in order to convert certain assets that the entity owns into funds yet still continue to use the assets. For example if a building is sold to an insurance entity or some other financial intermediary and then leased back from the purchaser, the entity has secured an immediate cash inflow. The only cash outflow is the rental payments that it now has to make. These rental payments are usually allowed as a tax-deductible expense. However, the entity may be subject to capital gains tax, which will arise if the sale price is in excess of the written-down value as agreed by the tax authorities.

It must be remembered, however, that the leased asset no longer belongs to the entity; the lease may one day come to an end and then alternative assets will have to be obtained.

This financing possibility is particularly applicable to assets that appreciate in value, such as land, buildings or some other forms of property. It is particularly appropriate to entities owning the properties freehold, and to institutions such as insurance entities or pension funds that are interested in holding long-term secure assets. The property is leased back at a negotiated annual rental, although with long leasebacks there will need to be a provision for the revision of the rental at certain intervals of time.

Operating leases

Operating leases are treated very much like contract hire. They do not appear on the lessee's balance sheet and the fee for the hire is charged directly against profits.

These agreements will usually not last for the full life of an asset. They are offered by entities who manufacture or deal in the particular product, often incorporating maintenance and other services. The lease can be cancelled and the equipment returned. Operating leases are common for office and business equipment, for example typewriters, photocopiers, computers and motor vehicles. The lessor will not recover his/her full investment on any one lease but will hope to lease a particular asset several times over its life.

Operating leases are particularly useful for industries where there is a rapid change in technology that makes it necessary to have the latest equipment, for example computers.

Hire purchase

Hire purchase is similar to leasing, except that the legal title to the asset passes to the hire purchase customer on payment of the final instalment payment. In a lease agreement ownership of the asset does not transfer to the lease.

Lease-or-buy decisions

The evaluation of the lease-or-buy decision is not a pure financing decision as it also involves interactions with the investment decision.

Operating leases

The evaluation of an operating lease is relatively straight forward. The process is as follows:

- Identify the lease payments payable over the life of the agreement.
- Adjust the lease payments for tax.
- Discount the after tax lease payments at a discount rate reflecting the asset's systematic risk.

Finance leases

The decision to lease or buy an asset is a financing decision that will be made only once the decision to invest in the asset has been taken. The decision to invest in the asset would be determined by discounting the operational costs and benefits from using the asset at the cost of capital normally used by the entity to evaluate projects, typically its weighted average cost of capital. Investing in the asset would be justified if a positive NPV is obtained.

The financing decision is then concerned with identifying the least-cost financing option. In evaluating the financing decision, it is usually assumed that the entity would have to borrow funds in order to purchase the asset.

Lease v buy evaluation

If an asset is needed for a major new investment, and the asset can be leased under a finance lease then a critical decision is:

- should the asset be leased?; or
- should the asset be purchased and the purchase cost financed by debt issue?

In the exam you may need to evaluate the lease against the borrowing to buy option to determine which would be better in financial terms.

The traditional approach to the evaluation is to use the NPV method i.e. determine the present value cost of leasing and compare this to the present value cost of borrowing to buy.

Note: the NPV method (Net Present Value) was covered earlier in the CIMA syllabus. A reminder of the method is covered in the later Chapter 'Investment Appraisal – basic techniques'.

Note on discount rate

In the lease v buy evaluation, it is considered that the risk associated with the lease option is comparable to the risk associated with the borrow to buy option. Hence the same discount rate should be used for both NPV calculations.

The discount rate to use is the **post tax cost of debt finance** - clearly this rate applies to the borrow to buy option, and it is considered to be appropriate to the leasing option too, since the post tax cost of debt is effectively the opportunity cost of leasing.

Example 5 – Simple lease example

Penny Co wishes to invest in new equipment costing $130,000. The equipment has a life of four years and no scrap proceeds are expected to be available after this period. Tax allowable depreciation is available at 25% on a reducing balance basis. The company can borrow at 12% pre-tax.

The equipment could alternatively be leased for a cost of $40,000 per annum payable in arrears over four years. Assume that the full lease payment is a tax deductible expense.Corporation tax is 33% payable one year in arrears

Required:

Determine whether the company should lease or purchase the asset.

Further calculations on lease interest

In the above example, to simplify the calculations, we were told specifically that the full lease payment was to be treated as a tax deductible expense.

In reality, it will usually be just the interest element of the lease payment which is tax deductible. In this case, the first step is to calculate the interest element, using either the actuarial method, or the sum of digits method.

The following illustration shows how both methods work.

Illustration 1

Assume that KL Co has the option to buy an asset for USD100,000, or to lease it under a finance lease by paying USD29,500 per year in arrears for 4 years.

Clearly, the interest element in the lease amounts to (4 × USD29,500) – USD100,000 = USD18,000 in total. This interest can be allocated to years using either the actuarial method, or the sum of digits method.

Actuarial method

Here the implied interest rate is found by using an IRR approach.

As a short cut, the 4 year annuity factor at the IRR can be found by dividing the cost of the asset by the annual interest payment (i.e. 100,000/29,500). This gives a 4 year annuity factor of 3.390, which (from tables) is very close to the 7% factor. Hence, the implied interest rate in the lease is (approximately) 7%.

Now, the interest can be allocated to individual years using the following table:

£	Year 1	Year 2	Year 3	Year 4
Opening balance	100,000	77,500	53,425	27,665
+ Interest (7% × Op Bal)	7,000	5,425	3,740	1,937
– Lease payment	(29,500)	(29,500)	(29,500)	(29,500)
Closing balance	77,500	53,425	27,665	102

Note: The closing balance at the end of year 4 should be zero. The difference is due to rounding.

The lease interest payments have now been allocated to years, so can be used to calculate the tax relief each year.

Sum of digits method

This is a simpler way of allocating interest, based on the sum of digits formula:

$$n(n+1)/2$$

In this example, the lease payments are to be made over 4 periods, so the sum of digits is 10 (working: 4 × 5 /2 = 10)

Hence, the interest allocation is:

Year 1	4/10 × 18,000	USD7,200
Year 2	3/10 × 18,000	USD5,400
Year 3	2/10 × 18,000	USD3,600
Year4	1/10 × 18,000	USD1,800

Once again, the tax relief on the lease interest can now be calculated easily.

Example 6 – More complex lease v buy evaluation

Following on from the information in the Illustration above:

Assume that KL Co has the option to buy an asset immediately for USD100,000, or to lease it under a finance lease by paying USD29,500 per year in arrears for 4 years.

Other information

- KL Co is liable to corporate tax at a marginal rate of 30% which is settled at the end of the year in which it arises.
- KL Co accounts for depreciation on a straight-line basis at the end of each year
- Under the buy option, tax depreciation allowances on the full capital cost are available in equal instalments over the first four years of operation.
- Under the lease option, both the accounting depreciation and the interest element of the finance lease payments are tax deductible.

Required:

Advise KL Co whether the asset should be leased or bought, assuming that the interest on the lease should be allocated using the actuarial method. Use a discount rate of 5% in your evaluation.

6 The Efficient Market Hypothesis (EMH)

Introduction to market efficiency

In theory, in a perfect market, the market value of a listed company should be a fair reflection of all the information which is known about that company. For example, a profitable company with good prospects should be worth more than an underperforming company.

In the real world, it is often argued that the market is not perfect, so the value of a listed company does not reflect all the information known about a company.

The extent to which market share prices are a fair reflection of a company's position depends on the efficiency of the market.

The Efficient Market Hypothesis (EMH)

The efficiency of a financial market may be examined in various ways, the most relevant here being in terms of information processing.

Information processing efficiency reflects the extent to which information regarding the future prospects of a company is reflected in its current price.

Information processing efficiency is of great importance to financial management as it means that the results of management decisions will be quickly and accurately reflected in share prices. For example, if a firm undertakes an investment project that will generate a large surplus, then in an efficient market it should see the value of its equity rise. Accordingly there have been many tests of the so-called Efficient Market Hypothesis (EMH) for the USA and the UK stock markets.

For the purposes of testing, the EMH is usually broken down into three categories, as follows.

- the weak form;
- the semi-strong form (which is closest to the real world situation);
- the strong form (which is assumed by many of the theories in Financial Strategy).

More detail on the EMH

Weak form

When a stock market displays weak form efficiency, share prices reflect all known publicly-available past information about companies and their shares. Share prices reflect this historical information, such as published financial results and dividend payments. If this hypothesis is correct, then it should be impossible to predict future share price movements from historical patterns (which is what so-called 'technical analysts' or 'chartists' attempt to do). For example, if a company's share price had increased steadily over the last few months to a current price of £2.50, this price will already fully reflect the currently available information about the company.

The next change in share price could be either upwards or downwards, with equal probability, depending on the nature of the next information made available to the market.

Because of this randomness in share price movements, this is frequently referred to as the random walk hypothesis. This means that the movements of share prices over time approximate a random walk. It also follows that because the current share price fully reflects past information about price changes it is the best estimate of the share's value.

Semi-strong form

The semi-strong form hypothesis of market efficiency is that current share prices reflect not only historical share price information and other historical information about a company, but also respond immediately to other current publicly-available information about the company.

For example, suppose that Alpha plc is a stock market company that announces its latest profits and dividends figures. If the stock market is efficient in its semi-strong form, the share price will react immediately to the news announcement and settle at a new level that reflects the new information. If the stock market does not display semi-strong form efficiency, it might be several days or weeks before the share price adjusts.

Thus a stock market specialist who attempts to use his expertise to use the publicly available information to predict which shares will be worth buying, would have little success in out-guessing the market.

The evidence also tends to confirm that the semi-strong form of efficiency does exist in leading stock markets.

Strong form

The strong form hypothesis of market efficiency states that the current share price reflects all the information relevant to the company, including information that has not yet been made public! If the hypothesis is correct then the mere publication of the information should have no impact on the share price, consequently it should not be possible to make profits by dealing in response to inside information. It would be impossible to make a profit by predicting future share price movements for reasons not yet known to the market, because the market knows everything. It would be impossible for individuals to make a profit from insider knowledge and insider dealing. (Insider dealing is illegal in both the UK and the US.) It is unlikely that the strong form exists.

Implications of the EMH for financial managers

If capital markets are efficient, the main implications for financial managers are:

- The timing of issues of debt or equity is not critical, as the prices quoted in the market are 'fair'.
- The entity's share price will reflect the net present value of its future cash flows, so managers must only ensure that all investments are expected to exceed the company's cost of capital.

7 Exam style questions

Test your understanding 1 – Rights issue and convertible bonds

(a) KB has a paid-up ordinary share capital of $1,500,000 represented by 6m shares of 25 cents each. It has no loan capital. Earnings after tax in the most recent year were $1,200,000. The P/E ratio of the entity is 12.

The company is planning to make a large new investment which will cost $5,040,000 and is considering raising the necessary finance through a rights issue at 192 cents.

Required:

(i) **Calculate the current market price of KB's ordinary shares.**

(2 marks)

(ii) **Calculate the theoretical ex-rights price, and state what factors in practice might invalidate your calculation.**

(6 marks)

(iii) **Briefly explain what is meant by a deep-discounted rights issue, identifying the main reasons why an entity might raise finance by this method.**

(3 marks)

(b) As an alternative to a rights issue KB might raise the $5,040,000 required by means of an issue of convertible bonds at par, with a coupon rate of 6%. The bonds would be redeemable in 7 years' time. Prior to redemption, the bonds may be converted at a rate of 35 ordinary shares per $100 nominal bonds.

Required:

(i) **Explain the term conversion premium and calculate the conversion premium at the date of issue implicit in the data given.**

(4 marks)

(ii) **Identify the advantages to KB of issuing convertible bonds instead of the rights issue to raise the necessary finance.**

(5 marks)

(Total 20 marks)

Test your understanding 2 – Financing options, inc. foreign

XTA plc is the parent entity of a transport and distribution group based in the United Kingdom. The group owns and operates a network of distribution centres and a fleet of trucks (large delivery vehicles) in the United Kingdom. It is currently planning to expand into Continental Europe, operating through a new subsidiary entity in Germany. The subsidiary will purchase distribution centres in Germany and invest in a new fleet of trucks to be based at those centres. The German subsidiary will be operationally independent of the UK parent.

Alternative proposals have been put forward by Messrs A, B and C, Board members of XTA plc on how best to structure the financing of the new German operation as follows:

Mr A: 'I would feel much more comfortable if we were to borrow in our base currency, sterling, where we already have long-standing banking relationships and a good reputation in the capital markets. Surely it would be much more complicated for us to borrow in euros?'

Mr B: 'I am concerned about the exposure of our consolidated balance sheet and investor ratios to sterling/euro exchange rate movements. How will we be able to explain large fluctuations to our shareholders? If we were to raise long-term euro borrowings, wouldn't this avoid exchange rate risk altogether? We would also benefit from euro interest rates which have been historically lower than sterling rates.'

Mr C: We know from our market research that we will be facing stiff competition in Germany from local distribution companies. This is a high-risk project with a lot of capital at stake and we should finance this new venture by XTA plc raising new equity finance to reflect this high risk.'

Assume that today is Saturday 1 October 20X5. A summary of the latest forecast consolidated statement of financial position (balance sheet) for the XTA Group at 31 December 20X5 is given below. It has been prepared BEFORE taking into account the proposed German investment:

	GBP (£) million
Assets	
Total assets	450
Equity and liabilities	
Equity	250
Long term borrowings	150
(there were no other non current liabilities)	
Current liabilities	50
Total equity and liabilities	450

The proposed investment in Germany is scheduled for the final quarter of 20X5 at a cost of £60m for the distribution centres, and £20m for the fleet of trucks when translated from euros at today's exchange rate of £/EUR1.50 (that is £1 = EUR (€) 1.50). There is a possibility that the euro could weaken against sterling to £/€2.00 by 31 December 20X5, but it can be assumed that this will not occur until after the investment has been made. The subsidiary's balance sheet at 31 December 20X5 will only contain the new distribution centres and fleet of trucks matched by an equal equity investment by XTA plc and will only become operationally active from 1 January 20X6.

Required

(a) **Write a memorandum to the Board of XTA plc to explain the advantages and disadvantages of using each of the following sources of finance:**

- **a rights issue versus a placing (assuming UK equity finance is chosen to fund the new German subsidiary); and**
- **a euro bank loan versus a euro-denominated eurobond (assuming euro borrowings are chosen).**

(8 marks)

(b) **Evaluate EACH of the alternative proposals of Messrs A, B and C for financing the new German subsidiary and recommend the most appropriate form of financing for the group. Support your discussion of each proposal with**

- **a summary forecast consolidated balance sheet for the XTA group at 31 December 20X5 incorporating the new investment; and**
- **calculations of gearing using book values**

using year end exchange rates of both £/€1.50 and £/€2.00.

(17 marks)

(Total 25 marks)

Test your understanding answers

Example 1

(a) The theoretical ex rights price (TERP) is:

$$\frac{(N \times \text{cum rights price}) + \text{Issue price}}{N+1}$$

= [(5 × 4.50) + 4.20]/6 =GBP4.45

Alternatively, TERP can be calculated by looking at the total value of all the shares as follows:

$$= \frac{\left((1m \times £4.50) + (\tfrac{1}{5} \times 1m \times £4.20)\right)}{\left(1m + \tfrac{1}{5} \times 1m\right)}$$

=GBP4.45

(b) The NPV of the project is GBP300,000, so in an efficient market, this will be the gain in wealth of the shareholders if the project is undertaken.

The total number of shares in issue is now

1 million + (1/5 x 1 million) = 1.2 million

Thus, the theoretical share price after the rights issue, and after undertaking the project is

4.45 + (300,000/1.2 million) = GBP4.70

Example 2 – more on TERPs

(a) (i) Current market price of shares already in issue:

EPS = 750,000 / 4m = EUR 0.1875

Therefore, since the P/E ratio is 8, the price per share is 8 × 0.1875 = EUR 1.50

(ii) Price at which rights issue will be made:

£1.50 × 75% = £1.125

(iii) Number of new shares that will be issued:

EUR2,025,000 / EUR 1.125 = 1.8 million

(iv) 1.8m new shares are being issued at EUR1.125 per share, 4m existing shares are in issue with a market price of EUR 1.50 per share, and the new project will have an NPV of EUR 402,400.

Hence, the TERP is

[(4m × 1.50) + (1.8m × 1.125) + 402,400] / 5.8m = EUR 1.453

Alternatively: ignoring the project initially, and using the formula from the formula sheet,

$$\text{TERP} = \frac{(\text{N} \times \text{cum rights price}) + \text{Issue price}}{\text{N+1}}$$

= [(4m/1.8m) × 1.50 + 1.125] / (4m/1.8m) + 1 = EUR 1.384

and with the new project worth NPV = EUR402,400, this increases to

1.384 + (402,400 / 5.8m) = EUR 1.453 as before

(b) This statement can be illustrated as follows:

For every 20 shares held, the rights issue means another 9 shares.

At least in theory, the selling price of the right to purchase one share will be £1.453 less £1.125, that is, £0.328.

A shareholder with 20 shares taking up the rights will have wealth of

	EUR
Market value of 29 shares at EUR1.453 each	42.137
Less: Cost of taking up rights of nine new shares at EUR1.125 each	(10.125)
	32.012

A shareholder with 20 shares selling the rights will have wealth of:

	EUR
Market value of 20 shares at EUR1.453 each	29.060
Add: Sale of nine rights at EUR0.328 each	2.952
	32.012

The above calculations, however, assume no transaction costs.

Furthermore, the market may read a particular message into the rights issue that would affect the calculations.

Example 3

YTM = (annual interest / current market value) × 100%

= (5/95) × 100% = 5.26%

Note that the coupon rate is applied to the nominal value to calculate the annual interest, but otherwise, the nominal value is not used in the calculation.

Example 4

The yield to maturity for these redeemable bonds is found by taking the IRR of the current market value (98 at t_0), the annual interest (7 per annum from t_1 to t_5), and the redemption amount (110 at t_5), as follows:

Time	GBP	DF 5%	PV	DF 10%	PV
t_0	(98)	1	(98)	1	(98)
t_1 - t_5	7	4.329	30.30	3.791	26.54
t_5	100	0.784	86.24	0.621	68.31
			18.54		(3.15)

Hence IRR = 5%+[5% × 18.54/(18.54+3.15)] = 9.27%

Example 5 – Simple lease example

The discount rate is the post tax cost of debt ∴ 12% (1 - 0.33) = 8.04% ≈ 8%.

Assumptions:

(1) Asset is purchased on first day of year 1.

(2) Tax is delayed by 1 year.

Buy asset

Tax allowable depreciation

		Tax @ 33%	*Date*
0	130,000		
1 TAD	32,500/97,500	10,725	2
2 TAD	24,375/73,125	8,044	3
3 TAD	18,281/54,844	6,033	4
4 SCRAP	0		
Balancing allowance	54,844	18,099	5

Year	Cash flow	PVF @ 8%	PV
0	(130,000)	1	(130,000)
1	–	–	–
2	10,725	0.857	9,191
3	8,044	0.794	6,387
4	6,033	0.735	4,434
5	18,099	0.681	12,325
			(97,663)

Lease asset

Year	Lease	Tax	Net	PVF @ 8%	PV
1	(40,000)		(40,000)	(0.926)	(37,040)
2	(40,000)	13,200	(26,800)	0.857	(22,968)
3	(40,000)	13,200	(26,800)	0.794	(21,279)
4	(40,000)	13,200	(26,800)	0.735	(19,698)
5		13,200	13,200	0.681	8,989
					(91,996)

Decision:

On purely financial grounds it is better to lease rather than buy the asset.

Example 6 – More complex lease v buy evaluation

Buy option

	T_0	T_1–T_4
Purchase cost	(100,000)	
Tax relief on tax depreciation (30% x 100,000/4)		7,500
Discount factor (5%)	1	3.546
Present value	(100,000)	26,595
Net present value	(73,405)	

i.e. Buying the asset to undertake the project will cost USD 73,405 in present value terms.

Lease option

	T_1	T_2	T_3	T_4
Lease payment	(29,500)	(29,500)	(29,500)	(29,500)
Tax relief on depreciation and lease interest (W1)	9,600	9,128	8,622	8,081
	(19,900)	(20,372)	(20,878)	(21,419)
Discount factors (5%)	0.952	0.907	0.864	0.823
Present value	(18,945)	(18,477)	(18,039)	(17,627)
Net present value	(73,088)			

i.e. Leasing the asset to undertake the project will cost USD 73,088 in present value terms.

(W1) Tax relief calculation

	T_1	T_2	T_3	T_4
Implied interest (from Illustration 1 earlier in the Chapter)	7,000	5,425	3,740	1,937
Depreciation	25,000	25,000	25,000	25,000
	32,000	30,425	28,740	26,937
Tax relief (30%)	9,600	9,128	8,622	8,081

Note: The tax relief on the lease interest is included in the evaluation as a relevant cashflow, but the lease interest itself is not a cashflow, so is not included.

Conclusion:

The lease option is cheaper so should be undertaken on financial grounds. However, the difference is so marginal that it will be important to undertake sensitivity analysis, and to consider other non financial factors before a final decision is made.

Note that we are assuming that the positive NPV of any cashflows arising from the new project must exceed the negative NPV associated with the cost of the asset, to give an overall positive NPV.

Test your understanding 1 – Rights issue and convertible bonds

(a) (i) Earnings per share (EPS) = Profit after taxation / No of shares = 1,200,000 / 6m = $0.20

Market price = EPS × P/E = 0.20 × 12 = $2.40

(ii) Number of shares issued in rights issue = 5,040,000 / $1.92 = 2,625,000

Therefore, TERP = [(6m × $2.40) + (2.625m × $1.92)] / (6m + 2.625m) = $2.254

Factors that may invalidate this calculation in practice include:

- adverse factors affecting the value of KB plc's shares between setting the terms of the rights issue and the issue date (e.g. a market crash);
- whether the market considers the forecast return from the new funds to be realistic;
- the increased number of shares in issue may affect their marketability, causing a further reduction in the ex-rights share price;
- if shareholders do not take up their rights, shares will be left with the underwriters, which will depress the share price;
- the new project may be seen by investors as more risky than existing projects, with no corresponding increase in return;
- investors' expectations of future dividends per share may change as a consequence of the increase in the share capital.

(iii) A deep-discounted rights issue is an issue where the issue price is set well below the current market price of the shares. In some cases, the discount has been as much as 40% on the pre-issue price. The issue price must still, however, be above the nominal value to comply with company law. If share prices are volatile, there is a risk that the market price will fall below the rights issue price, which would lead to undersubscription. A deep-discounted rights issue should avoid this potential problem.

The lower issue price does mean that more shares will need to be issued to raise the same level of finance, with a consequent impact on future dividends per share and earnings per share.

(b) (i) At a point in time, the price of convertible bonds is likely to be different from the price of the underlying ordinary shares. The conversion premium measures how much more expensive it would be to buy the convertible bonds than the corresponding underlying ordinary shares.

Conversion terms:

$100 nominal of bonds = 35 ordinary shares. Therefore, each share is worth (100/35=) $2.86 worth of bonds.

Share price = $2.40

Therefore, the conversion premium is 2.86 – 2.40 = $0.46, or (0.46/2.40=) 19% of the share price.

(ii)

- Convertible bonds will usually be a cheaper source of finance than equity because their greater security and prospective convertibility into ordinary shares reduces the risk premium required by an investor
- Interest on the bonds is a tax-deductible expense, whereas dividends on ordinary shares are an appropriation of profits
- The issue of convertible bonds will not immediately dilute existing shareholders' control
- Convertible bonds may be cheaper to issue than a rights issue
- Convertible bonds may be more appropriate for high-risk entities, because it offers investors the opportunity to benefit from long-term growth in the entity while providing short-term returns in the form of interest payments.

Test your understanding 2 – Financing options, inc. foreign

(a) **Rights issue versus placing**

Advantages of a rights issue

– no dilution of ownership by current shareholders

– reliable (can be underwritten)

Disadvantages of a rights issue

- limits potential investors to current shareholder base (placements can be marketed to a wider selection of institutional investors)
- more complex and more expensive than a placing
- takes longer to arrange than a placing

Euro bank loan versus euro-denominated eurobond

Advantages of a euro bank loan

- direct contact with lender
- flexible terms
- promotes good bank relationship
- access to a wider source of funds via syndicated credit from a panel of banks
- not dependent on a good rating
- relatively quick and cheap to arrange

Disadvantages of a euro bank loan

- does not give access to large, deep international capital markets which may support larger issues
- better rates possible from Eurobonds
- longer maturities may be harder to obtain from a bank (for example 20 years)

Examiner's Note

The answer to (a) above has been given in list form as a study aid, but in an examination, candidates would be expected to provide a memorandum, with short paragraphs (which could be in bullet point form) for each point.

(b) Revised statements of financial position (balance sheets)

The balance sheet of the German subsidiary is translated at closing rate since the company is operationally independent of the UK parent.

Table A: Mr A's proposal – long term borrowings in GBP (£)

	Ex rate £/€1.50	Ex rate £/€2.00
	GBP (£) million	GBP (£) million
Total assets	530	510
	(450 + 120/1.50)	(450 + 120/2.00)
Equity and liabilities		
Equity (balancing figure)	250	230
Long term borrowings	230	230
Current liabilities	50	50
Total equity and liabilities	530	510

Table B: Mr B's proposal – long term EUR (€) borrowings

	Ex rate £/€1.50	Ex rate £/€2.00
	GBP (£) million	GBP (£) million
Total assets	530	510
	(450 + 120/1.50)	(450 + 120/2.00)
Equity and liabilities		
Equity (balancing figure)	250	250
Long term borrowings	230	210
	(150 + 120/1.50)	(150 + 120/2.00)
Current liabilities	50	50
Total equity and liabilities	530	510

Table C: Mr C's proposal – UK (GBP) equity funding

	Ex rate £/€1.50	Ex rate £/€2.00
	GBP (£) million	GBP (£) million
Total assets	530	510
	(450 + 120/1.50)	(450 + 120/2.00)
Equity and liabilities		
Equity (balancing figure)	330	310
Long term borrowings	150	150
Current liabilities	50	50
Total equity and liabilities	530	510

Table D: Gearing levels

Current position (debt to debt plus equity) = 150 / (150 + 250) = 37.5%

Scenario:	**Ex rate £/€1.50**	**Ex rate £/€2.00**
Mr A	48%	50%
Mr B	48%	46%
Mr C	31%	33%

Evaluation of Board members' comments

Mr A: sterling-denominated borrowings

Reputation in the UK markets: Mr A's comment on the advantage of sterling borrowings due to reputation in the sterling capital markets is not valid since banks providing sterling loans should be equally willing to provide euro loans and a good reputation in the capital markets will extend beyond the United Kingdom.

Foreign exchange risk: There is, however, a major exchange risk arising from funding euro-based assets with sterling borrowings, arising mainly from the retranslation of the net investment in the subsidiary at the year end and the effect this has on equity values and gearing levels. This is illustrated in Table A, where the value of equity has fallen from £250m to £230m as a result of the weakening of the euro against sterling from a rate of £/€1.50 to £/€2.00. The effect on gearing is seen in Table D where a fall in the value of the euro leads to deterioration in gearing levels from 48% to 50%.

Impact on gearing: The use of borrowings has a major impact on gearing level, with debt/equity deteriorating from 37.5% to 48% (at £/€1.50). Euro-denominated borrowings have a similar impact at current exchange rates.

Other exchange risk: There is also an exchange risk on the sterling value of the repatriation of euro profits to the United Kingdom via dividends, interest and management charges.

Mr B: euro-denominated borrowings

Lower euro interest rates: This is not a valid argument since, under interest rate parity, spot rates are expected to move to compensate for lower euro interest rates and so any gain on interest payments is likely to be offset by a loss on the capital value of the loan when it is repaid.

Exchange risk and equity values: Euro borrowings provide a natural hedge by matching the currency of the assets with that of the funding used to finance those assets. At the balance sheet date, the exchange gain or loss on retranslating the net investement in the German subsidiary will be substantially matched by an equal and opposite gain or loss on retranslating the euro borrowings. This is illustrated in Table B, where a weakening of the euro borrowings against sterling is seen to have no impact on the value of equity.

Examiner's Note

Although outside the scope of the Financial Strategy Syllabus, it could be noted that the hedge accounting provisions of IAS39 can be applied to avoid volatility in reported profit figures. Without hedge accounting, gains and losses on the loan would be recognised in profit for the year whereas gains and losses on the investment in the German subsidiary would be recognised as part of equity under IAS21. If hedge accounting is permitted, the hedge provided by the loan can be designated as such and exchange rate movements on both the investment and the loan recognised as changes in the value of equity.

Exchange risk and gearing levels: The gearing ratio has again deteriorated markedly as a result of increased borrowing. In addition, gearing levels are exposed to exchange rate changes. In this case, gearing has improved from 48% to 46% as a result of a fall in the value of the euro, but a negative impact would have resulted from a strengthening of the euro against sterling.

Mr C: UK equity

Risk profile: Mr C is correct in his assertion that equity finance is more suitable than long-term borrowings for a high risk project, since dividends can be cut or reduced if profits are lower than expected, whereas the interest on borrowings always has to be paid in full at each due date.

Exchange risk: However, with equity finance denominated in sterling and the investment being linked to the value of the euro, there is no natural hedge of exchange rate risk arising on the revaluation of the net investment in Germany. Table C shows that the value of equity would fall from £330m to £310m as a result of a fall in the value of the euro from £/€1.50 to £/€2.00 and there would be a deterioration in gearing from 31% to 33%.

Gearing levels: These are at a much more acceptable level of around 31%. Indeed, additional long-term borrowings may not be practical if lenders are concerned about the already high gearing levels in the group and/or if the new venture has a high risk profile. In this case, the company may have no choice but to raise new equity finance.

Recommendation

The German distribution centre and transport fleet should be financed by long-term euro borrowings (which would be designated as a hedge under IAS 39 and hedge accounting provisions applied, as noted above) in order to match the currency and maturity of the assets to be funded and remove exposure of equity and reported profit to exchange rate gains and losses.

It would be preferable for such euro borrowings to be raised by the German subsidiary so that the euro loan interest can be paid out of euro earnings. This also provides the opportunity for reducing the cost of funding by securing the loans on the euro assets.

The proportion of new long-term borrowings may be restricted by the following:

- German tax authority regulations on minimum capitalisation levels.
- Value of assets in the German subsidiary that can be used for security.
- Level of parent company loan guarantees offered (where additional security is required).
- Debt capacity of the group (that is acceptable gearing level).

To the extent that long-term borrowings are not possible, the group should consider a rights issue or placing to raise additional equity finance.

chapter

5

Short Term Finance – Working Capital Management

Chapter learning objectives

Lead	Component
B1: Evaluate the financing requirements of an organisation and strategies for meeting those requirements.	(e) recommend optimal strategies for the management of working capital and satisfaction of longer term financing requirements.

Indicative syllabus content

- Working capital management strategies. (Note: No detailed testing of cash and stock management models will be set since these are covered at a lower level within the syllabus).
- Criteria for selecting sources of finance, including finance for international investments.
- The effect of financing decisions on balance sheet structure and on ratios of interest to investors and other financiers (gearing, earnings per share, price-earnings ratio, dividend yield, dividend cover gearing, interest cover).

1 Overview of Chapter

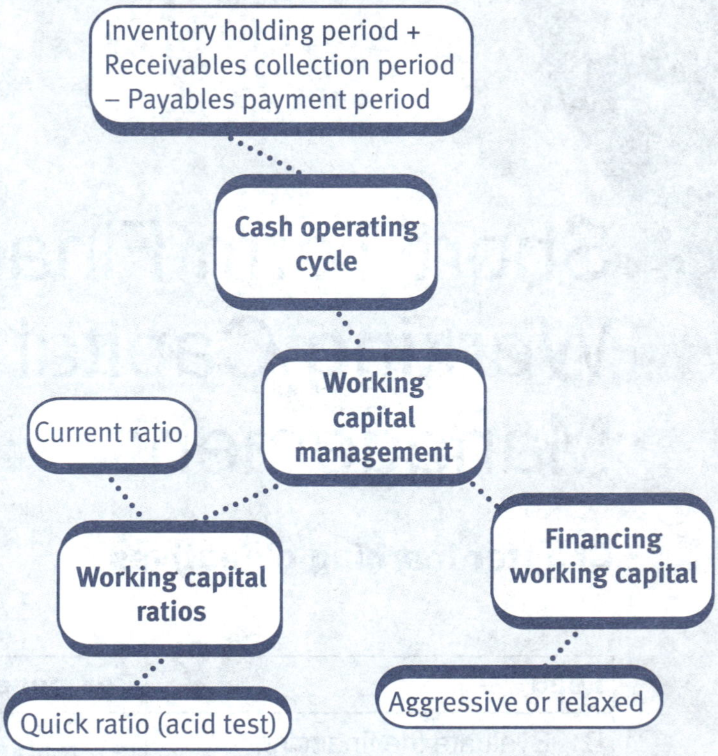

In CIMA's Official Terminology, working capital is defined as:

Working capital: The capital available for conducting the day-to-day operations of an entity; normally, the excess of current assets over current liabilities.

The key components of working capital are inventories, receivables, payables and cash.

2 The management of working capital

Liquidity and profitability

The efficient management of working capital is important from the points of view of both liquidity and profitability.

Poor management of working capital means that funds are unnecessarily tied up in idle assets, hence reducing liquidity, and also reducing the ability to invest in productive assets such as plant and machinery, so affecting profitability.

Examples of the liquidity v profitability trade off

Working capital is the firm's current assets, less its current liabilities, i.e. inventory, receivables, cash and payables. The firm faces a trade off with regard to each of these items, since too much or too little working capital can cause problems for the firm as follows:

Advantage of large inventories Few stockouts = good for sales (profitability)	**INVENTORY**	**Advantage of low inventories** Little cash tied up = good for preserving cash flow (liquidity)
Advantage of granting several months of credit Customers like credit = good for sales (profitability)	**RECEIVABLES**	**Advantage of granting little trade credit** Little cash tied up = good for preserving cash flow (liquidity)
Advantage of high cash balances Bills can be paid = good for relations with creditors	**CASH**	**Advantages of low cash balances** More cash can be invested = good for earning profits
Advantage of taking extended credit Preserves own cash (liquidity) = cheap source of finance	**PAYABLES**	**Advantage of adhering to reasonable credit terms** Suppliers are content = good relations and few disruptions

Investment and financing decision

An entity's working capital policy is a function of two decisions:

- The appropriate level of investment in, and mix of current assets to be decided upon, for a set level of activity – this is the investment decision.
- The methods of financing this investment – the financing decision.

3 The working capital investment decision

All entities require working capital, but there is no standard fixed requirement.

The actual amount required will depend on many factors, such as :

- the industry within which the firm operates - in some industries, customers expect long payment periods (impacting receivables) whereas in other industries cash payments are the norm (low receivables);
- the type of products sold – a business selling perishable products will have to keep a lower level of inventory;
- whether products are manufactured or bought in – a manufacturing company will have high levels of raw material and work in progress inventory as well as finished goods;
- the level of sales – if sales are high, it is likely that receivables will be high too;
- inventory management, receivables collection and payables payment policies – these impact on the length of the operating cycle – explained in detail later in this Chapter;
- the efficiency with which working capital is managed.

For example, a retail company will usually have very low receivables (because most sales are for cash) but high levels of inventories. In contrast, an IT support company will tend to have high levels of receivables (long credit terms offered to attract customers) and high levels of work in progress (inventories). Even comparing businesses in the same business sector can reveal different levels of working capital caused by different working capital management policies (aggressive, moderate and conservative policies are covered below), and one firm being more efficient at collecting debts than another.

It is essential that an appropriate amount of working capital is budgeted for to meet anticipated future needs.

In conditions of uncertainty, entities must hold some minimal level of cash and inventories based on expected revenue, plus an additional safety buffer.

Aggressive, moderate and conservative approaches

With an aggressive working capital policy, a firm would hold minimal inventory. Such a policy would minimise costs, but it could lower revenue because the firm may not be able to respond rapidly to increases in demand.

Conversely, a conservative working capital policy would call for large inventory. Generally, the expected return is lower under a conservative policy than under an aggressive one, but the risks are greater under the aggressive policy.

A moderate policy falls somewhere between the two extremes in terms of risk and returns.

More detail on aggressive, moderate and conservative policies

A company could pursue a more aggressive approach towards the management of working capital or a more conservative (relaxed) approach.

Benefits of a more aggressive approach:

(1) Lower levels of current assets therefore lower financing costs.

(2) The lower financing costs should result in better profitability.

(3) Quicker cash turnover may allow more reinvestment and hence allow the business to expand more quickly.

Benefits of a more conservative approach:

(1) Lower liquidity risk i.e. less risk of the company running out of cash or going into liquidation.

(2) Greater ability to meet a sudden surge in sales demand.

(3) More relaxed credit policy for receivables may improve sales.

Note:

Generally the more conservative the approach, the lower the risk, but the higher the cost in terms of money tied up in working capital.

4 The working capital financing decision

The traditional approach to working capital funding

Traditionally current assets were seen as fluctuating, originally with a seasonal pattern. Current assets would then be financed out of short-term credit, which could be paid off when not required, whilst non-current assets would be financed by long-term funds (debt or equity).

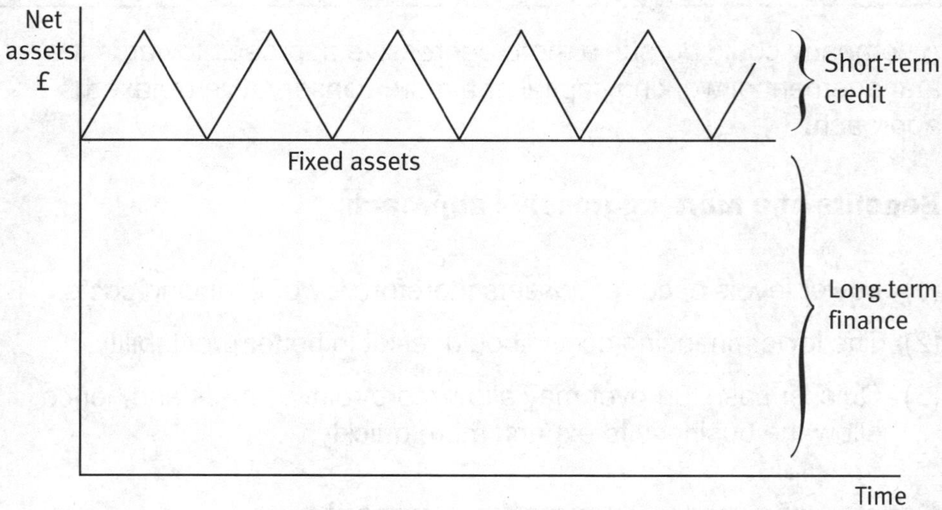

This analysis is rather simplistic. In most businesses a proportion of the current assets are fixed over time, being thus expressed as 'permanent'.

For example, certain base levels of inventory are always carried, or a certain level of trade credit is always extended. If growth were added to this situation a more realistic business picture would be as follows:

Working capital requirements with growth

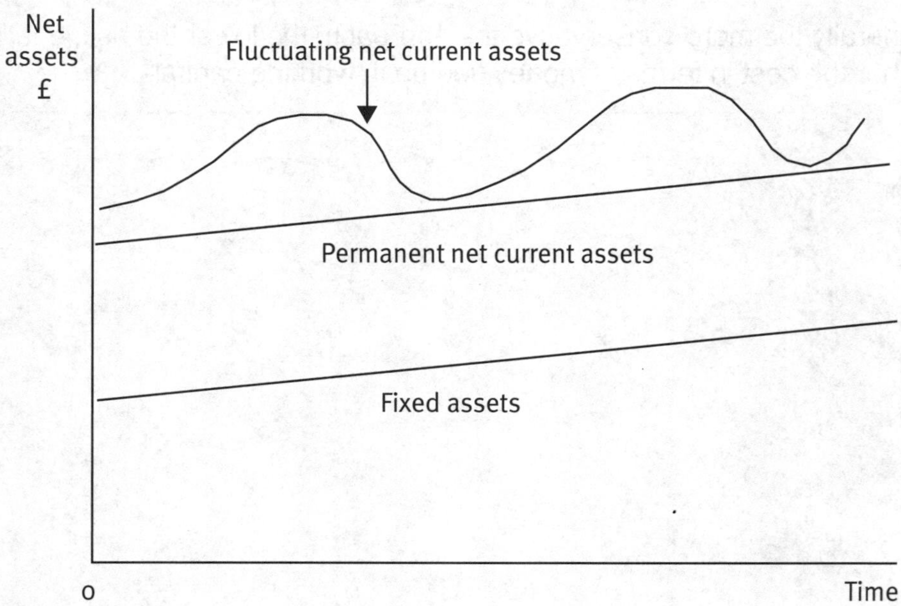

The modern approach to working capital funding

Given the permanent nature of a large proportion of current assets, it is generally felt prudent to fund a proportion of net current assets with long-term finance.

Short-term financing is generally cheaper than long-term finance, since short-term interest rates are generally lower than long-term rates. However, the price paid for reduced cost is increased risk for the borrower, because of:

- **Renewal problems** – short-term finance may need to be continually renegotiated as various facilities expire and renewal may not always be guaranteed.
- **Stability of interest rates** – if the company is constantly having to renew its funding arrangements it will be at the mercy of fluctuations in short-term interest rates.

The term structure of interest rates

One of the primary considerations in evaluating the use of borrowings is the likely movement in interest rates. This will affect the relative costs of long- and short-term borrowings, as well as increasing or decreasing the preference for fixed interest rates. In practice, long-term rates will normally be higher than short-term rates, owing to the additional risk borne by the lender. Hence an interest premium is required to attract investors to longer-term securities.

This effect may be magnified or reversed by investors' expectations of future rates, an anticipated rate rise producing higher longer-term rates. This difference between long- and short-term rates is known as term structure. The term structure of interest rates is shown by the yield curve (a graph of interest rates against time to maturity).

The yield curve

The yield curve will normally be upward-sloping in order to compensate investors for tying up their money for longer periods of time. In extreme cases, this may justify an entity, using short-dated borrowings which is replaced regularly – although the level of transaction costs makes this unlikely.

Sometimes the yield curve will be downward, or inverse, with short-term interest rates higher than long-term rates. In the UK, the Bank of England Monetary Policy Committee meets monthly to set interest rates. Their influence is directed primarily towards short-term interest rates, as a means of managing inflation in the economy. Short-term interest rates might be increased to combat inflation. If, however, interest rates are expected to fall in the future once the risk of inflation has been countered, long-term interest rates may be lower than short-term rates, and the yield curve would therefore be downward sloping.

Factors that influence term structure

In general terms, an increasing term structure results from two factors:

- increased risk of longer dated borrowings;
- anticipated general interest-rate rises.

Aggressive, moderate and conservative financing policies

The financing of working capital depends upon how current- and non-current asset funding is divided between long-term and short-term sources of funding.

The choice is a matter for managerial judgement, and depends to an extent on the cost v risk trade-off described above.

Three possible policies exist, as follows:

An **aggressive policy** for financing working capital uses short-term financing to fund all the fluctuating current assets as well as some of the permanent part of the current assets. This policy carries the greatest risk of illiquidity, as well as the greatest returns.

Aggressive financing policy

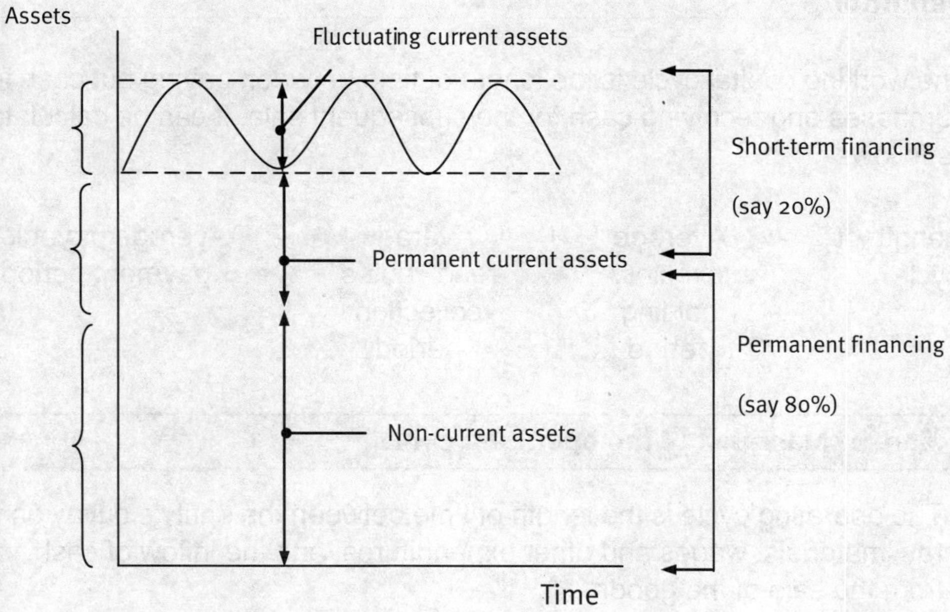

A **conservative policy** is where all of the permanent assets – both non-current assets and the permanent part of the current assets (i.e. the core level of investment in inventory and receivables, etc.) – are financed by long-term funding, as well as part of the fluctuating current assets. Short-term financing is used only for part of the fluctuating current assets.

Conservative financing policy

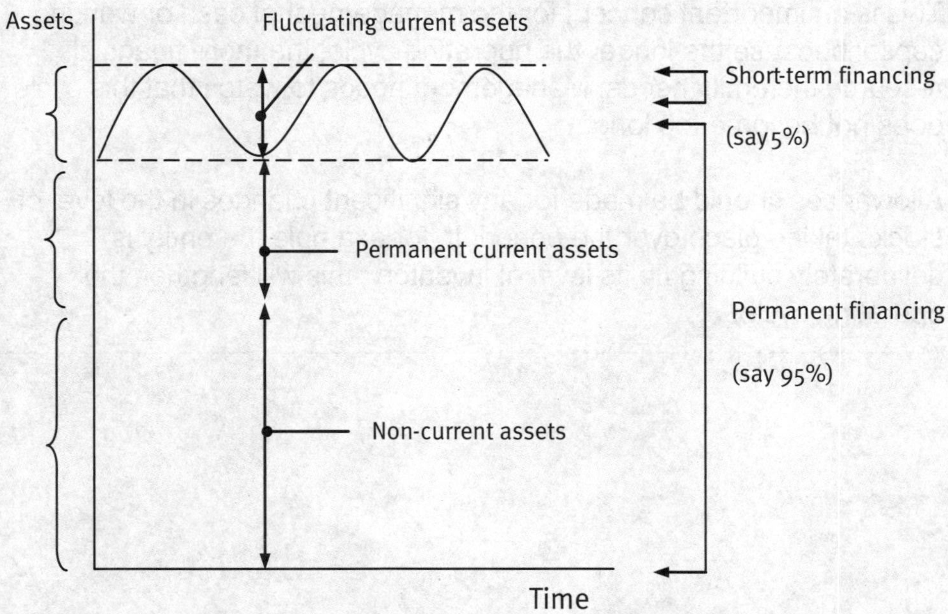

A **moderate policy** matches the short-term finance to the fluctuating current assets, and the long-term finance to the permanent part of current assets plus non-current assets.

5 The Working Capital Cycle (Operating Cycle)

Definition

The working capital cycle is the length of time between paying out cash for purchases and receiving cash for the subsequent sale. It can be calculated as follows:

Length of cycle	=	Average inventory holding period	+	Average receivables collection period	–	Average payables payment period

More explanation of the operating cycle

The operating cycle is the length of time between the entity's outlay on raw materials, wages and other expenditures, and the inflow of cash from the sale of the goods.

In a manufacturing business this is the average time that raw materials remain in stock less the period of credit taken from suppliers plus the time taken for producing the goods plus the time the goods remain in finished inventory plus the time taken by customers to pay for the goods. On some occasions this cycle is referred to as the cash cycle, or the working capital cycle.

This is an important concept for the management of cash or working capital because the longer the operating cycle, the more financial resource the entity needs. Management needs to watch that this cycle does not become too long.

Allowances should be made for any significant changes in the level of stocks taking place over the period. If, for example the entity is deliberately building up its level of inventory, this will lengthen the operating cycle.

Businesses will generally seek to shorten the operating cycle as much as possible consistent with:

(a) providing good customer service;

(b) allowing reasonable credit period for sales; and

(c) paying suppliers within an acceptable time.

As seen above, the management of working capital requires management to find an appropriate balance between profitability and liquidity.

A key consideration here is that shortening the operating cycle to improve liquidity may have an adverse effect on the entity's profitability.

Shortening the operating cycle

If the operating cycle can be shortened, this should improve the entity's liquidity.

In general terms, the volume of receivable balances could be cut by a quicker collection of debt, finished goods could be turned over more rapidly, the level of raw materials inventory could be reduced or the production period could be shortened.

More specifically, a number of steps could be taken to shorten the operating cycle, as follows:

- **Reduce raw materials stockholding** This may be done by reviewing slow-moving lines and reorder levels. Inventory control models may be considered if not already in use. More efficient links with suppliers could also help. Reducing inventory may involve loss of discounts for bulk purchases, loss of cost savings from price rises, or could lead to production delays due to stockouts.
- **Obtain more finance from suppliers by delaying payments** This could result in a deterioration in commercial relationships or even loss of reliable sources of supply. Discounts may be lost by this policy.
- **Reduce work in progress** by reducing production volume (with resultant loss of business and the need to cut back on labour resources) or improving production techniques and efficiency (with the human and practical problems of achieving such change).

- **Reduce finished goods inventory** perhaps by reorganising the production schedule and distribution methods. This may affect the efficiency with which customer demand can be satisfied and result ultimately in a reduction of revenue.
- **Reduce credit given to customers** by involving and following up outstanding amounts more quickly, or possibly offering discount incentives. The main disadvantages would be the potential loss of custom as a result of this policy.

6 Working Capital Ratios

Operating cycle calculations

Receivables collection period (in days) $\frac{\text{Average receivables}}{\text{Average daily sales}}$ or $\frac{\text{Average receivables} \times 365}{\text{Total sales}}$

Payables payment period (in days) $\frac{\text{Average payables}}{\text{Average daily purchases}}$ or $\frac{\text{Average payables} \times 365}{\text{Total purchases}}$

Inventory holding period (days)

(a) Raw materials (RM) $\frac{\text{Average inventory of RM}}{\text{Average daily purchases}}$ or $\frac{\text{Average inventory of RM} \times 365}{\text{Total purchases}}$

(b) Work in progress (WIP) $\frac{\text{Average WIP}}{\text{Average daily cost of production}}$ or $\frac{\text{Average work in progress} \times 365}{\text{Total cost of production}}$

(c) Finished goods (FG) $\frac{\text{Average inventory of FG}}{\text{Average daily cost of sales}}$ or $\frac{\text{Average inventory of FG} \times 365}{\text{Total cost of sales}}$

Other working capital ratios

Current ratio $\frac{\text{Current assets}}{\text{Current liabilities}}$

Quick ratio/Acid test $\frac{\text{Current assets} - \text{Inventory}}{\text{Current liabilities}}$

Inventory turnover $\frac{\text{Total cost of sales}}{\text{inventory + WIP}}$

Interpreting ratios

The **current ratio** provides a broad measure of liquidity.

A high current ratio would suggest that the business would have little difficulty meeting current liabilities from available assets. However, if a large proportion of current assets is represented by inventory, this may not be the case as inventory is less liquid than other current assets.

The **quick ratio**, or acid test, indicates the ability to pay suppliers in the short term. The quick ratio recognises that inventory may take some time to convert into cash and so focuses on those current assets that are relatively liquid.

There are no general norms for these ratios and 'ideal' levels vary depending on the type of business being examined.

Manufacturers will normally require much higher liquidity ratios, than retailers. When analysing these liquidity ratios, the absolute figure calculated for a particular year is less important than the trend over time.

e.g

Illustration 1 – The operating cycle

The table below gives information extracted from the annual accounts of Davis for the past 2 years.

Davis – Extracts from annual accounts

	Year 1 EUR	**Year 2 EUR**
Inventory: raw materials	108,000	145,800
Inventory: work in progress	75,600	97,200
Inventory: Finished goods	86,400	129,600
Purchases	518,400	702,000
Cost of goods sold	756,000	972,000
Revenue	864,000	1,080,000
Receivables	172,800	259,200
Accounts payable	86,400	105,300

Required:

Calculate the length of the operating cycle for each of the 2 years.

Solution:

Note that, owing to the nature of the simplified information provided, end-of-year values – rather than average values – have been used for inventories, receivables and payables.

	Year 1	Days	Year 2	Days
RM holding period	(108/518.4)×365	76	(145.8/702)×365	76
WIP (production) period	(75.6/756)×365	37	(97.2/972)×365	37
FG holding period	(86.4/756)/×365	42	(129.6/972)×365	49
Receivables collection period	(172.8/864)×365	73	(259.2/1,080)×365	88
Payables payment period	(86.4/518.4)×365	(61)	(105.3/702)×365	(55)
		167		195

Example 1

Income statement extract	GBP
Turnover	350,000
Cost of sales	(250,000)
Gross profit	100,000
Statement of financial position extract	GBP
Current assets	
Inventory	105,000
Receivables	35,000
Current liabilities	
Payables	55,000

Required:

Calculate the length of the operating cycle.

7 Overtrading

Interpreting ratios

Definition of overtrading

Overtrading is defined in CIMA's Official Terminology (2005) as follows:

The condition of an entity's which enters into commitments in excess of its available short-term resources. This can arise even if an entity is trading profitably and is typically caused by financing strains imposed by a lengthy operating cycle or production cycle. Undercapitalised new entities are prone to suffer from overtrading.

Overtrading can be a problem for new, or fast-growing firms.

As sales increase, the levels of inventories and receivables also increase, and the liquidity position of the firm deteriorates.

External finance is often needed to help the firm manage its liquidity position.

Careful working capital management, together with increased investment in non-current assets to support the higher level of sales, can help to overcome the problem of overtrading.

Symptoms of overtrading

The common symptoms of overtrading are:

- there is a fall in liquidity ratios;
- there is a rapid increase in revenue;
- there is a sharp increase in the sales to non-current assets ratio;
- there is an increase in inventory in relation to revenue;
- there is an increase in receivables;
- there is an increase in the accounts payable period;
- there is an increase in short-term borrowing and a decline in cash balances;
- there is an increase in gearing;
- the profit margin decreases.

Preventing overtrading

Overtrading can result in the failure of an entity through liquidity problems.

To prevent overtrading, an entity will have to formulate an immediate response, and then focus in the longer term on more efficient working capital management policies.

The longer term focus on efficient working capital management policies is covered above.

Potential immediate responses to the overtrading problem

- Introduce new capital. An overdraft is often used as a short term solution, since it is easy to negotiate with the bank, and very flexible. However, overdrafts are repayable on demand, so are risky. Alternatively, the entity could issue new share capital, or organise a long-term loan. The downside of long term financing options is that the entity will have to continue paying returns to investors for a long period after the immediate overtrading problem has been addressed.
- Reduce distributions. This may not be a welcome suggestion, but not paying dividends or taking less salary or fees if a partnership or sole trader may need to be considered.
- Cost cutting. Reducing costs or finding efficiencies should increase cash flow and reduce the impact of overtrading. This may include delaying capital expenditure if possible.
- Factoring or invoice discounting. Factoring involves selling invoices to a specialist finance entity who takes on the administration and cost of recovering the invoice payments. With invoice discounting, a loan is raised from a finance entity against the value of invoices, but the responsibility and cost of recovering invoice payments is not passed to the invoice discounter.
- Lease or hire purchase assets. Both approaches can help smooth cash flows to obtain non-current assets. Alternatively, a sale and leaseback agreement involves selling an asset to generate cash immediately, and then leasing it from the new owner for a period. The benefit is the immediate cash inflow, but the downside of a sale and leaseback is that the entity loses the potential appreciation in value of the asset (usually property) in the future.

Multinational working capital management

The aims of a multinational entity in relation to cash management will be similar to those for a purely domestic entity, which will be to:

- ensure fast collection of cash;
- take longer to pay out cash;
- optimise cash flow within the entity;
- generate the best return on cash surpluses.

Achieving these aims will be more difficult in a multinational entity due to the longer distances involved, the number of parties involved, and the risk of governments placing restrictions on the transfers of funds out of certain countries.

Granting credit is often an essential condition to undertake international business. In addition to the normal risks of default, firm granting credit, exchange rate fluctuations between the time of sale and the time the debt is collected provide an additional risk.

Management of inventory is also similar to but more complex than for a purely domestic enterprise. The balance between minimising inventory and being able to meet customer demands is more difficult to judge. The movement in exchange rates will also influence the timing of purchases, and the level of inventory held in a particular currency.

Political risk is a further consideration; multinationals will need to allow for the prospect of import or export quotas or tariffs being imposed. In certain countries, the risk of expropriation of inventory will lead to minimal inventory holdings being maintained. Some countries have property taxes on assets, including inventory, where the tax payable is based on holdings on a particular date in the year, which again will influence the strategy adopted for inventory management by a multinational.

8 Short term financing options

The working capital financing decision (discussed above) considers the balance between long-term and short-term finance.

Long-term financing options, such as equity, preference shares and bonds, were covered in the previous Chapter ('Long Term Finance').

Short-term financing options include:

Bank overdraft

With an overdraft, an entity arranges to borrow, through its current account, a fluctuating amount up to a pre-agreed amount. An overdraft is an extremely flexible form of finance, but technically it is repayable on demand.

Money market borrowings

The money market is the market for trading in relatively short-dated funds, usually for less than one year. These markets are dominated by the major banks and other financial institutions, but large profit-making entities will also borrow and lend on the money market.

Terms on short term money market borrowings may range from overnight to 12 months or more.

Term loan

A term loan is a bank loan which runs for a specified term, agreed with the bank when the money is borrowed. Term loans can be short-term, or indeed medium-term or long-term.

Under a term loan, a specified payment schedule has to be followed, to repay the capital and interest over the term of the loan (or sometimes at the end of the term).

Term loans are quick and easy to set up, and give certainty to the borrower that the money will be available for the whole of the term.

Supplier credit

By taking credit from suppliers, organisations reduce the amount of other short-term finance needed. Supplier credit can often be used on a very informal basis to deal with a short-term cashflow problem.

However, taking too much credit from suppliers can be expensive (if prompt payment discounts are foregone) and can adversely affect an entity's credit rating.

Bills of exchange

Bills of exchange enable suppliers to receive the benefit of payment well before the customer actually pays.

A bill of exchange is similar to a post-dated cheque in that it is a written commitment by the customer to pay a specified amount to the supplier of goods or services on a future specified date. The supplier can hold the bill until the maturity date, or it can be traded with a bank if the cash is needed earlier at a discount.

Debt factoring

In CIMA's Official Terminology, 2005, factoring is defined as follows:

'The sale of debts to a third party (the factor) at a discount, in return for prompt cash. A factoring service may be with recourse, in which case the supplier takes the risk of the debt not being paid, or without recourse when the factor takes the risk.'

More detail on factoring and invoice discounting

Debt factoring

Specialist finance entities (usually subsidiaries of banks) offering factoring arrangements will provide three main services:

- Provide finance by advancing, say, 80% of invoice value immediately, the remainder being settled when the client's customer settles the debt (but net of a charge for interest, for example 3% per annum above base rate).
- Take responsibility for the operation of the client's sales ledger, including assessment of creditworthiness and dealing with customers for an additional service charge, typically 2% of turnover.
- They may, for an additional fee, offer non-recourse finance, that is guarantee settlement even if they are not paid by the customer.

In order to do this economically, they have developed their expertise in credit control in term of market intelligence (including credit scoring), information management (sophisticated databases, processing and decision support systems) and the skills required for dealing with customers especially those who are in no hurry to pay.

Invoice discounting

Alternatively, they may offer a confidential invoice discounting facility under which they provide the finance as above, but do not get involved with the operation of the sales ledger or hence become known to the customers.

This has, to date, been more popular than the overt factoring arrangement. It is cheaper, and avoids creating a barrier between the entity and its customers. It is less attractive to the providers of finance, however, being in the nature of supplying a commodity rather than adding value through expertise.

9 Exam style questions

Test your understanding 1 – Overtrading and calculation of ratios

Ewden Co is a medium-sized company producing a range of engineering products which it sells to wholesale distributors. Recently, its sales have begun to rise rapidly following a general recovery in the economy as a whole. However, it is concerned about its liquidity position and is contemplating ways of improving its cash flow. Ewden's accounts for the past two years are summarised below.

Income statements for the year ended 31 December

	20X2	**20X3**
	USD000	USD000
Turnover	12,000	16,000
Cost of goods sold	7,000	9,150
Operating profit	5,000	6,850
Interest	200	250
Profit before tax	4,800	6,600
Taxation (after capital allowances)	1,000	1,600
Profit after tax	3,800	5,000
Dividends	1,500	2,000
Retained profit	2,300	3,000

Balance sheet as at 31 December

	20X2		20X3	
	USD000	USD000	USD000	USD000
Non-current assets		9,000		12,000
Current Assets				
Inventory	1,400		2,200	
Receivables	1,600		2,600	
Cash	1,500		100	
		4,500		4,900
Total Assets		13,500		16,900
Equity and liabilities	USD000	USD000	USD000	USD000
Current liabilities				
Overdraft	–		200	
Trade payables	1,500		2,000	
Other payables	500		200	
		2,000		2,400
10% loan stock		2,000		2,000
Ordinary shares (50 cents)		3,000		3,000
Profit and loss account		6,500		9,500
		13,500		16,900

Required:

Identify the reasons for the sharp decline in Ewden's liquidity and assess the extent to which the company can be said to be exhibiting the problem of 'overtrading'.

Illustrate your answer by reference to key performance and liquidity ratios.

Test your understanding 2 – Aggressive v conservative

UR is a privately owned machine tool manufacturing company based in the Republic of Ireland. For the past five years it has operated an aggressive policy in respect of the management of its working capital. The following information concerns the company's forecast end of year financial outcomes if it continues with this type of policy.

	€000
Receivables	5,200
Inventory	2,150
Cash at bank	350
Total current assets	7,700
Non-current assets	14,500
Trade payables	4,500
Sales	17,500
Operating costs	14,000
Operating profit	3,500
Earnings	2,625

There are 2.5 million shares in issue.

The company has been experiencing a series of problems because of the type of working capital management policy it has been following and is considering an alternative approach to working capital management.

The percentage figures shown below are changes to the above forecast. These changes are anticipated to occur if a more conservative policy is adopted.

Receivables	– 40%
Inventory	+ 20%
Cash (figures in €000)	Increase to €1,000
Non-current assets	No change
Current liabilities	– 30%
Forecast sales	– 5%
Operating profit and earnings	+ 5%

Required:

Evaluate the two working capital management policies described above and recommend a proposed course of action. Include in your evaluation a discussion of the problems that might have arisen as a result of operating aggressive working capital management policies and the key elements to consider and actions to take before making a decision to change.

You should calculate *appropriate* and *relevant* ratios or performance measures to support your arguments. [*The calculations will earn up to 8 marks.*]

(25 marks)

Test your understanding answers

Example 1

Operating cycle

		Days
Inventory holding period	$\frac{105{,}000}{250{,}000} \times 365 =$	153
Receivables period	$\frac{35{,}000}{350{,}000} \times 365 =$	37
Less: Period of credit taken (payables days)	$\frac{55{,}000}{250{,}000} \times 365 =$	(80)
Total		**110**

Test your understanding 1 – Overtrading and calculation of ratios

Liquidity measures the amount of cash the company can expect to realise in the short term. In this case, Ewden's cash balance has fallen from USD1.5 million in 20X2 to a net overdraft of USD0.1 million, a decline in liquidity of USD1.6 million. This is in stark contrast to the apparently healthy profit for the year, indicating that cash has been used to finance balance sheet assets.

Indeed, analysis of the balance sheet indicates that at least USD3 million has been ploughed into non-current assets. It is not possible to say whether this investment has been in new technology, or perhaps some kind of acquisition, but the result appears to be that turnover has increased by 33 per cent.

At the same time, the company's working capital has been funded, to the tune of USD0.8 million in inventory and USD1 million in receivables, probably at the expense of trade payables which have lengthened by USD0.5 million.

More significantly, no long-term finance has been raised which appears to be in conflict with the maxim that we should match the length of the finance with the length of the project.

This may be a case of overtrading where a company undergoes a rapid expansion without the support of long-term financing.

Growth here has been financed short term, at the expense of cash and payables. As sales increase, so too do inventory and receivables, leading to further liquidity problems.

We can now look at more specifics in the form of ratio analysis.

Current ratios

These have fallen from 2.3 to 2.0, but once we remove inventory to give us the acid test ratio the fall is from 1.6 to 1.1, which may be significant if Ewden experiences bad debts and therefore severe short-term liquidity constraints.

Operating cycle

Inventory days have increased from 73 in 20X2 to 88 days in 20X3, almost three months; this appears high but should be measured against the industry average.

Receivables days have lengthened from 49 days to 59 days, almost two months, which will significantly pressure liquidity. Credit terms may have to be reviewed and enforced.

Payables days have lengthened marginally from 78 to 80 days. Again this must be compared to the terms offered and industry averages, but any increase may result in a loss of goodwill from suppliers.

The net effect is that the operating cycle has lengthened from 44 days to 67 days.

Return on capital employed

The ROCE (operating profit as a percentage of shareholders' funds and long-term loans) has in fact risen from 43 per cent to 47 per cent. This could be explained either by the net profit margin or by the asset turnover.

The net profit margin has remained stable at 42 per cent versus 43 per cent, which indicates first that the turnover increase is not due to price reductions, and second that ROCE has improved due to asset turnover by 1.04 versus 1.10. This has not lengthened too much in that the increase in turnover appears to have been asset backed.

In summary although liquidity is certainly a problem, the expansion does appear to be backed by fixed assets and therefore Ewden may not necessarily overtrade.

It would perhaps be advantageous to obtain long-term financing if Ewden is to maintain its growth.

Note: The following ratios have been used.

$$\text{Current ratio} = \frac{\text{Current assets}}{\text{Current liabilities}}$$

$$\text{Acid ratio} = \frac{\text{Current assets} - \text{Inventory}}{\text{Current Liabilities}}$$

$$\text{Inventory days} = \frac{\text{Inventory}}{\text{Cost of sales}} \times 365$$

$$\text{Receivables days} = \frac{\text{Receivables}}{\text{Sales}} \times 365$$

$$\text{Payables days} = \frac{\text{Payables}}{\text{Cost of Sales}} \times 365$$

$$\text{ROCE} = \frac{\text{Operating profit}}{\text{Shareholders' funds + Long - term loans}}$$

$$\text{Net profit margin} = \frac{\text{Operating profit}}{\text{Sales}}$$

$$\text{Asset turnover} = \frac{\text{Sales}}{\text{Shareholders' funds + Long - term loans}}$$

If in doubt about using a ratio, always define the way you have calculated it.

Test your understanding 2 – Aggressive v conservative

UR COMPANY

First we calculate relevant accounting ratios:

	With aggressive policy	*With more conservative policy*
Current ratio	$\frac{7{,}770}{4{,}500} = 1.7$	$\frac{6{,}700}{3{,}150} = 2.1$
Acid test ratio	$\frac{5{,}550}{4{,}500} = 1.2$	$\frac{4{,}120}{3{,}150} = 1.3$
Receivable days	$\frac{5{,}200}{17{,}500} \times 365 = 108$ days	$\frac{3{,}120}{16{,}625} \times 365 = 68$ days
Inventory days	$\frac{2{,}150}{14{,}000} \times 365 = 56$ days	$\frac{2{,}580}{12{,}950} \times 365 = 73$ days
Non-current asset turnover	$\frac{17{,}500}{14{,}500} = 1.2$ times	$\frac{16{,}625}{14{,}500} = 1.1$ times
Return on capital employed	$\frac{3{,}500}{17{,}700} \times 100\% = 19.8\%$	$\frac{3{,}675}{18{,}050} \times 100\% = 20.4\%$
Earnings per share	$\frac{2{,}625}{2.5m} = 105$ cents	$\frac{2{,}756.25}{2.5m}$ 110 cents

Evaluation of the two policies considered

The aggressive policy to working capital management combines high receivables, low inventories, a low cash balance and high trade payables. The philosophy is to chase sales by offering lax trade credit to customers, while attempting to maintain adequate liquidity by taking extensive credit from suppliers. This is a risky policy since it involves the risk of:

- long-standing receivables balances going bad
- discouraging potential customers since the low inventory balances held increase the risk of goods being out of stock so that customers will take their business elsewhere

- the low cash balance meaning that unexpected expenditures (e.g. having to pay for a new roof for the factory if the old one starts leaking) cannot be paid for out of cash but that specific funds have to be organised (e.g. a bank overdraft)
- the high trade payables balances will upset suppliers who will then give a better service to other customers who pay more promptly. In extreme cases, suppliers might refuse to supply any more goods until the balance outstanding is paid.

The more conservative policy involves lower receivables, higher inventories, higher cash-in-hand and lower trade payables. The effect of not chasing marginal sales is that although the sales total falls, the forecast operating profit and earnings figure actually increase.

Consider the levels of the ratios calculated:

- The current ratio and acid test ratio both increase somewhat when the more conservative policy is adopted, but the levels of the ratios were not critical in the first place. In any case, liquidity is better judged by looking at cash budgets over the next year rather than by calculating accounting ratios. If anything, a current ratio of 2.1 is possibly too high and might suggest inefficient utilisation of current assets.
- The receivables days was worryingly large at 108 days under the aggressive policy. That is allowing customers on average more than three months before they pay what they owe. Since this is an average, it is likely that many customers will be taking considerably longer than three months which is out of control. There is a considerable risk of debts going bad under the aggressive policy and there is no point in struggling to make a sale if you will never get paid. The more conservative policy brings down the average receivables collection period to 68 days, or somewhat over two months, which is more acceptable. Often businesses are compelled to offer the credit terms that have become established in the particular business sector, so that if, for example, other competitor companies are offering 90 days' credit, then UR will struggle to enforce a new policy of 68 days' credit.
- It is impossible to calculate an accurate figure for inventory days since we are not given a purchases or a cost of sales figure. Instead we have used the total operating costs figure which will include many other costs as well as the cost of inventory. However, the trend between the policies can faithfully be seen: the increased inventory held under the conservative policy increases the inventory days and will therefore reduce the risk of stock-outs leading to customers going elsewhere.

- The fixed asset turnover ratio is hardly changed at all, which is not surprising since we are considering the management of the components of working capital. The non-current assets total is unaffected by any change in policy towards working capital.
- The return on capital employed (ROCE) is increased slightly, due to the greater profitability of the more conservative policy. The reduction in bad debts and the greater availability of inventory to good customers leads to greater operating profits.
- The earnings per share also increases slightly for the same reasons.

Recommended course of action

I recommend that the more conservative policy is adopted. The objective of all financial strategy techniques is generally assumed to be the maximisation of shareholder wealth. The conservative policy leads to reduced risk and greater earnings, so the share price should increase, other things being equal.

Elements to consider and actions to take before deciding

As long as a company's P/E ratio remains constant, then an increase in earnings should feed straight through to a corresponding increase in the share price which will increase shareholder wealth. However, the P/E ratio will only remain the same if the market's perceptions of the company stay the same. We should consider the market's reaction to the proposed change to the more conservative policy of working capital management. If the market thinks that management have 'gone soft' or 'lost their nerve' then the P/E ratio might be marked down. However, this is unlikely since the company should be able to demonstrate that the change in policy has actually increased earnings which must be a good thing.

Therefore it is important to inform key shareholders and the market as a whole before the change is undertaken, to brief them of the change and the likely benefits to be enjoyed, so that they can reflect these matters in the share price.

There is also the less enjoyable matter of informing debtors that a stricter line will be taken in future towards debt collection. It is always easy to loosen credit control, but tightening can be difficult. However, in the circumstances in the question it is clear that several debtors were taking far more credit than even they would admit is reasonable, so the 40% reduction in receivables balances may be achievable.

chapter

6

Cost of Capital

Chapter learning objectives

Lead	Component
B1: Evaluate the financing requirements of an organisation and strategies for meeting those requirements.	(c) evaluate the weighted average cost of capital of an organisation.

Indicative syllabus content

- The capital asset pricing model (CAPM): calculation of the cost of equity using the dividend growth model (knowledge of methods of calculating and estimating dividend growth will be expected), the ability to gear and un-gear betas and comparison to the arbitrage pricing model.
- The ideas of diversifiable risk (unsystematic risk) and systematic risk. (Note: use of the two-asset portfolio formula will not be tested).
- The cost of redeemable and irredeemable debt, including the tax shield on debt.
- The weighted average cost of capital (WACC): calculation, interpretation and uses.

1 Overview of Chapter

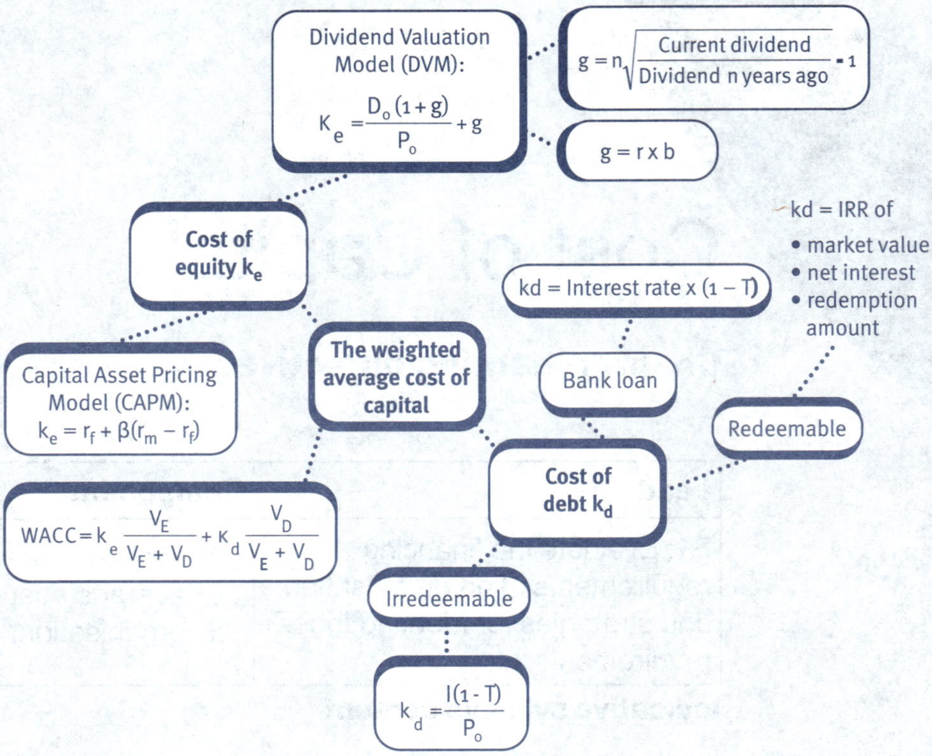

2 Introduction to the Weighted Average Cost of Capital (WACC)

In order to calculate the NPV of a project (covered in more detail in the later Chapter 'Investment Appraisal - basic techniques'), a company will need to determine an appropriate discount rate. In many cases, the company's WACC, which reflects the returns required by investors, will be used as a discount rate.

The WACC is derived by first estimating the cost of each source of finance separately (e.g. ordinary shares, debt, preference shares) and then taking a weighted average of these individual costs, using the following formula:

$$k_o = k_{eg}\left[\frac{V_E}{V_E + V_D}\right] + k_d\left[\frac{V_D}{V_E + V_D}\right]$$

3 The Cost of Equity – ke

The cost of equity is the rate of return that ordinary shareholders expect to receive on their investment. The two main methods of computing ke are:

- the dividend valuation model (DVM)
- the capital asset pricing model (CAPM)

4 The Cost of Equity – Dividend Valuation Model

The Dividend Valuation Model (DVM) states that the current share price is determined by the future dividends, discounted at the investors' required rate of return.

$$P_0 = \frac{d}{k_e}$$

where k_e = cost of equity

d = is the constant dividend

P_0 = the ex div market price of the share

This is a variant of the formula for a perpetuity.

We can re-arrange the formula to get the one below:

The dividend valuation model with constant dividends

$$k_e = \frac{d}{P_0}$$

More explanation of the DVM

The DVM is a method of calculating cost of equity.

This model makes the assumption that the market price of a share is related to the future dividend income stream from that share, in such a way that the market price is assumed to be the present value of that future dividend income stream.

This is known as the fundamental theory of share valuation.

Cum div and ex div share prices

The ex dividend ("ex div") value of a share is the value just after a dividend has been paid. Occasionally in questions, you may be given a share price just before the payment of a dividend (a "cum div" price). In this case, the value of the upcoming dividend should be deducted from the cum div price to give the ex div price.

For example, if a dividend of 20 cents is due to be paid on a share which has a cum div value of $3.45, the ex div share price to be entered into the DVM formula is $3.45 - $0.20 = $3.25.

Example 1

The ordinary shares of Jones plc are quoted at $4 per share. A dividend of 30 cents is about to be paid. There is expected to be no growth in dividends.

Required:

Calculate the cost of equity.

Introducing growth

The dividend valuation model with constant growth

$$k_e = \frac{d_1}{P_0} + g \quad \text{or} \quad k_e = \frac{d_0(1 + g)}{P_0} + g$$

where g = a constant rate of growth in dividends

d_1 = dividend to be paid in one year's time

d_0 = current dividend

Estimating growth

There are two main methods of determining growth (although the examiner will usually give the growth rate in the question if you need it):

(1) **The averaging method**

$$g = \sqrt[n]{\frac{d_o}{d_n}} - 1$$

Where d_o = current dividend

d_n = dividend n years ago

Example 2

A company paid a dividend of 8 cents per share eight years ago, and the current dividend is 13 cents. The current share price is $2.76 ex div.

Required:

Calculate the cost of equity.

(2) **Gordon's growth model**

$g = rb$

where r = return on reinvested funds

b = proportion of funds retained

Example 3

The ordinary shares of a company are quoted at $7.00 cum div. A dividend of 50 cents is just about to be paid. The company has an annual accounting rate of return of 12% and each year pays out 70% of its profits after tax as dividends.

Required:

Calculate the cost of equity.

Assumptions of Gordon's growth model

Gordon's growth model was developed by economist Myron Gordon. It attempts to derive a future growth rate, rather than the previous approach of extrapolating the historical growth rate.

Gordon argued that an increase in the level of investment by a company will give rise to an increase in future dividends. The two key elements in determining future dividend growth will be the rate of reinvestment by the company and the return generated by the investments.

There are a number of assumptions required to apply this model:

- the entity must be all equity financed;
- retained profits are the only source of additional investment;
- a constant proportion of each year's earnings is retained for reinvestment;
- projects financed from retained earnings earn a constant rate of return.

The cost of preference shares

Preference shares usually pay a constant level of dividend, which is quoted as a percentage of nominal value. Hence, the cost of preference shares (k_p) can be calculated using a formula very similar to the one covered earlier for k_e in a no growth situation.The formula is:

$$k_p = \frac{d}{P_0}$$

d = is the constant dividend

P_0 = the ex div market price of the share

k_p = the cost of preference shares

5 The Cost of Equity – Capital Asset Pricing Model

The Capital Asset Pricing Model (CAPM) is an alternative to the Dividend Valuation Model, which can be used to calculate the cost of equity. The CAPM derives cost of equity based on the risk perception of the investor.

Systematic and unsystematic risk

There are two elements that make up the risk associated with a company:

- Unsystematic (or specific) risk is the risk of the company's cash flows being affected by specific factors like strikes, R&D successes, systems failures, etc.
- Systematic (or market) risk is the risk of the company's cash flows being affected to some extent by general macro-economic factors such as tax rates, unemployment or interest rates.

TOTAL RISK

Unsystematic risk	**Systematic risk**
Company specific factors	General economic factors
Can be eliminated by diversification	Cannot be eliminated

The impact of diversification

By holding a portfolio of investments, the unsystematic risk is diversified away but the systematic risk is not, so will be present in all portfolios.

For example, the return from a single investment in an ice-cream entity will be subject to changes in the weather – sunny weather producing good returns, cold weather poor returns. By itself the investment could be considered a high risk. If a second investment were made in an umbrella entity, which is also subject to weather changes, but in the opposite way, then the return from the portfolio of the two investments will have a much-reduced risk level. This process is known as diversification, and when continued can reduce portfolio risk to a minimum.

If an investor enlarges his portfolio to include approximately 25 shares the unsystematic risk is reduced to close to zero, the implication being that we may eliminate the unsystematic portion of overall risk by spreading investment over a sufficiently diversified portfolio.

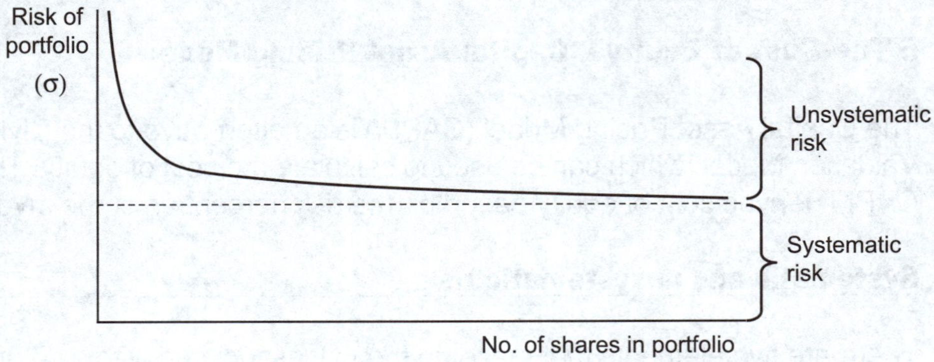

The capital asset pricing model (CAPM) enables us to calculate the required return for a well-diversified investor who is not subject to unsystematic risk.

If we can measure the systematic risk of a company or investment, the CAPM will enable us to calculate the level of required return.

ß (beta) factor

The method adopted by CAPM to measure systematic risk is an index, ß (beta). The ß factor is the measure of a share's volatility in terms of market risk.

The ß factor of the market as a whole is 1. Market risk makes market returns volatile and the ß factor is simply a yardstick against which the risk of other investments can be measured.

The ß factor is critical to applying the CAPM; it illustrates the relationship of an individual security to the market as a whole, or conversely the market return given the return on an individual security.

Beta values fall into four categories, with the following meanings:

(i)	ß > 1	The shares have **more** systematic risk than the stock market average.
(ii)	ß = 1	The shares have the **same** systematic risk as the stock market average.
(iii)	ß < 1	The shares have **less** systematic risk than the stock market average.
(iv)	ß = 0	The shares have **no** risk at all.

A share's beta value can be interpreted quite precisely:

ß = 1.25 : The shares have 25% **more** systematic risk than the average level on the stock market.

ß = 0.80 : The shares have 20% **less** systematic risks than the average. (i.e. they only have 80% of the average level).

The security market line

The security market line (SML) gives the relationship between systematic risk and return. We know two relationships:

(1) **The risk-free security**
This carries no risk and therefore no systematic risk and therefore has a **beta** of zero.

(2) **The market portfolio**
This represents the ultimate in diversification and therefore contains only systematic risk. It has a **beta** of 1.

The results may be plotted:

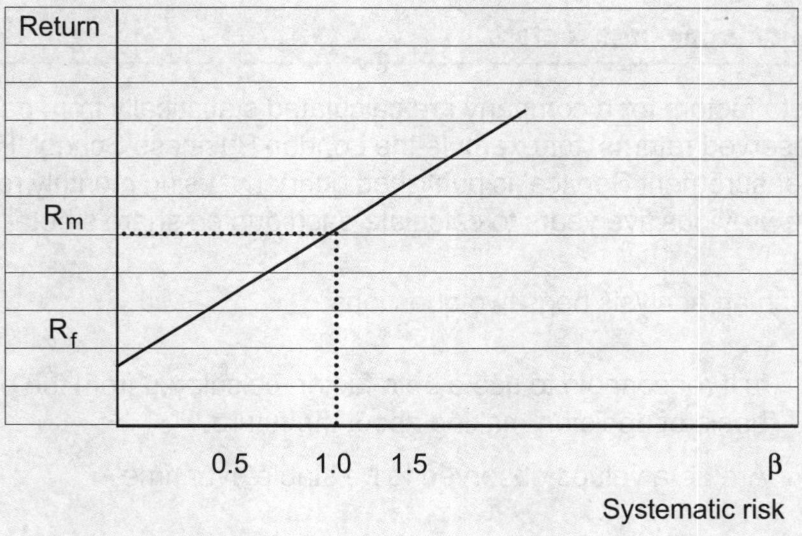

R_f is the point on the graph where the line intersects the axis, and then the higher the systematic risk, the higher the required rate of return.

The SML and the relationship between required return and risk can be shown using the following formula:

Formula – given in the exam

$$k_e = R_f + [R_m - R_f]\,ß$$

where

k_e = required return from individual security

ß = Beta factor of individual security

R_f = risk-free rate of interest

R_m = return on market portfolio

Note: In exams, the question will sometimes refer to the market premium – this is the difference between R_m and R_f. It is the long term market premium that should be used in CAPM if this is different from current market rates.

Calculating beta factors

Beta factors for a company are calculated statistically from past observed returns; for example the London Business School 'Risk Measurement Service' is published quarterly, using monthly returns from the previous five years to calculate each quoted share's beta.

Such an analysis begs two questions:

- Is it reasonable to use a beta factor, calculated from the past, as the basis of decision-making about the future?
- Are beta values observed to be stable over time?

If beta values were not observed to be almost stationary over time, the whole theory would collapse. Luckily the evidence is that both US and UK shares do exhibit stable betas, the stability being stronger for highly diversified shares such as investment trusts than for more focused companies. Naturally beta will only be stable if the company's systematic risk remains the same, i.e. the company carries on the same areas of business in the long term.

Since betas are calculated statistically, the calculated beta value will be more reliable the more separate data went into its calculation. Therefore the longer the period underlying the calculations the better. However if the beta will be used to estimate a required rate of return for a future project, it is important that the company's risk class in future will be more or less unchanged by accepting the project. Many businesses deal with this apparent paradox by using a sector average beta rather than using their own calculated beta.

Example 4

Data for three shares

	A	*B*	*C*
Beta	1.5	0.7	1
Risk-free rate	5%		

Expected return on the Market Portfolio 12%.

Required:

Calculate the required return for each investment.

Illustration 1

In Example 4 above, we calculated the required return for each investment separately.

Now assume that an investor intends to set up a portfolio, where he invests 50% of his funds into A's shares, and 25% each into B's and C's.

The individual company betas are exactly the same as in Example 4 above, and the risk free rate is still 5% and the expected return on the market portfolio is 12%.

Required:

Calculate the required return from the new portfolio.

Solution:

The beta factor for the portfolio will be the weighted average of the individual companies' beta factors, as follows:

ß (portfolio) = (50% × 1.5) + (25% × 0.7) + (25% × 1) = 1.175

So the required return from the portfolio is: 5% + (12%–5%)×1.175 = 13.2%

The CAPM gives a required return for a given level of risk (measured by the beta factor).

Therefore, if we can estimate the level of risk associated with a new investment project (the beta of the project), we can use CAPM to give a required return to shareholders.

This required return to shareholders is essentially the cost of equity which should be used to derive an appropriate WACC to use as a discount rate.

Alpha values

If the CAPM stated that we should expect, on average, an annual return of 16.5%, this does not mean that the shares will produce a return (dividend yield plus capital gain) of 16.5% each year. Remember, shares are a risky investment which produces an uncertain annual return.

Suppose in one particular year, Company A shares produce an actual return of 18%. The shares are said to have produced a positive 'abnormal' return of 1.5% – that is, 1.5% higher than the expected return.

The alpha value of a share is simply its average abnormal return. Suppose Company A shares have an alpha value of +2%, this implies that in the recent past the shares have, on average, produced a return of 16.5% + 2% = 18.5%.

Alpha values can be either positive or negative, and in a perfect world they should be zero. In other words the average return that the shares actually do produce **should** be the same as the return indicated by CAPM. However, the world isn't perfect and so that will not always happen. Hence we get positive and negative alpha values.

Criticisms of the CAPM

(1) CAPM is a single period model. This means that the values calculated are only valid for a finite period of time and will need to be recalculated or updated at regular intervals.

(2) CAPM assumes no transaction costs associated with trading securities.

(3) Any beta value calculated will be based on historic data which may not be appropriate currently. This is particularly so if the company has changed the capital structure of the business or the type of business it is trading in.

(4) The risk free rate may change considerably over short periods of time.

(5) CAPM assumes an efficient investment market where it is possible to diversify away risk. This is not necessarily the case, meaning that some unsystematic risk may remain.

(6) Additionally, the idea that all unsystematic risk is diversified away will not hold true if stocks change in terms of volatility. As stocks change over time it is very likely that the portfolio becomes less than optimal.

(7) CAPM assumes all stocks relate to going concerns, this may not be the case.

Arbitrage Pricing Theory (APT)

Arbitrage pricing theory (APT) is an alternative pricing model to CAPM, developed by Ross in 1976. It attempts to explain the risk–return relationship using several independent factors rather than a single index.

CAPM is a single index model in that the expected return from a security is a function of only one factor, its beta value:

$$R_s = R_f + \beta (R_m - R_f)$$

However APT is a multi-index model in that the expected return from a security is a linear function of several independent factors:

$$R_s = a + \beta_1 f_1 + \beta_2 f_2 + \ldots$$

where R_s = the expected return from a security

$a, \beta_1, \beta_2, \ldots$ are constants

$f_1, f_2, \ldots$ are the various factors that influence security returns

For example, f_1 could be the return on the market (as in CAPM), f_2 could be an industry index specific to the sector in which the company operates, f_3 could be an interest rate index, etc.

Ross showed that, if shares are assumed to form an efficient market, an equilibrium is reached when:

$$R_s = R_f + \beta_1 (R_1 - R_f) + \beta_2 (R_2 - R_f) + \ldots$$

where R_s = the expected return from a security

R_f = the risk-free rate

β_i = constants expressing the security's sensitivity to each factor

R_i = the expected return on a portfolio with unit sensitivity to factor i and zero sensitivity to any other factor

Research undertaken to date suggests that there are a small number of factors, or economic forces, that systematically affect the returns on assets. These are:

- inflation or deflation;
- long-run growth in profitability in the economy;
- industrial production;
- term structure of interest rates;
- default premium on bonds;
- price of oil.

Each factor must be independent of the other factors.

APT assumes that the process of arbitrage would ensure that two assets offering identical returns and risks will sell for the same price.

Intuitively, APT appears to improve on CAPM, as return is determined by a number of independent factors. The main practical difficulties are in determining what those factors are, as the model does not specify them, and forecasting their value. There have been few tests of APT, probably because of the difficulties in determining which variables to include in the model and how to weigh them.

APT has gained in popularity as empirical tests of CAPM in practice have raised significant doubts as to CAPM's validity. However it is fair to say that empirical testing of APT has to date been only limited, so its effectiveness remains to be proved. CAPM is certainly simpler than APT, being a single index rather than a multi-index model, so CAPM will remain popular for some time.

6 The Cost of Debt – kd

The cost of debt is the rate of return that debt providers require on the funds that they provide.

The value of debt is assumed to be the present value of its future cash flows.

Features

(1) Debt is tax deductible and hence interest payments are made net of tax.

(2) Debt is always quoted in $100 nominal units or blocks.

(3) Interest paid on the debt is stated as a percentage of nominal value. This is known as the coupon rate. It is not the same as the cost of debt. The amount of interest payable on the debt is fixed. The interest is calculated as the coupon rate multiplied by the nominal value of the debt.

(4) Debt can be:

(i) irredeemable;

(ii) redeemable at par (nominal value) or at a premium or discount.

(5) Interest can be either fixed or floating (variable).

k_d for irredeemable debt

Irredeemable debt is debt issued by the company where there is no intention to repay the principal. The company will simply pay interest on the debt for ever.

$$k_d = \frac{i(1-T)}{P_0}$$

where i = interest paid

T = marginal rate of tax

P_0 = ex interest market price of the debt

Note that if the current market price is the par value of $100, then the cost of debt is simply the after-tax interest rate i.e. i(1–T).

Example 5

The 10% irredeemable debentures of a company are quoted at $130 ex int. Corporation tax is payable at 30%.

Required:

Calculate the net of tax cost of debt.

k_d for redeemable debt

The k_d for redeemable debt is given by the IRR of the relevant cash flows.

Note: the IRR (Internal Rate of Return) was covered earlier in the CIMA syllabus. A reminder of the method is covered in the later Chapter 'Investment Appraisal – basic techniques'.

The relevant cash flows would be (assuming that there is no one year delay in the tax saving):

Year	*Cash flow*	
0	Market value of the loan	(P_0)
1 to n	Annual net interest payments	$i(1 - T)$
n	Redemption value of loan	RV

There are four steps to ensuring an accurate computation:

(1) Identify the cash flows.

(2) Estimate the IRR.

(3) Calculate two NPVs (preferably one -ve and one +ve).

(4) Calculate the IRR.

Example 6

A company has 10% debentures quoted at $95.00 ex int redeemable at par in five years' time. Corporation tax is paid at 31%.

Required:

Calculate the net of tax cost of debt.

Note: The cost of bank loans and debt trading at par can be calculated more simply by taking the net of tax interest payment.

$$kd = I\,(1 - t)$$

The cost of convertible debt

Convertible debentures are like redeemables, but they offer the investor a choice of cash or shares on the redemption date.

In practice, particularly if the value of the cash and shares option is very similar, some investors will choose cash for liquidity reasons, whereas other investors may choose shares, hoping for large dividend returns in the future.

In order to calculate the cost of convertible debt, we make a simplifying assumption that all investors will make the same decision.

Example

Consider a $100 debenture which is redeemable at par in 5 years, or convertible into 10 shares at that time. The current share price is $8.60 and historically, dividends (and hence share prices) have grown at 5% per annum.

To decide which option is likely to be chosen by investors, we compare:

- the value of the cash option, $100; with
- the value of the conversion option, i.e. $10 \times (\$8.60 \times 1.05^5) = \$109.76$

Hence, it is assumed that all investors will choose the conversion option, and the cost of the convertible debt is calculated in a similar way to the cost of redeemable debt, i.e. it is the IRR of :

Year	*Cash flow*	*$*
0	Market value of the loan	(P_0)
1 to n	Annual net interest payments	$i(1 - T)$
n	**The higher of the cash and the conversion option**	C

7 Weighted Average Cost of Capital (WACC)

The weighted average cost of capital (WACC) is the average of cost of the company's finance (equity, debentures, bank loans, and preference shares) weighted according to the proportion each element bears to the total pool of funds.

In the analysis so far carried out, each source of finance has been examined in isolation. However, the practical business situation is that there is a continuous raising of funds from various sources. These funds are used, partly in existing operations and partly to finance new projects. There is not normally any separation between funds from different sources and their application to specific projects.

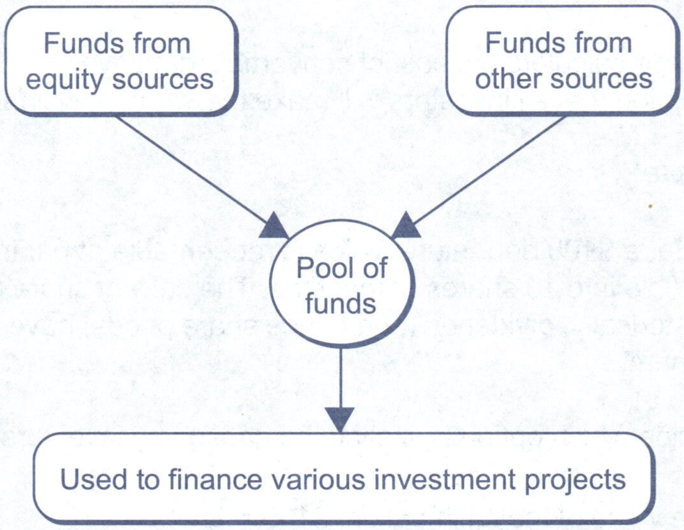

In order to provide a measure for evaluating these projects, the cost of the pool of funds is required. This is variously referred to as the combined or weighted average cost of capital (WACC).

The general approach is to calculate the cost of each source of finance, then to weight these according to their importance in the financing mix.

Procedure for calculating the WACC

The calculation involves a series of steps.

Step 1 Calculate weights for each source of capital.

Step 2 Estimate the cost of each source of capital.

Step 3 Multiply the proportion of the total of each source of capital by the cost of that source of capital.

Step 4 Sum the results of step 3 to give the weighted average cost of capital.

Formula – given in the exam

$$k_o = k_{eg}\left[\frac{V_E}{V_E + V_D}\right] + k_d\left[\frac{V_D}{V_E + V_D}\right]$$

Alternative WACC formula

Using market values for a firm with equity, debt and preference shares in its capital structure, the WACC would be:

$$k_0 = \frac{k_e V_e + k_P V_P + k_d V_d}{V_e + V_P + V_d}$$

where Ve, Vp and Vd are the market values of equity, preference shares and debt respectively.

Example 7

Rebmatt Co has a capital structure as follows.

	Cost of capital %	*Book value $m*	*Market value $m*
Bank loans	6	5	5
Debenture loans	10	8	5
Ordinary shares	15	18	30

Required:

Calculate Rebmatt's WACC, using market values as weights.

Example 8

The following is an extract from the statement of financial position (balance sheet) of Gate Co at 30 September 20X4:

	$
Ordinary shares of 25 cents each	250,000
Reserves	350,000
7% preference shares of $1 each	250,000
15% unsecured bonds	150,000
Total long-term funds	1,000,000

The ordinary shares are currently quoted at $1.25 each, the bonds trading at $85 per $100 nominal and the preference shares at 65 cents each. The ordinary dividend of 10 cents has just been paid, and the expected growth rate in the dividend is 10%. Corporation tax is at the rate of 33%.

Required:

Calculate the weighted average cost of capital for Gate Co.

Problems with the computation of WACC

Which sources of finance to include

The above examples have concentrated on the cost of long-term finance. Firms also raise finance from short-term sources, e.g. overdrafts, short-term loans, trade credit etc. It is possible to calculate a cost for short-term finance and we need to decide whether it should be included in our calculations. The usual argument is that the weighted average cost of capital is a tool for appraising long-term investments and as these should only be financed by long-term funds then the costs of short-term funds should be excluded. However, if it is clear that short-term finance is being used to fund long-term projects, then it should be included.

Loans without market values

Bank loans do not have market values in the same way as debentures. All we can do in this case is to take the book value of loans as an approximation of market value.

Cost of capital for small companies

There are important factors which are relevant to the cost of capital of small companies:

- If the company is unquoted, then obtaining the cost of finance is much more difficult.
- The lack of liquidity offered by the company's securities, plus the smaller size of the company, tend to make finance more expensive.

8 When can WACC be used as a discount rate?

The WACC is often used as a discount rate when using net present value or internal rate of return calculations. However, this is only appropriate if the following conditions are met:

(1) The capital structure is constant. If the capital structure changes, the weightings in the WACC will also change.

(2) The new investment does not carry a different business risk profile to the existing company's operations. If business risk is different, the CAPM would suggest that the required return of investors should be different.

(3) The new investment is marginal to the company. If we are only looking at a small investment then we would not expect any of k_e, k_d or the WACC to change materially. If the investment is substantial it will usually cause these values to change.

More details on the use of WACC as a discount rate

When discounting cash flows to present value, it is important to match the discount rate used to the cash flows being discounted.

Cost of equity

For example, the cost of equity capital should be used for valuing income flows (such as dividends, or earnings) which are attributable to the equity investor.

The NPV result is the value of equity.

WACC

The weighted average cost of capital is used when discounting after tax cash flows but before deducting finance charges such as interest. The WACC is the cost of capital required on the whole capital employed (debt plus equity capital invested in the company). This is therefore the appropriate discount rate to use to discount the cash flows attributable to all contributors to capital employed in the entity. For example, when valuing a project or a division of a company which does not have its own debt capital or finance charges.

The NPV result obtained is the value of the total capital employed in the entity – giving the total value of debt plus equity for a company.

NEW

Alternatives to the use of existing WACC as a discount rate in project appraisal

We have now established that the existing WACC should only be used as a discount rate for a new investment project if the business risk and the capital structure are likely to stay constant. Alternatively,

If the business risk of the new project differs from the entity's existing business risk

A risk-adjusted WACC can be calculated, by recalculating the cost of equity to reflect the business risk of the new project. This often involves the technique of 'degearing' and 'regearing' beta factors, covered in the later 'Capital Structure' Chapter.

If the capital structure is expected to change when the new project is undertaken

The simplest way of incorporating a change in capital structure is to recalculate the WACC using the new capital structure weightings. This is appropriate if the new investment project can be effectively treated as a new business, with its own long-term gearing level.

Alternatively, if the capital structure is expected to change significantly, the Adjusted Present Value method of project appraisal could be used. This approach separates the investment element of the decision from the financing element and appraises them independently. APV is only recommended when there are complex funding arrangements (e.g. subsidised loan, temporary or permanent change to debt capacity or choice of capital structure). APV is covered in detail in the later 'Investment Appraisal – further techniques' Chapter.

Finally, the Marginal Cost of Capital (MCC) could be used. Again, this is appropriate if the capital structure is forecast to change significantly. It is found by calculating the total additional cost of financing a new project, and it attempts to reflect the true incremental cost associated with the new financing.

More detail on the marginal cost of capital

As discussed above, the use of WACC assumes that the capital structure of an entity will remain unchanged and that any new investment will have a similar risk profile to existing investments.

If a large project is under consideration, and it would fundamentally affect the capital structure of an entity, these assumptions would mean that WACC is no longer the appropriate technique for investment appraisal. Use of WACC could lead to the acceptance of projects that reduce the entity's value.

The relevant cost of capital is now arguably the incremental cost, that is the marginal cost reflecting the changes in the total cost of the capital structure before and after the introduction of the new capital.

In theory, the marginal cost of capital is just the difference between the total cost with the existing capital structure and the total cost with the new capital structure once the investment has been undertaken.

Consider an entity with the following cost of capital (all currency in GBP, or £):

	Post tax cost	Value	Cost x value
	%	£m	
Equity	20	5	1.00
Preference	10	1	0.10
Debt	8	4	0.32
		10	1.42

So, WACC = (1.42/10) × 100% = 14.2%

It has a large investment project under consideration, to be financed by a major issue of funds which will alter the capital structure. The estimated project cost is £1,000,000, to be financed in equal proportions by a new share issue and a new issue of bonds.

The new capital structure will imply a new level of risk for holders of bonds and equity shares, causing the cost of capital for the company to change.

The new cost of capital may be as follows (if we assume that the cost of equity will rise to 22% and the new bonds will have a post-tax cost of 10%):

	Post tax cost	Value	Cost x value
	%	$m	
Equity	22	5.5	1.21
Preference	10	1.0	0.10
Bonds	8	4.0	0.32
New Bonds	10	0.5	0.05
		11	1.68

So, WACC = (1.68/11) × 100% = 15.3%

Marginal Cost of Capital = (1.68-0.42) / (11-10) × 100% = 26%

The total cost of capital has increased by £260,000 as a result of raising £1,000,000 of funds. The incremental cost of capital is therefore 26%.

It might be thought that by raising £500,000 of equity with a cost of 22%, and £500,000 of bonds with a cost of 10%, the marginal cost of capital would be:

(0.50 × 22) + (0.5 × 10) = 16%

but this would ignore the change in the cost of original capital.

The approach illustrated here is appropriate only if the investment project is large relative to the current size of the entity and undertaking the project causes an identifiable difference in the capital structure.

In practice, entities rarely raise funds from a particular source for a particular purpose, which makes this approach difficult to use.

e.g

Illustration 2 – The marginal cost of capital

Marsh has a current capital structure of $5m equity and $5m debt finance. Its cost of equity is 13% and its post tax cost of debt is 6%.

It intends to raise $1m of new debt finance to fund a new project. The new debt finance will have a post tax cost of 8%, and the cost of equity of Marsh is expected to rise to 15% when the new project is undertaken.

Required:

Calculate the WACC of Marsh before and after undertaking the project, and calculate the Marginal Cost of Capital.

Solution:

Current WACC

	Post tax cost	Value	Cost x value
	%	$m	
Equity	13	5	0.65
Debt	6	5	0.30
		10	0.95

So, WACC = (0.95/10) × 100% = 9.5%

New WACC

	Post tax cost	Value	Cost x value
	%	$m	
Equity	15	5	0.75
Existing Debt	6	5	0.30
New Debt	8	1	0.08
		11	1.13

So, WACC = (1.13/11) × 100% = 10.3%

Marginal Cost of Capital = (1.13–0.95) / (11-10) × 100% = 18%

9 Exam style questions

Test your understanding 1 – Basic WACC calculation

L Co
Balance sheet as at 31st December 20X5

	$m
Net assets	50
Capital and reserves	
Ordinary share capital (50c shares)	15
Reserves	25
10% irredeemable debentures	10
	50

The current share price is $1.32 cum div and a dividend of 12c has been paid for many years. The debentures are trading at 90 ex int. The corporation tax rate is 30%.

Required:

Calculate the WACC at 31st December 20X5.

Test your understanding 2 – More complex WACC calculation

Weird plc is a company which specialises in elocution courses based in Preston and Oxford in England.

The recently appointed finance director, Mr Cook, has asked for your assistance in obtaining a cost of capital which Weird plc can use in appraising its long-term investment opportunities. Mr Cook has provided you with the following information regarding the capital structure of the company.

(1) 2 million 25p ordinary shares valued @ 87p. The annual dividend of GBP180,000, which represents 70% of the amount available for distribution, has just been paid. The company expects to achieve a return of 26% on its retained profits.

(2) 1 million 9% preference shares of 10p each valued at GBP80,000 cum div.

(3) GBP1 million 8% debentures which are redeemable in eight years' time at a premium of 5%. Mr Cook estimates that the debenture holders require a return of 11%.

Corporation tax is at a rate of 35%.

Required:

Calculate for Weird plc its:

(a) **cost of equity share capital;**

(b) **cost of preference share capital;**

(c) **market value of debentures;**

(d) **cost of debentures;**

(e) **weighted average cost of capital (WACC).**

Test your understanding 3 – Detailed WACC calculation

The capital structure of Rock Co as at 1st January 20X3 is as follows:

	$m
Issue ordinary shares (50c shares)	500
6% debenture 20X6	700
11% bank term loan	500

The ordinary shares have a current market price of $2 each. The dividend for 20X2 has just been paid. Dividends per share in the five preceding years were as follows:

20W8	6.8 cents
20W9	7.2 cents
20X0	8.8 cents
20X1	9.6 cents
20X2	10.4 cents

Dividends are paid once a year and are expected to grow in future at the same annual rate as they have since 20W8. The debenture stock has a market price of $90. Redemption will be at par in four years time. The company pays corporation tax at a rate of 30%.

Required:

Estimate the cost of capital of Rock Co.

Test your understanding 4 – WACC and financing discussion

The summarised statement of financial position (balance sheet) of D Co at 30 June 20X9 was as follows:

Assets	**USD'000**
Non current assets	15,350
Current assets	5,900
Total assets	21,250
Equity and liabilities	
Ordinary shares (25 cents)	2,000
7% Preference shares (USD 1)	1,000
Share premium	1,100
Retained earnings	6,550
Total equity	10,650
Long term liabilities: 5% debentures	8,000
Current liabilities	2,600
	21,250

The current price of the ordinary shares is 135 cents ex-dividend.

The dividend of 10 cents is payable during the next few days. The expected rate of growth of the dividend is 9% per annum. The current price of the preference shares is 77 cents and the dividend has recently been paid. The debenture interest has also been paid recently and the debentures are currently trading at USD80 per USD100 nominal. Corporate tax is at the rate of 30%.

Required:

(a) **Calculate the gearing ratio for D Co using:**

(i) book values

(ii) market values

(6 marks)

(b) **Calculate the entity's WACC, using the respective market values as weighting factors.**

(8 marks)

Assume that D plc issued the debentures one year ago to finance a new investment.

(c) **Discuss the reasons why D plc may have issued debentures rather than preference shares to raise the required finance.**

(4 marks)

(d) **Explain what services a merchant bank may have provided to D plc in connection with the raising of this finance.**

(7 marks)

(Total 25 marks)

Test your understanding 5 – Discussion of risk and diversification

You are the company accountant with a medium-sized, privately-owned company. The company has surplus funds which it does not believe it will be able to invest in company operations for at least five years. The majority shareholders are also the directors of the company and they do not wish the surplus funds to be distributed as dividends. A board meeting has therefore been called to discuss the proposal that the funds be invested in a portfolio of medium-to long-term securities.

Three of the directors have recently attended a short course at the local university on *'Investment and the Management of Risk'*. They make the following comments at the meeting, based on their interpretations of what they have learnt on the course:

'If we hold a portfolio of stocks, we need only consider the systematic risk of the securities.'

'As a cautious investor we must always consider total risk.'

'We should not buy anything if the expected return is less than that on the market as a whole, and certainly not if it is below the return on the risk-free asset.'

Required:

(a) **Explain to the members of the board the meaning of systematic, unsystematic and total risk and advise them, briefly, how all three types of risk can be measured.**

(b) **Discuss the directors' comments.**

(15 marks)

Test your understanding 6 – Portfolio management and investing

Carlham has short-term investments in the shares of four listed entities:

Company	**Holding**
Teval	100,000 shares, 50 cents par value
Undal	155,000 shares, $1 par value
Veral	260,000 shares, 20 cents par value
Wirtal	430,000 shares, 10 cents par value

	Geared (equity) beta	**Market price (cents)**	**Latest dividend yield (%)**	**Expected annual return on investment (%)**
Teval	1.55	280	6.8	21.0
Undal	0.65	340	3.6	12.5
Veral	1.26	150	6.4	18.0
Wirtal	1.14	95	7.2	18.5

The yield on UK Treasury bills is 6% per year, and the market return is 16% per year.

Required:

(a) **Estimate the risk of Carlham's short-term investment portfolio relative to the market.**

(4 marks)

(b) **Recommend, giving your reasons, whether the composition of Carlham's short-term investment portfolio should be changed. Relevant calculations must be shown.**

(10 marks)

(c) **Discuss the factors that a financial manager should take into account when investing surplus funds.**

(6 marks)

(Total 20 marks)

Test your understanding answers

Example 1

$$k_e = \frac{30}{400 - 30} = 8.1\%$$

Example 2

(A) $g = (13/8)^{1/8} - 1 = 6.26\%$

(B) $k_e = \frac{13 \times 1.0625}{276} + 0.0625 = 11.26\%$

Example 3

(A) $g = 12\% \times 30\% = 3.6\%$

(B) $k_e = \frac{50 \times 1.036}{700 - 50} + 0.036 = 11.57\%$

Example 4

(a) 15.5%

(b) 9.9%

(c) 12%

Example 5

$$k_d = \frac{10(1 - 0.30)}{130} = 5.4\%$$

Example 6

Cash flows

Year 0	$95.00
Year 1 – 5	$10 (1 – 0.31) = $6.90
Year 5	$100.00

Discounting

Year	*Cash flow*	*Disc. fact. @ 6%*	*Present value*	*Disc. fact. @ 10%*	*Present value*
0	(95.00)	1,000	(95.00)	1.000	(95.00)
1 – 5	6.90	4,212	29.06	3.791	26.16
5	100	0.747	74.7	0.621	62.10
Total			+8.76		–6.74

$$\text{IRR} = 6\% + (10\% - 6\%) \times \frac{8.76}{(8.76 - 6.74)} = 8.26\%$$

Example 7

The calculation is carried out as follows:

	Market value		*Cost of capital*	*Weighted cost*
Source	*$m*	*Proportions*	*%*	*%*
Bank loans	5	0.125	× 6 =	0.75
Debenture loans	5	0.125	× 10 =	1.25
Ordinary shares	30	0.75	× 15 =	11.25
	40	1.00		13.25

WACC = 13.25%

Example 8

Solution:

Market values of the securities:

Equity (Ve) = 1,000,000 × 1.25 = $1,250,000

Preference (Vp) = 250,000 × 65 cents = $162,500

Bonds (Vd) = 150,000 × 85% = $127,500

So total value = 1,250,000 + 162,500 + 127,500 = $1,540,000

Cost of equity (ke) =

$$\frac{10 \times 1.10}{125} + 0.10 = 18.8\%$$

Cost of preference shares (kp) =

$$\frac{7}{65} = 10.8\%$$

Cost of bonds (kd(1-t)) =

$$\frac{15(1 - 0.30)}{85} = 12.4\%$$

Weighted average cost of capital

	Market value		Cost of capital	Weighted cost
Source	$000	*Proportions*	%	%
Equity	1,250	0.812	× 18.8 =	15.27
Preference shares	162.5	0.106	× 10.8 =	1.14
Bonds	127.5	0.082	× 12.4 =	1.02
	1,540	1.00		17.43

WACC = 17.43%

Test your understanding 1 – Basic WACC calculation

(1) ke = 12/120 = 10%

(2) kd = 10(1–0.30) /90 = 7.78%

(3) Market values: Equity 15/.5 × 1.20 = $36m

Debt 10 x (90/100) = $ 9m

Equity and Debt = $45m

(4) WACC = 10% × (36/45) + 7.78% × (9/45) = 9.56%

Test your understanding 2 – More complex WACC calculation

(a) Using the dividend valuation model (DVM)

$$ke = \frac{\text{Dividend in 1 year}}{\text{MV (XD)}} + g$$

where g = growth rate = rb, and

r = return on new investment = 0.26

b = proportion of earnings retained = 0.3

hence g = 0.26 × 0.3 = 0.078.

Dividend in 1 year = Current dividend × (1 + g)

= 180,000 × 1.078

= GBP194,040

MV (XD) = 2 million × 0.87

= GBP1,740,000

The market value is ex div since the dividend has just been paid.

$$ke = \frac{194.040}{1{,}740{,}000} + 0.078$$

= 18.95%, say 19%

(b) Again using the DVM

$$k_p = \frac{9{,}000}{80{,}000 - 9{,}000} = 12.68\%, \text{ say } 12.7\%$$

(c) The DVM gives the market value of debentures as the present value (at the debenture holder's required rate of return) of the payments to debenture holders gross of tax.

Hence:

Time		*Cash flow*	*DF @ 11%*	*PV @ 11%*
		GBP		*GBP*
1–8	Interest	80,000	5.146	411,680
8	Redemption	1,050,000	0.434	455,700
	MV ex interest debentures			867,380

(d) The cost of debt k_d is equal to the discount rate which, when applied to the interest flows net of tax and the redemption costs, produces a PV of GBP867,380.

i.e. the internal rate of return of the following flows:

Time		*Cash flow*	*DF @ 7%*	*PV @ 7%*
		GBP		*GBP*
0	Market value	(867,380)	1	(867,380)
1–8	Net interest	52,000	5.971	310,492
8	Redemption	1,050,000	0.582	611,100
				54,212

We chose 7% as our first estimate of the IRR since 11% × (1 – 0.35) = 7.15%. Since the result is positive, the second estimate is higher, say 8%.

Time	*Cash flow*	*DF @ 8%*	*PV @ 8%*
	GBP		*GBP*
0	(867,380)	1	(867,380)
1-8	52,000	5.747	298,844
8	1,050,000	0.540	567,000
			(1,536)

Hence IRR is approximately 8%.

(e)

	Market value GBP	Cost of capital %	Weighted cost %
Equity	1,740,000	19	12.34
Preference	71,000	12.7	0.34
Debentures	867,380	8	2.59
Total	2,678,380		15.27

Weighted average cost of capital is approximately 15.3%.

Test your understanding 3 – Detailed WACC calculation

(1) Ke

$$k_e = \frac{d_0\,(1+g)}{P_0} + g$$

$$\text{where} \quad g = \sqrt[4]{\frac{10.4}{6.8}} - 1 = 11.2\%$$

$$\text{Therefore} \quad k_e = \frac{10.4 \times 1.112}{200} + 0.112 = 17.0\%$$

(2) kd – redeemable debt – IRR of Market Value, net interest and redemption amount:

		Cash flow	DF	PV	DF	PV
			@ 10%		@ 5%	
0	Market value	**(90.0)**	1.000	(90.00)	1.000	(90.00)
1-4	Interest payments	**4.2**	3.170	13.31	3.546	14.89
4	Capital repayment	**100.0**	0.683	68.30	0.823	82.30
	NPV			(8.39)		7.19

$$IRR = 5\% + \left[\frac{7.19}{7.19 + 8.39} \times (10\% - 5\%)\right] = 7.3\%$$

(3) Market Values

		$m
Equity	500/0.50 × 2	2,000
Debentures	700 × 0.90	630
Bank loan (assuming the loan can be repaid without penalty at any time)		500
Total		3,130

(4) WACC

$$= \left(\frac{2000}{3130} \times 17.0\%\right) + \left(\frac{630}{3130} \times 7.3\%\right) + \left(\frac{500}{3130} \times 11\% \times (1 - 0.30)\right) = 13.6\%$$

Test your understanding 4 – WACC and financing discussion

(a) Gearing = debt / (debt + equity)

Using **book values**, gearing = 8,000 / (8,000 + 10,650) = 43%

(assuming that the preference shares are irredeemable and therefore treated as equity)

Tutorial note: Gearing measured as (debt / equity) would be equally acceptable. Show your workings clearly.

Market values

Ordinary shares 2m × (1.35 / 0.25)	10,800,000
Preference shares 1m × 0.77	770,000
Debentures 8m × 80%	6,400,000
	17,970,000

So gearing = 6,400 / (6,400 + 770 + 10,800) = 36%

(b) **Cost of equity**

$$ke = \frac{10(1.09)}{135} + 0.09$$

= 17.1%

Cost of preference shares

$$k_p = \frac{7}{77} = 9.1\%$$

Cost of debentures

$$k_d\,(1–t) = \frac{5(1–0.30)}{80} = 4.4\%$$

So the weighted average cost of capital is:

	Market value	Cost of capital	Weighted cost
	USD	%	%
Equity	10,800,000	17.1	10.3
Preference	770,000	9.1	0.4
Debentures	6,400,000	4.4	1.6
Total	17,970,000		12.3%

(c) The debentures are a cheaper source of finance than the preference shares. The interest is a tax-deductible expense, whereas the preference dividend is an appropriation from post-tax profits.

The debentures will be secured on the company's assets, which makes them more attractive to investors than preference shares.

Preference shares cannot be secured.

Debenture-holders will rank before preference shareholders in a liquidation.

(d) A merchant bank may have provided the following services:

- advice on the type of capital to be issued, that is debt, equity or preference shares;
- advice on the form of debt issued, that is secured or unsecured, and on the use of sweeteners such as a conversion option or warrants;
- advising on the coupon rate, issue price and maturity of the debenture;
- marketing and administration of the issue;
- identifying potential investors;
- recommendations about any derivatives that may be available to hedge interest-rate exposure;
- ensuring that D Co complied with any statutory and regulatory requirements relating to the new issue.

Test your understanding 5 – Discussion of risk and diversification

MEMORANDUM

To: The Board of Directors

From: The Company Accountant

Date: X June 20XX

Subject: Investing funds in a portfolio of securities

(a) This memorandum starts with some definitions:

Systematic risk is risk that cannot be eliminated by diversification.

Unsystematic risk is risk that can be eliminated by diversification.

Total risk is the sum of systematic and unsystematic risk.

These definitions can be explained as follows. There will be some uncertainty normally inherent in the future returns of any investment that is made. This uncertainty can be measured as the total risk of the investment by calculating the standard deviation of the investment's possible returns.

Some of this total risk can be diversified away by combining the investment with other different investments; this component of total risk is called unsystematic risk and relates to factors unique to the company itself or the business sector it is in.

The remainder of the total risk cannot be diversified away; this component of total risk is called systematic risk and relates to factors affecting the stock market as a whole e.g. the risk that interest rates rise.

Total risk is measured as the standard deviation of investment returns.

If future returns are unclear, the standard deviation of past returns over recent periods can be calculated as a measure of the investment's total risk.

Systematic risk is measured by looking at an investment's beta value. An investment with no systematic risk has a beta value of zero. An investment with the same systematic risk as the market as a whole has a beta of one. An investment with systematic risk twice that of the market as a whole has a beta of two, etc.

Unsystematic risk is normally measured as the difference between systematic risk and total risk i.e. as a balancing figure, although it is possible to calculate it separately.

(b) The expected return from any investment should compensate for its risk. If the investment is held alone, it is the total risk that is relevant. But if the investment is held as one unit in a widely diversified portfolio, the unsystematic risk will be eliminated, and it is only the systematic risk that is relevant.

Thus it is acceptable to buy investments with expected returns less than the expected return on the market as a whole, as long as those investments possess less risk than the market as a whole. It might be felt prudent, for example, to hold a proportion of a portfolio in cash on deposit, effectively as a risk-free asset, although the expected return will be lower than the return expected for investing in shares on the stock market.

It is even acceptable to buy investments with expected returns less than the risk-free rate of return, as long as those investments contribute sufficiently to the overall diversification of the portfolio held. Investments with negative beta values fall particularly into this category; their expected return is low but they offer substantial diversification opportunities.

Test your understanding 6 – Portfolio management and investing

(a) The risk of Carlham's short-term investment portfolio may be measured by the weighted average beta equity coefficient of the four shares. The weighting is by the market value of the shares.

	Geared (equity) beta	Market value ($)	Beta x MV
Teval	1.55	280,000	434,000
Undal	0.65	527,000	342,550
Veral	1.26	390,000	491,400
Wirtal	1.14	408,500	465,490
Total		1,605,500	1,733,640

So the portfolio beta is 1,733,640 / 1,605,500 = 1.08

Carlham's short-term investment portfolio is slightly more risky than the market.

(b) The composition of the short-term investment portfolio may be considered from two viewpoints:

(i) Is the expected performance of the individual investments within the portfolio satisfactory?

(ii) Does the portfolio provide the most suitable form of short-term investments for Carlham plc?

(i) The individual shares may be examined to establish if they are expected to provide a satisfactory return for the systematic risk they involve. The required return is:

$R_f + [R_m - R_f]$ ß

where Rf is the risk-free rate (assumed to be the yield on UK Treasury bills) and Rm is the market return.

Company	Required return
Teval	6% + ((16% – 6%) 1.55) = 21.5%
Undal	6% + ((16% – 6%) 0.65) = 12.5%
Veral	6% + ((16% – 6%) 1.26) = 18.6%
Wirtal	6% + ((16% – 6%) 1.14) = 17.4%

	Required return (%)	Expected return (%)	Abnormal return (alpha value)	Recommendation
Teval	21.5	21	–0.5	Sell shares
Undal	12.5	12.5	0	Hold
Veral	18.6	18	–0.6	Sell shares
Wirtal	17.4	18.5	1.1	Buy more shares

If the above data are accurate, the shares in Teval and Veral are not expected to give a satisfactory return relative to their systematic risk, and should be sold. The shares of Undal should be held and further shares should be purchased in Wirtal, which has an expected positive abnormal return.

(However, none of the abnormal returns are large and any decision to buy or sell might be influenced by this, as well as by the existence of transaction costs.)

This analysis considers only systematic risk. If Carlham does not have other investments and is not well diversified, systematic risk is likely to underestimate the risk to Carlham of these investments.

(ii) The portfolio is unusual for a short-term investment portfolio. Short-term investments are usually made for a specific purpose, for example to ensure cash is available for purchase of assets, payment of dividends, taxes or creditors where a known amount of funds is required. Most companies are not willing to tolerate much risk of price movement in their short-term investments. This portfolio of investments in ordinary shares is exposed to substantial price movements as share prices change in response to the possibility that one or more of the companies could fail. Although the expected returns are relatively high, the risk of this portfolio is very high relative to most portfolios of marketable securities. Unless Carlham is happy to take such risks, it is recommended that short-term investments should concentrate upon fixed-interest marketable securities such as goernment bonds and certificates of deposit. Such investments involve much less risk of price movement and default and, if held short term, possible inflation is not a concern.

(c) The factors that a financial manager should take into account when investing surplus funds include the following:

(i) Default risk. The risk that interest and/or principal will not be paid on schedule on fixed-interest investments. Most short-term investment in marketable securities is confined to investments with negligible risk of default.

(ii) Price risk. The risk of the value of the investment changing, for example when interest rates change. Financial managers normally wish to avoid substantial price risk.

(iii) Marketability. Securities should normally be marketable at short notice at close to the quoted market price.

(iv) Taxation. Are there any special tax effects of the selected investments?

(v) Yield. Managers will usually try to achieve the maximum yield possible, consistent with a satisfactory level of risk and marketability.

(vi) Foreign exchange risk. If investments are not denominated in the domestic currency of the investor, foreign exchange risk must be taken into account.

(vii) The amount of funds to be invested. Some types of investment require a minimum size of investment.

(viii) The period for which the investment is to be made. The type of investment should be matched with the timing requirements of the future need for funds.

chapter

7

Capital Structure

Chapter learning objectives

Lead	Component
B1: Evaluate the financing requirements of an organisation and strategies for meeting those requirements.	(b) evaluate alternative methods of meeting financing requirements, taking account of the implications for the organisation's financial statements, its tax position and financial stakeholders. (c) evaluate the weighted average cost of capital of an organisation.

Indicative syllabus content

- The impact of changing capital structure on the market value of a company. (Note: An understanding of Modigliani and Miller's theory of gearing, with and without taxes, will be expected, but proof of their theory will not be examined).
- The capital asset pricing model (CAPM): the ability to gear and un-gear betas.
- The effect of financing decisions on balance sheet structure and on ratios of interest to investors and other financiers (gearing, earnings per share, price-earnings ratio, dividend yield, dividend cover gearing, interest cover).

1 Overview of Chapter

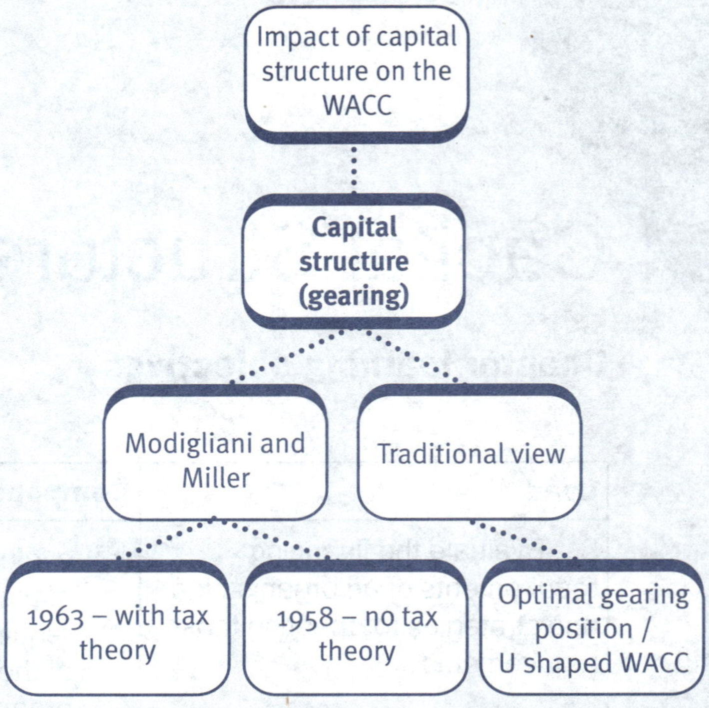

2 Changing Capital Structure

The impact of capital structure on WACC and company value

When we consider the WACC formula which was introduced in the earlier 'Cost of Capital' Chapter, it is clear that if a company changes its capital structure (gearing level), the WACC will change, since the ratio of debt to equity is a key variable in the formula.

Also, since the value of an entire company (debt plus equity) can be calculated as the present value of its post tax operating cash flows (before financing) discounted at the WACC, when the WACC changes so does the value. (See the later Chapter on 'Business Valuation' for more details on this.)

Several studies have focused on this link between capital structure and company value. The key question is:

> "What capital structure should the company aim for in order to maximise the company's value?"

The main studies are:

- the traditional view;
- the Modigliani-Miller view, ignoring taxation;
- the Modigliani-Miller view, taking into account the tax relief on debt interest payments.

These studies are based on different assumptions and come to different conclusions. They are covered below.

In order to understand the different views, it is vital to understand the two opposing forces which impact on the WACC as capital structure changes.

The two opposing forces which impact WACC

By introducing debt

Downward force on WACC

– Debt is cheaper than equity and would cause the WACC to fall

Upward force on WACC

– K_e increases because of financial risk and would cause the WACC to rise

Impact on WACC of an increase in gearing

As an entity increases the amount of debt in its capital structure, two opposing forces impact on the weighted average cost of capital:

Downward force on the WACC

In general, the entity's cost of debt finance is cheaper than its cost of equity finance, for two reasons:

- Interest is an obligation which has to be paid out each year, whereas dividends are paid only if the company can afford them. This means that debt holders face less risk, so accept lower returns.
- Interest is a tax deductible expense, whereas dividends are paid out of post tax profits. This further reduces the cost of debt for the company.

Therefore, as the entity increases its gearing by raising more debt finance, the greater proportion of (cheaper) debt in the capital structure exerts a downward force on the WACC.

Upward force on the WACC

As the gearing level increases, the extra interest payments to debt holders mean that the likelihood of the entity being able to afford to pay dividends to shareholders reduces. This increases the risk perception of the shareholders, so they demand higher returns to compensate for the increased risk.

This increase in the cost of equity exerts an upward force on the WACC.

Net effect

Clearly, the two factors identified have opposing impacts on the weighted average cost of capital. The key questions are:

Which of the two forces is stronger?

What is the net effect of these two factors?

There is no simple answer to these questions. In fact, the different gearing theories propose different answers to the questions, based on different assumptions.

However, an understanding of these two factors, and these key questions, is crucial to a sound understanding of the capital structure theories covered in this Chapter.

Impact of capital structure on the equity investor

High gearing exists when an entity has a large proportion of prior charge capital in relation to equity and low gearing exists when there is a small proportion of prior charge capital. High gearing increases the financial risk of the equity investor but the reward can be in the form of increased dividends when profits rise. If, however, profits falter, the equity investor can expect to be the first to feel the effect of the reduction in profits.

Low gearing or no gearing may not necessarily be in the equity investor's best interests because the entity might then be failing to exploit the benefits which borrowing can bring.

Provided that the return generated from borrowed funds is greater than the cost of those funds, capital gearing could be increased. The extent to which it is prudent for an entity to increase its capital gearing will depend upon many variables such as the type of industry within which the entity operates, the cost of funds in the market, the availability of investment opportunities and the extent to which the company can continue to benefit from the 'tax shield'.

The ordinary share price of highly geared entities will tend to be depressed in times of rising interest rates.

3 Traditional View

According to the 'traditional' view of gearing and the cost of capital, as an organisation introduces debt into its capital structure the weighted average cost of capital will fall because initially the benefit of cheap debt finance more than outweighs any increases in the cost of equity required to compensate equity holders for higher financial risk.

As gearing continues to increase the equity holders will ask for increasingly higher returns. The cost of equity therefore rises as gearing increases. Eventually this increase in the cost of equity will start to outweigh the benefit of cheap debt finance, and the weighted average cost of capital will rise. At extreme levels of gearing the cost of debt will also start to rise (as debt holders become worried about the security of their loans) and this will also contribute to an increasing weighted average cost of capital.

The diagram below demonstrates this position in which:

- k_e is the cost of equity;
- k_d is the cost of debt;
- k_o is the overall or weighted average cost of capital.

Traditional view of gearing and the cost of capital

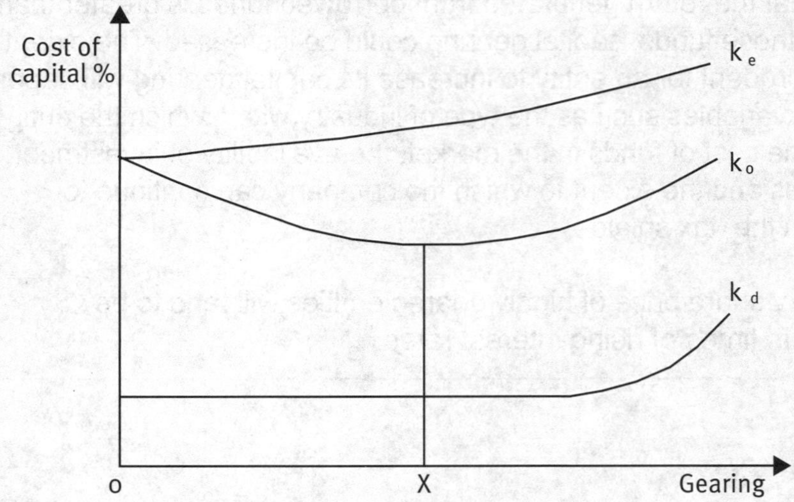

X = optimal level of gearing, where k_o is at a minimum.

The traditional view therefore claims that there is an optimal capital structure where the weighted average cost of capital is at a minimum. This is at point X in the above diagram.

At point X the overall return required by investors (debt and equity) is minimised.

It follows that at this point the combined market value of the entity's debt and equity securities will also be maximised (because the value of the entity's debt and equity and the WACC are inversely related - discounting the future operating cash flows at a lower cost of capital will give a higher value.)

Optimal capital structure

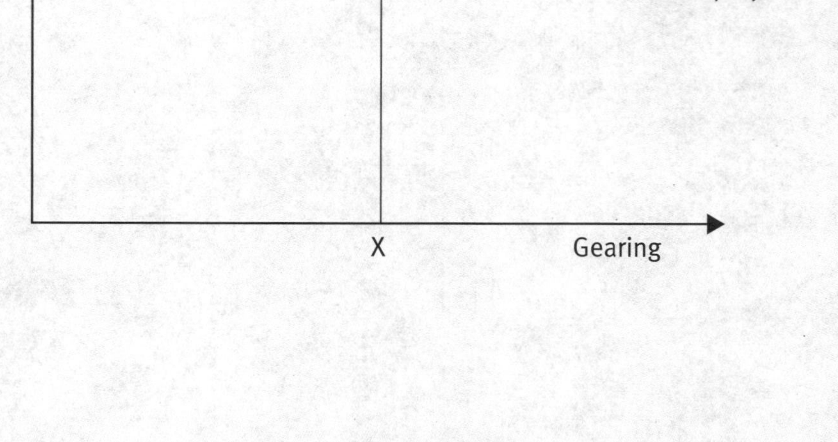

4 Capital Structure – Modigliani And Miller's View

In 1958, the two American economists, Professors Modigliani and Miller, challenged the traditional view of gearing and the cost of capital. Over a 20-year period they put forward a number of propositions as to why the traditional view of gearing might be wrong.

They began by assuming that the effect of tax relief on debt interest could be ignored.

Modigliani and Miller without tax (1958)

The 1958 proposition was that companies which operate in the same type of business and which have similar operating risks must have the same total value, irrespective of their capital structures.

Their view is based on the belief that the value of a company depends solely upon the future post tax (pre financing) operating income generated by its assets.

The way in which the funding is split between debt and equity should make no difference to the total value of the company (equity plus debt). In fact, one of M & M's assumptions is that the investors are indifferent between personal and corporate gearing.

Thus, the total value of the company will not change with gearing. This means that its weighted average cost of capital will not change with gearing, and will be the same at all levels of gearing.

Their view is represented in the following diagrams.

Modigliani and Miller view (no taxation)

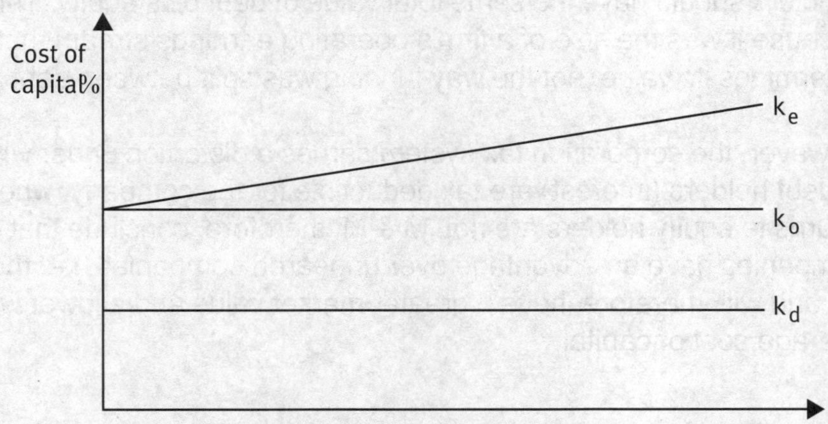

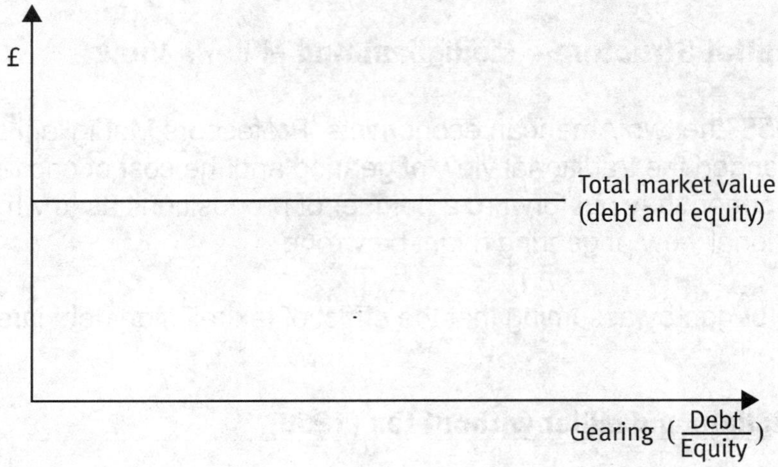

If the weighted average cost of capital is to remain constant at all levels of gearing, it follows that any benefit from the increased proportion of cheaper debt finance (downward force on the WACC) must be exactly offset by the increase in the cost of equity (upward force on the WACC).

The essential point made by M & M is that, ignoring taxation, a company should be indifferent between all possible capital structures. This is at odds with the beliefs of the traditionalists.

M & M support their case by demonstrating that market pressures will ensure that two companies identical in every aspect apart from their gearing level will have the same overall market value.

Modigliani and Miller with tax (1963)

In 1963, M & M amended their model to include the impact of corporation tax. This alteration changes the results of their analysis significantly.

Previously they argued that companies that differ only in their capital structure should have the same total value of debt plus equity. This was because it was the size of a firm's operating earnings stream that determines its value, not the way funding was split between debt and equity.

However, the corporation tax system carries a distortion under which returns to debt holders (interest) are tax deductible for the company, whereas returns to equity holders are not. M & M, therefore, conclude that geared companies have an advantage over ungeared companies, i.e. they pay less tax and will, therefore, have a greater market value and a lower weighted average cost of capital.

Graph of M & M model with tax

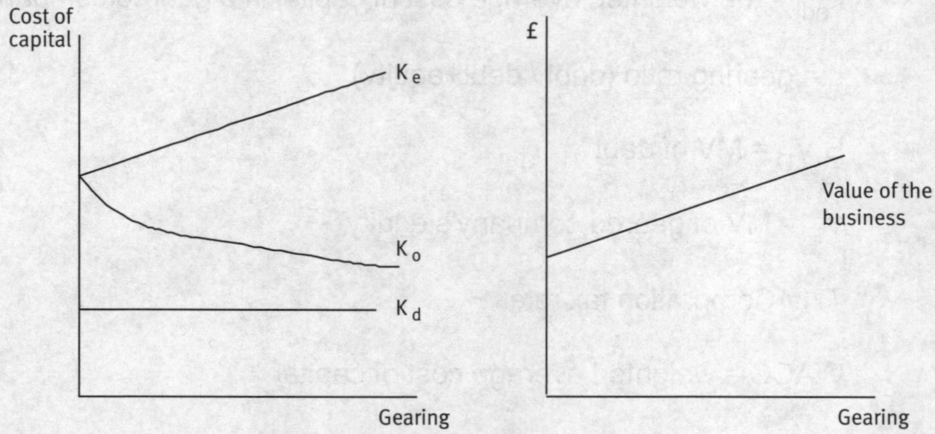

As gearing increases, the WACC steadily decreases, and hence the value of the company (debt plus equity) increases.

In the presence of tax, the downward force on the WACC (the impact of the greater proportion of debt finance) is stronger than the upward force (the increase in cost of equity).

If the other implications of the M & M view are accepted, the introduction of taxation suggests that the higher the level of taxation, the lower the combined cost of capital.

Modigliani and Miller (M & M) formulae

M & M developed the following formulae that can be applied to finding the value, cost of equity or WACC of companies that have a given level of business risk, but changing capital structure.

	With tax
Value of the company (debt+equity)	$V_g = V_u + TB$
Cost of equity	$k_{eg} = k_{eu} + (k_{eu} - k_d)\ V_D(1 - t) / V_E$
WACC	$k_{adj} = k_{eu}\ (1 - tL)$

where V = Value of company (V_g = value of geared company, V_u = value of ungeared company)

k_e = Cost of equity (k_{eg} = cost of equity in geared co, k_{eu} = cost of equity in ungeared co)

k_d = Cost of debt (must be gross of tax)

k_{adj} = the weighted average cost of capital in a geared company

L = gearing ratio (debt / debt+equity)

B,V_D = MV of debt

V_E = MV of geared company's equity

T, t= Corporation tax rate

WACC = weighted average cost of capital

The without-tax formulae are simply a special case of the with-tax formulae, where t = 0.

Interpreting the M & M graphs and formulae

Without tax

Company value (V_g = V_u)

The graph showed a horizontal line for company value in the M & M without tax theory.

This is backed up by the formula, which shows that if T=0, the values of an ungeared company and an equivalent ungeared company are the same.

WACC (k_{adj} = k_{eu})

The graph also showed a horizontal line for WACC in the M & M without tax theory.

Again, the formula backs this up. If t=0, the formula reduces to k_{adj} = $k_{eu.}$ This shows that the WACC of the geared company is always the same as the WACC of an equivalent ungeared company, irrespective of the level of gearing.

With tax

Company value ($V_g = V_u + TB$)

The graph showed an upward sloping line for company value in the M & M with tax theory.

This is backed up by the formula, which shows that the higher the value of B (value of debt), the greater the value of the entire company should be.

As the company increases its gearing, the value of the entire company (debt plus equity) increases.

Cost of equity ($k_{eg} = k_{eu} + (k_{eu} - k_d) V_D(1 - t) / V_E$)

The cost of equity slopes upwards as gearing increases under M & M's assumptions, because shareholders face higher risk so demand higher returns.

We can see from the formula that the k_{eg} increases as the amount of debt (V_D) increases relative to the value of equity (V_E).

Note that the inclusion of (1-t) in the formula has the impact of reducing the slope of the line if the tax rate increases. Most importantly, this means that the cost of equity in the M & M with tax theory will always increase less steeply than in the without tax theory. This helps to explain why the upward force on WACC is smaller in the with tax theory, and hence why the downward force on the WACC caused by the (net of tax) cheap debt finance is the net stronger force in the with tax theory.

WACC ($k_{adj} = k_{eu}(1 - tL)$)

The formula shows that WACC will reduce as gearing (measured by L) increases. This is seen on the graph as a downward sloping line.

Example 1 – M & M without tax

X Co is identical in all operating and risk characteristics to Y Co, except that X Co is all equity financed and Y Co is financed by equity valued at $2.1m and debt valued at $0.9m based on market values. X Co and Y Co operate in a country where no tax is payable.

The interest paid on Y Co's debt is $72,000 per annum, and it pays a dividend to shareholders of $378,000 per annum. X Co pays an annual dividend of $450,000.

Required:

(a) **Calculate the value of X Co.**

(b) **Calculate the cost of capital for X Co.**

(c) **Calculate the cost of equity for Y Co, and the cost of debt for Y Co.**

(d) **Calculate the weighted average cost of capital for Y Co.**

Example 2 – M & M with tax

X Co is identical in all operating and risk characteristics to Y Co, except that X Co is financed only by equity valued at $3m whereas Y Co has debt valued at $0.9m (based on market value) as part of its capital structure. X Co and Y Co operate in a country where tax is payable at 33%.

The interest paid on Y Co's debt is $72,000 per annum, and it pays a dividend to shareholders of $378,000 per annum. X Co pays an annual dividend of $450,000.

Required:

(a) **Calculate the value of the equity of Y Co.**

(b) **Calculate the cost of capital for X Co.**

(c) **Calculate the cost of equity for Y Co, and the cost of debt for Y Co.**

(d) **Calculate the weighted average cost of capital for Y Co.**

M & M's key assumptions

- There exists a perfect capital market in which there are no information costs or transaction costs.
- Debt is risk free and k_d remains constant at all levels of gearing.
- Investors are indifferent between personal and corporate gearing.
- Investors and companies can borrow at the same rate of interest.

5 Capital Structure in the Real World

Introduction

We need to adjust M & M 's theories to also take into account real life factors.

The most unrealistic of M & M's key assumptions is that debt is risk free.

In reality, there is a greater risk to both the lenders and shareholders with very high levels of gearing. This is the risk that the company is unable to service the debt and end up in financial distress or even insolvent.

In reality, lenders will ask for higher interest if they perceive that there is a greater risk of default.

Practical considerations

This then leaves the problem of how companies determine their capital structures in the real world.

The main practical considerations are:

- The company's ability to borrow money (the company's 'debt capacity')
- Existing debt covenants
- Increasing costs of debt finance as gearing rises
- Views of other stakeholders and rating agencies
- Tax exhaustion

More detail on practical considerations

The company's ability to borrow money (the company's 'debt capacity')

- The maximum level of borrowing that a company can comfortably support is referred to as its debt capacity. (**Definition** of debt capacity from CIMA Official Terminology, 2005 is the "extent to which an entity can support and / or obtain loan finance.")
- A company can only increase its gearing if it can find a lender who will provide it with debt finance. In recessionary times, this should not be taken for granted.
- A company's capacity to borrow is increased if it is able to offer good quality, valuable assets as collateral.

- Debt capacity is function of a company's credit-worthiness (introduced in an earlier Chapter) and credit scoring. (**Definition** of credit scoring from CIMA Official Terminology, 2005 is the "assessment of the credit-worthiness of an individual or company by rating numerically a number of both financial and non-financial aspects of the target's present position and performance.")

Existing debt covenants

- Debt covenants reduce the flexibility of management. Existing debt covenants may even prevent the company from borrowing more.
- Management must keep the company well within the terms of the existing covenants (keeping plenty of "leeway" or "headroom") to ensure that the flexibility of the company is maximised.

Increasing costs of debt finance as gearing rises

- M & M assumed that debt was risk free, and that k_d would be constant at all levels of gearing. In reality, an increased level of gearing is likely to be perceived as risky by lenders, so the interest rates on loans generally increase as gearing increases.

Views of other stakeholders and rating agencies

- The gearing theories focus on the position of the shareholders and the lenders at different levels of gearing. In reality, the views of other stakeholders should also be considered. In particular, many stakeholders perceive high levels of gearing to be risky. This could impact on the credit score or credit worthiness of the company. A reduction in credit worthiness may be evidenced by a credit rating downgrade by one of the credit rating agencies.
- For example,
  - customers may be concerned about buying goods from companies that have poor credit worthiness (due to concerns about warranties and guarantees being honoured)
  - suppliers might not want to supply, or advance credit (due to the risk of default)
  - employees and managers might choose to leave if they fear for their job security.
- All these factors will damage the company's prospects and reputation.

Tax exhaustion

- M & M's with tax theory suggests that the benefits of tax relief on debt interest will help to reduce the company's cost of capital at all levels of gearing. This is not the case in practice.

- At some level of gearing the interest payable will be so high that taxable profit will be reduced to zero. Beyond this point, there will be no further benefit of raising debt finance.
- However, in order for tax exhaustion to apply, the company must be making a loss and will have breached any interest cover covenants. The company is therefore likely to have much greater problems to contend with than the loss of tax relief.

NEW

6 Risk adjusted WACC – a project specific cost of capital

Introduction

An important application of the M & M theories and formulae is in the calculation of project specific discount rates.

In the earlier Chapter on 'Cost of Capital' it was noted that the existing cost of capital (WACC) of an entity is unsuitable as a project discount rate if the business risk of the new project and / or the entity's capital structure will change as a consequence of taking on the project.

Using the M & M theories and the CAPM model, a project specific discount rate (or risk adjusted WACC) can be calculated in these circumstances.

Asset betas, equity betas and debt betas

In order to understand the risk adjusted WACC method, we first need to expand our understanding of beta factors which were introduced earlier in the 'Cost of Capital' Chapter.

- The beta factor is a measure of the systematic risk of an investment relative to the market.
- This risk will be dependent on the level of business risk and the level of financial risk (gearing) associated with an investment.
- Hence, the beta factor for a geared company will be greater than the beta factor for an equivalent ungeared company.

The relationship between the beta factors for ungeared and geared companies is given by the following formula (given in the exam):

$$\beta_u = \beta_g\left[\frac{V_E}{V_E + V_D[1-t]}\right] + \beta_d\left[\frac{V_D[1-t]}{V_E + V_D[1-t]}\right]$$

where

β_g = the equity (geared) beta measures the systematic business risk and the systematic financial risk of a company's shares

$ß_u$ = the asset (ungeared) beta measures the systematic business risk *only*

$ß_d$ = the debt beta measures the risk associated with the debt finance. Usually we assume that debt is risk free and hence the debt beta is zero. If this is the case, the second term in the given formula disappears and the formula becomes:

$$\beta_u = \beta_g \left[\frac{V_E}{V_E + V_D[1-t]} \right]$$

More on systematic risk

We know from the earlier 'Cost of Capital' Chapter that what is important is an investment's systematic risk.

Remember:

- Shareholders are only interested in systematic risk because they hold well-diversified portfolios. Systematic risk of a project is measured by its beta.
- Shareholders in a geared company suffer two types of systematic risk i.e. business and financial risk.
- The business risk of a company refers to the risk of the operating cash flows.
- Financial risk is the increased volatility of dividend payments to shareholders as gearing increases.

From the M & M analysis, we know that a share's systematic risk can be split up between the systematic *business* risk and the systematic *financial* risk.

Systematic business risk arises out of the risky nature of the company's business caused by:

- revenue sensitivity;
- proportion of fixed to variable production costs.

Systematic financial risk arises out of how the company has financed itself – its gearing or capital structure.

Use of the formula

For example, suppose a question tells you that the ABC company has a gearing ratio (D : E) of 1 : 2; the shares have a beta value of 1.45 (the equity beta); and the corporation tax rate is 30%. Then:

$$\beta_u = 1.45 \times \frac{2}{2 + 1 \times (1 - 0.30)} = 1.074$$

Note: If a question only states the beta, assume it is an equity beta. Also, if there is no mention of a debt beta, assume it is zero.

This indicates that shareholders in ABC have a beta value/systematic risk exposure of 1.45. Of this value, 1.074 arises out of the risky nature of the company's business (its business risk) and the rest (i.e. 1.45 – 1.074 = 0.376) arises out of the financial risk caused by the company's capital structure.

Notice four very important implications of this analysis:

(1) A company's equity beta will always be greater than its asset beta, except

(2) If it is all equity financed (and so has no financial risk), when its equity beta and asset beta will be the same.

(3) Companies in the same 'area of business' (i.e. same business risk) will have the same *asset* beta, but

(4) Companies in the same area of business will *not* have the same *equity* beta unless they also happen to have the same capital structure.

As we shall see, the *third* of these points is particularly important.

Risk adjusted WACC – Gearing and ungearing beta factors

There are two ways in which the gearing / degearing formula above can be used in order to derive a project specific cost of capital:

Method 1: Use the formula (if necessary) to derive the ungeared beta factor, then regear this beta to reflect the entity's capital structure. Then use CAPM to derive a risk adjusted cost of equity and use this k_e in the standard WACC formula to find risk adjusted WACC.

Method 2: Use the formula (if necessary) to derive the ungeared beta factor, then use CAPM to find an "ungeared cost of equity" (k_{eu}). Finally, use M & M's WACC formula (introduced earlier in this Chapter) to calculate the risk adjusted WACC.

Both methods will now be illustrated, to show that they give the same answer.

e.g

Illustration 1 – Risk adjusted WACC

Garvey Co is planning to undertake a new project in a new business sector. Information for Garvey Co and for Rocket Co, a listed company in the new business sector is as follows:

	Garvey Co	**Rocket Co**
Current geared (equity) beta	1.25	1.86
Current capital structure ratio (D:E by market value)	1:2	1:1

Garvey Co intends to finance the project to maintain its existing gearing ratio.

The tax rate is 30% and the return on the stock market has been 12% per annum in recent years. Debt is assumed to be risk free and has a pre tax cost of 5% per annum.

Required:

Calculate a suitable cost of capital for the new project.

Solution

Method 1:

Step 1

Rocket Co's ungeared / asset beta is calculated and then used as an estimate of the project's asset beta (because the project and Rocket Co are in the same area of business and so will have the same *asset* beta). Since debt is risk free, use

$$ßu = ßg \times \frac{V_E}{V_E + V_D(1-t)}$$

$$ßu = 1.86 \times \frac{1}{1 + 1(1-0.30)} = 1.09$$

Step 2

A geared / equity beta for the project is calculated next. As we know, an equity beta reflects both systematic business risk *and* systematic financial risk. The project's equity beta will reflect the project's business risk and the capital structure of Garvey Co - the company that is to undertake the project.

Using: $$ßu = ßg \times \frac{V_E}{V_E + V_D(1-t)}$$

$$1.09 = ßg \times \frac{2}{2 + 1 \times (1-0.30)}$$

So ßg = 1.47

Step 3

This equity beta is then input into the CAPM to give a cost of equity capital for the project (the return required on the shareholders' funds invested by Garvey Co in the new project:

$k_e = R_F + [R_M - R_F]$ ßg

$ke_{PROJECT} = 5\% + [12\% - 5\%] \times 1.47 = 15.3\%$

Step 4

The risk adjusted WACC is now calculated using the standard WACC formula:

$$k_o = k_{eg}\left[\frac{V_E}{V_E + V_D}\right] + k_d\left[\frac{V_D}{V_E + V_D}\right]$$

$= 15.3\% \times (2/3) + 5\% \times (1\text{-}0.30) \times (1/3) = 11.4\%$

Method 2:

Step 1

As above, the existing geared / equity beta of Rocket Co is degeared, to give an ungeared / asset beta of 1.09.

Step 2

Input this ungeared beta into the CAPM formula to give an ungeared cost of equity (k_{eu})

k_{eu}= 5%+ [12% – 5%] × 1.09 = 12.6%

Step 3

Use the M & M WACC formula to find the risk adjusted WACC

$k_{adj} = k_{eu} (1 – tL)$

=12.6% (1 – 30% × (1/3)) = 11.4% as before.

Example 3

ABC is a cement company with a D : E ratio of 1 : 3. It wishes to evaluate a project in the telecoms industry and does not intend to change its capital structure.

XYZ is a 'typical' telecoms company. It has an *equity* beta of 1.25 and a D : E ratio of 1 : 2.

Assume that R_F = 6%, R_M = 14%, and the tax rate is 30%. It is assumed that corporate debt is risk-free (and so the debt beta is zero).

Required:

Calculate a risk adjusted WACC for the new project.

7 Exam style questions

Test your understanding 1 – M & M's formulae

The finance director of Netra plc, a company listed on the UK's AIM (Alternative Investment Market), wishes to estimate what impact the introduction of debt finance is likely to have on the company's overall cost of capital. The company is currently financed only by equity.

Netra plc Summarised capital structure

	£000
Ordinary shares (25 pence par value)	500
Reserves	1,100
	1,600

The company's current share price is 420 pence, and up to £4 million of fixed rate irredeemable debt could be raised at an interest rate of 10% per annum. The corporate tax rate is 33%.

Netra's current earnings before interest and tax are £2.5 million. These earnings are not expected to change significantly for the foreseeable future.

The company is considering raising either:

(i) £2 million in debt finance;

(ii) £4 million in debt finance

In either case the debt finance will be used to re-purchase ordinary shares.

Required:

(a) **Using Miller and Modigliani's model in a world with corporate tax, estimate the impact on Netra's cost of capital of raising:**

(i) **£2 million; and**

(ii) **£4 million in debt finance.**

State clearly any assumptions that you make.

(b) **Briefly discuss whether or not the estimates produced in part (a) are likely to be accurate.**

Test your understanding 2 – WACC and M & M's formulae

Berlan Co has annual earnings before interest and tax of GBP15 million. These earnings are expected to remain constant. The market price of the company's ordinary shares is 86 pence per share cum div and of debentures GBP105.50 per debenture ex interest. An interim dividend of six pence per share has been declared. Corporate tax is at the rate of 35% and all available earnings are distributed as dividends.

Berlan's long-term capital structure is shown below:

	GBP000
Ordinary shares (25 pence par value)	12,500
Reserves	24,300
	36,800
16% debenture 31.12. X4 (GBP100 par value)	23,697
	60,497

Required:

(a) **Calculate the cost of capital of Berlan Co according to the traditional theory of capital structure. Assume that it is now 31 December 20X1.**

(8 marks)

(b) Canalot Co is an all equity company with an equilibrium market value of GBP32.5 million and a cost of capital of 18% per year.

The company proposes to re-purchase GBP5 million of equity and to replace it with 13% irredeemable bonds.

Canalot's earnings before interest and tax are expected to be constant for the foreseeable future. Corporate tax is at the rate of 35%. All profits are paid out as dividends.

Explain and demonstrate how this change in capital structure will affect:

(i) **the market value;**

(ii) **the cost of equity; and**

(iii) **the cost of capital**

of Canalot Co, using the assumptions of Modigliani and Miller.

(7 marks)

(c) **Explain any weaknesses of both the traditional and Modigliani and Miller theories and discuss how useful they might be in the determination of the appropriate capital structure for a company.**

(10 marks)

(Total: 25 marks)

Test your understanding 3 – Comparison of financing options

RH Co manufactures machine tools. It has 2 million ordinary $1 shares in issue, quoted at 168 cents each, and $1 million 10% secured debentures quoted at par. To finance expansion the directors of the company want to raise $1 million for additional working capital.

Cash flow from trading before interest and tax is currently $1 million per annum. It is expected to rise to $1.3 million per annum if the expansion programme goes ahead.

To simplify placing a valuation on the company's equity, you should assume that:

- the forecast level of cash flow, and a tax rate of 33%, will continue indefinitely;
- the required rate of return on the market value of equity, 18% post tax, will be unaffected by the new financing;
- there is no difference between taxable profits and cash flow.

The company's directors are considering two forms of finance - equity via a rights issue at 15% discount to current share price, or 12% unsecured bonds at par.

Required:

(a) **Calculate for both financing options, the expected:**

(i) **increase in the market value of equity;**

(ii) **debt: debt + equity ratio;**

(iii) **weighted average cost of capital.**

(13 marks)

(b) **Assume you are the financial manager for RH Co. Write a report to the board advising which of the two types of financing is to be preferred. Include in your report brief comments on non-financial factors which should be considered by the directors before deciding how to raise the $1 million finance.**

(12 marks)

(Total: 25 marks)

Test your understanding 4 – WACC and risk adjusted WACC

A colleague has been taken ill. Your managing director has asked you to take over from the colleague and to provide urgently-needed estimates of the discount rate to be used in appraising a large new capital investment. You have been given your colleague's working notes, which you believe to be numerically accurate.

Working notes

Estimates for the next five years (annual averages)

Stock market total return on equity	16%
Own company dividend yield	7%
Own company share price rise	14%
Own company equity (geared) beta	1.4
Growth rate of own company earnings	12%
Growth rate of own company dividends	11%
Growth rate of own company sales	13%
Treasury bill yield	12%

The company's gearing level (by market values) is 1 : 2 debt to equity, and after-tax earnings available to ordinary shareholders in the most recent year were $5,400,000, of which $2,140,000 was distributed as ordinary dividends. The company has 10 million issued ordinary shares which are currently trading on the Stock Exchange at 321 cents. Corporate debt may be assumed to be risk-free. The company pays tax at 35% and personal taxation may be ignored.

Required:

(a) **Estimate the company's weighted average cost of capital using:**

(i) **the dividend valuation model**

(ii) **the capital asset pricing model.**

State clearly any assumptions that you make.

Under what circumstances would these models be expected to produce similar values for the weighted average cost of capital?

(10 marks)

(b) You are now informed that the proposed investment is a major diversification into a new industry, and are provided with the following information about the new industry:

Average industry gearing level (by market value)	1 : 3 debt to equity
Average pay-out ratio	55%
Average beta coefficient (ß equity)	1.50

Using any relevant information from parts (a) and (b), prepare a brief report recommending which discount rate should be used for the investment. Any relevant calculations not included in your answer to part (a) should form part of your report.

(7 marks)

(c) **Discuss the practical problems of using the capital asset pricing model in investment appraisal.**

(8 marks)

(Total: 25 marks)

Test your understanding answers

Example 1 – M & M without tax

(a) $V_g = V_u + TB$

so given that T = 0,

$V_g = V_u$

so the value of X Co is the same as the value of Y Co, ($2.1m + $0.9m) $3m

(b) Assuming no growth in dividends, using the dividend valuation model,

k_{eu} = Dividend / V_E = 450,000 / 3,000,000 = 15%

(c) **Cost of debt for Y Co** (assuming debt is irredeemable)

k_d = Interest / V_D = 72,000 / 900,000 = 8%

Cost of equity for Y Co:

Using M & M's formula:

$k_{eg} = k_{eu} + (k_{eu} – k_d) V_D(1 - t) / V_E$

k_{eg} = 15% + (15%–8%)×0.9/2.1 = 18%

(Alternatively, using the dividend valuation model,

k_{eg} = Dividend / V_E = 378,000 / 2,100,000 = 18%)

As shown on the graphs, the geared company has a higher cost of equity.

(d) Weighted average cost of capital:

WACC = (18% × 2.1 / 3) + (8% × 0.9 /3) = 15%

Again, notice that this corresponds to the graphs seen above. In the no tax case, the WACC is constant irrespective of capital structure.

Example 2 – M & M with tax

(a) $V_g = V_u + TB$

so given that T = 0.33,

V_g = 3,000,000 + (33% × 900,000) = $3,297,000

so the value of the equity = 3,297,000 – 900,000 (value of debt) = $2,397,000

(b) Assuming no growth in dividends, using the dividend valuation model,

k_{eu} = Dividend / V_E = 450,000 / 3,000,000 = 15%

(c) **Cost of debt for Y Co** (assuming debt is irredeemable)

k_d = Interest / V_D = 72,000 / 900,000 = 8%

Cost of equity for Y Co:

Using M & M's formula:

$k_{eg} = k_{eu} + (k_{eu} - k_d)\, V_D(1 - t) / V_E$

k_{eg} = 15% + (15%–8%)×900,000×(1 – 0.33)/2,397,000 = 16.76%

As shown on the graphs, the geared company has a higher cost of equity.

(d) Weighted average cost of capital:

WACC = (16.76% × 2,397 / 3,297) + (8% × (1 – 0.33) 900 /3,297) = 13.65%

Alternatively, using M & M's formula:

$k_{adj} = k_{eu}(1 - tL)$ = 15% (1 - 33% × 900 / 3,297) = 13.65%

Again, notice that this corresponds to the graphs seen above. In the with tax case, the WACC reduces as the level of debt in the capital structure increases.

Example 3

Method 1:

Step 1

XYZ's asset beta is calculated and then used as an estimate of the project's asset beta (because the project and XYZ are in the same area of business and so will have the same *asset* beta).

Using: $ßu = ßg \times \frac{E}{E + D(1 - t)}$

$ßu = 1.25 \times \frac{2}{2 + 1(1 - 0.30)} = 0.926$

Step 2

An equity beta for the project is calculated next. As we know, an equity beta reflects both systematic business risk *and* systematic financial risk. The project's equity beta will reflect the project's business risk and the financial risk of ABC – the company that is to undertake the project.

Using: $ßu = ßg \times \frac{E}{E + D(1 - t)}$

$0.926 = ßg \times \frac{3}{3 + 1 \times (1 - 0.30)}$

$0.926 = ßg \times 0.811$

$\frac{0.926}{0.811} = ßg = 1.14$

Step 3

This equity beta is then input into CAPM to give a cost of equity capital for the project (the return required on the shareholders' funds invested by ABC in the telecoms project) using:

$k_e = R_F + [R_M - R_F]\,ßg$

$Ke_{PROJECT} = 6\% + [14\% - 6\%] \times 1.14 = 15.12\%$

Step 4

ABC's WACC is now calculated but, instead of using ABC's k_e, we use the *project's* k_e so as to give a risk-adjusted WACC.

However, before we can do this calculation, we need to identify ABC's after-tax cost of debt capital. In many questions this information is given, but here it is not.

If you need a cost of debt in order to answer a question, but are not given one, then you can make use of the fact that we are allowed to assume 'corporate debt is risk-free'. In these circumstances:

$$k_d = R_F$$

$$\text{and } kd(1 - t) = R_F (1 - T)$$

Therefore: kd(1 – t) = 6% (1 – 0.3) = 4.2%

Hence the risk-adjusted WACC can be calculated using:

$$k_0 = k_e \times \frac{E}{V} + kd(1\text{-}t) \times \frac{D}{V} = 15.12\% \times \frac{3}{4} + 4.2\% \times \frac{1}{4} = 12.4\%$$

Alternatively: Method 2:

Step 1

As above, the existing geared / equity beta of XYZ is degeared, to give an ungeared / asset beta of 0.926.

Step 2

Input this ungeared beta into the CAPM formula to give an ungeared cost of equity (k_{eu})

k_{eu}= 6% + [14% – 6%] × 0.926 = 13.4%

Step 3

Use the M & M WACC formula to find the risk adjusted WACC

$k_{adj} = k_{eu} (1 - tL)$

=13.4% (1 – 30% × (1/4)) = 12.4% as before.

Test your understanding 1 – M & M's formulae

(a) Assuming that all earnings are paid out as dividends, the current cost of equity (and overall cost of capital) is total earnings divided by the market value of the company's shares:

	£000
Earnings before finance charges and tax	2,500
Taxation	825
Earnings = dividends	1,675

The market value of equity is two million shares × 420 pence per share = £8.4 million.

$$K_e = \frac{£1,675,000}{£8,400,000} = 19.94\%$$

If equity is replaced by debt the value of the company will increase.

V geared = V ungeared + TB (tax rate x amount of debt)

With £2 million debt

V geared = 8,400 + (2,000 × 0.33) = 9,060.

	£000
Total value of the company	9,060
Market value of debt	2,000
Value of equity	7,060

With £4 million debt

V geared = 8,400 + (4,000 × 0.33) = 9,720

	£000
Total value of the company	9,720
Market value of debt	4,000
Value of equity	5,720

Cost of equity	£2 million debt	£4 million debt
	£000	£000
Earnings before f.charges and tax	2,500	2,500
Finance charges	200	400
		2,100
Taxation (33%)		693
Earnings/dividends	1,541	1,407
Cost of equity Ke =	1,541/7,060 = 21.83%	1,407/5,720 =24.60%

WACC

£2 million debt:

$$WACC = 21.83 \times \frac{7,060}{9,060} + 10\,(1 - 0.33)\frac{2,000}{9,060} = 18.49\%$$

£4 million debt:

$$WACC = 24.60 \times \frac{5,720}{9,720} + 10\,(1 - 0.33)\frac{4,000}{9,720} = 17.23\%$$

Alternative method of calculation

Or alternatively using $WACC = K_{eu}\left(1 - \frac{Dt}{E + D}\right)$

£2 million debt:

$$\text{WACC} = 19.94\left(1 - \frac{2{,}000 \times 0.33}{7{,}060 + 2{,}000}\right) = 18.49\%$$

£4 million debt:

$$\text{WACC} = 19.94\left(1 - \frac{4{,}000 \times 0.33}{5{,}720 + 4{,}000}\right) = 17.23\%$$

The higher the level of gearing, the lower the cost of capital becomes, due to the benefit from tax relief on finance charges.

(b) As debt is introduced into the capital structure it is likely that the cost of capital will initially fall. However, the estimates produced in (a) may not be accurate because:

(i) They rely on the assumptions of the Modigliani and Miller (M & M) model, many of which are unrealistic such as the capital market is perfectly efficient, debt is risk free, information is costless and readily available, there are no transaction costs, investors are rational and make the same forecasts about the performance of companies, and investors and companies can borrow at the risk-free rate.

(ii) Only corporate taxation is considered and not the impact of other forms of taxation including personal taxation.

(iii) M & M assumed that debt is permanent.

(iv) The estimates ignore possible costs that might be incurred as gearing increases, which would reduce share price and increase the cost of equity (and possibly debt). These include bankruptcy costs, agency costs and tax exhaustion.

(v) Inaccuracies exist in the measurement of the data required for the model.

Test your understanding 2 – WACC and M & M's formulae

(a) **Cost of equity**

All available earnings are distributed as dividends and earnings are expected to remain constant.

$$\therefore Ke = \frac{D}{Ve}\text{, where D is the annual dividend}$$

V_e is the ex dividend market value of equity

V_e = (Cum div share price – interim dividend) number of shares

= (0.86 – 0.06) × (12,500,000 ÷ 0.25)

= GBP40 million

The dividends may be calculated as follows:

	GBP000
Earnings before finance charges and tax	15,000
Debenture interest (GBP23,697,000 16%)	(3,792)
	11,208
Tax @ 35%	(3,923)
	7,285

$$K_e = \frac{7,285}{40,000} \equiv 18.2\%$$

Cost of debt

The cost of debt is equivalent to the internal rate of return of the following cash flows:

31 Dec 20X1	Market value ex int	(105.50)
31 Dec 20X1 – X4	Finance charge less tax	16 × 0.65 = 10.40
31 Dec 20X4	Redemption value	100.

The net present values are calculated using discount rates of 8% and 10% as follows:

			At 8%		At 10%
t_0	(105.50)	(105.50) × 1 =	(105.50)	(105.50) × 1 =	(105.50)
t_{1-3}	10.40	10.40 × 2.577 =	26.80	10.40 × 2.487 =	25.86
t_3	100	100 × 0.794 =	79.40	100 × 0.751 =	75.10
			0.70		(4.54)

The internal rate of return is given by:

$$8\% + \frac{0.70}{0.70 + 4.54} \times 2\% = 8.2\%$$

$$\therefore Kd \approx 8.2\%$$

Cost of capital

The market value of equity = GBP40m from above.

The market value of debt = GBP23.697m × 1.055 = GBP25m.

The weighted average cost of capital is therefore given by:

$$WACC = K_e \times \frac{40}{65} + K_d \times \frac{25}{65}$$

$$= 18.2\% \times \frac{40}{65} + 8.2\% \times \frac{25}{65} = 14.4\%$$

(b)

(i) **Market value**

Modigliani and Miller's hypothesis including the effects of corporation tax suggests that:

$$V_g = V_u + TB$$

Where V_g is the value of the geared company

V_u is the value of an equivalent ungeared company

B is the market value of debt

T is the rate of corporation tax

In the case of Canalot:

V_u = GBP32.5 million

B = GBP5 million

T= 35%

$\therefore V_g$ = 32.5m + 5m x 35% = GBP34.25m

The original value was GBP32.5 million.

This therefore represents an increase of GBP1.75 million.

(ii) **Cost of equity**

Modigliani and Miller propose the following formula for calculating the cost of equity of a geared company:

$$K_{eg} = K_{eu} + (K_{eu} - K_d) \times \frac{V_d}{V_e} \times (l - t)$$

where K_{eg} is the cost of equity of the geared company

K_{eu} is the cost of equity of an equivalent ungeared company

K_d is the cost of debt before tax

V_d is the market value of debt

V_e is the market value of equity

t is the rate of corporation tax

K_{eu} = 18% (given)

K_d = 13%

V_d = 5m

$V_e = V_g - D$ = 34.25m - 5m = 29.25m

$$\therefore Ke = 18\% + (18\% - 13\%)\ \frac{5}{29.25} \times (1 - 0.35)$$

= 18.56%.

The cost of equity has increased by 0.56%, reflecting the increase in financial risk as a result of gearing.

(iii) **Cost of capital**

Using Modigliani and Miller's formula:

$$WACC = K_{eu}\left[1 - \frac{Dt}{D + Ve}\right]$$

$$= 18\%\ \left[1 - \frac{5 \times 0.35}{34.25}\right]$$

$$= 17.08\%$$

Alternatively the traditional weighted average cost of capital formula may be used, i.e.

$$WACC = 18.56\% \times \frac{29.25}{34.25} + 13\%(1 - 0.35) \times \frac{5}{34.25}$$

= 17.08%

The previous WACC was equal to K_{eu}, i.e. 18%. It has therefore decreased by 0.92%, reflecting the tax benefits of increased gearing.

(c) The traditional view of capital structure theory is intuitive only; it is not based on any empirical evidence or computation and therein lies its major weakness.

It argues that there exists an optimal capital structure where the overall cost of capital is minimised and thus the company value is maximised. This is based on the following propositions:

- as gearing increases the cost of equity rises due to the increase in financial risk, but this is outweighed by the lower cost of debt and so the overall cost of capital decreases;
- as gearing continues to increase the cost of equity rises more sharply, such that this effect is greater than the effect of the lower cost of debt and the cost of capital rises;
- therefore there exists a minimum optimal cost of capital.

The theory is useful in as much as it highlights the fact that financing and capital structure may affect a company's value but it gives no suggestion as to where that optimal level lies.

Modigliani and Miller's theory, however, was initially based on empirical evidence and followed by quantification. Their hypothesis which includes the effects of corporate taxes (an adjustment to their original model) suggests that the optimal capital structure comprises 99.9% debt. Since this policy is not adopted by companies there must be certain flaws in this theory, the most important of which was later corrected by Miller himself, i.e. the effect of personal taxes.

Other common criticisms of the model include the following:

- the use of unrealistic assumptions, for instance:
  - there are no transaction costs;
  - information is freely available;
  - individuals can borrow on the same terms as companies;
  - individuals are prepared to exchange personal gearing for corporate gearing;
- costs associated with high levels of gearing are not considered. These may include the following:

(1) **Bankruptcy costs**

As gearing reaches high levels the probability of bankruptcy increases and if bankruptcy occurs there will be associated costs. These include the liquidation fees and the loss on the disposal of assets in a forced sales situation.

(2) **Tax exhaustion**

The benefit derived from increasing the level of gearing relates to the tax relief obtained by companies on returns paid to debt, i.e. interest. However, at very high levels of gearing there is the possibility that the company will not have sufficient taxable profits from which to deduct the debt interest. In this situation the advantage of gearing up will be lost.

(3) **Agency costs**

These relate to constraints imposed on the company by providers of finance through restrictive covenants contained within terms of agreement. Such constraints are aimed to protect the interest of (primarily) the debt holders when a company finds itself in a potentially difficult situation close to bankruptcy.

As a result of the above and the effect of personal taxes, it is clear that benefits related to increased gearing do not continue indefinitely. The final position is not well defined, but it may be possible that there exists a point where the cost of capital is minimised before the additional costs of high gearing outweigh the benefits. Thus, if managers are able to quantify such costs and benefits, this adapted theory may be of use to them in identifying an appropriate level of gearing to adopt.

Test your understanding 3 – Comparison of financing options

(a)

(i)

	Rights issue	Bonds
MV equity		
Extra dividends	300,000 × 67%	(300,000 – 120,000) × 67%
	= 201,000	= 120,600
PV at 18%	$\frac{201,000}{0.18}$	$\frac{120,000}{0.18}$
	= $1,116,667	= $670,000

The market value of equity will rise by $1.117m under the rights issue financing option (yielding a net gain to shareholders of $0.117m after the rights price of $1m) and by $0.67m under the bonds option (which is also their gain).

(ii) Debt: debt + equity ratio

Current MV equity = 2m × 1.68 = $3.36m

	Rights issue	Bonds
Market values after expansion ($m)		
Equity	3.36 + 1.117 = 4.477	3.36 + 0.67 = 4.03
10% secured debentures	1000	1.00
12% unsecured bonds	–	1.00
	5.477	6.03
Debt: debt + equity ratio	1: 5.477 (18.3%)	2 : 6.03 (33.2%)

(iii) WACC

	Rights issue			Bonds		
	MV ($m)	*Cost (%)*	*WACC (%)*	*MV ($m)*	*Cost (%)*	*WACC (%)*
Equity	4.477	18	14.71	4.03	18	12.03
10% secured	1.000	6.7	1.22	1.00	6.7	1.11
12% unsecured bonds	–			1.00	8.04	1.33
	5.477		15.93	6.03		14.47

The WACC will be 15.93% under the rights issue option and 14.47% under the bonds option.

(b)

Report

To: Board of Directors, RH Co

From: Financial manager

Date: XX/XX/XX

Re: Finance options for expansion project

The company wishes to raise $1m to fund our proposed expansion. This report initially assesses the two methods of finance currently being considered - a rights issue or issue of unsecured bonds. I will then outline non-financial factors that I believe you should consider before making the final decision.

Evaluation of the two methods of finance

I have assessed the two proposed methods on the basis of their impact on the market value of equity, the gearing level and the WACC.

The results of my computations are as follows:

	Current	*With project and* rights issue	*With project* and bonds
MV equity ($m)	3.36	4.477	4.03
representing			
an increase of		1.117	0.67
a gain to shareholders of		0.117	0.67
Gearing			
(debt:debt + equity)	1:4.36	1:5.477	2:6.03
	(22.9%)	(18.3%)	(33.2%)
WACC	15.41%	15.93%	14.47%

On the basis of these figures, to give maximum gain to our shareholders, the bonds option should be chosen. This will also raise our gearing level and lower our WACC.

However, it should be noted that the impact of changes in gearing on the cost of equity has been ignored in this analysis. It is likely that an approximate 50% rise in gearing (from 22.9% to 33.2%) under the bonds option will lead to an increase in the cost of equity above the current 18%, to compensate for the additional risk borne by the shareholders.

This will have the effect of lowering the value placed on the additional dividends by shareholders (thus reducing their gain) and limiting the fall in WACC (although, with tax relief on debt interest, this is still likely to be below the current cost).

Other considerations

First, alternative methods of finance that may be considered, (particularly as it is to fund working capital), include a bank overdraft, a medium-term loan or invoice discounting.

Other non-financial factors:

- whether the issue of bonds now will limit the availability of such finance in the future, when this longer term form of finance may be more appropriate;
- whether the rights issue is likely to be successful in the current market climate. If the company has a small number of shareholders, it may be possible to talk to them directly;

– whether the rights issue will be regarded as a positive move by the market or whether it might signal financial difficulties - this can be pre-empted by ensuring shareholders are made fully aware of the reasons for the additional finance being needed;

– the extent to which you feel you can rely on the cash flow estimates built into the appraisal.

Test your understanding 4 – WACC and risk adjusted WACC

Key answer tips

Note in part (b) that a major diversification into a new industry is likely to involve a different level of systematic risk from that of the company's existing investment portfolio. In these circumstances a project specific discount rate should be estimated, and the company's weighted average cost of capital is not appropriate. The project specific discount rate will need to reflect both the systematic risk of operating cash flows and the financial gearing of the company as a whole.

(a)

(i) **Dividend valuation model**

If we assume a constant growth in dividends, we may estimate the cost of equity by using:

$$Ke = \frac{D1}{P0} + g$$

As $$Do = \frac{2{,}140{,}000}{10{,}000{,}000 \text{ shares}}$$

$$= 21.4 \text{ cents}$$

then $$D1 = 21.4(1.11)$$

$$= 23.75 \text{ cents}$$

hence $$Ke = \frac{23.75}{321} + 0.11$$

$$= 0.184 \text{ or } 18.4\%$$

Cost of debt (Kd), as corporate debt is assumed to be risk free, is 12%, the Treasury bill yield.

The after-tax cost is 12(1 – 0.35) = 7.8%

The weighted average cost of capital (WACC) is the Cost of debt after tax × Proportion of debt financing + Cost of equity × Proportion of equity financing.

WACC	=	7.8% × 1/3 + 18.4% × 2/3
	=	14.87%

(ii) **Capital asset pricing model**

Cost of equity may be estimated using E(re) = rf + (E(rm) – rf) ße

E(re)	=	12% + (16% – 12%)1.4
	=	17.6%
Kd	=	7.8% as in part (i)
WACC	=	7.8% × 1/3 + 17.6% × 2/3
	=	14.33%

If the stock market is in equilibrium, and the inputs into the models are correctly specified (e.g. the dividend valuation model reflects only systematic risk), then the cost of equity Ke from the dividend valuation model should approximately equal the expected return on equity E(re) of the CAPM.

(b) **Report on the discount rate to be used in the appraisal of a major diversification into a new industry**

A pragmatic, although not completely accurate, way of identifying the systematic risk of operating cash flows is to use the published equity beta coefficients of other companies within the industry. These equity betas are considered to reflect the systematic risk of our company's major investment in the industry. However, if the average gearing level of the companies in the industry differs from our company's gearing, the beta coefficient will need to be adjusted to reflect the gearing level (financial risk) of our company.

The ß equity of the industry is 1.50.

Using $\text{ß asset} = \text{ß equity} \frac{E}{E + D(1 - t)} + \text{ßdebt} \frac{D(1 - t)}{E + D(1 - t)}$

As ß debt is 0.

$$\text{ß asset} = 1.50 \times \frac{3}{3 + 1(1 - 0.35)} + 0$$

ß asset (= ß equity for an ungeared project) = 1.233

Adjustment for the company's gearing level may be achieved by 're-gearing' the ß asset.

$$\beta \text{ geared} = 1.233 \times \frac{2.65}{2} \left(\frac{E + D(1-t)}{E} \right) = 1.634$$

$$\text{Project E(r equity)} = 12 + (16 - 12)1.634$$

$$= 18.54\%$$

Project weighted average cost of capital is $7.8\% \times \frac{1}{3} + 18.54\% \times \frac{2}{3} = 14.96\%$

14.96% or approximately 15% is the suggested discount rate for the project. This discount rate must only be regarded as a rough approximation.

(c) **Practical problems of the CAPM**

(i) The CAPM is an ex-ante model. It is difficult, if not impossible, to forecast accurate future returns of the company, project, or the market. For practical purposes ex-post data is normally used in the CAPM.

(ii) Even if the use of ex-post data is considered to be acceptable, it is difficult to estimate the appropriate data inputs.

Rf What is the appropriate risk-free rate? A short-term government bill? A long-term government stock?

Rm What is the market return? Do returns on companies comprising the FTSE All Share Index (or similar) provide a satisfactory estimate of returns on the market as a whole?

beta The use of an historical beta assumes that future risk is the same as past risk. Evidence for individual companies suggests that this is not the case.

Over what period should historic data be considered? How frequently should returns be calculated?

There is considerable subjectivity involved in the ex-post calculation of ß

(iii) CAPM only considers systematic risk. This may not be satisfactory to the management of a company that is not fully diversified.

(iv) CAPM is a one-period model, investment appraisal is multi-period. Attempts have, however, been made to produce multi-period extensions of the basic CAPM.

(v) CAPM considers only the level of return, not how the return is received by the providers of finance, and the significance to shareholders of whether return is in the form of dividends, interest or capital gains.

chapter

8

The Role of Treasury

Chapter learning objectives

Lead	Component
B2: Discuss the treasury function.	(a) discuss the role and management of the treasury function.

Indicative syllabus content

- The role of the treasury function in terms of setting corporate objectives, liquidity management, funding management, and currency management.
- The advantages and disadvantages of establishing treasury departments as profit centres or cost centres, and their control.

1 Overview of Chapter

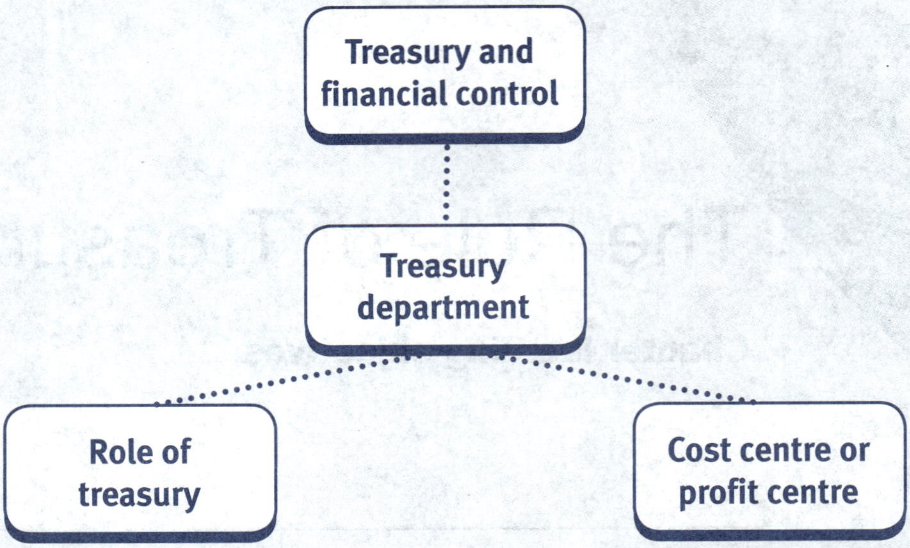

Many businesses have a separate treasury function within the finance department.

Developments in technology, the breakdown of exchange controls, increasing volatility in interest rates and exchange rates, combined with the increasing globalisation of business have all contributed to greater opportunities and risks for entities. To survive in today's complex financial environment, entities need to be able to actively manage both their ability to undertake these opportunities, and their exposure to risks.

A separate treasury function is more likely to develop the appropriate skills, and it should also be easier to achieve economies of scale; for instance in achieving lower borrowing rates, or netting-off balances.

Introduction to treasury

The website of the Association of Corporate Treasurers (ACT) gives the following introduction to treasury:

> Treasury in a company is key in determining the firm's financial strategy and financial policy – advising on what businesses to invest in, organising the appropriate funding for this, and controlling the risk in the organisation.

Dependent on the risk environment, treasury will create an appropriate capital structure of debt and equity in order to fund the business, getting the optimum balance between cost and risk. This translates into the need to ensure that at all times the company has the liquidity and cash to meet its obligations as they fall due, taking in funding from equity or debt capital markets activities, bank borrowings, through to day-to-day cash management and investment.

Treasury is responsible for the identification of risks associated with this activity and for controlling risks that could erode financial strength, using mitigation and hedging techniques and encouraging a culture of sound financial practice.

In essence treasury management is all about handling the banking requirements, the funding for the business and managing financial risk. It therefore incorporates raising and managing money, currency, commodity and interest rate risk management and dealing, and, in some organisations, the related areas of insurance, pensions, property and taxation.

NEW

2 Treasury and financial control

In a large entity the finance function may be split between treasury and financial control, with both functions reporting to the chief financial officer.

The financial control function will be concerned primarily with the allocation and effective use of resources, and will have responsibility for investment decisions.

The treasury function is usually responsible for obtaining finance and managing relations with the financial stakeholders of the entity who will include shareholders and lenders.

Close liaison is often required between financial control and treasury, for example:

- In investment appraisal decisions, the treasurer is best able to assess the cost of capital and quantify the entity's aversion to risk, while the financial controller relates these factors to group strategy;
- When managing currency risks, the financial controller will play an important role in identifying the entity's currency risks, while the treasurer advises on the best means to hedge the risk.

In larger entities, treasury will usually be centralised at head office, providing a service to all the various units of the entity and thereby achieving more effective control over financial risks and also achieving economies of scale (for example, by obtaining better borrowing rates).

Financial control is frequently delegated to individual units, where it can more closely impact on customers and suppliers and relate more specifically to the competition that those units have to face.

As a result, treasury and financial control may often tend to be separated by location as well as by responsibilities.

e.g

Illustration 1 – roles of treasury and financial control

When an entity is considering investing in a new project, the roles of treasury and financial control will include the following:

Treasury

- Advising on interest, currency and credit risks arising on the project;
- Agreeing a suitable discount factor for the NPV calculations;
- Liaising with lenders, arranging new debt or equity finance.

Financial control

- Collecting information on costs and revenues;
- Project appraisal using NPV and other methods;
- Reviewing project implementation and investigating variances;
- Negotiating contracts.

Although the two departments work in very different areas, it will be very important for them to liaise with each other.

3 The role of the treasury function

The Association of Corporate Treasurers (ACT) identifies the following five core roles of the treasury function:

- Capital markets and funding
- Cash and liquidity management
- Corporate financial management
- Risk management
- Treasury operations and controls

The treasurer's responsibilities can also be categorised according to the three levels of management:

- Strategic, for example matters concerning the capital structure of the entity and distribution/retention policies, the actual raising of capital, including share issues, corporate finance decisions such as mergers and acquisitions and investment projects, the assessment of the likely return from each source and the appropriate proportions of funds from each source, the decision as to the level of dividends, and consideration of alternative forms of finance.
- Tactical, for example the management of cash/investments and decisions as to the hedging of currency or interest rate risk.
- Operational, for example the transmission of cash, placing of 'surplus' cash and other dealings with banks.

Details on the role of the treasury function

Capital markets and funding

Capital markets and funding covers all the different techniques and sources for raising funding to finance the business, from bank debt to equity finance.

There are choices to be made between the different forms of borrowing, their structures, terms and conditions and relative costs.

The relationships with lenders and investors will need to be built and the borrower's business and risk characteristics explained to credit analysts and credit rating agencies.

Cash and liquidity management

Cash and liquidity management is about forecasting the company's cash needs to run its businesses and then managing the group wide cashflows, short-term borrowings and cash in the most efficient manner to ensure that those cash needs can be met.

With the help of IT and communications systems, cash can be pooled internationally and used to best advantage.

Funding and liquidity needs are intimately connected with understanding and managing working capital and the payments and cash reporting systems to best advantage.

Corporate financial management

Corporate financial management looks at the organisation's business strategy and financial strategy and seeks to determine the optimum solution to mesh the two together.

It answers the fundamental questions as to what assets the business should invest in – including major projects, acquisitions, mergers and divestments – and what capital structure should be put in place to raise the money to make the investments.

Risk management

Risk management is about understanding what business and financial risks the company is exposed to and considering whether the returns generated are sufficient to justify taking those risks.

The risks need to be evaluated and assessed so that decisions can be made on whether to retain them, or to employ techniques to mitigate or transfer risk.

The underlying risks can be managed to limit risk, they can be hedged with counterbalancing exposures, often created through the financial markets, or insurance taken out to protect the company's financial health.

Risks that are of particular interest to treasury include:

- Currency risk
- Interest risk
- Credit risk
- Liquidity risk
- Pensions risk

Treasury operations and controls

Treasury operations and controls looks at the running of a treasury function, taking in its overall policies, the procedures, staffing, systems and controls, and the relationships with parties within and outside the group.

Specific skills required

Treasurers require specialist skills to be able to handle effectively an ever growing range of capital instruments, for example convertible preference shares issued in the name of an offshore subsidiary, and to determine the most suitable way to protect their entity from foreign exchange risk, which demands a good knowledge of forward markets and an ability to select the most appropriate methods of hedging and foreign exchange cover.

They also need a knowledge of taxation in all areas in which the entity operates and, deriving from that, the ability to advise effectively on policies such as transfer pricing in permissible ways to minimise overall tax liability, and to be able to liaise competently with the entity's taxation department.

The capacity to make large gains or losses is enormous: a treasurer can wipe out, in a few hours, all the profit made from making and selling things over several months. It is important, therefore, that authority and responsibility associated with the treasury function are carefully defined and monitored. This becomes even more important as the range of derivatives increases. Senior managers need to be aware of which risks are being carried, which laid off, and, where appropriate, taken on.

4 Advantages of a specialised central treasury function

Establishing the treasury function as a centralised service at head office has the following advantages:

- Control of cash will be recognised as a separate and significant activity, concentrating on the most efficient use of this resource.
- Central funding arrangement provides greater control to ensure that adequate funding is in place and that debt covenants are monitored and standardised as far as possible. It also allows for economies of scale.
- Central risk management is clearly advantageous in improving visibility and control of corporate-wide risk. It also allows netting of risks and economies of scale to obtain finer pricing on external hedge transactions.
- As a specialist user, treasury can ensure that information technology software is made available to meet the specific needs of cash and currency management.
- Corporate planning staff will be aided by expert advice and quick feedback from specialists in such matters as interest rates and currency movements.
- Marketing management will be given a competitive edge by specialist expertise and speed of response in making important cash based decisions.

5 Cost centre or profit centre

The contribution made by treasury to company performance and risk management is difficult to quantify and will not be accurately reflected in the accounting profit figure.

The treasury centre will not usually be set up as a separate profit centre unless it acts as an 'in-house' bank, a set-up that is only appropriate for the very largest of multi-national groups.

Some revenue will be achieved from, for example, the difference between rates charged to subsidiaries and paid on external deals or on transaction costs and bank margins saved by netting off equal and opposite positions in different areas of the business.

However, the primary focus of treasury is in providing liquidity and managing risk rather than generating profit.

The treasury is primarily a service centre for the subsidiary companies, providing finance etc at reasonable rates and investing surplus cash and arranging external hedge cover on their behalf.

e.g

Illustration 2

Treasury management in the real world:

The annual report of J Sainsbury for 2010 states:

"Financial strategy and treasury risk

The main financial risks are the availability of short- and long-term funding to meet business' needs, and fluctuations in interest and foreign currency rates, which continue to be impacted by the turbulence in the financial markets.

The central treasury function is responsible for managing the Group's liquid resources, funding requirements, and interest rate and currency exposures and the associated risks .... Additional funding was secured through a capital raise in the summer of 2009 to support the business' space expansion plans. The treasury function has clear policies and operating procedures which are regularly reviewed and audited."

6 Exam style questions

Test your understanding 1 – Objectives and role of treasury

HG is a privately-owned toy manufacturer based in a country in the European Union, but which is not in euroland (the countries who have adoped the euro as their currency). It trades internationally, both, as a supplier and a customer. Although HG is privately owned, it has revenue and assets equivalent in amount to some public listed companies. It has a large number of shareholders, but has no intention of seeking a listing at the present time. In fact, the major shareholders have often expressed a wish to buy out some of the smaller investors.

The entity has a long history of sound, if unspectacular, profitability. The directors and shareholders are reasonably happy with this situation and are averse to adopting strategies that they think might involve a substantial increase in risk, for example acquisition or setting up manufacturing capability overseas, as some of HG's European competitors have done. As a consequence, HG accepts its growth rate will be relatively low, compared with some of its competitors.

The entity is financed 70% equity and 30% debt (based on book values). The debt is a mixture of secured and unsecured bonds carrying interest rates of between 7% and 8.5% and repayable in 5 to 10 years' time. Inflation in HG's country is near zero and interest rates are low and possibly falling.

The Company Treasurer is investigating the opportunities for, and consequences of, re-financing.

HG's main financial objective is simply to increase dividends each year. It has one non-financial objective, which is to treat all stakeholders in the organisation with 'fairness and equality'. The Board has decided to review these objectives. The new Finance Director believes maximisation of shareholder wealth should be the sole objective, but the other directors do not agree and think a range of objectives should be considered, for example profits after tax and return on investment and performance improvement across a number of operational areas.

Required:

(a) **Evaluate the appropriateness of HG's current objectives and the Finance Director's suggestion, and discuss the issues that the HG Board should consider when determining the new corporate objectives. Conclude with a recommendation.**

(15 marks)

(b) **Discuss the factors that the treasury department should consider when determining financing, or re-financing strategies in the context of the economic environment described in the scenario and explain how these might impact on the determination of corporate objectives.**

(10 marks)

(Total 25 marks)

Test your understanding answers

Test your understanding 1 – Objectives and role of treasury

(a) **Evaluation**

Theory supports the Finance Director, suggesting that maximisation of shareholder wealth is the only true objective of the entity – now considered an extreme view – and one which may have contributed to some of the corporate scandals in recent years that have occasioned the increase in corporate governance requirements.

Many entities now establish objectives that aim to maximise shareholder wealth while recognising constraints, legally enforceable or voluntary, imposed by society.

A major problem with this objective in the circumstances of HG is that this is a private entity that does not have a quoted share price. Shareholder wealth, as traditionally valued, is difficult to determine.

Looking only at dividends as an objective has its limitations, for example dividends could increase while earnings fall. The dividend ratio therefore needs to be considered alongside dividend payout. Alternatives, such as those being considered by other directors, are therefore worth further consideration.

For example: profitability as measured by returns after tax and return on investment.

The main advantages are:

- Well understood measures and recognised guidelines are available in the form of International Accounting Standards.
- Shareholders expect profitability – and indeed the current objective is to increase earnings.

Disadvantages are:

- Accounting ratios are historic and backward-looking;
- They are subject to manipulation;
- A variety of accounting policies are available – even within Accounting Standards;
- Tax can be affected by factors outside the control of managers.

Recommendation

Maximisation of shareholder wealth, using the theoretical definition, is difficult to apply in the circumstances of HG. As a minimum, it would be worth introducing an objective that incorporates earnings growth as well as dividend growth.

A range of objectives could be considered, such as risk-related returns to investors, but again this is more difficult with a private entity than one with a share listing.

The entity needs to consult its shareholders and, possibly, consider using a balanced scorecard approach to determine a range of objectives appropriate for an entity such as HG.

(b) The scenario in this question concerns a large privately owned entity based in the EU, but not in euroland. It trades internationally, both as supplier and customer. Inflation is zero and interest rates are low and, possibly, falling. The treasury department needs to decide how to deal with the challenges and opportunities the specific set of circumstances provide and evaluate the impact on the entity's capital structure.

Finance theory suggests that entities should use a judicious amount of debt in their capital structure to lower cost of capital. Debt is cheaper than equity because interest payments attract tax relief and are (generally) cheaper than equity. This is because providers of debt do not participate in profits. Here we have a mixture of secured and unsecured debt, but the entity appears sound and of high credit worthiness and so should be able to borrow at comparatively favourable rates.

This might even be an argument in favour of increasing gearing which will provide the ability to pay a special dividend or undertake a share buyback, as seems to be the desire of the major shareholders.

The opposite argument is that in a period of low inflation, debt becomes a burden. Some of the reasons are as follows:

(i) The real value of debt is not being eroded when there is low or no inflation, so one of the benefits of debt disappears.

(ii) The equity risk premium will tend to be less in inflationary times, so equity is relatively less expensive. In addition, fixed rate debt may lead to lack of competitiveness if competitors can access debt at lower rates in an environment of falling interest rates. The company should also carefully consider what types of finance (e.g. bank or capital markets) and what currency profile (e.g. to match currency profile of foreign assets) might be appropriate.

(iii) Raising equity is safer if profits really dive; dividends do not have to be paid and the shareholders do not get their money back in a liquidation. However, raising new equity in a private entity is more difficult than in a public entity, where shares are listed so there is a ready benchmark for the price of new shares.

Floating rate debt overcomes some of these concerns, but if markets are efficient then the interest rate obtainable should reflect expectations.

In theory (according to M & M), the mix of debt and equity does not affect the value of the entity, other than the value of the tax shield, but it does have an effect on the attribution of profits to three groups of stakeholders: lenders, government (taxers) and owners (shareholders).

The main question is therefore what combination of dividend policy and capital structure is likely to maximise the present value of cash flows to shareholders. This is where the financing strategies adopted contribute to the achievement of the objectives of the entity.

The treasury department needs to specifically look at

- Terms of existing borrowing to see if re-financing at lower rates is feasible, recognising any possible penalties for early retirement of loans.
- Discuss with the directors and major shareholders the possibility (or even probability) that returns are likely to be lower; the lower the rate of interest, the lower the cost of capital and therefore the return that can be expected – not least because the rate sought by competitors will be lower.
- The different threats and opportunities that might be presented if HG's country joins the ECCA. For example, there is a larger market for sourcing funds, which may mean increased competition and therefore access to cheaper finance. On the downside, ECCA rates might increase if this country joins the ECCA and/or if other countries join from less-developed parts of the continent.

chapter

9

Investment Appraisal – basic techniques

Chapter learning objectives

Lead	Component
C1: Evaluate investment choices.	(a) analyse relevant costs, benefits and risks of an investment project. (b) evaluate investment projects, including their financial and strategic implications.

Indicative syllabus content

- Identification of a project's relevant costs (e.g. infrastructure, marketing and human resource development needs), benefits (including incremental effects on other activities as well as direct cash flows) and risks (i.e. financial and non-financial, including reputation risk arising from ethical considerations and risks of legal change or uncertainty).
- Calculation of a project's net present value and internal rate of return, including use of the weighted average cost of capital.
- The modified internal rate of return based on a project's "terminal value" (reflecting an assumed reinvestment rate).
- The effects of taxation and inflation.

1 Overview of Chapter

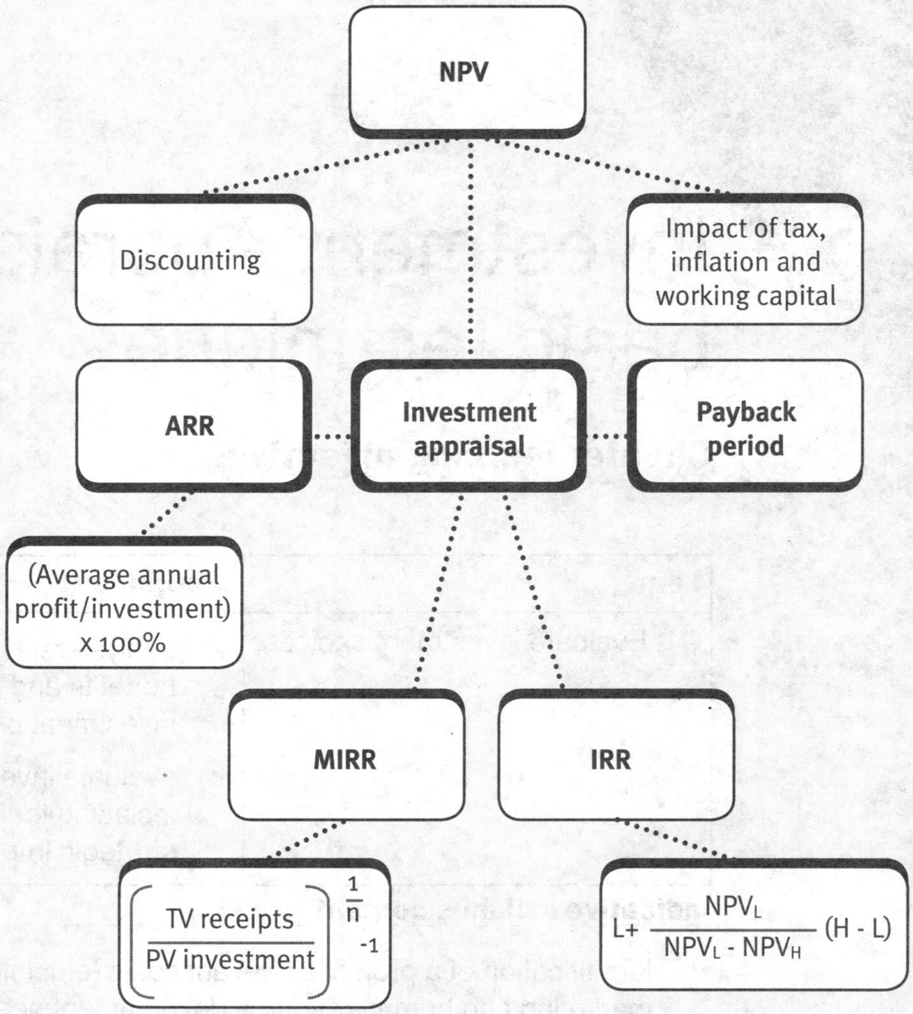

2 Investment Appraisal

The investment decision was identified in the earlier Chapter 'An Introduction to Financial Strategy' as one of the three key elements of financial strategy.

An entity will only be able to provide appropriate returns to investors if it can identify suitable projects which provide appropriate returns to the entity itself.

It is therefore critically important that the financial manager understands how to appraise different investments and decide whether they are acceptable to the firm.

An introduction to investment appraisal

In this Chapter, we discuss various methods of evaluating investment projects. These methods are, in the main, concerned with quantitative aspects, but first you need to be clear that methods of evaluation are by no means the only factors to be taken into account in investment appraisal.

Consideration of stakeholders

Thus, we might define investment appraisal as being concerned with maximising shareholder wealth, but we must be careful to qualify this concept by making it subject to constraints associated with issues of social responsibility, such as effective controls over pollution.

So, shareholders' wealth in this context needs to be linked with the wider view of stakeholder theory, whereby many other interested parties apart from shareholders – for example, suppliers, lenders, employees, managers, as well as the general public – need to be taken into account in assessing a project's viability.

Incidentally, in the case of 'not-for-profit' entities, we should follow a similar path, but by substituting maximising benefits in place of shareholders' wealth.

We must also be clear that maximising wealth is not the same as maximising profit from a project by minimising costs regardless of the wider implications of doing so. Shareholders will best be served by action being taken to ensure that a project will meet an economic want while maintaining a good and respected image of the entity, and indeed projects which damage that image can negate the benefits of otherwise effective marketing and promotional activities.

Investment appraisal data requirements

Clearly, then, qualitative aspects of a proposal are very important, and this leads us on to the data content needed to evaluate a project effectively.

Bear in mind that the cash inflows and outflows involved are simply the standard means of translating into a common base of numbers all the underlying quantitative and qualitative assumptions which are the real determinants of a project's viability. The management accountant needs to consider carefully the strengths and weaknesses of these assumptions before finally converting them to cash flows.

The investment appraisal methods

It is useful to use a number of different methods for evaluating a project, especially for a major project, as different methods may well throw valuable light on various and different aspects of a project's value, bearing in mind the strengths and limitations of each method, as set out throughout this Chapter.

This Chapter covers the five main investment appraisal methods:

- payback period
- accounting rate of return (ARR)
- net present value (NPV)
- internal rate of return
- modified internal rate of return (MIRR).

In the next Chapter, we shall explore the use of the methods in various specific circumstances.

The five investment appraisal methods

Payback period

The payback period measures the time taken for the net cash inflows from a project to equal its initial investment.

Given that future cashflows are often difficult to predict accurately, a project with a short payback period would be considered to be a low risk project.

The payback period should never be used as the sole investment appraisal method, since it ignores later cashflows which arise after the payback period. However, when used alongside other methods, it can provide useful information about the likely risk of a project and its liquidity.

Accounting rate of return (ARR)

The ARR is the only investment appraisal method in this Chapter which is based on profits rather than cashflows. Since profits are more subjective than cashflows, the ARR should not be used in isolation.

However, the concept of profit and its relationship to the amount of capital invested in a project is widely understood, and is closely related to performance measures such as Return on Capital Employed (covered in the earlier Chapter on 'Performance Measurement in Financial Strategy'). Therefore the ARR is often used to consider how a new project compares to the existing ROCE of a business.

Net present value (NPV)

In the NPV method, future cashflows are discounted to present value to recognise the time value of money. The sum of the discounted cashflows is the NPV.

The NPV method is theoretically the best method of investment appraisal, because it calculates the absolute gain (or loss) in wealth of the shareholders if a project is undertaken.

In the earlier Chapter 'Introduction to Financial Strategy' it was noted that the maximisation of shareholder wealth is the assumed objective of any company. Since NPV links directly to that objective, it is the primary investment appraisal method used in practice, and it is superior to the payback period and ARR explained above.

Internal rate of return (IRR)

The IRR is the discount rate at which a project has a zero NPV. In most cases, the IRR represents the highest cost of capital at which a project would be acceptable (because at lower costs of capital the project would have a positive NPV).

It is a useful investment appraisal method in circumstances where it is difficult to identify an appropriate cost of capital, and it is particularly useful as a follow up to the NPV method when performing sensitivity analysis (more details in the next Chapter).

Modified internal rate of return (MIRR)

The MIRR gives the percentage return from a project, on the assumption that any cash inflows can be reinvested at the entity's cost of capital.

As a percentage return figure, it is arguably easier to understand than the absolute figure given by an NPV analysis (in many other contexts the return from an investment is given as a percentage, so the concept of a percentage return is well understood).

The investment appraisal methods are separated below into basic methods and discounted cash flow methods.

3 Basic Investment Appraisal Methods

Payback period

Definition

This method involves calculating the period of time likely to recoup the initial outlay on a project, and then comparing this with the 'acceptable period'. If the payback period is less than 'acceptable', and there are no other constraints, for example capital rationing, the project will be accepted.

Also alternative projects can be ranked according to the length of expected payback period.

More details on payback period

Payback is a simple investment appraisal technique which involves determining how long will be needed before the initial investment is 'paid back'.

Unlike ARR (explained in detail below), which is bound by accounting definitions of 'profit' and 'investment', payback concentrates on the specific cash flows which an investment will generate. (In this respect, payback is superior to ARR because the management accounting theory of decision-making is based on whether the wealth of the decision-maker will be increased if a particular decision is made. The definitions and conventions of financial accounting should not be allowed to muddy the waters of this essentially simple problem.)

The well-documented drawbacks of the payback technique are based on the fact that future cash flows, in themselves, do not indicate increased wealth. This is because a money flow in the future is not worth as much as the same money flow now. (Cash available now can be invested and so is worth more than the same cash flow at a later date.)

Advantages and disadvantages of using payback period

The disadvantages of payback are:

- all cash flows within the payback period are given equal weight;
- cash flows outside the payback period are ignored;
- it is not easy to determine how long the payback period should be.

Although one might expect payback to be little used because of these disadvantages, in practice, it is used extensively. Its simplicity probably explains its popularity:

- decision-makers understand information presented to them;
- calculations are straightforward and likely to be error-free;
- since data in itself is unreliable (estimates of future cash flows), sophisticated analysis may not be justified.

Payback can also be recommended if the business requires liquid funds at some date in the future – a project which 'pays back' before this date would be preferable to one which needs to be funded for a longer period.

A further advantage is the 'risk aversion' of payback – early cash flows are given full value, and later cash flows are ignored.

Summary of strengths and limitations of payback period

The payback period is a very useful starting point in an investment appraisal, in that it is simple to understand and it can help to screen projects before more detailed analysis is performed.

For example, a project with a very long payback period might be perceived as too risky, so might be rejected before more time and money is spent on its evaluation.

The main problem with payback period is that it ignores any cashflows which arise after the payback period and therefore it does not relate to the primary financial objective of maximising shareholder wealth.

Accounting Rate of Return (ARR)

Definition

This is a method of estimating the rate of return from an investment without discounting or compounding. The investment inflows are totalled and the investment costs subtracted to derive the profit.

The profit is divided by the number of years invested (to establish the average annual profit), then by the average investment cost to establish an annual rate of return, e.g.

$$\frac{\text{Average annual profit}}{\text{Average investment}} \times 100$$

where average investment = the average book value of the capital employed in the project (i.e. the average of the initial investment and the residual value)

Note: in some cases, the initial investment will be used instead of average investment.

Explanation of the ARR formula

Accounting rate of return (ARR) is calculated in basically the same way as 'return on investment' as (Profit / Investment), but whether 'profit' is before or after interest charges and whether 'investment' is the initial outlay or is averaged over the life of the project is unclear.

This lack of clarity seems strange.

The point of this technique is that it is based on the same principles as the published financial statements. Entities (and managers) are often evaluated by the 'return on investment' or 'return on capital employed' ratio derived from the published income statement and balance sheet. (The two ratios are identical, merely reflecting the two sides of the balance sheet; 'capital employed' reflects the financing of the business, 'investment' reflects the use of that finance.) It is therefore logical that it should be calculated in a way which makes it comparable with these ratios. As the balance sheet contains written-down asset values one would expect ARR to be calculated as (Profit / Average written down investment).

This accords with common sense, because if profit is after depreciation, then one would expect that depreciation to affect the value of the investment.

Summary of the strengths and limitations of the ARR method

The ARR is the only one of the investment appraisal methods covered in this Chapter which focuses on profits rather than cashflows.

Consequently, it is affected by different accounting policies and assumptions, which make it a less useful measure than the cash based methods.

However, it is expressed in terms familiar to managers - profit and capital employed. This means that the ARR is a similar measure to the widely understood ROCE.

Example of payback period and ARR

Blake Co is considering investing in a project with a cost of $100,000.

Cash inflows from the project are expected to be as follows:

	$000
Year 1	20
Year 2	30
Year 3	40
Year 4	40
Year 5	10

Straight line depreciation will be charged on the capital expenditure, over the 5 year life of the project.

Required:

Calculate the payback period for the proposed investment, and the ARR (based on the average investment).

Solution:

Payback period:

The payback period is calculated by looking at the cumulative cash position at the end of each year, as follows:

	$000
Year 0	(100)
Year 1 – add $20,000	(80)
Year 2 – add $30,000	(50)
Year 3 – add $40,000	(10)
Year 4 – add $40,000	30

So the payback period is 4 years (if we assume that cashflows arise at the end of each year) or 3.25 years if we assume that cashflows accumulate evenly over the course of each year.

ARR:

Total cash inflow over the five years = $20,000 + $30,000 + $40,000 + $40,000 + $10,000

= $140,000

So total profit = $140,000 – (depreciation) $100,000 = $40,000

Hence average profit = $40,000 / 5 = $8,000

The average investment here is $50,000 – average of initial $100,000 and final (fully depreciated) $0.

Therefore ARR based on the average investment is $8,000 / $50,000 = 16%

Discounted payback period

One of the disadvantages of payback is its failure to take into account the time value of money, but this can be overcome by first discounting the cash flows to their present values and then using these discounted values to calculate the discounted payback period.

Note: Discounting has been covered earlier in the CIMA syllabus, but a reminder of the detailed method follows later in this Chapter.

Taking the cash flow data from the Example above, and using a discount rate of 10%, we can calculate the discounted payback period as follows:

Discounted payback period:

The discounted payback period is calculated by looking at the cumulative discounted cash position at the end of each year, as follows:

	$000
Year 0	(100)
Year 1 – add 20 × 0.909 = 18.2	(81.8)
Year 2 – add 30 × 0.826 = 24.8	(57.0)
Year 3 – add 40 × 0.751 = 30.0	(27.0)
Year 4 – add 40 × 0.683 = 27.3	0.3

So the payback period is just under 4 years.

Although this is an improvement over basic payback period, in that it takes account of the time value of money, the technique is also not suitable as a sole method of investment appraisal because it does not take into account all project cash flows.

4 Discounted Cash Flow (DCF) Investment Appraisal Methods

Basic revision of DCF methods

Compounding

To calculate the value of an amount X in n years time, with an annual interest rate of r, use the compounding formula:

$X \times (1+r)^n$

For example, an amount of $10 in 2 years with an interest rate of 10% will be worth

$\$10 \times 1.10^2 = \$12.10$

Discounting

Discounting is the opposite to compounding i.e. it allows us to calculate the equivalent "present value" of a given future amount. The formula is below, but most of the time the present value (PV) tables will be used.

$$PV = \frac{1}{(1+r)^n} = (1+r)^{-n}$$

where r is the discount rate for a single time period (normally a year) and n is the number of time periods in the discount period (usually the number of years before the cashflow occurs).

For example, an amount of $100 receivable in 6 years with an interest rate of 10% has a present value of $100 × 1.10^{-6} = $56.45.

Also, an amount of $100 receivable in 3 months' time at a quoted annual interest rate of 10%, or 2.5% paid every quarter (where 2.5% = 10% x 3/12), has a present value of $100/1.025 = $97.56.

Present value of cumulative flows (Annuity)

The formula is below, but most of the time the cumulative present value tables will be used.

$$PV = \frac{1-(1+r)^{-n}}{r} \quad \text{or} \quad \frac{1}{r}\left(1 - \frac{1}{(1+r)^n}\right)$$

where r is the discount rate for a single time period (normally a year), and n is the number of time periods of cash flows.

Notation: AF(1–n)(r%) =Annuity factor for n years at an annual interest rate of r %.

e.g

Illustration 1 – Annuities

The present value of GBP1,000 received next year and for the following 4 years if the annual interest rate is 10% is:

AF1-5(10%) = 3.791

PV = 3.791 × GBP1,000 = GBP3,791

Examination twist: The deferred annuity. This is where the first cash flow takes place not at time 1 but at a later date.

Consider a receipt of GBP1,000 each year for five years starting at time 3. The annual interest rate is 10%.

Since the receipt is for five years the five-year annuity factor is used. This gives the present value 1 year prior to the first receipt i.e. time 2. This is then discounted back to time 0.

3.791 × GBP1,000 × 0.826 = GBP3,131

Present value of a perpetuity

$$PV = \frac{1}{r}$$

Hence, the present value of $1,000 received every year from year 1 onwards if interest rates are 10% is $1,000 / 0.10 = $10,000.

Present value of a growing perpetuity

$$PV = \frac{1}{r-g}$$

where r is the annual interest rate and g is the estimated annual growth rate.

Hence, the present value of a perpetuity which will be $1,000 in 1 year and then will grow at 3% per annum thereafter is $1,000 / (0.10–0.03) = $14,286 (assuming that interest rates are 10%).

e.g

Illustration 2 – Complex perpetuities and annuities

Calculate the present value of the following cash flows in each of the specified circumstances:

Year	*Cash flow*
1	1,000
2	1,500
3	1,600
4	1,800

(1) the USD1,800 will arise annually each year from year 4, for the next ten years (last year – year 13).

(2) the USD1,800 will arise each year in perpetuity.

(3) the USD1,800 arises in perpetuity but grows at 2% per annum.

The annual cost of capital is 10%.

Answer

1

Year	*Cash flow*	*DF*	*PV*
1	1,000	0.909	909
2	1,500	0.826	1,239
3	1,600	0.751	1,202
4-13	1,800	7.103 – 2.487 or 6.145 × 0.751	8,309

Note: the annuity factors have been taken from the annuity tables which will be provided in the exam.

Total PV = USD11,659

2

Year	*Cash flow*	*DF*	*PV*
1	1,000	0.909	909
2	1,500	0.826	1,239
3	1,600	0.751	1,202
4- ∞	1,800	1/0.10 – 2.487 or 1/0.10 × 0.751	13,523

Total PV = USD16,873

3 Year	Cash flow	DF	PV
1	1,000	0.909	909
2	1,500	0.826	1,239
3	1,600	0.751	1,202
4- ∞	1,800	(1/(0.10-0.02)) × 0.751	16,898

Total PV = USD20,248

Net Present Value (NPV)

Definition

This is a method of determining whether the expected financial performance of a proposed investment promises to be adequate when measured against a cost of capital.

It is the most theoretically accurate method of investment appraisal.

The NPV of a proposed investment is calculated by discounting future cash flows to present value and summing (or netting) them together.

Identification of a project's relevant costs and benefits

A common difficulty experienced by students is how to choose which cash flows to include and which to exclude in the investment appraisal calculations.

Some of the main points to look out for are:

- Accounting adjustments such as depreciation do not represent cash outflows, as no physical movement of cash takes place. However, tax allowances do represent inflows as they reduce the amount of tax actually to be paid in cash.
- Cash inflows should be after-tax.
- Financing decisions can be analysed separately from operational project decisions, so financing charges should not be included as a cash flow in the investment appraisal.
- Any incidental effects of undertaking a project need to be included if they represent cash movements.

- Working capital movements need to be included (see examples later in this Chapter), but bear in mind that there will usually be a release of working capital (a terminal value) at the end of the project.
- Sunk costs, which have already been incurred, should be excluded as they do not involve a new cash movement created by the project.
- Opportunity cost could be defined as 'the value of a benefit sacrificed in favour of an alternative course of action'. For example, if by undertaking a project, we use some materials which would otherwise have been sold for $1,000, the $1,000 sale proceeds foregone would need to be recorded as a cost of the new project.
- Residual values for any assets utilised in the project should be included in the final year of the appraisal period. The residual value will reflect the remaining useful life in the asset or its disposal value. The residual value should be net of disposal costs.

In general terms, an item should be included in an NPV analysis if it represents a **future, incremental cashflow** which will arise as a consequence of the project being undertaken.

The meaning of NPV

A positive NPV indicates that expected return on a project more than compensates the investor for the perceived level of (systematic) risk i.e. that the expected return is greater than the required return.

The value of the NPV equals the gain (or loss) to shareholders if the project is undertaken.

Recommended format

Year	0	1	2	3	4	5
	$000	$000	$000	$000	$000	$000
Receipts		X	X	X	X	
Payments:						
Wages		(X)	(X)	(X)	(X)	
Materials		(X)	(X)	(X)	(X)	
Variable/Fixed overheads		(X)	(X)	(X)	(X)	
Administration/Distribution expenses		(X)	(X)	(X)	(X)	
Taxable cash flows		X	X	X	X	
Tax: Corporation tax			(X)	(X)	(X)	(X)
: Tax depn allowances			X	X	X	X
Initial outlay	(X)					
Net Realisable Value					**X**	
Working capital	(X)				X	
Net cash flows	(X)	X	X	X	X	(X)
Discount rate (e.g.10%)	1	0.909	0.826	0.751	0.683	0.621
Present value	(X)	X	X	X	X	(X)
Net Present Value (NPV)	**XXX**					

Strengths and limitations of the NPV method

Any project with a positive NPV increases the value of the company. The primary financial aim is to maximise the wealth of the ordinary shareholders, and selection of projects on an NPV basis is consistent with this objective.

The discount rate can be adjusted to take account of the different level of risk inherent in different projects. Alternatively, the technique can be combined with sensitivity analysis (see the next Chapter) to quantify the risk of the project's results being different from those expected.

The main limitation of the NPV method is that the result of an NPV analysis (an absolute figure) is not as easy to understand as the percentage return figures given by ARR, IRR and MIRR. This is particularly a problem for non-financially minded managers, who will normally be more happy with the concept of a percentage return.

The impact of taxation on the NPV analysis

There are three important tax effects to consider:

(a) tax payments on operating profits;

(b) tax benefit from tax depreciation allowances;

(c) tax relief on interest payments on debt.

Tax relief on interest payments on debt is taken into account by adjusting the discount rate.

Depreciation and tax depreciation allowances

Depreciation

The Financial Strategy syllabus is not specifically concerned with the accounting treatment or methods of depreciation.

Depreciation is not cash and the key point to remember is that if a question requiring a DCF calculation includes depreciation (or other non-cash items, including accruals and prepayments), these items have to be added back to profits or losses to arrive at operational cash flows.

Tax depreciation allowances

However, tax depreciation allowances do have an impact on the cash flows of a business.

The important point is that tax depreciation allowances themselves are not cash, but they affect the tax liability of an entity, which in turn affects tax payable or refundable. Tax depreciation allowances do therefore have an effect on cash flow.

Tax depreciation allowances are sometimes given in the form of first-year allowance followed by allowances at a lower rate in subsequent years.

'Capital allowances' is the term used in the United Kingdom for tax depreciation allowances. Most countries have similar schemes.

Assumptions

(a) Tax is normally assumed to be payable in the same year as, or one year after, the relevant cash flow. You will be told in a question which assumption to make.

(b) It is normally assumed that the company is generating sufficient taxable profits so as to be able to absorb all tax depreciation allowances in full at the earliest opportunity.

(c) Tax depreciation allowances

Two alternative assumptions are possible:

(i) the expenditure arises just before a company's year end. The first allowances can therefore be claimed immediately;

(ii) the expenditure arises at the beginning of a new accounting period. The first allowance will therefore be claimed at time 1.

Also, assume that in the year of disposal, a balancing allowance (BA) or balancing charge (BC) will arise, being the difference between the tax written down value and the sale proceeds.

e.g

Illustration 3 – Tax depreciation allowances

A company purchases a machine at the beginning of the year in order to undertake a new investment project.

The machine costs EUR30,000, it has a life of four years and a scrap value of EUR5,000 in year 4.

Tax depreciation allowances can be claimed on the machine on a reducing balance basis at 20% per annum. The tax rate is 30% and tax is payable in the same year as profits are generated.

Required:

Calculate the annual tax depreciation allowances, and the associated tax relief.

Solution:

Tax depreciation allowances

	WDV	*Benefit*
	30,000	
WDA Y1	(6,000) @ 30%	1,800 at T_1
	24,000	
WDA Y2	(4,800) @ 30%	1,440 at T_2
	19,200	
WDA Y3	(3,840) @ 30%	1,152 at T_3
	15,360	
Proceeds	(5,000)	
	10,360	
BA Y4	(10,360) @ 30%	3,108 at T_4
	Nil	

Example 1 – Taxation

A company purchases a machine at a cost of $100,000.

It has a life of four years and a scrap value of $20,000 in year 4.

Tax depreciation allowances can be claimed on the machine on a reducing balance basis at 25% per annum.

The machine will generate the following annual net income:

year 1 – $30,000
year 2 – $40,000
year 3 – $50,000
year 4 – $40,000

The cost of capital is 12% net of corporation tax at 33%, payable in arrears.

Required:

Evaluate whether the machine should be acquired.

The impact of inflation on the NPV analysis

There are two acceptable approaches to incorporating inflation into an NPV analysis:

(a) **The "real" method**

In this case ***cash flows are not inflated*** i.e. we consider future cash flows which will be generated, but in today's prices. When discounting the cash flows, however, we must use a discount rate which is adjusted for inflation. This is called a ***real discount rate*** or a real cost of capital.

(b) **The "money" method**

In this case ***adjust future cash flows for the effect of inflation*** i.e. inflate the cash flows, and then discount by using ***a money or nominal*** cost of capital.

We will consider how to discount using each approach. If you need to get from a money cost of capital to a real cost of capital or vice versa then the relationship between the two is as follows:

$$(1 + m) = (1 + r)(1 + i)$$

where m = money cost

r = real cost

i = inflation rate

Note: In an exam question, assume that both the discount rate and cashflows are given in money / nominal terms unless told otherwise.

Inflation terminology explained

A common source of confusion and misunderstanding in DCF calculations is the treatment of inflation.

Money and real costs of capital

Typically, the discount rate is the money cost of capital (often referred to as the nominal cost of capital), that is the rate payable on borrowed money (the source of funds may be a bank loan, bonds, equity or some combination of sources).

Such a rate includes an allowance for inflation, in the sense that the lender cannot expect any more than the interest rate. (The lender may charge a 15% rate assuming that inflation will be 8% and so a 'real return' of approximately 7% will be generated.)

Money and real cashflows

If a money cost of capital is employed, then the cash flows on which the analysis is performed should also include any inflation which is expected. (And, if different rates of inflation are expected on revenues and costs, then this should be reflected in the cash flows.)

In practice, cash flows are often projected in so-called 'real' terms, that is excluding inflation. Given the uncertain nature of estimated future cash flows this is not surprising – inflating estimated future cash flows may introduce the potential for greater confusion.

And, since inflation might be expected to affect all entities equally, it can reasonably be assumed that, if there are unexpected inflationary pressures, they will be compensated by price adjustments.

There are therefore arguable reasons for the use of cash flows in 'real' terms in DCF analysis. However, it therefore follows that the discount rate should also be in 'real' terms.

The interaction of tax and inflation in an NPV analysis

Finally, there is the problem of using the real rate when there are taxation implications in an examination question.

If there are any taxation implications in an investment appraisal, it would not usually be appropriate to leave the cash flows in terms of present-day prices and discount those cash flows at the real cost of capital.

This would understate the overall tax liability as tax depreciation allowances are based on original, rather than replacement cost, and do not change in line with changing prices. The cash flows will have to be adjusted by the appropriate estimate of price change.

Example of inflation in an NPV calculation

Brooker has under review a project involving an outlay of $55,000 and expected to yield the following net cash flows in current terms:

	$
Year 1	10,000
Year 2	20,000
Year 3	30,000
Year 4	5,000

The company's money cost of capital is 20% and the expected rate of inflation is 5% per annum.

Required:

Evaluate the project using both of the recognised approaches to dealing with inflation.

Solution:

The real method:

First, calculate the real rate of interest.

$(1+m) = (1+r)(1+i)$

$1.20 = (1+r) \times 1.05$

So r = 14.29%, which should be used to discount the current terms cash flows:

	Cash	Discount factor	*PV*
0	(55,000)	1	(55,000)
1	10,000	1/1.1429	8,750
2	20,000	$1/1.1429^2$	15,311
3	30,000	$1/1.1429^3$	20,095
4	5,000	$1/1.1429^4$	2,930
			(7,914)

The money method:

Discount the inflated cashflows at 20%:

	Cash	Discount factor	PV
0	(55,000)	1	(55,000)
1	10,500(10,000 ×1.05)	1/1.20	8,750
2	22,050 (20,000 ×1.05^2)	1/1.20^2	15,313
3	34,729 (30,000 ×1.05^3)	1/1.20^3	20,098
4	6,078 (5,000×1.05^4)	1/1.20^4	2,931
			(7,908)

N.B. The small difference between the two methods is caused by rounding.

Example 2 – Inflation

Boris Nicholaevich is considering investing in a new machine.

The machine costs $100,000.

It will generate income of $50,000 per annum for the next three years in current prices.

The selling price is expected to increase in line with the rate of inflation at 10% per annum.

The money cost of capital is 20%.

Required:

Calculate the NPV at the real cost of capital.

Calculate the NPV at the money cost of capital.

Note:

(1) If the rate of inflation affecting all the cash flows and the cost of capital is the same, then the NPV in money terms will equal the NPV in real terms. In this case it does not matter whether you discount in money or in real terms.

(2) In the exam you are much more likely to have to approach things in money rather than real terms. If there are different rates of inflation quoted for different cash flows e.g. for sales compared to cost of sales, then you will have to discount in money terms. Likewise if tax depreciation allowances are given in a question then you will have to discount in money terms. Basically, if in doubt assume that you have to discount in money terms.

(3) Assume that a discount rate is a money rate unless told otherwise.

(4) The only time when you are likely to have to discount in real terms is if you are given annuities for a long period of time. e.g. 10 years. By discounting in real terms you can use the cumulative annuity factors.

The working capital adjustment in an NPV analysis

The investment in working capital necessary to undertake a project will appear as a negative cashflow in the early years of an NPV analysis and then a positive cashflow in the later years as the normal assumption is that working capital reduces to zero at the end of a project.

Explanation of the working capital adjustment

Most projects not only involve an investment in non-current assets, but also an investment in working capital items such as raw materials, finished goods or trade receivables.

At the end of the project's life the working capital is usually assumed to be recovered in full. This is because at the end of the project the entity should be able to run down inventories or utilise the items in other projects, and outstanding trade receivables should be cleared.

This is shown in the Illustration below.

The existence of inflation means that additional cash is needed each year to finance the increased money value of working capital.

Any real changes to the level of working capital invested in a project will require incremental cash flows in the relevant years as will any changes in the level of working capital brought about by inflation.

e.g

Illustration 4 – Working capital

A project requires the following levels of cumulative working capital investment (the working capital is required at the start of each year):

Year 1	*Year 2*	*Year 3*	*Year 4*
500	600	700	800

NPV – cash flows – put only the incremental cash flows at the start of each year, then release the total amount invested at the end of the project:

Time 0	*Time 1*	*Time 2*	*Time 3*	*Time 4*
(500)	(100)	(100)	(100)	800

Example of NPV with taxation, inflation and working capital

PQ Co, a UK based motor components subsidiary of a conglomerate entity, has to decide whether to invest in a new production line. The project involves an initial investment in equipment costing GBP600,000 and working capital costing GBP180,000

The projected net cash inflows for the products are GBP200,000 per annum for 5 years at current price levels. At the end of 5 years it is projected that the equipment will have a terminal value of GBP50,000, and that the elimination of working capital will provide an inflow equal to its initial book value.

PQ Co's post-tax cost of capital is 14% in nominal (money) terms and the inflation rate is projected to be 5% per annum.

Taxation data is as follows:

(i) The equipment will be subject to tax depreciation allowances of 25% per annum on a reducing-balance basis, which can be claimed against taxable profits as from the current year (year 0) which is shortly to end. A balancing charge or allowance will arise on disposal.

(ii) The rate of corporate tax is 35% payable 1 year in arrears.

Required:

Determine whether or not the NPV of the project will justify the investment.

Solution:

You should note that the figures required are in nominal (money) terms, but in this case, while it is possible to convert net cash flows back from nominal to real terms, it is not possible to ascertain a discount rate in real terms, from the data given, because of the mixture of inflated and non-inflated cash flows in the projections. If PQ Co's planners wished the figures to be in real terms, then the company's real discount rate would have to be separately determined. Care would also be required in adjusting the tax savings on tax depreciation allowances.

	Capital	Working capital	Net inflows	Tax 35%	Tax relief on tax depn	Net cash flow	DF @14%	Present value
	GBP	GBP	GBP	GBP	GBP	GBP		GBP
0	(600,000)	(180,000)				(780,000)	1.000	(780,000)
1			210,000		52,500	262,500	0.877	230,213
2			220,500	(73,500)	39,375	186,375	0.769	143,322
3			231,525	(77,175)	29,531	183,881	0.675	124,120
4			243,101	(81,034)	22,148	184,215	0.592	109,055
5	50,000	180,000	255,256	(85,085)	16,611	416,782	0.519	216,310
6				(89,340)	32,335	(57,005)	0.456	(25,994)
							NPV	17,026

The NPV is positive and therefore the investment should be accepted.

Workings

Tax saved on tax depreciation allowances

Time		GBP	Tax relief @ 35%	Timing
0	Purchase	600,000		
0	Tax depn 25%	(150,000)	52,500	1
		450,000		
1	Tax depn 25%	(112,500)	39,375	2
		337,500		
2	Tax depn 25%	(84,375)	29,531	3
		253,125		
3	Tax depn 25%	(63,281)	22,148	4
		189,844		
4	Tax depn 25%	(47,461)	16,611	5
		142,383		
5	Sale proceeds	(50,000)		
	Balancing allowance	92,383	32,334	6

The internal rate of return (IRR)

Definition

The IRR is the discount rate which gives a zero NPV.

In many cases this is the maximum discount rate at which a project would be acceptable (because in most cases, the NPV is positive at all discount rates less than the IRR).

Calculation

It can be estimated by working out the NPV at two different rates (L, the lower rate, and H, the higher rate) and then using the following (linear interpolation) formula:

$$L + \left(\frac{NPV_L}{NPV_L - NP_H}\right)(H - L)$$

Limitations of the IRR method

- The IRR method assumes that earnings throughout the period of the investment are reinvested at the IRR. If the cost of capital is different from the IRR (as in most cases) this is an incorrect assumption which means that the IRR overestimates the project's return.
- For a project having irregular cash flows there can be more than one IRR for that project. This can make comparison of projects using IRR vey confusing. For example, consider the following project:

	$
Initial investment at t_0	(50,000)
t_1 cash inflow	127,500
t_2 cash outflow	(78,750)

  This project has IRRs of 5% and 50% (i.e. NPV = 0 when discounted at either of these rates).

- Ranking projects according to the size of their IRRs can give a different ranking from the ranking using NPV. This is because IRR is a relative figure and NPV is an absolute figure. For example, a project giving a $1,000 return in 1 year from a $900 investment immediately, has the same IRR as a project which gives a $1m return in 1 year from a $900,000 investment. Clearly the larger project would have a much bigger NPV.

More on the limitations of IRR

Decision rule

The decision rule for IRR is:

- accept the project if its IRR is greater than the cost of capital;
- reject if the IRR is less than the cost of capital.

If a decision has to be made about a single project with 'conventional' cash flows (i.e. a single outlay followed by a series of inflows) IRR will lead to the same decision as NPV.

However, in more complex circumstances IRR and NPV can lead to different decisions.

Multiple IRRs

If project cash flows reverse during the life of the project – there may, for example, be an initial outflow followed by several inflows before another major outflow (as plant undergoes major refurbishment, for example) – there may be more than one IRR. A graph of discount rate versus NPV might appear as follows:

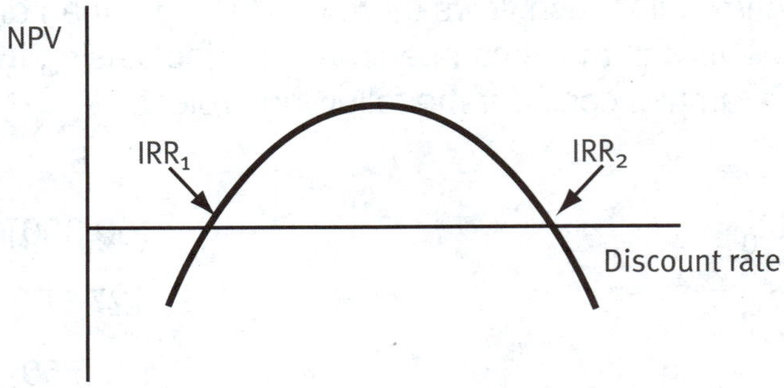

Discount rate and NPV - more than one IRR

In such an example, the IRR decision rule (accept if cost of capital is less than IRR) is misleading because the project should only be accepted if cost of capital is between IRR1 and IRR2.

To explain this result it is necessary to understand the reinvestment assumptions implicit in the NPV and IRR calculations.

The reinvestment assumptions

All NPV calculations assume that incoming cash can be reinvested at the rate which is used in the NPV calculation.

This means that the calculation of IRR1 assumes reinvestment at IRR1 while the calculation of IRR2 assumes reinvestment at IRR2. Only at rates between IRR1 and IRR2 can the incoming cash be reinvested at a rate which is sufficient to offset both the initial cash outflow and the eventual second cash outflow. This analysis is perfectly sound and, arguably, the project is acceptable only if the cost of capital lies between IRR1 and IRR2.

Unfortunately, however, it means that the IRR decision rule – accept if cost of capital is less than IRR – can be applied only to projects having conventional cash flows.

The NPV approach avoids this problem quite simply. By using the cost of capital as the discount rate in the NPV formula, a negative NPV is generated if cost of capital is less than IRR1, a positive NPV is obtained if cost of capital is between IRR1 and IRR2, and the NPV is negative again if cost of capital is greater than IRR2.

The possibility of multiple IRRs is cited as a disadvantage of the IRR technique. However, the problem can be overcome. Multiple IRRs arise only when cash flows reverse more than once. In these circumstances, it is only necessary to identify the (possibly) several IRRs (some calculators will draw the graph of NPV versus discount rate in a few seconds) and draw the correct conclusions.

IRR and mutually exclusive projects

Another problem with IRR concerns the selection of a favoured project from two or more projects which are 'mutually exclusive' (i.e. if one is chosen the others are automatically ruled out).

Suppose, instead of our project (A) being a simple accept/reject decision we have to choose between it and another project (B) which can be compared with project A as follows:

	Project A	**Project B**
Initial investment ($000)	100.0	50.0
NPV ($000)	6.5	5.0
IRR (%)	12.7	18.0

The IRR approach would favour project B (18.0% compared with 12.7%). However, provided that funds are freely available, project A would maximise wealth because, if chosen, it could generate $6,500 NPV compared with project B's $5,000.

In essence, IRR can mislead because it may select a lower investment with higher 'earning potential', when it may be preferable to invest a greater sum which generates a lower 'return' but (because of its scale) produces a greater sum in the end.

This limitation of IRR does mean that IRR must be used with caution if a choice has to be made between mutually exclusive projects.

Conclusion

While the IRR technique assumes that cash flows can be reinvested at the IRR, the NPV technique assumes that cash flows can be reinvested at the cost of capital used in the discounting process. This difference has two repercussions:

(1) Even if mutually exclusive projects have the same initial investment, NPV and IRR can give conflicting results. IRR may prefer a project with high early cash flows (assumed reinvestment at the IRR), while NPV may prefer a different project – with higher flows later.

(2) If IRR is used to rank projects in a capital-rationing situation the ranking may be different from that obtained using the profitability index because IRR will favour early cash inflows (assuming reinvestment at the IRR), while the profitability index (being based on NPV) may produce a different ranking. (Capital rationing is covered in more detail in the later Chapter 'Investment appraisal – further techniques'.)

It is usually assumed that NPV provides the best guidance because the cost of capital reinvestment assumption is more conservative and likely to be more realistic.

To address these limitations, we can compute the Modified Internal Rate of Return (see below), which is a percentage measure (like IRR) but it is unique for each project and it measures the actual return generated by the project.

NEW

5 Modified IRR (MIRR)

Definition and explanation of MIRR

Modified internal rate of return (MIRR) is that rate of return which, when the initial outlay is compared with the terminal value of the project's net cash flows reinvested at the cost of capital, gives an NPV of zero.

The MIRR gives the percentage return from a project, on the assumption that any cash inflows can be reinvested at the entity's cost of capital.

As a percentage return figure, it is arguably easier to understand than the absolute figure given by an NPV analysis (in many other contexts the return from an investment is given as a percentage, so the concept of a percentage return is well understood).

The process for calculating MIRR

- Cash inflows from the project are converted to a single cash inflow in the last year of the project (a "terminal value" or TV) by assuming that the cash flows are reinvested at the cost of capital.
- MIRR is calculated as the annual return which equates the present value of the outflows to this TV.
- i.e. the MIRR is found by taking (TV / PV of cash outflows) $^{(1/n)}$ – 1 (Note: n is the length of the project in years.)

Note: This calculation identifies the rate of interest that equates the terminal value with the initial investment.

e.g

Illustration 5 – MIRR

Initial investment		(5,000)
Cash flows	at t_1	2,000
	at t_2	(1,000)
	at t_3	3,500
	at t_4	3,800

Cost of capital 10%

NPV = 1,216

IRR ≈ 19%

Required:

Calculate the MIRR of this project.

Solution:

MIRR calculation

	Inflow		*TV of inflows*
1	2,000	$(1.10)^3$	2,662
3	3,500	$(1.10)^1$	3,850
4	3,800	1.0	3,800
			10,312

	Outflow	*DF*	*PV of outflows*
0	5,000	1	5,000
2	1,000	$1/1.10^2$	826
			5,826

MIRR = $(10,312 / 5,826)^{(1/4)} - 1 = 0.1534$ (15.34%)

This is a better measure of the financial return from the project than the IRR of 19% which was given.

Strengths of the MIRR approach

- MIRR is unique for each project and it assumes that reinvestment takes place at the cost of capital, so it is a much more accurate measure of the return from a project than IRR.
- MIRR represents the actual return generated by a project.

Discussion of investment appraisal methods

Discussion of techniques

In using discounting and other techniques of investment appraisal, you must always be aware that financial analysis is only a part of the decision-making process and that, often, social and other factors may also be of considerable importance.

However, accepting this point and the need for a rounded, pragmatic approach to investment decisions, it is still essential that a management accountant should thoroughly understand the application of the 'tools of his trade'.

The arguments put forward here suggest that all the techniques of investment appraisal need to be well understood if they are to be wisely used.

In summary:

(1) NPV is the principal theoretical recommendation and should be used if the cost of capital is a realistic reinvestment assumption.

(2) IRR, like NPV, incorporates discounting principles and, for some managers, may be more meaningful than the absolute NPV of the project. However, IRR needs to be thoroughly understood because of possible difficulties concerning multiple IRRs and its use if projects are mutually exclusive. MIRR is a recent innovation worthy of consideration.

(3) Payback is much used in practice and, aside from its obvious simplicity, it can also be recommended if a risk-averse decision is needed (or if liquidity is a major problem).

(4) ARR takes no account of the time value of money and could lead to an incorrect decision if compared with the cost of capital. However, because of the extensive use of the return on capital employed or return on investment ratio, in practice it could be foolish not to calculate it.

The analysis suggests that there may be a place for all the techniques of investment appraisal in the management accountant's armoury. However, a thorough understanding of their strengths and limitations is important.

How is risk incorporated using the different methods?

The usual textbook advice is to take account of risk in the following ways:

(1) If payback is used, reduce the required payback period;

(2) If IRR is used, increase the required 'cut-off' rate;

(3) If NPV is used, increase the discount rate to take account of the 'risk' associated with the project. The capital asset pricing model can be used to provide a means of assessing the premium which ought to be added to the 'risk-free' discount rate;

(4) Assign probabilities to 'best', 'most likely' and 'worst' values for each variable and calculate a range of possible outcomes together with their probabilities. (This approach can be refined by establishing distributions for the input variables and 'simulating' the project many times in order to build up a distribution of possible outcomes.)

The relatively straightforward methods of handling risk if payback or IRR are used are cited as advantages of these techniques.

However, none of the techniques described above deals with the important point that early cash flows are likely to be more certain than late ones. The discounting techniques take account of the time value of money but they assume that whatever cash flows are projected are certain. Only the payback technique clearly favours early inflows much more than later ones and this may partially account for its popularity.

The issue of risk in investment appraisal is dealt with more fully in the next Chapter.

6 Conclusion – Which investment appraisal method should be used?

To some extent, the decision as to which investment appraisal methods to use depends on the circumstances.

For example, if the company has short term liquidity problems, the payback period may well provide useful information. Alternatively, if a manager is being appraised based on the ROCE generated, he may decide to use the ARR method as an important investment appraisal method.

However, in most cases, the NPV method is considered to be the best investment appraisal method, because it measures the absolute gain in shareholders' wealth if a project is undertaken. This links to the primary financial objective of all companies – to maximise the wealth of the shareholders.

The IRR is useful as a follow up to NPV when trying to assess the sensitivity of the project to changes in input factors (see next Chapter for more details). However, if it is difficult to interpret the IRR (perhaps because there is more than one IRR), the MIRR gives a unique percentage measure of project return and should be used if trying to explain the concept of return from a project to a non-financially minded audience.

Financial and strategic considerations in investment appraisal

The investment appraisal methods shown in this Chapter are, in the main, concerned with financial aspects.

However, you need to be clear that financial methods of evaluation are by no means the only factors to be taken into account in investment appraisal.

Maximising shareholder wealth

We might define investment appraisal as being concerned with maximising shareholder wealth, but we must be careful to qualify this concept by making it subject to constraints associated with issues of social responsibility, such as effective controls over pollution.

Stakeholder considerations

Shareholders' wealth in this context needs to be linked with the wider view of stakeholder theory which was introduced in the earlier Chapter on 'Introduction to Financial Strategy').

The key point here is that many other interested parties apart from shareholders – for example, suppliers, lenders, employees, managers, as well as the general public – need to be taken into account in assessing a project's viability.

For example, a project with a large positive NPV would normally be considered to be acceptable. However, if undertaking the project would lead to job losses within the entity, or would increase pollution levels, the decision is not so clear cut.

In situations such as this, the competing needs of stakeholders would need to be assessed and compared.

Although it may seem to go against the key "maximise shareholder wealth" objective to reject a project with a positive NPV, it is worth considering that a project which fails to achieve the objectives of the other stakeholders might ultimately undermine the entity's position and may lead to negative publicity which might adversely impact shareholder wealth in the future.

Strategic considerations

The financial appraisal of a project must also be balanced against its strategic benefits to the entity.

For example, if a project has been appraised which has a small positive (or negative) NPV, usually the project would be rejected. However, if the project would help to consolidate the entity's competitive position, or give it the opportunity to expand into a new, attractive market, the decision is not so clear cut.

In this case, management would have to try to balance the financial requirements of the entity against the long-term strategic requirements.

If it is felt that undertaking a project now would improve the entity's prospects and likely shareholder wealth in the future, a project with a small positive (or negative) NPV might sometimes be accepted.

Note: Real options theory (covered in the next Chapter) is one way of trying to formalise the process, by assigning values to strategic factors so that they can be incorporated more easily in the decision making process.

7 Exam style questions

Test your understanding 1 – Detailed investment appraisal

Assume that you have been appointed finance director of Breckall. The company is considering investing in the production of an electronic security device, with an expected market life of five years.

The previous finance director has undertaken an analysis of the proposed project; the main features of his analysis are shown below.

He has recommended that the project should not be undertaken because the estimated annual accounting rate of return is only 12.3%.

	Year 0 $000	*Year 1* $000	*Year 2* $000	*Year 3* $000	*Year 4* $000	*Year 5* $000
Investment in depreciable fixed assets	4,500					
Cumulative investment in working capital	300	400	500	600	700	700
Sales		3,500	4,900	5,320	5,740	5,320
Materials		535	750	900	1,050	900
Labour		1,070	1,500	1,800	2,100	1,800
Overhead		50	100	100	100	100
Finance charges		576	576	576	576	576
Depreciation		900	900	900	900	900
		3,131	3,826	4,276	4,726	4,276
Taxable profit		369	1,074	1,044	1,014	1,044
Taxation		129	376	365	355	365
Profit after tax		240	698	679	659	679

Total initial investment is $4,800,000.

Average annual after tax profit is $591,000.

All of the above cash flow and profit estimates have been prepared in terms of present day costs and prices as the previous finance director assumed that the sales price could be increased to compensate for any increase in costs.

You have available the following additional information:

(a) Selling prices, working capital requirements and overhead expenses are expected to increase by 5% per year.

(b) Material costs and labour costs are expected to increase by 10% per year.

(c) Tax depreciation allowances are allowable for taxation purposes against profits at 25% per year on a reducing balance basis.

(d) Taxation of profits is at a rate of 35% payable one year in arrears.

(e) The fixed assets have no expected salvage value at the end of five years.

(f) The company's real after-tax discount rate (or weighted average cost of capital) is estimated to be 8% per year, and nominal after-tax discount rate 15% per year. Assume that all receipts and payments arise at the end of the year to which they relate except those in year 0 which occur immediately.

Required:

(a) **Estimate the net present value of the proposed project. State clearly any assumptions that you make.**

(20 marks)

(b) **Calculate by how much the discount rate would have to change to result in a net present value of approximately zero.**

(5 marks)

(Total: 25 marks)

Test your understanding 2 – NPV (project specific discount rate)

Ceely plc, a UK based company, is evaluating a high risk project in a new industry. The company is temporarily short of accountants, and has asked an unqualified trainee to produce a draft financial evaluation of the project. This draft is shown below:

Year	*0*	*1*	*2*	*3*	*4*	*5*	*6*
	£000	£000	£000	£000	£000	£000	£000
Cash outflows							
Long-term capital:							
Land and building	500	600					
Plant and machinery	700	1,700					
Working capital							
(cumulative requirement)	230	570	680	700	720	740	740
Sales		2,950	3,820	5,200	5,400	5,600	5,800
Direct costs:							
Materials		487	630	858	891	924	957
Labour		805	1,043	1,420	1,474	1,529	1,583
Selling and distribution		207	267	364	378	392	406
		1,499	1,940	2,642	2,743	2,845	2,946
Overheads		370	480	630	642	655	660
Finance Charges		214	610	610	610	610	610
Depreciation		240	700	700	700	700	460
Total cost		2,323	3,730	4,582	4,695	4,810	4,676
Net profit before tax		627	90	618	705	790	1,124
Taxation at 40%		251	36	247	282	316	450
Net profit after tax		376	54	371	423	474	674
Net cash flows	(1,200)	(1,924)	54	371	423	474	674
Cash flows discounted							
at 30% per year	(1,200)	(1,480)	32	169	148	124	140

The net present value is –£2,067,000.

Conclusion: the project is not financially viable and should not be undertaken.

Notes: Year 0 is the present time, year 1 is one year in the future, etc.

Cash flows have been discounted at a high rate because of the high risk of the project. Assume that you have been engaged as a financial consultant to Ceely plc. The following additional information is made available to you.

(1) The company has a six-year planning horizon for capital investments. The value of the investment at the end of six years is estimated to be five times the after-tax operating cash flows of the sixth year.

(2) The project would be financed by two 15% debentures, one issued almost immediately and one in a year's time. The debentures would both have a maturity of 10 years.

(3) 50% of the overheads would be incurred as a direct result of undertaking this project.

(4) Corporate taxation is at the rate of 40% payable one year in arrears.

(5) Tax allowable depreciation is on a straight-line basis at a rate of 20% per year on the full historic cost of depreciable fixed assets. Land and buildings are not depreciable fixed assets.

(6) The company is listed on the AIM. Its current share price is 273 pence, and its equity beta coefficient value is 1.1.

(7) The yield on Treasury Bills is 12% per year, and the average total yield from companies forming the FTSE All Share Index is 20% per year.

(8) Interest rates are not expected to change significantly.

(9) The equity beta value of a company whose major activity is the manufacture of a similar product to that proposed in Ceely's new project is 1.5. Both companies have gearing levels of 60% equity and 40% debt (by market values). Ceely's gearing includes the new debentures issues.

Required:

(a) **Modify the draft financial evaluation of the project, where appropriate, to produce a revised estimate of the net present value of the project. Recommend whether the project should be accepted, and briefly discuss any reservations you have about the accuracy of your revised appraisal. State clearly any assumptions that you make.**

(20 marks)

(b) **You are later told that the draft cash flow estimates did not include the effects of changing prices. Discuss whether, on the basis of this new information, any further amendments to your analysis might be necessary.**

(5 marks)

(Total: 25 marks)

Test your understanding answers

Example 1 – Taxation

Assumptions:

(1) Asset is purchased on the first day of year 1.

(2) Tax is payable 1 year in arrears.

Working – Tax depreciation allowances

	WDV	*Benefit*
	100,000	
WDA Y1	(25,000) @ 33%	8,250 at T2
	75,000	
WDA Y2	(18,750) @ 33%	6,188 at T3
	56,250	
WDA Y3	(14,063) @ 33%	4,641 at T4
	42,187	
Proceeds	(20,000)	
	22,187	
BA Y4	(22,187) @ 33%	7,322 at T5
	Nil	

Net present value

	0	1	2	3	4	5
Revenue flows	–	30,000	40,000	50,000	40,000	–
Tax@ 33%			(9,900)	(13,200)	(16,500)	(13,200)
TDA (Working)			8,250	6,188	4,641	7,322
Scrap					20,000	
Capital	(100,000)					
	(100,000)	30,000	38,350	42,988	48,141	(5,878)

NPV at 12% = $15,247.

Example 2 – Inflation

NPV in real terms

1.2 = (1 + r)(1 + 0.1)

r = 9.1%

AF 1–3 9.1% = $(1 - (1.091)^{-3}) / 0.091 = 2.5268$

Time	*Flow*	*DF @9.1%*	*NPV*
0	(100,000)	1.000	(100,000)
1–3	50,000	2.5268	126340
		NPV	26,340

NPV in money terms

Time	*Flow*	*DF @ 20%*	*NPV*
0	(100,000)	1.000	(100,000)
1	50,000 × 1.10	0.833	45,815
2	$50,000 \times 1.10^2$	0.694	41,987
3	$50,000 \times 1.10^3$	0.579	38,532
		NPV	26,334

Note: Difference is due to rounding

Test your understanding 1 – Detailed investment appraisal

Tutorial notes: As different items are inflating at different rates the only realistic approach is to discount money cash flows at the nominal (money) discount rate. This is particularly true as taxation is involved and the amount of tax payable will be based upon a taxable profit figure that in turn is determined by items subject to various rates of inflation.

The general procedure will be as follows:

- Determine the corporation tax liability.
- Determine other relevant cash flows (in money terms).
- Discount these cash flows to present value at the nominal WACC.

(a) Calculation of corporation tax liability

	1	*2*	*3*	*4*	*5*	
	$000	$000	$000	$000	$000	
Sales (5% rise pa)	3,675	5,402	6,159	6,977	6,790	
Materials (10% rise pa)	588	907	1,198	1,537	1,449	
Labour (10% rise pa)	1,177	1,815	2,396	3,075	2,899	
Overheads (5% rise pa)	52	110	116	122	128	
Tax depn allowances	1,125	844	633	475	1,423	note 1,2
	–––––	–––––	–––––	–––––	–––––	
Taxable	733	1,726	1,816	1,768	891	
Tax (35%)	256	604	636	619	312	

Notes:

(1) **Tax depreciation allowances**

	Opening balance	*Allowance*
	$000	$000
Year 1	4,500	1,125
Year 2	3,375	844
Year 3	2,531	633
Year 4	1,898	475
Year 5	1,423	1,423

This assumes that the first allowance is available in the first year and that the balancing allowance is taken in year 5. Note that allowances are based upon original cost of assets.

(2) **Depreciation is replaced by the tax depreciation allowance**

Interest is not deducted in calculating the tax liability. The tax deductibility of interest will have been allowed for in the calculation of the weighted average cost of capital.

Discount relevant cash flows to present value

Year **Inflows**	*0*	*1*	*2*	*3*	*4*	*5*	*6*
Sales	–	3,675	5,402	6,159	6,977	6,790	–
Outflows							
Materials	–	(588)	(907)	(1,198)	(1,537)	(1,449)	–
Labour	–	(1,177)	(1,815)	(2,396)	(3,075)	(2,899)	–
Overheads (note 3)	–	(52)	(110)	(116)	(122)	(128)	–
Fixed assets	(4,500)						
Working capital (note 4)	(300)	(120)	(131)	(144)	(156)	851	–
Taxation (note 5)			(256)	(604)	(636)	(619)	(312)
Net cash flows	(4,800)	1,738	2,183	1,701	1,451	2,546	(312)
Discount factors at 15%		0.870	0.756	0.658	0.572	0.497	0.432
Present values	(4,800)	1,512	1,650	1,119	830	1,265	(135)

NPV = $1,441,000 and on this basis the project should be accepted.

(3) Once again interest is not included. The cost of interest is taken care of in the discounting process. If we were to charge interest against cash flow and include it in the discounting process we would be double counting. This is a very common examination trap and should be avoided.

(4) We require the incremental investment in working capital each year. Adjusting for inflation, this is:

Year 0	300	
Year 1	(400 × 1.05) – 300 =	120
Year 2	$(500 \times 1.05^2) – (400 \times 1.05)$ =	131
Year 3	$(600 \times 1.05^3) – (500 \times 1.05^2)$ =	144
Year 4	$(700 \times 1.05^4) – (600 \times 1.05^3)$ =	156
Year 5	Refund of working capital assumed =	851
	Net	0

(5) Tax payment lagged by one year

(b) **Tutorial note:** This is a roundabout way of asking what is the IRR of the project. By normal trial and error procedures this may be determined as follows:

Year	*Cash flow* $000	*20% discount factor*	*PV* $000	*27% discount factor*	*PV* $000
0	(4,800)		(4,800)		(4,800)
1	1,738	0.833	1,448	0.787	1,368
2	2,183	0.694	1,515	0.620	1,353
3	1,701	0.579	985	0.488	830
4	1,451	0.482	699	0.384	557
5	2,546	0.402	1,023	0.303	771
6	(312)	0.335	(105)	0.238	(74)
			765		5

The discount rate would have to change from 15% to approximately 27% to produce a net present value of zero. This is a change of approximately 80%.

Test your understanding 2 – NPV (project specific discount rate)

(a) **Suitable discount rate**

Ceely's current WACC is not suitable as the project is a 'high risk'. Using the equity ß of the company whose major activity is manufacturing a product similar to Ceely's:

$k_e = R_f + ß\ (R_m - R_f)$

12% + 1.5 (20% – 12%) = 24%

$k_d = 15\%(1 - t) = 15\%(1 - 0.4) = 9\%$

WACC = 24% × 0.6 + 9% × 0.4 = 18%

Note: No gearing adjustment needs be made to the cost of equity as the two firms have the same level of gearing.

Project cash flows

	0	1	2	3	4	5	6	7	*Notes*
	£000	£000	£000	£000	£000	£000	£000	£000	
Sales		2,950	3,820	5,200	5,400	5,600	5,800		
Direct costs		(1,499)	(1,940)	(2,642)	(2,743)	(2,845)	(2,946)		
Fixed costs		(185)	(240)	(315)	(321)	(328)	(330)		(1)
Working Capital	(230)	(340)	(110)	(20)	(20)	(20)	740		(2)
Taxation			(450)	(464)	(705)	(742)	(779)	(874)	(3)
Land and buildings	(500)	(600)							
Plant and machinery	(700)	(1,700)							
Closing value							8,725		(4)
Tax on closing Value								(3,490)	(5)
Net	(1,430)	(1,374)	1,080	1,759	1,611	1,665	11,210	(4,364)	
18% PV factors	1	0.847	0.718	0.609	0.516	0.437	0.37	0.314	
Present value	(1,430)	(1,164)	775	1,071	831	728	4,148	(1,370)	

Net present value = +£3,589,000 and the project should therefore be accepted.

Notes

(1) Only 50% of overheads are incremental to the project.

(2) Incremental investment in working capital. It is assumed that the cumulative investment is released in year 6.

(3) Tax calculation

	Year					
	1	*2*	*3*	*4*	*5*	*6*
(Sales – Direct costs 50% of fixed costs)	1,266	1,640	2,243	2,336	2,427	2,524
Depreciation (Straight line)	140	480	480	480	480	340
Taxable	1,126	1,160	1,763	1,856	1,947	2,184
Tax (40%)	450	464	705	742	779	874

(4) We must include some allowance for the value of the project at the end of the planning horizon.

(After tax operating cash flow in year 6) × 5

= (5,800 – 2,946 – 330 – 779) × 5 = 8,725

(5) This potential cash flow (4) would be taxable. Plant and machinery has been fully depreciated so we will base the tax charge on gross value less the initial cost of land and buildings.

8,725 × 0.4 = £3,490

Tutorial note:

Other sensible approaches would be allowed; the main point is to recognise that a liability could exist.

(6) Note debenture interest and the tax relief thereon has been excluded from the above cash flows. The net of tax cost of interest is allowed for in the discount rate. The inclusion of interest as a project expense is a very common 'trap' set by examiners – don't fall into it!

Possible reservations

(i) How accurate is the closing value of the project?

(ii) How reliable are the estimates of cash flows?

(iii) Is the discount rate suitable? Is the comparative company's line of operations truly similar to Ceely's?

(iv) Do all cash flows occur at year ends?

(b) The analysis would probably need to be amended.

The discount rate is market derived and would therefore be the nominal rate i.e. it would include a premium for inflation.

Cash flows have been specified in real terms and therefore do not include the effect of inflation. This means that the project has been charged with the cost of inflation (in the discounting process) but not its benefits in terms of increased cash flow.

To correct this, the simplest approach would be to restate cash flows by applying expected inflation rates to each item.

If different categories of cost and revenues seem set to inflate at different rates this would in fact be the only practical way of handling the problem. In the unusual circumstances of all items inflating at the general rate of inflation we could alternatively discount real cash flows at the real discount rate.

chapter

10

Investment Appraisal – further techniques

Chapter learning objectives

Lead	Component
C1: Evaluate investment choices.	(a) analyse relevant costs, benefits and risks of an investment project. (b) evaluate investment projects, including their financial and strategic implications. (d) recommend investment choice in the presence of capital rationing and / or real options.

Indicative syllabus content

- Linking investments with customer requirements and product/service design.
- Linking investment in IS/IT with strategic, operational and control needs (particularly where risks and benefits are difficult to quantify).
- Recognising risk using the certainty equivalent method (when given a risk free rate and certainty equivalent values).
- Adjusted present value. (Note:The two step method may be tested for debt introduced permanently and debt in place for the duration of the project).
- Capital investment real options (i.e. to make follow-on investment, abandon or wait).
- Single period capital rationing for divisible and non-divisible projects. (Note: Multi-period rationing will not be tested).
- Selection of an appropriate cost of capital for use in valuation.

1 Overview of Chapter

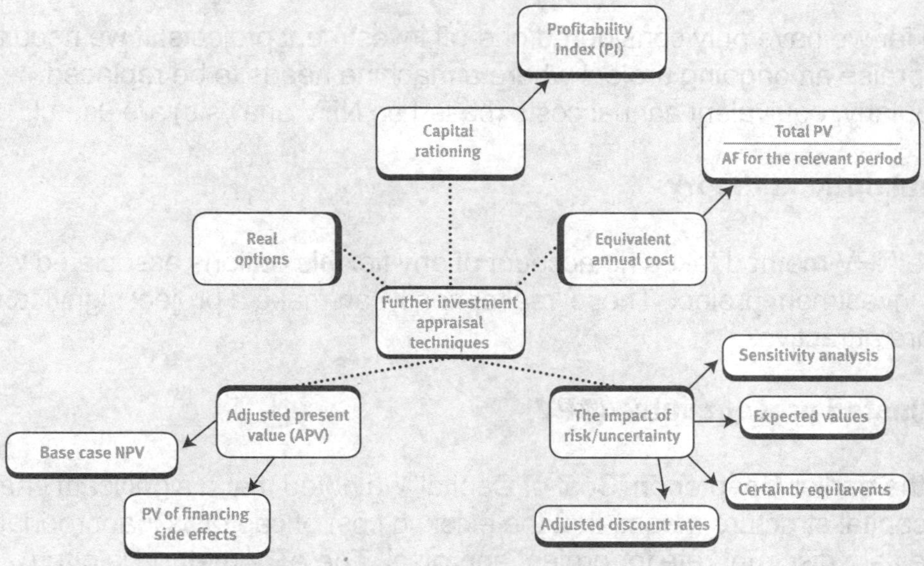

The previous Chapter introduced various investment appraisal techniques, most notably the Net Present Value (NPV) method.

This Chapter introduces some further considerations, many of which incorporate the use of NPV is different situations.

The main topics covered are:

Capital rationing

This considers how the investment decision is affected by a restriction in the amount of capital available. The key consideration is which project to choose if we have a choice of positive NPV projects available but insufficient finance to undertake them all.

The impact of risk

All the investment appraisal techniques in the previous Chapter were based on estimating future cash flows and / or profits. We need to also consider the potential for inaccuracies in our estimates.

Sensitivity analysis is often performed to assess the likely impact on a project of certain estimates being inaccurate.

We shall also see how to use probabilities and certainty equivalents to address potential uncertainties in cashflows, and how to derive risk adjusted discount rates if a new project is deemed to have a different risk from an entity's existing operations.

Equivalent annual costs

So far we have only considered one-off investment projects. If we need to appraise an ongoing project where a machine needs to be replaced regularly, equivalent annual costs (based on NPV analysis) are useful.

Real options theory

The NPV method takes no account of any flexible options associated with an investment project. These 'real options' can make a project significantly more attractive.

Adjusted present value (APV)

In the earlier Chapter on 'Cost of Capital' we noted that a significant change in capital structure means that the existing cost of capital is inappropriate to use as a discount rate for project appraisal. The APV method is often proposed as an alternative investment appraisal method in these circumstances.

Investment appraisal in specific contexts (e.g. IT investments, and investment in design)

In the modern business environment, the traditional investment appraisal methods need to be adapted when faced with projects such as IT investments where some of the benefits may be difficult to quantify.

NEW

2 Capital Rationing

Introduction

This is a situation where the funds available for new projects are limited to an amount which prevents acceptance of all new projects with a positive NPV.

Capital rationing needs to be recognised as a constraint during the capital budgeting cycle.

The methods below show how to decide between projects in different capital rationing situations.

Definition of capital rationing

Capital rationing definition

A restriction on an entity's ability to invest capital funds, caused by an internal budget ceiling being imposed on such expenditure by the management (soft capital rationing), or by external limitations being applied to the entity, as when additional borrowed funds cannot be obtained (hard capital rationing).

(CIMA Official Terminology, 2005)

More details on the capital rationing problem

If capital is not rationed there is no problem; all projects which meet the cut-off criteria are accepted.

When capital is rationed the ranking of projects becomes important. The various methods of investment appraisal – payback, IRR, NPV, etc. – often give conflicting rankings of investment priorities.

Methods of determining how the investment decision should be made will depend on the type of capital rationing.

Single-period capital rationing is a situation where capital is rationed at present (year 0), but will be freely available in the future.

Multi-period capital rationing is a situation where capital is rationed over a number of periods.

This syllabus concentrates on single-period capital rationing.

Capital budgeting and control

The capital budgeting cycle

A common feature of industrial activity is the need to commit funds by purchasing land, buildings, machinery, etc, in anticipation of being able to earn, in the future, an income greater than the funds committed. This indicates the need for an assessment of the size of the outflows and inflows of funds, the life of the investment, the degree of risk attached (greater risk being justified perhaps by greater returns) and the cost of obtaining funds.

Basic stages in the capital budgeting cycle may be identified as follows:

(a) Needs for expenditure are forecast.

(b) Projects to meet those needs are distinguished.

(c) Alternatives are appraised.

(d) Best alternatives are selected and approved.

(e) Expenditure is made and monitored.

(f) Deviations from estimates are examined as part of a post completion audit (PCA)

Types of capital project

Reasons for capital expenditure vary widely. Projects may be classified into the following categories.

- Maintenance – replacement of worn-out or obsolete assets, safety and security, etc.
- Profitability – cost savings, quality improvement, productivity, relocation, etc.
- Expansion – new products, new outlets, research and development, etc.
- Indirect – office buildings, welfare facilities, etc.

A particular investment project, of course, could combine any number or all of the above classifications.

Capital expenditure forecast

In preparing budgets, it is necessary to consider how much money can or must be allocated to capital expenditure. Capital development schemes may be started because a surplus of cash resources is revealed by the long-term plan, but usually management decides on a capital development scheme and then seeks the means to finance it. Initially, the budget will be an expression of management's intention to allocate funds for certain broad purposes. In the budget period, money will be required as follows:

- for previously authorised existing projects;
- for new projects, full details of which may not yet be available.

The forecasts will indicate whether sufficient funds are available, and perhaps when additional funds will need to be obtained. It is advisable, therefore, for managers to submit long-term capital expenditure forecasts, say for two to five years ahead. Consequently, the possibility of obsolescence (and the direction of the future development of the firm) must be borne in mind.

Capital expenditure committee

A capital expenditure committee may be formed, either as a sub-committee of the budget committee or as a separate meeting of the entire budget committee. The responsibilities of the capital expenditure committee are to:

- co-ordinate capital expenditure policy;
- appraise and authorise capital expenditure on specific projects;
- review actual expenditure on capital projects against the budget.

Capital expenditure decision

Capital expenditure requiring approval by the committee must be formulated by the managers. The amount of detail should be stipulated by the committee and would generally cover the following:

- Outline of the project, including the budget classification and how it is linked, if at all, with other projects.
- Reason for the expenditure, if a new project, and the departments affected. An assessment of intangible benefits or disadvantages.
- The amount of capital expenditure required (fixed and working capital), including a breakdown by budget periods, and an estimate of any internal work required.
- A complete statement of incremental costs and revenue arising from the project, and the budget periods affected. An assessment of the effect of taxation ought to be made.
- Estimated life of the project.
- Assessment of risks to which the project is sensitive – political, economic, competitors, natural hazards, etc.
- Projects that are feasible alternatives, and comparative data.
- Effect of postponement or rejection of project.

Major projects would probably be subjected to a comprehensive financial evaluation, as part of the committee's consideration. Less important projects could be submitted, accompanied by an economic justification.

Types of capital rationing

Hard rationing

This refers to an external constraint on the amount of capital available. It may arise because of:

- problems raising bank loans due to tight lending criteria being applied
- problems raising equity or bond finance in a depressed stock market
- prohibitively high costs of raising small amounts of finance.

Soft rationing

This is where the constraint is internally imposed. It may be because:

- management are reluctant to issue share capital because it might dilute the earnings per share, or lead to an unwanted change in the ownership structure of the business.
- management don't want to raise additional debt finance because of concerns about the level of gearing, or the potential problem of meeting higher interest payments.
- the capital expenditure budget may place a limit on the level of spending permitted (perhaps for a subsidiary or a division).

Single period capital rationing

(a) If projects are mutually exclusive, pick the project with the largest positive NPV.

(b) If projects are divisible, rank projects via the profitability index.

The profitability index is calculated as:

NPV of project/Capital investment

(c) If projects are indivisible, rank projects and combinations of projects via total NPV. The optimal solution is found by using trial and error i .e identify the possible combinations of investments and pick the one with the highest NPV.

Justification for the use of profitability index

The NPV technique is the academic recommendation and it is theoretically sound.

However, its use in practice implies that the decision-maker must judge a project by an absolute number and while it is easy to give the 'rule' – any project generating positive NPV is acceptable – a decision-maker will be interested not only in the final NPV 'payoff' but also in the size of the initial investment and the length of time before the project 'matures'.

Use of the NPV rule becomes problematic if capital is rationed, because not all projects can then be accepted.

In this situation, it becomes necessary to rank projects according to their 'earning power' – placing the project which generates the maximum NPV per pound invested at the top of the list.

Conventionally, the profitability index is calculated in order to rank projects.

More details on terminology

Mutually exclusive, divisible and indivisible projects

The key to a single period capital rationing problem is to identify first whether projects are mutually exclusive, divisible or indivisible.

If projects are mutually exclusive, only one of the projects can be undertaken. In this case the decision rule is clear cut - choose the available project with the highest positive NPV.

A divisible project is one where a fraction of the project can be undertaken and the same fraction of total NPV generated.

For example, if an entity is considering buying 10 machines to undertake a manufacturing project, it may be possible to only buy five of the machines and still generate half of the NPV.

An indivisible project is one which has to be done in total or not at all.

For example, a company buying a single machine to undertake a manufacturing project will not be able to invest in a fraction of the project.

Implications for a capital rationing scenario

When faced with a limiting factor (capital in this case), management should follow the decision rule of maximising the return per unit of the limiting factor. This is called the profitability index (PI).

Hence, if possible, projects should always be ranked using PIs.

However, whereas the PI approach works in a situation where projects are divisible, it is not appropriate when projects are indivisible or mutually exclusive.

This is because:

- when projects are mutually exclusive, the decision should be to undertake the project with the highest absolute return (i.e. NPV) rather than considering the relative measure of PI.
- when projects are indivisible, there will often be some unused capital left over when allocating finance to projects, because finance can only be allocated to full projects. It may be that a better absolute return (NPV) can be generated by investing in two projects with low PIs, rather than investing in the project with the best PI and then having surplus funds left over which cannot be invested in any other project.

Multiple period rationing

To rank projects, linear programming techniques must be used. The examiner has stated that candidates will not be expected to solve a linear programming problem in the exam.

Example 1 – Capital rationing

Bob plc has USD60,000 available to invest at time zero.

Data is available about the following four projects:

	A	*B*	*C*	*D*
Initial cost	30,000	20,000	40,000	10,000
PV of subsequent cashflows	52,000	25,000	56,000	18,000

Determine the optimum investment plan if:

(a) projects are mutually exclusive

(b) projects are divisible;

(c) projects are not divisible.

Assume that any surplus funds cannot be invested elsewhere.

3 Dealing with risk / uncertainty

Many projects are subject to risk or uncertainty and it is important that this can be evaluated and incorporated into the evaluation process.

Note that, in F3, you can usually expect to see the term 'risk' used in examination questions in the context of the possibility of an outcome that affects us in a negative manner, whereas the term 'uncertainty' would refer to the possibility of both positive and negative outcomes or inputs.

This follows common use of the term in practice.

For example, the possibility of a travel delay would normally be referred to as a 'risk' and lack of certainty over the actual departure date as 'uncertainty', whereas the possibility of a higher revenue than expected would be likely to be referred to as an 'opportunity' rather than as a 'risk'.

We set out below brief descriptions of procedures that can be used to help evaluate projects which are subject to risk.

Sensitivity analysis

Definition of sensitivity analysis

Sensitivity analysis definition

A modelling and risk assessment procedure in which changes are made to significant variables in order to determine the effect of these changes on the planned outcome. Particular attention is thereafter paid to variables identified as being of special significance.

(CIMA Official Terminology, 2005)

When undertaking an NPV analysis of a project, the accuracy of the NPV depends on the accuracy of the input factors in the calculation (e.g. estimates of cost of capital, sales, expenses, tax rates).

After computing the NPV of a project, sensitivity analysis can be used:

- to identify which of the input variables of the project could have the most adverse impact on the NPV of the project if they were to change.
- to assess the impact on the NPV of a certain change in a particular input factor.
- to consider by how much each input variable could change before the NPV of the project became zero (and hence the project became unacceptable).

Interpretation of sensitivity analysis results

A company has calculated the NPV of a project, and has subsequently identified the following sensitivities:

> Sales can fall by 10% or costs may rise by 20%, or the discount rate can increase by 1% before the NPV becomes zero.

In this case we would conclude that the project NPV is very sensitive to changes in discount rate (small percentage sensitivity) but not very sensitive to changes in costs (if costs were to change, unless they changed by more than 20% the NPV would still be positive.

Limitations of sensitivity analysis

The major problem is that we normally consider the impact of only one variable at a time. Management may be more interested in the risk of some key factors changing at the same time. For example, if the selling price changes, there is likely to be an impact on sales volume too. Sensitivity analysis can only deal with one of these variables changing at a time.

Also, sensitivity analysis does not include any assessment of the probability of certain variables changing.

It is therefore useful as an aid to decision making, rather than a decision rule in itself.

Two basic approaches to sensitivity analysis

(1) An analysis can be made of all the key input factors to ascertain by how much each factor must change before the NPV reaches zero, the indifference point.

(2) Alternatively specific changes can be calculated, such as the sales decreasing by 5%, in order to determine the effect on NPV.

Both approaches will be shown in the Illustration below.

e.g

Illustration 1 – Sensitivity

A project has an NPV of $1m. The PV of material costs (included in the NPV calculation) are $5m.

Sensitivity = (NPV / PV of cashflows affected by the estimate) × 100%

= 1m / 5m = 0.2 (20%)

i.e. the material costs could rise by up to 20% and the project remains viable. A rise of greater than 20% will produce a negative NPV and the project would not be worthwhile.

Alternatively, sensitivity analysis could be used to assess the impact of a given percentage change in a variable.

To continue with the above example, if the material costs were to change by 10% (from a PV of $5m to $5.5m – a change of $0.5m) the NPV would reduce by $0.5m from $1m to $0.5m (a fall of 50%).

More detailed example of sensitivity analysis

AVI Co is evaluating a new investment project as follows:

$000	t_0	t_1	t_2	t_3	t_4
Sales		1,000	1,000	1,000	1,000
Costs		600	600	600	600
		400	400	400	400
Tax (30%)		(120)	(120)	(120)	(120)
Net		280	280	280	280
CapEx	(600)				
Tax relief on depreciation		45	45	45	45
(30% x 600/4)					
Net cash flow	(600)	325	325	325	325
DF @ 10%	1	0.909	0.826	0.751	0.683

NPV = $430,000

Sensitivity to sales (i.e. by how much could sales fall before NPV becomes zero)

= (NPV / PV of cashflows affected by the estimate of sales) × 100%

= [430 / (1,000 × (1 – 0.30) × 3.170)] × 100%

=19.4%

i.e. if sales were to fall by 19.4% (to $806,000 per annum) then the NPV would be zero.

Sensitivity to tax rate

= (NPV / PV of cashflows affected by the estimate of tax rate) × 100%

= [430 / ((45-120) × 3.170)] × 100%

=181%

i.e. if the tax rate were to rise by 181% (from 30% to 30 x 2.82 = 84.6%) then the NPV would fall to zero.

Sensitivity to discount rate

This cannot be calculated in the same way. Instead the IRR of the project should be calculated and the difference between the existing cost of capital and the IRR then indicates the sensitivity to the discount rate.

Here the IRR is approximately 40%.

Interpretation of sensitivity calculations

AVI Co would initially be inclined to accept the project due to its positive NPV.

However, before making a final decision, the sensitivities would be considered. Any factors with small percentage sensitivities will have to be carefully assessed, because if the estimates of these factors turn out to be incorrect, the result may be a negative NPV.

In this example, the project NPV is not very sensitive to changes in the tax rate or the discount rate. The likelihood of sales falling by 19.4% would need to be assessed before making a final decision, but assuming that management decide that this is not a major risk, the project would be undertaken.

Probabilities

If forecasts are uncertain and probabilities can be attached to the possible outcomes, expected values (EV) can be calculated.

EV = (outcome 1 × probability 1) + (outcome 2 × probability 2) etc

Examples of probabilities

Simple example

GH Co is trying to estimate sales in the coming year.

It has been predicted that there is a 30% chance of sales being $20,000, a 50% chance of sales being $30,000 and a 20% chance of sales being $40,000.

Required:

Calculate the expected sales in the coming year.

Solution:

Expected sales = (0.30 × 20,000) + (0.50 × 30,000) + (0.20 × 40,000) = $29,000

More complex example (dependent probabilities)

Following on from the example above, assume that the sales in year 2 are dependent on the level of sales achieved in the first year, as follows:

Sales in year 1 (as above)	Probability (as above)	Sales in year 2
$20,000	30%	Could be $20,000 (probability 70%) or $10,000 (probability 30%)
$30,000	50%	Will also be $30,000
$40,000	20%	Could be $40,000 (probability 60%) or $50,000 (probability 40%)

Required:

Calculate the expected sales in year 2.

Solution:

Expected sales in year 2

= 0.30 × [(0.70 × 20,000) + (0.30 × 10,000)]

+ 0.50 × 30,000

+ 0.20 × [(0.60 × 40,000) + (0.40 × 50,000)]

= $28,900

Decision trees

In appraisal situations where uncertainty can apply to more than one variable, and values of the variables can be interdependent, many different outcomes are possible. The decision tree is a useful tool for reviewing a multiplicity of choices and outcomes.

Imagine the trunk of the tree as representing a project to be appraised, perhaps a new product to be added to a range, then the first branches (of which there may be two, three or more) may represent alternative predictions as to expected volume of revenue to each of which probabilities are assigned. Each revenue volume branch then creates secondary branches to represent contributions, to which again probabilities are assigned, and finally these branches create tertiary branches with allied probabilities to represent fixed costs.

The probabilities of each branch sequence are then multiplied and the joint probabilities thus obtained are applied in turn to each sequential set of values to give a series of pay-offs or outcomes as shown below:

Sales ('000 units)	Contribution $	Fixed costs $000	Joint probabilities	Pay-offs $
100 0.4	7 0.5	400 (0.4)	0.08	24,000
		500 (0.6)	0.12	24,000
	5 0.5	400 (0.4)	0.08	8,000
		500 (0.6)	0.12	NIL
80 0.6	7 0.5	400 (0.4)	0.12	19,200
		500 (0.6)	0.18	10,800
	5 0.5	400 (0.4)	0.12	NIL
		500 (0.6)	0.18	(18,000)
			1.00	68,000

Decision tree

As can be seen from the diagram, we arrive at eight joint probabilities leading to eight outcomes arising from 2 × 2 × 2 branches, representing 2 sales volumes × 2 contributions × 2 fixed cost values.

By relating the joint probabilities to the value figures, we obtain the eight pay-offs which are added to give an overall predicted net contribution of $68,000.

The pay-offs also show a range of net contributions from $24,000 positive to $18,000 negative, and by adding the joint probabilities there is a 58% chance of a positive outcome, 24% of a breakeven and 18% of a negative result.

Certainty equivalents

The cash flows of the project are calculated as per normal but then adjusted downwards by a certainty equivalent factor. This in effect decreases the cash flow. The cash flows are then discounted at a risk-free rate. In practice the major problem is that the use of certainty equivalents is subjective.

Definition of certainty equivalents

Certainty equivalent method – definition

An approach to dealing with risk in a capital budgeting context. It involves expressing risky future cash flows in terms of the certain cashflow which would be considered, by the decision maker, as their equivalent, that is the decision maker would be indifferent between the risky amount and the (lower) riskless amount considered to be its equivalent.

(CIMA Official Terminology, 2005)

Illustration 2 – Certainty equivalents

Year	*Cash flow*	*Certainty equivalent*	*RF DF, 6%*	*PV*
0	(1,000)	1	1	(1,000)
1	900	0.95	0.943	806
2	750	0.9	0.89	601

NPV = 407

More detail on certainty equivalents

The certainty equivalents method adjusts for risk by incorporating the decision maker's risk attitude into the investment decision by converting the expected cashflows of the project into equivalent riskless amounts.

The danger of using certainty equivalents lies in the high level of subjective judgement required from the decision-maker, while it could also be argued that risk-averse management might be better off using a high cut-off rate.

Nevertheless, certainty equivalents do represent a useful tool in the investment appraisal armoury, especially in assessing cases where an apparently small change in a key variable can interact with others to create significant falls in inflows, with a possible cumulative effect over the life of the project.

Risk adjusted discount rate

Discount rate considerations

In all the examples considered so far in this section on risk, a constant discount rate has been used, on the assumption that the cost of capital will remain the same over the life of the project. As the factors which influence the cost of capital, such as interest rates and inflation, can change considerably over a short period of time an organisation may wish to use different rates over the life of the project. Net present value and discounted present value allow this, but IRR and ARR present a uniform rate of return. Using NPV, for example, a different discount factor can be used for each year if so desired.

Perhaps, one of the major problems in using a discounted cash flow method is deciding on the correct discount rate to use.

It is difficult enough in year 1 but deciding on the rate for, say, year 4 may be very difficult because of changes in the economy, etc. If a very low rate is chosen almost all projects will be accepted, whereas if a very high discount rate is chosen very few projects will be accepted.

Looking back over the years, it would appear that the majority of managers have probably used too high a discount rate and have, as a consequence, not invested in projects that would have helped their organisation to grow in relation to their competitors. There are no prizes for being too conservative; it is just as much a failing as being too optimistic.

If there is any doubt over the correct discount rate to be used, sensitivity analysis can help.

A premium to the normal discount rate may be added to evaluate projects that are considered more risky.

Then, more marginal projects would be less likely to have a positive NPV.

More detail on adjusted discount rates

A useful scheme is to have a risk category schedule providing different risk gradings. For example, a "normal" project could be discounted at the usual cost of capital, with more risky projects being discounted at perhaps 2% more than this.

The difficulty with risk-adjusted discount rates lies mainly in the need for skilful management judgement as to the risk category, even though considerable product and market research may have been undertaken.

The capital asset pricing model (CAPM) is often used to calculate risk adjusted discount rates, as shown in the earlier Chapter on "Capital Structure".

4 Equivalent Annual Cost

This is sometimes useful for comparing projects when the assets of the project need replacing periodically by new assets.

Definition

The Equivalent Annual Cost (EAC) is the equivalent annuity which has the same present value as the project if paid for the same number of years as the project's life.

Formula

$$\text{EAC} = \frac{\text{Total present value}}{\text{Annuity factor for life of asset}}$$

Further details on the use of annual equivalent cost

When the present value (of a capital project) is expressed as an annual amount, this is called annual equivalent cost and is used to compare projects having different life cycles.

Calculating equivalent annual costs is basically a method of discounting especially for asset replacement decisions, but it also has value when comparing the sensitivity of variables where projects have unequal lives.

Unequal lives

When two or more mutually exclusive investments with unequal lives are being compared, consideration must be given to the time period over which a comparison of the investments is to be made.

Before making a comparison between mutually exclusive projects with differing lives, an explicit decision must be taken as to whether it is necessary to equalise the lives.

A choice should be made on the basis of NPV, whether equalisation is required or not, although the process of equalisation may alter the ranking of the projects under consideration.

Asset replacement cycles

The concept of equivalent annual costs can be used in determining the optimum replacement cycle for an asset.

This decision involves how long to continue operating the existing asset before it is replaced with an identical one. As the asset gets older, it may become less efficient, its operating costs may increase and the resale value will reduce.

e.g

Illustration 3 – Equivalent annual cost

Assume that the NPV of cash outflows for asset replacement project A is USD64,300, with discounting at 12% and an asset life of 4 years, while for project B, the NPV of outflows is USD79,355, also after discounting at 12% but with an asset life of 6 years.

Annual equivalent costs are:

Project A: 64,300 / 3.037 (AF for 4 years at 12%) = 21,172

Project B: 79,355 / 4.111 (AF for 6 years at 12%) = 19,303

So on an annualised basis, project B has the lower cost and would be preferred even though on a non-annualised basis project A would have seemed more advantageous.

Note that the cashflows and discount rates must always be in real terms in order to deal with inflation accurately.

Detailed example of the use of equivalent annual cost

Lita Co operates a delivery vehicle, which cost $20,000 and has a useful life of 3 years. Lita Co has a cost of capital of 5%. The details of the vehicle's cash operating costs for each year and the resale value at the end of each year are as follows.

	Year 1	Year 2	Year 3
	$	$	$
Cash operating costs	9,000	10,500	11,900
End of year resale value	14,000	11,500	8,400

Required:

Determine how frequently the vehicle should be replaced.

Solution

The first step is to calculate the present value of the total costs incurred if the vehicle is kept for 1, 2 or 3 years, respectively.

Keep for 1 year

NPV = –20,000 + (5,000 × 0.952) = –15,240

Keep for 2 years

NPV = –20,000 – (9,000 × 0.952) + (1,000 × 0.907) = –27,661

Keep for 3 years

NPV = –20,000 – (9,000 × 0.952) – (10,500 × 0.907) – (3,500 × 0.864) = –41,116

These present value figures are not comparable because they relate to different time periods.

To render them comparable they must be converted to average annual figures, or equivalent annual costs, by dividing by the cumulative discount factors:

Keep for 1 year

EAC = 15,240 / 0.952 = 16,008

Keep for 2 years

EAC = 27,661 / 1.859 = 14,880

Keep for 3 years

EAC = 41,116 / 2.723 = 15,100

The lowest equivalent annual cost occurs if the vehicle is kept for 2 years. Therefore, the optimum replacement cycle is to replace the vehicle every 2 years.

5 Real Options

Introduction to real options

Traditional approaches to investment appraisal tend to treat investments as one-off decisions which must be taken at a single point in time, with the opportunity otherwise being lost.

While this may typify some investment decisions, it certainly does not apply to them all.

In many situations it may be possible to delay and gain further valuable information, which could be influential in the viability or otherwise of the investment decision.

In such cases the opportunity to invest can be thought of as being very similar to a call option. It gives a right, but not an obligation, to a stream of cash flows associated with the project at some future date. When a company either decides to go ahead or completely rejects an investment proposal it effectively brings this option to an end.

While the option is open it has a value, and recent research would suggest that the NPV rule should be modified to take account of the value of this option.

Such options are called 'real options' because they are options on real physical assets, to distinguish them from financial options which are options on financial assets.

Detailed explanation of real options

Introduction

Option-pricing theory is not part of the syllabus, but it is useful to consider the option-like features found in investment decisions. When a project is slipping behind forecast, managers can take action in an attempt to achieve the original NPV target. In other words, they can create options, or take action to mitigate losses or exploit new opportunities presented by capital investments.

Terminology – call and put options

Before discussing investment decisions as options on future cash flows, it may be useful to identity the meaning of call and put options:

- a call option is an option to buy a specified asset at a specified exercise price on or before a specified exercise date;
- a put option is an option to sell a specified asset at a specified exercise price on or before a specified exercise date.

Application to investment appraisal

The NPV approach to investment appraisal makes two assumptions that may be questioned:

(1) a project is reversible;

(2) a project cannot be delayed.

The assumption that a project is reversible implies that if the project does not work out, the original investment can be recovered and applied to a new project. This is flawed, as in most significant projects the original investment will either be wholly or partly irreversible.

In some instances, it may not be possible to delay an investment decision, but in the majority of cases a delay is possible – although there may be costs associated with delay. If a project is irreversible to some degree, the ability to delay the investment decision in order to obtain new information is valuable. The additional costs associated with delay should be assessed against the benefits associated with that new information.

Investment projects can be related to financial call options, in that the project provides the right, but not the obligation, to purchase an asset (or commit to a series of cash flows) in the future. When an irreversible investment decision is made, the call option becomes exercised. The opportunity to delay an investment and keep the option alive has a value, which is not normally reflected in an NPV calculation.

The real options approach suggests that decisions that increase flexibility by creating and preserving options should be pursued. Decisions that reduce flexibility by exercising options and irreversibly committing resources should be valued at a lower figure than conventional NPV would suggest.

Categorisation of real options

In the context of investment decisions there are three options to be considered:

(1) The abandonment option (financial put option).

(2) Timing options (financial call option) – sometimes referred to as "wait and see options".

(3) Strategic investment options (financial call option) – sometimes referred to as "follow-on options".

Different types of real options

The abandonment option

Major investment decisions involve heavy capital commitments and are largely irreversible: once the initial capital expenditure is incurred, management cannot turn the clock back and act differently.

Because the management is committing large sums of money in pursuit of higher, but uncertain, payoffs, the ability to abandon, or 'bail out', should things look grim, can be valuable.

Timing options (or "wait and see options")

Management may view an investment as a 'now or never' opportunity, arguing that in highly competitive markets there is no scope for delay.

In effect, this amounts to viewing the decision as a call option which is about to expire. If a positive NPV is expected, the option will be exercised, otherwise the option lapses and no investment is made. However, delaying the decision by a year to gain valuable new information is likely to be a more valuable option.

This helps us to understand why entities sometimes do not take up apparently wealth-creating opportunities: the option to wait and gather new information is sufficiently valuable to warrant such delay.

Strategic investment options (or "follow-on options")

Certain investment decisions give rise to follow-on opportunities which are wealth-creating.

For example, new technology investment, involving large-scale research and development, is particularly difficult to evaluate, and many such projects would show negative NPVs as the uncertainty involved would demand the use of high discount rates. However, they offer the potential to access a large market in the future.

The negative NPV can be viewed as the option cost, or premium on the follow-on option. The value of the option is the value of the flexibility associated with the project.

Simple real options example

Cardiff Components Co is considering building a new plant to produce components for the nuclear defence industry.

Proposal A is to build a custom-designed plant using the latest technology, but applicable only to nuclear defence contracts.

A less profitable scheme, B, is to build a plant using standard machine tools, giving greater flexibility in application.

The outcome of a general election to be held one year hence has a major impact on the decision. If the current government is returned to office, their commitment to nuclear defence is likely to give rise to new orders, making proposal A the better choice. If, however, the current opposition party is elected, its commitment to run down the nuclear defence industry would make proposal B the better course of action.

Proposal B has, in effect, a put option attached to it, giving the flexibility to abandon the proposed operation in favour of some other activity.

(Illustration adapted from Pike and Neale)

Numerical illustration of real options

Initial scenario

A project, P, has expected cash flows as shown below:

Year 0	Year 1		Year 2		Year 3	
$	p	$	p	$	p	$
(3,500)	1/3	3,000	1/3	3,000	1/3	3,000
	1/3	2,000	1/3	2,000	1/3	2,000
	1/3	1,000	1/3	1,000	1/3	1,000
Expected values		2,000		2,000		2,000

Note that p = probability of each outcome.

The project's NPV at a discount rate of 10%, based on the expected value of its cashflows is:

Year	Cash flow ($)	DF 10%	PV ($)
0	(3,500)	1	(3,500)
1	2,000	0.909	1,818
2	2,000	0.826	1,653
3	2,000	0.751	1,503
			1,474

More details regarding the project

The initial investment of $3,500 in project P represents the purchase of a customised machine, the price of which is known with certainty.

Because it is a customised machine its resale value is low; it can only be sold for $2,000 up to 1 year after purchase. Thereafter, its resale value will be zero.

The option to abandon the project immediately

Once the machine is bought, the expected value of abandoning the project immediately would be $2,000 (1 × $2,000).

This must be compared with the expected value of continuing with the project, which is $4,974 ($1,818 + $1,653 + $1,503).

In this case, the expected benefits of continuing with the project far outweigh the returns from abandoning it immediately.

The option to abandon the project in 1 year's time

Once the machine has been in operation for a year, the first year's cashflow will be known with certainty.

Assume that in this scenario, the year 1 outcome determines the years 2 and 3 outcomes with certainty (i.e. if the outcome is $1,000 in year 1, it will also be $1,000 in year 2 and year 3, etc).

Note: if this were not to be the case, a decision tree could be used to identify all the potential combinations of outcomes.

Given that the machine can be sold for $2,000 at this point, the three possible outcomes if the project is abandoned in 1 year's time are:

Year	**Cash flow ($)**	**DF 10%**	**PV ($)**
New 0	2,000	1	2,000
1	(1,000)	0.909	(909)
2	(1,000)	0.826	(826)
			265

Year	**Cash flow ($)**	**DF 10%**	**PV ($)**
New 0	2,000	1	2,000
1	(2,000)	0.909	(1,818)
2	(2,000)	0.826	(1,652)
			(1,470)

Year	Cash flow ($)	DF 10%	PV ($)
New 0	2,000	1	2,000
1	(3,000)	0.909	(2,727)
2	(3,000)	0.826	(2,478)
			(3,205)

Note that in each case it has been assumed that the project has been abandoned, and therefore all the future cashflows have been foregone.

It can be seen that if the future cashflows are expected to be $2,000 per annum or $3,000 per annum, the project should not be abandoned in 1 year's time, since the value of the future cashflows foregone would be higher than the disposal value of $2,000.

However, if the future cashflows are expected to be $1,000, the project should be abandoned since the abandonment option has a positive NPV.

Assessing the value of the abandonment option

The fact that the project can be abandoned in 1 year's time if cashflows turn out to be at the low end of expectations ($1,000 per annum) gives an additional value to the overall project.

The value of this can be incorporated into the NPV of the project by recomputing the NPV based on the cashflows if the abandonment takes place, as follows:

Year 0	Year 1		Year 2		Year 3	
$	p	$	p	$	p	$
(3,500)	1/3	3,000	1/3	3,000	1/3	3,000
	1/3	2,000	1/3	2,000	1/3	2,000
	1/3	1,000+2,000	1/3	NIL	1/3	NIL
Expected values		2,667		1,667		1,667

The NPV of the project now becomes:

Year	Cash flow ($)	DF 10%	PV ($)
0	(3,500)	1	(3,500)
1	2,667	0.909	2,424
2	1,667	0.826	1,377
3	1,667	0.751	1,252
			1,553

i.e. the option to abandon the project in 1 year's time increases the NPV of the project by $79 ($1,553 – $1,474).

Valuing real options

Option valuation

Calculations on option pricing are not part of the syllabus, but it is worth noting that the Black-Scholes option pricing model can be used to value real options if the following five factors can be identified and entered into the model:

(1) present value of the future cash flows from the investment;

(2) initial outlay on the investment;

(3) time until the investment opportunity disappears, that is the length of time that an investment decision can be deferred without losing the opportunity to invest;

(4) variability of project returns;

(5) risk-free rate of interest.

In practice, however, the time to expiry and the variability of project returns may be difficult to measure.

Pricing an option using values for these factors will arguably provide more information about the value of a project than using NPV. However, quantifying these factors objectively is not straightforward.

NEW

6 Adjusted Present Value (APV)

Introduction

We saw in the earlier Chapter on 'Cost of Capital' that a significant change in capital structure renders an entity's existing cost of capital unsuitable as a discount rate in an NPV analysis. This is because the existing cost of capital is a function of the entity's existing capital structure ratio.

The discount rate to be used in the investment decisions should, in theory, be a specific risk-adjusted discount rate which reflects the business risk of the project.

This adjusted rate is the basis of the concept of adjusted present value (APV), which suggests that the NPV of a project can be increased or decreased by the side-effects of financing.

More details on when to use APV

It is not appropriate or necessary to use the APV method if there is just a simple change in the capital structure when a project is undertaken. In this case, it is simpler to recalculate the WACC based on the new capital structure and to use the risk adjusted WACC as a discount rate for the project cashflows.

APV should be used in the following circumstances:

(1) if the project is to be funded using a subsidised loan. The benefit of the subsidy can be separately identified in the APV calculations, so the APV method gives a more accurate assessment of the project and the associated financing;

(2) if there is to be a change in the debt capacity of the company. The APV method values separately the benefit to the company of the tax relief generated on the new finance.

(3) if the project is to be modelled under a number of capital structure options. A risk adjusted WACC could be recalculated for each potential capital structure position, but this would be a much more time consuming process than using APV.

Note that the calculation of APV usually takes the form of first calculating NPV as if the project financing was all by equity, and then incorporating adjustments to allow for the effects of the financing method to be actually used.

Bear in mind that difficulties in using APV may arise either in determining the costs involved in the financing method to be used, or in finding a suitable cost of equity for the basic NPV calculation. Nevertheless, APV often has the advantage of being a more positive approach than making an arbitrary adjustment to the entity's discount rate.

APV calculations

APV consists of two different elements:

APV = Investment element ('Base case NPV') + Financing element

(i.e. Value of a geared project = value of an all equity financed project + PV of financing side-effects)

Three step approach

APV takes a three-stage approach:

- **Stage One:** the project is evaluated as if it is all equity financed.
- **Stage Two:** the project's 'finance package' is evaluated
- **Stage Three:** Stages One and Two are combined to produce the APV.

Stage One

Stage One is a standard NPV analysis of the project, *except* for the discount rate used.

In APV, a special discount rate is used, to reflect the risk of an all equity financed company undertaking the new project (the 'base-case discount rate').

More details on the base case NPV discount rate

Sometimes a suitable ungeared cost of equity is provided in the question or the company's geared cost of equity can be adjusted to find a suitable ungeared cost of equity. For example, it may be possible to use one of the Modigliani & Miller formulae to convert a geared cost of equity to an ungeared cost of equity or, alternatively, to use the CAPM formula to calculate an ungeared cost of equity from an ungeared beta. Both of these methods are explained the earlier Chapter on 'Capital Structure'. The choice of method will depend on the information provided in the question.

In other cases, the project may have a different business risk from that of the company making the investment or the company itself may not be listed and so may not have its own cost of equity. It may then be necessary to use a proxy company to calculate an appropriate ungeared cost of equity for use in the base case NPV. If proxy company beta information is provided, use this to obtain the ungeared/asset beta value of the proxy company and then put this into the CAPM formula to obtain an appropriate ungeared cost of equity to use as the base case discount rate.

Only then can you move on to calculate the base case NPV (project cash flows discounted at the base case discount rate).

Stage Two

In Stage Two, the present value of the costs and benefits associated with the financing package is calculated.

The side-effects of financing can be numerous, and may include:

- tax relief on the interest paid on debt capital used;
- after tax issue costs of the finance needed for the project;
- tax relief of surplus debt capacity created by the project;
- government grants;
- tax relief on subsidised loans.

The discount rate to apply to the financing side-effects should reflect the systematic risk level involved for those side-effects identified above, it is usually assumed that the **pre-tax cost of debt** should be used.

This rate reflects the low risk nature of the tax benefits and avoids double-counting the tax relief on debt interest.

Details of financing costs and benefits

Issue costs

Equity issue costs are not tax deductible but debt issue costs tend to be (however, the examiner will generally tell you what to assume here).

Sometimes the amount raised has to cover the issue costs. For example, if it says in a question that $480,000 of finance is needed for a project, net of issue costs of 4%, the total amount of finance raised will have to be 480,000 × (100/96) = $500,000 (hence the issue costs are $20,000).

PV of tax relief on interest payments = PV of tax shield

This is a calculation of an annuity, or a deferred annuity if tax relief is first received in year 2.

Annual tax relief = total loan x interest rate x tax rate

Subsidised / Cheap Loan

Like all loans, calculate the tax shield. In addition, you need to calculate the opportunity benefit of the cheap loan as follows:

PV of interest saved	X
Less PV of tax relief lost	(X)
PV of the cheap loan	X

Debt capacity

A project's debt capacity denotes its ability to act as security for a loan. It is the tax relief available on such a loan, which gives debt capacity its value.

When calculating the present value of the tax shield (tax relief on interest) one should base it on the project's theoretical debt capacity and not the actual amount of the debt used.

The company accrues a tax benefit from a project of each pound of debt finance that project can support, even if the debt is used on some other project. Therefore we use the theoretical debt capacity to match the tax benefit to the specific project.

This technique assumes that the theoretical debt capacity is fully utilised within the company as a whole.

Stage Three

Having calculated the project's base-case net present value and also the present value of the financing side effects, these are then combined to find the project's Adjusted Present Value or APV.

Basic APV illustration

A project requires $1m capital investment. The project will save $220,000 per year after taxes. Assume the savings are in perpetuity.

The business risk of the venture requires a 20% discount rate (based on a calculation of a suitable ungeared beta for the project). In this case, the project's base case NPV is just positive:

Base case NPV = –1,000,000 + (220,000 / 0.2) = $100,000

However, assume that this project has one financial side-effect: it expands the firm's borrowing power by $400,000. The project lasts indefinitely, so we treat it as supporting perpetual (i.e. undated) debt.

If we assume that the borrowing rate is 14% and the tax rate is 35%, the project supports debt which generates an interest tax shield of 0.35 × 0.14 × $400,000, which is $19,600 per annum for ever.

The **PV of the tax shield** is:

$19,600 / 0.14 = $140,000

The **project's APV** is therefore:

APV = Base case NPV + PV shield

= $100,000 + $140,000 = $240,000

Comprehensive APV illustration

Scrumpy is considering a project that requires an initial investment of $400,000 and is expected to generate annual net cash flows after tax of $175,000 over its 3 year life. The investment will have no residual value.

20% of the initial investment will be financed by equity. A further 40% of the initial investment will be financed by a subsidised loan at an interest rate of 5%. The balance will be met by a loan at the rate of 9% per annum. Issue costs for the equity are expected to be 3% of the amount raised, but can be assumed to be zero for the debt.

The project is in a sector which has an equity beta of 1.7 and an average debt:equity ratio of 1:3.

The risk free rate of return is 5% after tax and the market return is 13% after tax.

Corporate tax is at the rate of 30%. Assume that tax is paid at each year end without delay and there is no tax relief on capital expenditure or issue costs.

Required:

Evaluate the project using the APV approach.

Solution

Base-case NPV

$$\beta_{asset} = 1.70 \times \frac{3}{3 + 1(1 - 0.3)} = 1.38$$

Base-case discount rate = 5% + (13%–5%) × 1.38 = 16%

Year	Cash flow ($)	DF 16%	PV ($)
0	(400,000)	1	(400,000)
1	175,000	0.862	150,850
2	175,000	0.743	130,025
3	175,000	0.641	112,175
			(6,950)

Financing side effects

PV of tax relief on debt interest

$400,000 × 0.4 × 0.09 × 0.3 × annuity factor years 1–3 @ 9% = $4,320 × 2.531 = $10,934

$400,000 × 0.4 × 0.05 × 0.3 × annuity factor years 1–3 @ 9% = $2,400 × 2.531 = $6,074

Total = $17,008

PV subsidised loan

Interest saving

= $400,000 × 0.4 × (0.09 – 0.05)(1 – 0.3) × Annuity factor years 1–3 @ 9%

= $4,480 × 2.531 = $11,338

Issue costs

$400,000 × 0.2 × 0.03 = $2,400

Adjusted present value

Base case NPV +/– PV of financing side effects

= –6,950 + 17,008 + 11,338 – 2,400 = $18,996

The project should be accepted as it has a positive APV of $18,996

Example 2 : APV

DT plc is a UK quoted company. The directors have been evaluating a cost saving project which will require £1.9 million capital expenditure on new machinery. The directors expect the capital investment to provide cost savings of £300,000 per annum indefinitely. Both of these figures are given **net** of any tax implications.

The company is at present all equity financed.

The discount rate which should be applied to the project is 16% (based on an estimate of a suitable ungeared beta for the project).

The directors believe the current capital structure fails to take advantage of the tax benefits of debt and propose to finance the new project with undated debt secured on the company's assets. The current rate of interest required by the market on corporate debt of this risk and maturity is 9%, but half of the loan will be subject to an interest rate of 3% under a Government subsidy scheme. For the purposes of this example, assume that the Government subsidy will be received into perpetuity.

The costs of issue, which are not tax deductible, are expected to be 5% of the gross proceeds of issue. The company intends to issue sufficient debt to cover the cost of capital expenditure and the costs of issue.

The company's tax rate is 33%.

Required:

Using the information given for DT plc, calculate the APV of the investment.

Comparison of the APV method and the NPV method

APV can be used to appraise a project when there is a significant change in an entity's capital structure. However, following on from earlier work in the 'Cost of Capital', 'Capital Structure' and 'Investment Appraisal – basic techniques' Chapters, we know that a project can also be appraised more directly by discounting its cashflows using an appropriate cost of capital.

The following worked example will compare the APV method with the standard NPV method.

Example

XX Co, a US based company, is considering diversifying its operations away from its main area of business (food manufacturing) by setting up a brand new plastics division.

Its first potential plastics project is an investment project which involves the purchase of a moulding machine which costs USD100,000. The project is expected to produce net post tax annual operating cash flows of USD15,000 into perpetuity.

The assets of the project will support debt finance of 40% of its initial cost. The loan will be irredeemable, and will carry an interest rate of 10% per annum. The balance of finance will be provided by a placing of new equity. Assume that there will be no issue costs associated with the new finance.

The plastics industry has an average geared (equity) beta of 1.368 and an average debt:equity ratio of 1:5 by market values. XX Co's current geared (equity) beta is 1.8 and 20% of its long-term capital is represented by debt which is generally regarded to be risk-free.

The risk-free rate is 10% p.a. and the expected return on an average market portfolio is 15%. Corporation tax is at a rate of 30%.

Evaluation of the project

Three approaches will be considered:

- Method 1: using the current WACC as a discount rate
- Method 2: using an adjusted WACC as a discount rate
- Method 3: adjusted present value (APV).

Method 1: Using the current WACC as a discount rate

The entity's current WACC would be:

$[ke \times 0.8] + [kd(1 - t) \times 0.2]$

$= [(10\% + 1.8\ (15\% - 10\%)) \times 0.8] + [(10\%\ (1 - 0.30)) \times 0.2]$

$= 16.6\%$

However, if this figure were used to discount the post tax operating cash flows of the project we would be making several errors:

- The current WACC is based upon XX Co's existing business risk (i.e. that of the food manufacturing industry). The plastics project involves considerably different business risk and should therefore be evaluated at a discount rate appropriate to its own business risk.
- The capital structure associated with the new plastics division is significantly different from XX Co's existing capital structure, so the weightings used in this WACC calculation are not relevant to the new investment.

In conclusion, it is not appropriate to use this WACC as a discount rate for the new project.

Before considering alternative Methods 2 and 3, let's consider the issues of business risk and capital structure separately.

Impact of a change in business risk

First, consider the issue of business risk.

The plastics project will have a different level of business risk from XX Co's existing operations, so we need to derive a suitable cost of equity for the plastics project, based on shareholders' expectations of the risk they are likely to face. Since no beta factor exists for the new project yet, we shall use a proxy beta factor based on the plastics industry to enable us to approximate the risk of the new project, and hence (using the CAPM model) the adjusted cost of equity.

The given plastics industry beta is a geared beta, so we first degear this to remove the impact of industry average gearing:

Using: $$ßu = ßg \times \frac{E}{E + D(1 - t)}$$

$$ßu = 1.368 \times \frac{5}{5 + 1(1 - 0.30)} = 1.2$$

So the ungeared beta for an entity in the plastics business = 1.2

Impact of a change in capital structure

Now, consider the issue of capital structure.

The assumption here is that the new project undertaken by XX Co effectively represents the setting up of a new division, whose future capital structure will be 40% debt : 60% equity (in common with the initial financing of the project). In this case, there are two options:

- the ungeared beta calculated above can be regeared to this new level of capital structure (40% debt:60% equity), and then used to find an adjusted WACC to be used for discounting – see Method 2 below.
- the Adjusted Present Value (APV) method can be used, where the ungeared beta is used to find an ungeared cost of equity, which is used for discounting the project cash flows before the impacts of financing are dealt with separately – see Method 3 below.

Alternatively, if the assumption is that the new project is likely to significantly alter the entire entity's capital structure level, the marginal cost of capital approach can be used instead (covered in the earlier Chapter on 'Cost of Capital').

Method 2: Using an adjusted WACC as a discount rate

First, regear the ungeared beta (1.2) from above to reflect the 40% debt:60% equity gearing ratio associated with the new project.

Using: $$ß_u = ß_g \times \frac{E}{E + D(1 - t)}$$

$$1.2 = ß_g \times \frac{0.6}{0.6 + 0.4 \times (1 - 0.30)}$$

$$1.2 = ß_g \times 0.682$$

$$\frac{1.2}{0.682} = ß_g = 1.76$$

Then, the CAPM model can be used to derive a risk adjusted cost of equity, and this cost of equity can be inserted into the WACC formula along with the new capital structure level (40% debt : 60% equity) to give a risk adjusted WACC for discounting as follows:

Cost of equity of 10% + 1.76 (15% - 10%) = 18.8% and a WACC for the plastics project is:

$$k_o = k_{eg}\left[\frac{V_E}{V_E + V_D}\right] + k_d\left[\frac{V_D}{V_E + V_D}\right]$$

i.e. (60/100) × 18.8% + (40/100) × 7% = 14.08%

Therefore the project NPV, at 14.08%, would be:

–USD100,000 + USD15,000 / 0.1408 = USD6,534

Note here that when discounting the project flows using the WACC, the post tax cash flows before financing charges are used, because financing charges are incorporated in the calculation of WACC, so deducting them as part of the cash flows would mean double counting their impact.

Method 3: Adjusted present value approach

As an alternative to adjusting the WACC as shown in Method 2 above, we sometimes use the Adjusted Present Value (APV) approach.

Step 1 Base case net present value

First compute a suitable (ungeared) cost of equity for the new project, based on the ungeared beta (1.2) derived above:

Required return of project = 10% + (15% – 10%) 1.2 = 16% p.a.

Then discount the project cash flows at 16%, to give a base case NPV of
–USD100,000 + USD15,000 / 0.16 = –USD6,250 (negative figure).

Step 2 The financing side effects

In this case, the financing side effects comprise just the tax relief on the debt interest (benefit of financing). The present value of this element now needs to be computed as follows, using the pre tax cost of debt (10%) as a discount rate, since this rate accurately reflects the risk associated with the debt cashflows and hence the tax relief.

Debt interest = 10% x (40% x USD100,000) = USD4,000 per annum

Therefore tax relief = USD4,000 x 30% = USD1,200 per annum.

So PV of tax relief at 10% = USD1,200 / 0.10 = USD12,000

Adjusted present value

	USD
Base case NPV	(6,250)
Tax shield / relief on debt interest	12,000
APV	5,750

Comparison of Methods 2 and 3

Method 2 (discounting using a risk adjusted WACC) and Method 3 (APV) give slightly different results for the project appraisal (USD 6,534 and USD 5,750 respectively). This is because the amount of debt entered into the APV calculation in this case (USD40,000) represents 40% of the initial investment required, while the risk adjusted WACC calculation also incorporates the tax benefit on the additional debt capacity generated by the positive NPV of the project. If the APV calculation had used this higher level of debt capacity , the two methods would have given the same answer.

The two methods have the following relative advantages.

Advantages of the risk adjusted WACC method:

- the risk adjusted WACC method is conceptually easier to understand.
- it requires the calculation of a single hurdle rate which can be used for different projects, and to compare with other businesses.

Advantages of APV:

- APV can deal with other financing side effects such as subsidies on loans in a more transparent way than in a risk adjusted WACC calculation.
- using APV means less recalculating if assumptions regarding capital structure change. The base case NPV is calculated independently of any financing issues.

However, both methods share the following **limitations**:

- because the methods are both based on Modigliani and Miller's theories, they do not deal with the increased financial risk that comes with increasing gearing. Adjusting the beta for gearing simply recognises the impact of the change in capital structure on the cost of capital (because of the tax shield on debt). It does not deal with the "U-shaped" graph of WACC under the Traditional View of gearing which is more applicable in the real world.
- both methods assume that cost of capital stays constant into perpetuity, whereas in practice the various input components may well fluctuate as real world economic factors change.

Conclusion

Despite these limitations, both methods of investment appraisal can be used to give a useful insight into the viability or otherwise of a potential investment project.

As long as we are aware of the limitations, we can make sure that any marginal projects are evaluated using other methods too (such as payback period, modified internal rate of return, or non-quantitative methods) before a final decision is made.

NEW

7 Linking investment in IS/IT with strategic, operational and control needs

Introduction to IS/IT projects

A particular problem is experienced in appraising investment projects concerned with Information Systems (IS) and Information Technology (IT).

Businesses have always used information systems, even before computers became widespread, as methods to collect data about the company and its competitors, which is then made available to the managers of the company to help them in their decision-making.

Recent developments in IT including the prevalence of cheap powerful computers and database technology have allowed such systems to help managers:

- at the strategic level, to plan for the achievement of the organisation's overall objectives (e.g. competitive advantage)
- at the operational level, to ensure that the processes currently carried out are efficient and effective (e.g. fewer delays, better service to customers, reduced staff levels)
- to control the business, to provide feedback on performance (e.g. exception reporting and comparison of performance against budget, leading to better decision-making).

Problems in appraising IS/IT projects

While the cost of a computer or a software application is a known amount, the benefits of IT are hard to tie down.

Some senior managers simply believe that expenditure on IT is a 'good thing' and that money must be spent as an 'act of faith', but the pressure on all budget areas in recent years has led to blind faith no longer being an acceptable policy.

Top managers today insist on IT spending being justified in the same way as any other proposed expenditure.

The problem in applying conventional DCF analysis to IS/IT projects is that, even if the up-front cost is known, the benefits will be both tangible and intangible, and selecting a discount rate to reflect the risk of the project will also prove difficult. Nevertheless, the exercise can still be carried out, even if it will only be possible in approximate terms.

More details on IS/IT investment projects

IS/IT strategy

Until quite recently, most entities regarded their IT systems and their information systems as a resource that was necessary but not strategically significant. The IT department was treated like any other collection of overheads, and the information systems allowed to evolve rather than being formally planned.

Many entities now realise that the information system is a strategic resource, and should be treated as such. This often includes having a formal strategy.

IS, IT and IM strategy

Some authors distinguish between three components (or levels) of strategy as follows:

IS strategy, which looks at the way in which the information systems in various parts of the entity are organised;

IT strategy, which looks at the technology infrastructure of the systems; and

IM strategy, which considers how the systems support management processes.
In this chapter, we use the term 'information systems strategy' to encompass all three of these components.

Content of information systems strategy

It is unlikely that the information systems strategy will remain unchanged within an entity over any significant period of time. Strategies may need amending for various reasons including:

- change in the overall objectives of the entity;
- development of new information technologies;
- update of existing hardware and software;
- change in the number of employees, resulting in existing systems not coping with new information requirements.

Whatever the reason for the change, it is important that some formal process is followed to ensure that the IS and business objectives remain in alignment. In the worst case scenario, the IT department may decide that some new technology is useful, and implement this. However, if it does not support the overall business objectives of the entity, then the business may not be able to operate successfully.

A general strategy to follow when information systems require amendment is outlined below.

General approach

Initially, the business strategy of the entity must be determined. Checking this strategy is essential, because the IT strategy must support this strategy and not drive it. Just because new IT systems may be available does not mean that they have to be used in the entity. Also, new IT systems may not be compatible with other software or hardware used in the entity. Additional checks will be necessary to confirm compatibility.

Within any entity, amending part of the information strategy may have an impact on other sections. For example, if information is suddenly provided in a different format, it may no longer be accessible by other divisions or branches. Amendments to the information strategy must be checked against the business plan and individual requirements of each part of the organisation.

Having decided to amend the IS strategy in some way, a plan for developing and implementing the system will have to be developed. As well as setting out the plan in an appropriate manner, alternative hardware and software as well as development methods may need to be considered. The choice will be between development in-house or outsourcing. A full cost–benefit analysis (CBA) may also be used now, or earlier in the change process, to check that the change will provide the necessary benefits to the organisation at an acceptable cost.

Having determined the overall strategy for change, this can be implemented and systems amended. Checks may also be required to ensure that staff and customers are kept fully informed. Particularly where the change will result in some competitive advantage, advertising that the change has taken place will be essential.

Finally, a review will be necessary to ensure that the initial objectives of the change have been met. If this is not the case, then further review may be required to determine why and confirm what additional changes are actually required.

Cost-benefit analysis

Traditional CBA tends to be focused on costs and benefits derived from the accounting system. With many of the costs and benefits of information being intangible, this analysis may not form a suitable way of assessing the value of information.

This section summarises the benefits and limitations of CBA, and these are given below:

Which tangible costs to include in the CBA?

The main issue is identifying which costs are actually attributable to producing the new information. Most entities have a network of some description, so distributing any additional information for a new system should not be a problem. However, increase in network traffic will result from the new information, along with growth in information transfer from other applications. When the network bandwidth needs upgrading, which specific project pays for this?

How to measure intangible costs

Many intangible costs arise from not having information available for a specific decision. For example, lack of information about competitors may result in incorrect decision making within the entity. The issue is how to measure the cost of not having all the information to make a decision. As the accounting system does not trap these costs, they may be excluded from the CBA.

Diminishing returns from benefits

Some of the benefits of enhanced information systems can be seen in terms of the improvement in quality of information being provided. For example, if information is provided in 2 seconds rather than 20 seconds, then the information is probably timelier. Placing some value on this benefit may be difficult, although it could be included in the CBA under a heading of 'other benefits' and a guess made as to the value.

However, there will be significant diminishing returns to this provision, for example providing information in 0.2 of a second rather than 2 seconds will attract a much smaller amount of benefit. Humans cannot necessarily react to information this quickly. There are limits to benefits from automation so the benefits of improving the quality of information should not be overstated.

How to measure intangible benefits

Enhanced information may be provided by a new system, however placing a value on how that information helps people make better decisions is more difficult. The benefits of having additional information may be measured in terms of improved customer service, competitive advantage gained, etc. Again, these items are not identified in the accounting system and it may be very difficult to place any value on them.

The benefits from providing more or better information may also take a long time to accrue. Information systems have to be accepted by the staff, and time will be taken for historical analysis to build up to any meaningful level. Traditional measures of CBA such as Payback or ROI may be inappropriate, because they provide too short a timeframe for assessing the benefits of information.

Evaluating system performance

Given the weaknesses of the decision-making techniques outlined above, how are we to assess the performance of an information system?

There are three approaches we might take:

(1) Ignore the benefits. If we choose to ignore those benefits or savings that are 'too difficult' to quantify, information systems will almost always appear to have negative cash-flow effects. This is obviously misleading, so this approach would be meaningless.

(2) Quantify the benefits. We can attempt to take each of the benefits and turn it, by means of some educated guesswork and dubious assumptions, into a cash-flow stream. There are two problems with this approach:

- our colleagues will dispute our rationale and assumptions;
- it will be difficult, or impossible, to post-audit the system in order to prove that the claimed benefits have been realised.

(3) Change the approach. Probably the best approach is to recognise and accept the qualitative nature of the benefits, and find some reasonable (but non-financial) way of assessing them.

The non-financial benefits could be assessed by means of an information audit. The issue then becomes determining appropriate ways to measure those benefits.

Example 3

List the main costs (one-off and continuing) of an information system implementation project, and the major benefits we might expect from it.

Linking investment appraisal to customer requirements

Primary objective

By this stage, you should be entirely happy with the assumed primary objective of companies to maximise their shareholder wealth. Any investment decision should be appraised with this objective foremost in mind.

Link to customer requirements and product / service design

The capital budgeting decision faced by entities is to identify the range of projects that, within the capital funding available, will maximise shareholder wealth. The quantitative aspects of this process involves identifying the mix of projects that produces the highest NPV. In addition to the initial capital investment, working capital must also be made available throughout the life of the selected projects.

Investment in new products will result in cash outflows for the entity. Design and development of new products or services often demands significant cash investment, regardless of whether the product or service is ultimately accepted for manufacture or implementation.

There will be a minimum size of entity that can afford certain types of research and development activity. This will be determined by the nature of the industry and the pace of technological change.

Decisions will have to be made at a number of stages in the development of a product or service on whether the expected future benefits justify the commitment of further investment. This applies to all new products or services, regardless of the amount of design and development expenditure required.

The investment decision for the new product or service requires the forecasting of expected cash inflows and outflows throughout the expected life of the product or service, and discounting to give a NPV.

Reasons for developing new products or services

There are a number of reasons why an entity will invest in developing new products and services. These include:

- to meet changing customer demands;
- to take advantage of developing technology;
- to maintain or improve competitive position;
- to respond to emerging environmental or safety issues;
- to diversify the product range or geographical outreach;
- to attract new customers to the brand.

8 Exam style questions

Test your understanding 1 – APV and CAPM

Polycalc plc is an internationally diversified company, whose head office is located in the UK (currency GBP, or £).

It is considering undertaking a capital investment in Australia to manufacture agricultural fertilisers. The project would require immediate capital expenditure of A$ 15m, plus A$ 5m of working capital which would be recovered at the end of the project's four year life. It is estimated that an annual revenue of A$ 18m would be generated by the project, with annual operating costs of A$ 5m. Straight-line depreciation over the life of the project is an allowable expense against company tax in Australia which is charged at a rate of 50%, payable at each year-end without delay. The project can be assumed to have a zero scrap value.

Polycalc plans to finance the project with a £5m four-year loan at 10% from the Euro-sterling market, plus £5m of retained earnings. The proposed financing scheme reflects the belief that the project would have a debt capacity of two-thirds of capital cost. Issue costs on the Euro debt will be 2½% and are tax deductible.

In the UK the fertiliser industry has an equity beta of 1.40 and an average debt: equity gearing ratio of 1:4. Debt capital can be assumed to be virtually risk-free. The current return on UK government stock is 9% and the excess market return is 9.17%.

Corporate tax in the UK is at 35% and can be assumed to be payable at each year-end without delay. Because of a double-taxation agreement, Polycalc will not have to pay any UK tax on the project. The company is expected to have a substantial UK tax liability from other operations for the foreseeable future.

The current spot rate is £/A$2.0000 (that is £1 = A$2.0000) and the A$ is expected to depreciate against the £ at an annual rate of 10%.

Required:

(a) **Using the Adjusted Present Value technique, advise the management of Polycalc on the project's desirability.**

(12 marks)

(b) **What are the limitations and difficulties of using the Capital Asset Pricing Model to generate discount rates for project appraisal?**

(8 marks)

(Total: 20 marks)

Test your understanding 2 – Financing, APV, discount rates

AB plc is a UK company which manufactures products for children.

The entity's turnover and earnings last year were GBP56m (£56m) and £3.5m, respectively. Its shares are not listed but they occasionally change hands in private transactions.

AB plc's weighted average cost of capital (WACC) is 13% net of tax.

The directors believe that an appropriate gearing ratio (debt to debt + equity) for a company such as AB plc is 30%, which is the industry average. Currently, AB plc's gearing ratio is slightly higher than this at 35%. Its debt comprises two secured long-term bank loans and a permanent overdraft, secured by a floating charge on the company's current assets. The current cost of debt to an entity such as AB plc is 10% before tax.

The entity is considering expansion outside the United Kingdom, in particular in an Eastern European (EE) country where its products have become popular. The EE government has offered AB plc a financing deal to establish a manufacturing operation. The financing would take the form of an EE marks 30m 6-year loan at a subsidised rate of only 2.5% each year interest. The current exchange rate is £/EEmarks 20 (that is EE marks 20 to £1).

Interest would be payable at the end of each year and the principal repaid at the end of 6 years. The exchange rate of EE marks to the £ would be fixed at the current rate for the whole 6-year period of the loan.

The marginal corporate tax rate in both countries is 25%.

Required:

(a) **Calculate the entity's present cost of equity and the present value of the EE government subsidy implicit in the loan. Comment briefly on the method used and any assumptions you have made in your calculations.**

(7 marks)

(b) **Discuss the relevance of both the cost of equity you have calculated in answer to (a) above and the WACC given in the scenario, to the entity's investment decision. Include comment on an alternative discount rate that could be used appropriately in the scenario's circumstances.**

(6 marks)

(c) **Discuss the advantages and disadvantages of using the EE government subsidy in AB plc's international investment decision. Recommend alternative methods of financing that might be suitable for AB plc in the circumstances of the scenario.**

(12 marks)

(Total 25 marks)

Test your understanding answers

Example 1 – Capital rationing

(a) Project A has the largest positive NPV (being PV of subsequent cashflows minus initial cost) so should be chosen if projects are mutually exclusive.

(b)

USD000	*A*	*B*	*C*	*D*
NPV	22	5	16	8
Initial cost	30	20	40	10
NPV/USD invested	0.73	0.25	0.40	0.80
Rank	2	4	3	1

Bob plc should invest the USD60,000 as follows:

(1) Do project D leaving USD50,000.

(2) Do project A leaving USD20,000.

(3) Do half of project C, using up the remaining funds.

(c) Bob plc can afford to invest in the following combinations:

	NPV
A + B + D	35
B + C	21
C + D	24

By trial and error the optimal investment is A + B + D.

Example 2 : APV

APV = Base case NPV ± PV of financing side effects

$$\text{Base case NPV} = \frac{£300,000}{0.16} - £1,900,000 = (£25,000)$$

The side effects of financing are:

Tax relief on debt interest

Debt issued = £1.9m + issue costs (= 5% debt issued)

∴95% debt issued = £1.9m

∴debt issued = £1.9m/0.95 = £2m

Tax relief on interest = [(£1m × 9%) + (£1m × 3%)] × 33% = £39,600 pa

$$\text{This has a PV of } \frac{£39,600}{0.09} = £440,000$$

(**Note:** A discount rate appropriate to the level of risk of the flow is used to find the PV.)

Value of subsidy

The subsidy saves 6% p.a. in interest (9% – 3%). The post tax value of this subsidy in perpetuity is therefore:

$$6\% \times £1m \times (1–0.33) \times \frac{1}{0.09} = £446,667$$

Issue costs

Issue costs = 5% of £2m = £100,000

These arise at time 0, and thus have a PV of (£100,000)

The **adjusted present** value is thus:

–£25,000 + £440,000 + £446,667 – £100,000 = **£761,667**

Example 3

One-off costs

- purchase of hardware and software;
- project team costs (feasibility, design, testing, etc.);
- production of documentation;
- training.

Running costs

- staff salaries;
- overheads;
- training;
- maintenance;
- financing.

Benefits

- better decision-making;
- fewer delays;
- better service to customers;
- competitive advantage;
- reduced staff levels.

The most noticeable thing is that, with the exception of staff reductions (which hardly ever happen in real life), the benefits are difficult or impossible to quantify. This is the major problem that we must address if we are to provide a meaningful evaluation of information system performance.

Test your understanding 1 – APV and CAPM

(a) First we must calculate the base-case present value.

Base-case discount rate

$$\beta_{asset} = 1.40 \times \frac{4}{4 + 1(1 - 0.35)} = 1.20$$

Base-case discount rate = 9% + (9.17% × 1.20) = 20%

A$ Project tax charge (A$m)

	1 – 4
Revenue	18
– Operating costs	(5)
– Depreciation	(3.75)
= Taxable profit	9.25
Tax charge	4.625

A$ Project cash flows (A$m)

Year	*0*	*1*	*2*	*3*	*4*
Capital equipment	(15)				
Working capital	(5)				5
Revenues		18	18	18	18
Costs		(5)	(5)	(5)	(5)
Taxation		(4.625)	(4.625)	(4.625)	(4.625)
Net cash flow	(20)	8.375	8.375	8.375	13.375

£m Base-case present value calculation

Year	A$m		Exchange rate		£m		20% Discount factor		£m PV Cash flows
0	(20)	÷	2	=	(10)	×	1	=	(10)
1	8.375	÷	$2(1.10)^1$	=	3.807	×	0.833	=	3.171
2	8.375	÷	$2(1.10)^2$	=	3.461	×	0.694	=	2.402
3	8.375	÷	$2(1.10)^3$	=	3.146	×	0.579	=	1.821
4	13.375	÷	$2(1.10)^4$	=	4.568	×	0.482	=	2.202
					Base Case PV			=	(£0.404m)

PV of financing side-effects

PV of tax shield

£5m × 0.10 = £500,000 = Annual interest

£500,000 × 0.35 = £175,000 = Annual tax relief

PV of tax relief: 175,000 A4 0.10 = £554,750

PV of issue costs

£5m × 0.025 × (1 – 0.35) = £81,250

Adjusted present value

		£m
Base-case PV	:	(0.404)
PV tax shield	:	0.555
PV issue costs	:	(0.081)
Adjusted present value	:	£0.07m or + £70,000 approx

Therefore accept.

(b) There are **two main limitations** to the use of CAPM for generating project discount rates. The first is that the model only generates a **single-period rate of return** (i.e. no discounting is involved) and so, strictly speaking, it should not be used to generate a discount rate for a multi-period analysis such as NPV. However, if it can reasonably be assumed that both the risk-free return and the excess market return will remain approximately constant over the life of the project then the limitation can be overcome.

The second limitation is that there is some evidence to suggest that the CAPM is an **incomplete model** in that there are other determinants of risk besides beta. However evidence on this point is somewhat mixed and even if beta is not the sole determinant of systematic risk, it would appear to be by far the most important determinant.

The difficulties met in attempting to use the CAPM to generate project appraisal discount rates are mainly caused by data identification difficulties of the three inputs: the risk-free return, the excess market return and the project beta.

With the **risk-free return** the problem is to identify a genuinely risk-free, after-tax rate of return. Normally, what is used is the return on government bonds with a similar maturity to the life of the project, after personal tax at the basic rate. The difficulty with the excess market return is its volatility over time which means that a long-run average after-tax excess market return is normally used.

Finally, and perhaps most difficult of all, is the identification of the correct beta value. Usually what is used is the beta value of the industry group into which the project falls, but difficulties may arise either if the project does not fall into a neat industry group or if the project's characteristics (in relation to its revenue sensitivity and ratio of fixed to variable operating costs) are not typical of the industry. In such circumstances a considerable element of judgement enters into the determination of the beta figure.

Test your understanding 2 – Financing, APV, discount rates

(a) The cost of equity can be determined using the WACC formula:

$$k_o = k_{eg}\left[\frac{V_E}{V_E + V_D}\right] + k_d\left[\frac{V_D}{V_E + V_D}\right]$$

13% = ke × 0.65 + 10%(1 – 0.25) × 0.35

Therefore, ke = 16%

These calculations use AB plc's current debt ratio. If the ratio were to fall to the company's stated optimum, the cost of new debt might also fall and, as a consequence, the WACC.

The value of the subsidy is the result of the difference between the interest payments that AB plc would have to make if the subsidised loan were not available and the interest it will have to pay with subsidy. The PV of the after-tax benefit over the 6-year period must be computed at the pre-tax (regular) rate of interest.

Annual difference of interest payments

= (0.10 – 0.025) × £1.5m (30m EE marks /20)

= £112,500

After tax, this equals

=£112,500 × (1 – 0.25)

=£84,375

So the PV of the benefits at 10% is

=£84,375 × 6 year annuity factor at 10% (4.355)

= £367,453

The PV of the benefits has been calculated using the cost of debt as the discount rate. An argument could be made that the WACC is the more appropriate rate, representing as it does the opportunity cost of the benefits. This would have the effect of reducing the value.

It is also necessary to assume that AB plc will continue to be able to offset interest payments against tax.

(b) Neither rate is entirely relevant to the investment decision. The rate calculated in (a) could only be used if the new investment was of the same risk as the company overall. The WACC could only be used if the investment was not only in the same risk class, but financed in the same way as the company.

The rate that should be used is a risk-adjusted cost of capital that reflects the risk of the investment. The CAPM could be used by finding a proxy company's published beta, adjusting for the differences in gearing and using the formula to calculate a discount rate.

However, the idea that one constant discount rate can be used that compensates for uncertainty and risk over the entire life of the project is doubtful in today's volatile market conditions.

(c) The advantage of using the EE government subsidy is obvious: that the company obtains cheap finance. Another advantage is that the company does not need to provide security for this loan. There may be other advantages such as having the government as a 'partner' might ease issues such as applications for planning permission. The potential problems are that:

- The domestic rates change downwards over the 6-year period, making the savings less attractive;
- The exchange rate EE marks/£ improves, making the interest payments more expensive;
- The EE government does not honour its commitments;
- The investment fails in less than 6 years and the company is tied into a 6-year loan agreement (this would also be true of any term loan agreement);
- Conditions attached to the loan might be commercially restrictive;
- Tax laws in both countries need to be examined for any hidden penalties.

The requirements are for long-term finance and assume that AB plc wishes to continue operations in the EE country. The fact that the EE government loan is for 6 years raises the question of how the venture will be financed after that time.

Alternative methods that might be considered are:

Long-term bonds/bank loan

The company already has two loans and an overdraft. Its debt ratio is higher than it would like and higher than the industry average. Further debt might be considered too risky, especially for a relatively risky business venture into a new market in a region still developing economically.

Supplier credit

The scenario does not give details of how AB plc sources its raw materials, but it is possible that suppliers would provide some funding if there were business opportunities for their products.

Cash/disposal

AB plc clearly has no cash on hand as it is using overdraft facilities. It could review its assets to determine whether there is any surplus that could be disposed of.

Leasing

Finance leases are the equivalent of secured medium-term bank loans and suffer the same disadvantages. Operating leases may be possible for some equipment, but this is an unlikely source in the circumstances.

Equity

The amount required is too small for a new issue, but a rights issue might be a possibility. The scenario does not say how many shareholders there are, but it does say shares change hands occasionally which suggests there are more than just family members. This might be an expensive option because of the fees involved.

Venture capital/joint venture

This is the type of venture that venture capitalists ought to be interested in. The disadvantage from AB plc's point of view would be the return required by the investor if the finance is in the form of equity. The investor would almost certainly demand some level of control over the company's entire operations. However, venture capitalists do provide debt finance and this might be an option.

Recommendation

All the alternatives carry advantages and disadvantages. In these circumstances, there is no obvious preferred type of finance. The decision will rest with the directors' attitudes to risk and control. Their future objectives for the entire company, not just their overseas expansion plans, should be established and evaluated. Subsequently, a financing, or possibly re-financing, plan should be discussed with the company's bankers and, if appropriate, its shareholders.

chapter

11

International Investment Appraisal

Chapter learning objectives

Lead	Component
C1: Evaluate investment choices.	(b) evaluate investment projects (domestic and international) including their financial and strategic implications.

Indicative syllabus content

- Calculation of a project's net present value and internal rate of return, including techniques for dealing with cash flows denominated in a foreign currency and use of the weighted average cost of capital.
- The effects of taxation (including foreign direct and withholding taxes), potential changes in economic factors (inflation, interest and exchange rates) and potential restrictions on remittances on these calculations.
- Selection of an appropriate cost of capital for use in valuation.
- Criteria for selecting sources of finance, including finance for international investments.

1 Overview of Chapter

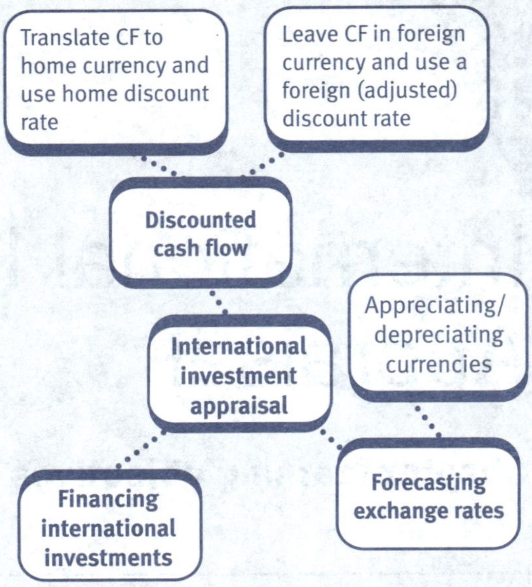

Introduction

Increasingly in the modern business environment, entities are expanding across national boundaries into many different countries.

Although there are risks associated with such strategies, the strategic and financial benefits to an entity can be enormous.

This Chapter covers the methods of investment appraisal for international projects, and considers the likely risks and benefits associated with international expansion. It also looks at the financing options available for foreign investment projects.

Risks of international expansion

Dealing with risk and individuals' attitudes to risk is vital to any decision-making process, and when multinationals look to evaluate international investments they have to compare the risks with the rewards.

The main factors to consider are:

- knowledge of the country's operational environment; economic and financial, cultural and political;
- availability of local technical expertise;

- travelling distances and difficulties between the location of the investment and the home base;
- language problems;
- competition;
- alternative investment opportunities.

Categories of risk

Risks fall into four main categories: transaction, translation, economic and political.

Translation risk is an accounting issue and of little consequence to the investment decision, unless foreign borrowings are at a high level, and the providers of debt have imposed restrictions on gearing levels.

Transaction risk is the risk of adverse exchange-rate movements between the date of a transaction and the date of settlement. This can be managed by using internal or external hedging techniques, for example:

- forward contracts, currency options and currency futures (external techniques)
- invoicing in home currency and netting (internal techniques).

Economic risk is the risk of actions by governments and reactions of markets that have economy-wide implications. This type of risk might best be managed by raising finance in the country where the investment is being made, as discussed later in this Chapter, or by manufacturing in that country.

Political risk refers to the risk that political action will affect the operations and value of an entity. Action may include import quotas, health and safety standards, changes in taxation, exchange controls or even nationalisation or expropriation of assets.

Methods of international expansion

International expansion is often a sequential process as outlined below. Entities reduce the risk of expansion by learning more about the new market place at each stage of the expansion, and adapting their strategies accordingly.

The expansion methods are explained below.

Exporting

The simplest way to develop a presence in a foreign market is by exporting goods, either directly through an entity's own export division, or by using foreign agents or distributors.

Exporting enables the entity to access new customers without the expense and risk of setting up a permanent base in the new country.

However, it could be difficult if there are import quotas or tariffs in the target country. Also, if using foreign agents and distributors the profit margins on sales will have to be shared.

Overall, exporting is only suitable for small scale international expansion.

Licensing

In order to quickly expand internationally, entities often use licensing.

This is where the entity (licensor) finds a local producer (licensee) and grants a licence to that company to give it the right to make and sell the licensor's products in return for a royalty payment.

Many of the world's breweries use licensing to avoid the need to set up production and bottling facilities in countries where they want to sell their beers.

Licensing can enable an entity to expand rapidly, because it avoids the time and expense associated with direct investment (see below). It also helps an entity avoid the quotas / tariffs issue which may restrict the exporting strategy explained above.

However, the licensor will have to share some of the profits from product sales with the licensee, so a licensing strategy might not be as lucrative as direct investment in the long run.

Joint venture

A joint venture is a contractual arrangement whereby two or more parties undertake an economic activity that is subject to joint control.

A joint venture is controlled by a management team consisting of representatives of the two or more parent entities. For example, a foreign company wanting to invest in a new country but wanting to benefit from the local knowledge of a local company's management might enter into a joint venture with the local company.

Joint ventures are often used to share expertise such as technology, marketing and local knowledge. They can also be a useful means of sharing high research and development costs.

Joint ventures may also provide a means of investing in certain countries where full foreign ownership is discouraged.

Direct investment – foreign subsidiary

International investment may be achieved through establishing a subsidiary entity in a foreign country.

The subsidiary may be created by the parent entity as a start-up investment, or if more rapid market entry is required, a takeover or merger with established foreign entities may be undertaken.

Setting up a foreign subsidiary requires an entity to commit substantial resources to the expansion strategy, but the strategy of direct investment is likely to be the most lucrative of all the methods of international expansion in the long run because the entity is now not having to share the profits generated in the foreign country with any other parties (e.g. export agents, licensees, joint venture partners).

It is however, far more risky than the other methods of international expansion, which is why the other methods are usually implemented first, as a way of developing knowledge and reducing the risk of direct investment if and when it finally happens.

Strategic and financial implications of international expansion

Strategic implications of international expansion

The main strategic implications of international expansion are:

Competition

Foreign markets may have weaker competition. A firm facing a competitive domestic market will benefit from finding a foreign market where it has a monopoly.

Country factors

Some countries have cheap sources of natural raw materials and cheap labour costs. Locating production facilities in these countries will bring significant cost savings. Also, some countries' governments offer grants and cheap loans to foreign investors to attract inward investment.

Benefits to the customer

Locating in a different country could move an entity closer to existing customers, so reducing delivery times and improving relationships. Also, it is likely to bring an entity closer to a pool of potential new customers.

Economies of scale

As the entity gets bigger, international expansion might be the best way of continuing to generate economies of scale.

Risk management

International expansion will leave an entity less exposed to a single economy. Factors such as interest rates, inflation, government policy and exchange rates from more than one economy will impact a business with international operations. This will reduce the economic and political risk to the entity.

Financial implications of international expansion

The primary corporate objective – to maximise shareholder wealth – has been referred to in several earlier Chapters.

The main financial benefit of an international investment is the positive NPV and consequent gain to shareholders of undertaking an attractive project.

However, also consider the following other financial implications of international investment:

Impact on the financial statements

If the foreign project assets are denominated in foreign currency, they will have to be converted into the domestic currency for the purposes of consolidation. If exchange rates fluctuate from one year to the next, the value of these assets will also fluctuate, giving (unrealised) exchange gains or losses in the entity's accounts. This is known as translation risk, and it can be mitigated by raising finance in the foreign currency too (matching). Financing options for foreign investments are covered in more detail later in this Chapter.

Impact on the cost of capital

International investments will often be more risky to an entity than its normal domestic investments. Therefore, it is likely that the entity's cost of capital will change to reflect this increased risk.

NEW

2 Basic Foreign Project Appraisal

In practice this is a difficult and highly controversial area; however, the exam treats the subject in a very straightforward way.

As a starting point it is assumed that candidates bring through their knowledge of basic investment appraisal, and in particular NPV analysis (covered in the earlier Chapter 'Investment Appraisal – basic techniques').

The NPV analysis of a foreign / international project – (foreign direct investment, or FDI) – requires some additional complexities to those found with an NPV analysis of a domestic project.

Definition of FDI

Foreign direct investment (FDI) is defined as:

Establishment of new overseas facilities or the expansion of existing overseas facilities by an investor. FDI may be inward (domestic investment by overseas companies) or outward (overseas investment by domestic companies).

(CIMA Official Terminology, 2005)

Overview of the international investment appraisal (NPV) method

An international project will generate a stream of net cash flows in the currency of its host country.

The normal discounting approach for an international investment is:

(1) forecast the project's cashflows (denominated in the foreign currency);

(2) subtotal the foreign denominated cashflows;

(3) translate the foreign currency cashflows into the domestic currency;

(4) adjust for any additional domestic currency cashflows which will also be incurred as a consequence of undertaking the project;

(5) discount the cashflows to present value using an appropriate discount rate (perhaps adjusted from the entity's standard cost of capital to reflect the different risk of the international project).

Standard layout for an international investment appraisal

The table below shows the layout for a UK company (domestic currency the British pound, £) investing in an international project denominated in US dollars ($):

Year	0	1	2	3	4	5
	$000	$000	$000	$000	$000	$000
Receipts		X	X	X	X	
Payments:						
Wages		(X)	(X)	(X)	(X)	
Materials		(X)	(X)	(X)	(X)	
Variable / Fixed overheads		(X)	(X)	(X)	(X)	
Administration / Distribution expenses		(X)	(X)	(X)	(X)	
Taxable cash flows		X	X	X	X	
Tax: Corporation tax			(X)	(X)	(X)	(X)
: Capital allowances			X	X	X	X
Initial outlay	(X)					
Net Realisable Value					**X**	
Working capital	(X)				X	
Net Cash Flows in $	(X)	X	X	X	X	X
Exchange rate	(X)	X	X	X	X	X
Net Cash Flows in £	x	x	x	x	x	x
Discount rate (e.g. 10%)	1	0.909	0.826	0.751	0.683	0.621
Present value	(X)	X	X	X	X	(X)
Net Present Value	**£XXX**					

But you could discount here and convert at the spot

The differences between international project appraisal and domestic project appraisal (highlighted in this table) are explained in detail in the next section.

Note on international currency symbols

The CIMA exam questions will use international currency symbols, or international currency codes.

For example:

Currency	**Symbol**	**Code**
US dollar	$	USD
British pound (sterling)	£	GBP
Euro	€	EUR

Note on exchange rate notation

In general, if an exchange rate is quoted as "A$/B$" followed by a number, the number represents the number of B$ which are equivalent to 1A$.

So, for example, a spot rate of £/€1.1500 means that £1 = €1.15, and a rate of GBP / USD1.5000 means that GBP 1 = USD 1.5000.

In general, exchange rates will be quoted to four decimal places, but in an exam you should follow the lead of the information quoted in the question to determine how accurately you should compute the rates. For example, if the question gives rates to three decimal places, prepare your answer to three decimal places too.

3 Additional complexities in foreign NPV calculations

In particular, in exam questions, look out for complexities involving:

- tax;
- inter-company cash flows (such as management charges or royalties);
- remittance restrictions where the foreign government restricts the amount of the project's cash flow that can be remitted back each year to the parent;
- forecasting future spot rates.

Taxation

There are three possible tax scenarios for an exam question:

	Home tax rate	*Foreign tax rate*
(i)	33%	< 40%
(ii)	33%	= 33%
(iii)	33%	> 25%

The question will always assume a double-tax treaty. Therefore a project's profits get taxed at whatever is the **higher** rate between the two countries.

In scenarios (i) and (ii) there would be no further domestic tax to pay on the project's foreign profits. But in scenario (iii) the project's profits would be taxed at 33% : 25% in the foreign country and a further 8% tax payable in the home country.

The effect of taxation

Tax planning for global organisations is complex, and beyond the scope of this syllabus. Most countries have a system of tax credits for taxes on income paid to the host country to avoid the same income being taxed twice.

Double taxation relief

Double taxation occurs when income is taxed both by the taxpayer's country of residence and in another country where the income rises.

The purpose of double taxation relief is to remove or reduce the disincentive that this double taxation represents to outward investment. Another important objective is to try to ensure that taxpayers do not exploit the terms of double taxation agreements and differing tax systems in each country for tax avoidance purposes.

Double taxation of income could discourage residents of one country from investing and expanding their business activities in other countries.

In order to ease the burden of double taxation many countries provide for relief. This is achieved either by virtue of the provisions of a double taxation agreement or under the country's own domestic legislation.

There are two main methods:

(1) exemption. Income or gains are exempted from tax in the country where the income or gains arise; exemption may also be given in the country of the recipient's residence.

(2) credit. Where the income or gains are taxed in both countries, the country in which the recipient is resident gives credit for the other country's tax against its own tax.

Where income remains taxable in both countries, the country in which it arises may agree, under a double taxation agreement, to tax it at a lower rate than its normal domestic rate.

Inter-company cash flows

Inter-company cash flows also impact the tax computations. In reality the whole issue of whether or not an inter-company cash flow (such as royalty payments made by an international project to the foreign parent) are or are not allowable for tax purposes is a very politically sensitive issue.

In the exam assume such cash flows **are** allowable (and state it) unless the question says otherwise.

The key point to remember is that, if an inter-company cash flow is allowable for tax **relief** in the foreign country, there will be a corresponding tax **liability** in the home country.

Inter company transfer prices

Transfer prices are particularly problematical. By manipulating the transfer prices charged it may be possible to minimise the global taxation cost for the group. For instance, suppose we have two companies within a group that are based in different countries.

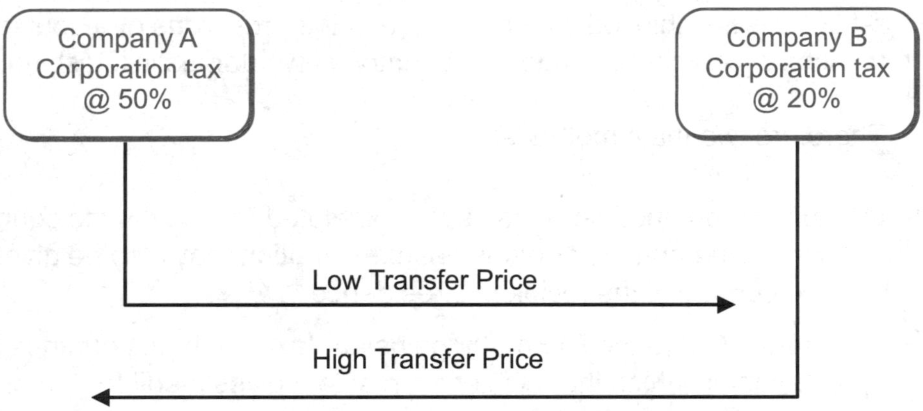

Company A will report low income therefore limiting its tax charge where as company B will be reporting high income as it pays less tax.

By manipulating the transfer price the overall tax charge can be lowered. The problem is that the government of country A will not look favourably on this action.

Assume that the tax authorities will only allow 'arm's length' / open-market prices for tax relief and will not allow an artificially high or low transfer price.

A second problem may also arise. Although the above may decrease the taxation, the profits will end up in country B. If the currency of country B is weak relative to the holding company, then loss from the depreciation of the currency may be more than the tax saving.

e.g

Illustration 1

An example helps to illustrate these points.

Take just the Year 2 cash flow of a US project which is being evaluated by a UK company; assume tax is paid at 25% in the US and 33% in the UK; assume royalty payments of $10m; and assume a forecast spot rate of £/$ 1.5000 (that is £1 = $1.5000).

Year 2	
	$m
Revenues	100
Costs	(30)
Royalties	(10)
	–––
Pre-tax profit	60
25% US tax	(15)
Remit to parent	45
÷ $/£ Spot	÷ 1.50
£ Cash flow	30
Royalties	6.7
UK Tax	(5.4)*
	–––
After tax cash flow	£31.3 m
	–––

$10m
÷1.50$/£
= £6.7m

UK tax computation:

8% UK tax on $ profits:	$60m × 0.08	$4.8m
33%@ UK tax on royalties:	$10m × 0.33	$3.3m
Total UK tax liability		= $8.1m
÷ spot rate		÷ 1.5000
UK tax payable		= £5.4 m*

Remittance restrictions

Remittance restrictions are where the foreign government places a limit on the funds that can be repatriated back to the holding company. By doing so, this may change the cash flows that are received by the holding company.

The effect of restrictions on remittances

When a foreign subsidiary makes a profit, that profit will be included in the total profits generated by the multinational entity. Investors in the parent entity will be concerned to see not just how much profit is made, but how much cash is available for distribution as dividends. This will require the subsidiary entity remitting cash to the parent entity. There are various ways by which the parent may obtain a cash return from its foreign subsidiary:

- capital flows comprising dividends and monies to servicing debt capital provided by the parent;
- payments for merchandise supplied, and
- management charges.

The ability to convert these cash flows from local currency into the parent's currency will depend on local legislation. Some countries place restrictions on the remittance of profits out of the country as part of a policy designed to protect the strength of their currency. Such restrictions work against the long-term interests of the country concerned, as freedom to withdraw funds is a key determinant of investors' willingness to commit in the first place.

For dividends there may be a requirement to reinvest a certain proportion of the profit, which limits dividends. Loan servicing should be less restricted subject to the reasonableness of interest rates.

Payments for merchandise will usually be permitted subject to transfer pricing restrictions, which will ensure that goods sold between the parent entity and a subsidiary are priced at 'arm's length', and not so as to minimise the profits of the subsidiary to manipulate how the total profit of the entity is divided between the parent and subsidiaries.

Management charges are usually restricted to avoid them from being used as a way of avoiding dividend restrictions and it will often be necessary to justify them to the authorities.
In all cases, there is a risk that all foreign currency remittances will be placed under severe restriction and this possibility should be carefully considered before an investment decision is undertaken, as should the tax implications of various systems of remitting profits back to the parent entity.

Suppose there are no tax complications. The project's after-foreign tax $ cash flow is as follows ($m):

Year	*0*	*1*	*2*	*3*
	(10)	3	4	6

In any one year, only 50% of cash flows generated can be remitted back to the parent. The blocked funds can be released back to the parent in the year after the end of the project.

Cash flows to parent:

Year	*1*	*2*	*3*	*4*
	1.5	2	3	6.5

It is these cash flows that have to be put through the NPV calculation.

It is the parent company's cash flow that should now be converted into home currency terms and discounted to NPV as we always need to evaluate the foreign investment from the parent company's viewpoint (and that of their shareholders): what money does the parent put in and what money is available for the parent company to take out?

Forecasting future spot rates

The exam question may provide you with estimated exchange rates over the life of the project, but it is more likely you will have to estimate them.

Appreciating and depreciating currencies

You may be asked to calculate exchange rates given currency appreciation / depreciation rates.

More details on currency appreciation / depreciation

Definitions

Currency Appreciation

An increase in the value of one currency with respect to another. This means that one unit of the appreciating currency buys more units of the other currency than it did previously. While this can be a good sign, as it may indicate a low rate of inflation, it also makes exports from the country with the appreciating currency more expensive, while making imports less expensive.

Currency Depreciation

A decrease in the value of a currency with respect to other currencies. This means that the depreciated currency is worth fewer units of some other currency. While depreciation means a reduction in value, it can be advantageous as it makes exports in the depreciated currency less expensive.

Example of the impact of currency appreciation / depreciation

For example, suppose one unit of Currency A is worth one unit of Currency B. If Currency A depreciates such that it becomes worth half of one unit of Currency B, then exports denominated in Currency A are only half as expensive when trading in a Currency B market.

e.g

Illustration 2

The spot rate is GBP/USD 2.0000 (that is GBP1 = USD 2.0000) and the USD is depreciating against the GBP at 10% per annum.

This means that, in future years, the GBP can buy more USD. The exchange rate in 1 year's time will be GBP 1 to USD 2.2000 (2.0000 x 1.10) and in two years' time it will be GBP 1 = USD 2.4200.

Notice that the exchange rate at the end of one year becomes the basis of the next year's calculation.

Forecasting appreciation / depreciation using parity theories

The amount by which a currency is expected to appreciate or depreciate can be estimated using the parity theories:

- Purchasing Power Parity; or
- Interest Rate Parity.

The formulae are given in the exam as follows:

Purchasing Power Parity (PPP)

$$\text{Future spot rate A\$/B\$} = \text{Spot rate A\$/B\$} \times \frac{1 + \text{inflation B\$}}{1 + \text{inflation A\$}}$$

Interest Rate Parity (IRP)

$$\text{Future spot rate A\$/B\$} = \text{Spot rate A\$/B\$} \times \frac{1 + \text{interest B\$}}{1 + \text{interest A\$}}$$

Although the parity theories are covered more fully in the P3 (Performance Strategy) syllabus, it is useful to note here how they can be used to forecast the expected appreciation or depreciation of a currency. Also, it is useful to consider the parity theories in this syllabus in the context of the impact of interest rates and inflation rates on an entity's financial strategy. This topic was addressed in the earlier Chapter 'Introduction to Financial Strategy'.

Predicting future appreciation or depreciation of a currency using IRP

If the spot rate of exchange is GBP / USD 1.6000 (that is GBP 1 = USD 1.6000) and interest rates in the UK and the US are expected to be 1% and 3% respectively, the predicted exchange rate in 1 year (using the above formula) is:

$$= 1.6000 \times \frac{1.03}{1.01}$$

i.e. the forecast rate is GBP 1 = USD 1.6317.

This is an appreciation of 1.98% in the value of the British pound (GBP).

Working: [(1.6317 – 1.6000) / 1.6000 = 0.0198]

By rearranging the IRP formula, the appreciation (or depreciation) can be identified more directly as follows:

$$1 + \text{expected change in value of A\$} = \frac{1 + \text{interest B\$}}{1 + \text{interest A\$}} = \frac{\text{Future exchange rate}}{\text{Current spot rate}}$$

Alternative approach to computations

We saw earlier that the most commonly used method of appraising foreign projects is to identify the cashflows in the foreign currency initially, and then to convert these cashflows into the home currency before discounting at the company's normal, domestic cost of capital.

However, there is an alternative approach, as follows:

Step 1 Estimate the project's relevant cash flows in the foreign currency.

Step 2 Convert the domestic cost of capital to the foreign equivalent, by manipulating the given information concerning appreciation / depreciation of currencies using the formula below (derived from interest rate parity):

$$1 + \text{expected change in value of A\$} = \frac{1 + \text{B\$ discount or interest rate}}{1 + \text{A\$ discount or interest rate}}$$

and

(1 + B$ discount rate)/(1 + A$ discount rate) = (1 + B$ interest)/(1 + A$ interest)

Step 3 Use this adjusted cost of capital to discount the foreign cash flows to produce an NPV in foreign currency.

Step 4 Convert the NPV into its domestic equivalent using the spot rate for translation.

This will give the same domestic NPV as the more commonly used approach explained earlier.

Example of foreign NPV calculations

Butler plc, a UK company, is considering undertaking a new project in Australia.

The project would require immediate capital expenditure of A$10m, plus A$5m of working capital which would be recovered at the end of the project's 4-year life. The net cash flows expected to be generated from the project are A$13m before tax.

Straight-line depreciation over the life of the project is an allowable expense against corporate tax in Australia, which is charged at the rate of 50%, payable at each year-end without delay. The project will have zero scrap value.

Butler plc will not have to pay any UK tax on the project due to a double-taxation agreement.

The spot rate is GBP / A$2.00 (that is 1 GBP = A$2.00) and the A$ is expected to depreciate against the GBP by 10% per year.

A similar risk, UK-based project would be expected to generate a minimum return of 20% after tax.

Required:

Calculate the project's NPV.

Solution:

1st method: Translate foreign cashflows to domestic cashflows, then discount at the normal, domestic rate:

Time	Capital	Contribution	Tax	Net CF	Ex rate	Net CF	DF20%	NPV
	A$m	A$m	A$m	A$m		GBPm		GBPm
0	(15)			(15)	2.00	(7.50)	1.000	(7.50)
1		13	(5.25)	7.75	2.20	3.52	0.833	2.93
2		13	(5.25)	7.75	2.42	3.20	0.694	2.22
3		13	(5.25)	7.75	2.66	2.91	0.579	1.68
4	5	13	(5.25)	12.75	2.93	4.35	0.482	2.10
			(W1)					
								1.43

(W1) Tax on profit = 50% × (13m – 2.5m depreciation) = A$5.25m

2nd method: Use a foreign discount rate to discount foreign cashflows, then convert to GBP at the end. If the A$ is going to depreciate by 10% per year, the British pound will appreciate by 10% per year.

Therefore,

$$1.10 = \frac{1 + \text{A\$ interest rate}}{1.20}$$

since 10% is the expected appreciation of the GBP, and 20% is the domestic (GBP) interest rate.

Therefore the A$ interest rate = 32%

Hence, the NPV in A$ using a 32% discount rate is

–15m + (7.75m × 0.758) + (7.75m × 0.574) +(7.75m × 0.435) + (12.75m × 0.329)

= 2.88m

At spot rate, A$2.88m ÷ 2 00 = GBP1.44m, which shows that both approaches to appraising investments lead to the same outcome.

Example 1

A manufacturing company based in the United Kingdom is evaluating an investment project overseas – in Rebmatt a politically stable country. It will cost an initial 5.0 million Rebmatt dollars (RM$) and it is expected to earn post-tax cash flows as follows:

Year	*1*	*2*	*3*	*4*
Cash flow (RM$000)	1,500	1,900	2,500	2,700

The following information is available:

- The current spot rate is £ / RM$ 2.0000 (that is £1 = RM$ 2.0000).
- The risk-free rate of interest in Rebmatt is 7% and in the UK 9%.
- The company requires a UK return from this project of 16%.

Required:

Calculate the £ net present value of the project using both the following methods:

(a) **by discounting annual cash flows in £;**

(b) **by discounting annual cash flows in Rebmatt $.**

4 Financing international investments

Introduction

This Chapter has considered the possibility that an entity might decide to set up a foreign subsidiary to invest in a foreign project. In the modern business world, this is becoming an increasingly common strategy.

The financing of these international ventures is obviously of key importance if the risks of trading internationally are to be minimised.

The earlier Chapter 'Long Term Finance' covered the general criteria which need to be considered when an entity is considering which financing options to use for a new investment. All these criteria (such as, cost of finance, gearing level, availability of finance, and impact on financial statements) are still relevant when considering the financing options for a foreign project.

However, for a foreign investment, the key additional consideration is whether the finance should be denominated in the entity's domestic currency or the foreign currency.

Financing options for foreign investments

The main options are:

- use the investment's own free cashflows;
- use finance raised in the parent entity's home country (denominated in either the parent's currency or the currency of the subsidiary);
- use finance raised in the subsidiary's country;
- use finance raised in a completely separate country.

More detail on the financing of international investment projects

Using free cashflows

A foreign subsidiary could rely upon its own internally generated funds.

This would avoid many of the problems of international financing, but is unlikely to result in the necessary level of expansion to meet high growth objectives, and is not suitable for new foreign ventures whose cashflows may be low at first.

Finance raised by the parent

Funds could be raised by the parent company and transferred to subsidiary entities by way of a combination of equity and loans.

The main advantage of this method is that the parent company is more likely to have a better reputation and credit-worthiness than the subsidiary and therefore have better access to funds at finer rates. A centralised treasury function at the parent may also have the expertise to and financial backing to be able to choose to access funds from a wider range of sources, including more complex products. Indeed, it may be possible to extend funds to a foreign subsidiary as part of a larger bond issue or bank debt arrangement.

However, if exchange controls exist this method can become difficult and expensive.

If the borrowing is denominated in the parent's domestic currency, this will in no way reduce foreign exchange risk through matching. However, if the funds are denominated in the subsidiary's currency, the foreign currency borrowing can be designated as a hedge of the net investment in the foreign subsidiary for hedge accounting purposes to reduce the impact of fluctuations in value due to currency movements. Interest payable on the foreign currency borrowing can also be set against income from the subsidiary, again reducing currency exposure to some extent.

General disadvantages of this method (whether the funds are denominated in the domestic or the foreign currency) are:

- The entity will also be more exposed to political risk. If the investment is lost, perhaps through a war or expropriation by a foreign government, the liability will still remain intact.
- Also, if the investment is a subsidiary entity, failure of the subsidiary would leave the parent entity with the liability in the same way.

Finance raised by the subsidiary

Finance raised by the subsidiary is likely to be denominated in the subsidiary's currency.

This method will result in a reduction in risk. Foreign exchange risk will again be reduced, since the exposure of the parent company to the net worth of the subsidiary will be reduced by the amount of the foreign currency borrowing. However, complete elimination of the risk through matching will not be possible due to the likelihood of thin capitalisation rules in the foreign country which may restrict the proportion of debt capital allowed. The currency exposure of the parent to annual reported foreign currency profits from the subsidiary would also be reduced by the extent of the interest charges paid by the foreign subsidiary on the borrowings.

Political risk can also be reduced since, if the investment is lost, the liability will be eliminated as well.

Difficulties may be experienced with this method of finance if the subsidiary company does not have sufficient history or reputation to be able to raise bank debt or the country concerned does not have a well-developed capital market.

On the other hand, financing in the subsidiary's country can make such investments more acceptable to that country since it is then seen that not all of the profits made are sent to the parent entity's country.

Most governments take steps to encourage international investors since they are beneficial to that country's economy, creating employment and wealth. Such encouragement often takes the form of grants, subsidies and cheap or guaranteed finance. These incentives should be taken into account when considering international investments and their financing.

Finance raised in a third currency

Finance can today be raised in a variety of different currencies, from a variety of capital markets in many different countries.

The main reason for raising money in other currencies is that interest rates may be substantially lower than in the entity's home country or in the country where an investment is intended.

However, if the interest cost is lower, then it is likely that the currency borrowed is strong, and will therefore appreciate with respect to sterling and other currencies (as per the interest parity theory introduced earlier). The expected exchange loss on the borrowings would therefore offset any benefit through a lower interest rate.

5 Exam style questions

Test your understanding 1 – Simple foreign NPV

KH is a large food and drink retailer based in the USA. To date, the entity has operated only in the US but is planning to expand into South America by acquiring a group of stores similar to those operated in the US. Projected cash flows in the US and South America for the first 3 years of the project, in real terms, are estimated as follows:

	Year 0	Year 1	Year 2	Year 3
US cashflows (USD 000)	(10,000)	(300)	(400)	(500)
South American cashflows (SA currency millions)	(1,000)	250	350	450

USD cash flows are mainly incremental administration costs associated with the project. SA currency cash flows are cash receipts from sales less all related cash costs and expenses.

The exchange rate for the South American country's currency is extremely volatile. Best estimates by KH's treasurer suggest that the USD is likely to appreciate in value by 34.6% per annum against the SA currency for the foreseeable future.

The current exchange rate is USD/SA currency 30 (that is USD1 = SA currency 30).

The following information is relevant:

- KH evaluates all investments using nominal cash flows and a nominal discount rate;
- SA currency cash flows are converted into USD and discounted at a risk-adjusted US rate;
- All USD cash flows for this project should be discounted at 20%, a nominal rate judged to reflect the project's high risk;
- Inflation is currently 40% per year in South America, and 4% per year in the USA;
- For the purposes of evaluation, assume the year 3 USD nominal cash flows (both converted cashflows and extra USD cashflows) will continue to be earned each year indefinitely.

Note: Ignore taxation.

Required:

Assume that you are the Financial Manager of KH. Prepare a report to the Finance Director that evaluates the proposed investment. Include in your report a calculation of the NPV of the proposed investment and a recommendation as to whether the entity should proceed with the investment, supported by your reasons for the recommendation.

(10 marks)

Test your understanding 2 – Complex foreign NPV

Allmodcoms plc is a listed company within the UK involved in the manufacture and supply of modems for the domestic PC market. It has recently been presented with a proposal by the government of Republica, a country in Eastern Europe with a developing economy. The proposal would involve Allmodcoms supplying Republica with modems over a five-year period, during which time the supply and price of the modems would be monitored by the Republica government.

The recently elected government is keen on encouraging inward investment into the country in order to boost growth in the economy. In recent years, growth has been sluggish or non- existent as the previous regime insisted on restricting trade with its neighbours. Republica's traditional industries of farming and mining did manage to grow, but technologically the country is now lagging significantly behind the rest of Europe.

After its narrow victory in the election, the government is keen to make good on its pledge to double economic growth during its three-year term, and has offered what it believes are attractive terms for the supply of modems into its domestic market.

Under the terms of the agreement Allmodcoms would need to make an initial investment of 400 million Republica Francs (RF), none of which is likely to be recovered at the end of the project. In addition it is estimated that a one-off injection of working capital in the region of RF250 million would be required, although this would be recovered at the end of the five-year project.

Local labour and materials would be used to assemble the modems and the present day cost per unit is estimated to be RF2000 and RF1000 respectively.

Allmodcoms estimates that other local costs would be equivalent to the material cost per unit and all local costs are expected to rise in line with local inflation for the year. In addition, Allmodcoms would take a fixed royalty payment of £2.00 sterling per unit throughout the five-year project.

The sales price and volume will be fixed by the local government under the terms of the agreement. For the first two years of the agreement Allmodcoms will be allowed to charge £30.00 per unit, rising to £40 per unit for the last three years. Sales volumes will be restricted to 80,000 units in year 1, increasing by 20,000 a year from then on.

The government has guaranteed the volume figures and hence will buy any units which are not purchased. The fixed sterling price is guaranteed as long as local inflation targets are met.

The sales and marketing directors have both suggested that the Republica market is significantly bigger than the projected volumes under the agreement and have suggested that Allmodcoms exports into the Republica market rather than undertaking the direct investment.

As an incentive to undertake the investment, the Republica regime have agreed to tax profits at a rate of only 10% throughout the project. This will be payable in the year in which the income arises. The initial investment will also attract a tax allowable depreciation of 25% per year on a straight-line basis.

The directors of Allmodcoms are considering undertaking the investment, but have concerns over the inflationary record of past Republica regimes. Over the last ten years the inflation level in the country has averaged 15%, although the new government has pledged to get it under control in the immediate future. It aims to halve inflation from its current levels within three years.

Other relevant information

(i) UK tax is payable at 30% in the year in which the income arises. A bilateral tax treaty exists between the UK and Republica.

(ii) All net cash flows arising from the Republica project will be remitted back to the UK at the end of the year in which they arise.

(iii) The relevant UK risk-free rate is 2% and UK market return is 10%.

(iv) Allmodcoms is 100% equity financed and will use a beta of 1.5 to estimate the appropriate discount rate for the converted £ cashflows from this project.

(v) Undertaking the project would mean abandoning a plan to open up a new factory in the UK. Allmodcoms had already spent £0.5million surveying potential sites. Two employees taken on last year to oversee the project would also need to be made redundant.

It is estimated that the redundancy package would be £40,000 in total, half payable now and half in one year.

(vi) The exchange rate is currently £/RF 195.5 (that is £1 =RF195.5) and predicted interest rates in the two countries for the length of the project are as follows:

Year	*UK (%)*	*Republica (%)*
1	2	10
2	2	10
3	2	5
4	3	5
5	3	5

Required:

(a) **Advise the directors of Allmodcoms as to whether it is financially advisable to undertake the project. State any assumptions you make.**

(18 marks)

(b) **What other considerations should the company take into account before agreeing to the project?**

(7 marks)

(Total: 25 marks)

Test your understanding answers

Example 1

Method 1

Calculation of exchange rates

(1+ expected appreciation / depreciation of £) = (1+ RM$ rate) / (1+ £ rate)

= 1.07 / 1.09 = 0.9817

Therefore the £ is expected to depreciate by (1 – 0.9817=) 0.0183, or 1.83% per annum.

Year 1	2.0000 × 0.9817	=	1.9634
Year 2	1.9633 × 0.9817	=	1.9275
Year 3	1.9273 × 0.9817	=	1.8922
Year 4	1.8919 × 0.9817	=	1.8576

Year	*0*	*1*	*2*	*3*	*4*
Cash flow (RM$000)	(5,000)	1,500	1,900	2,500	2,700
Exchange rate	2.000	1.9634	1.9275	1.8922	1.8576
Cash flow £	(2,500)	764	986	1,321	1,453
PV factor 16%	1.000	0.862	0.743	0.641	0.552
PV	(2,500)	659	733	847	802

NPV = £541k

Method 2

Calculate the adjusted discount rate:

(1 + RM$ interest rate) / (1 + £ interest rate)

= (1 + discount rate RM$) / (1 + discount rate £)

So 1.07 / 1.09 = (1 + discount rate RM$) /1.16

So the RM$ discount rate = 13.87%

Year	*Cash flow RM $*	*PVF 13.87%*	*PV*
0	(5,000)	1.000	(5,000)
1	1,500	0.878	1,317
2	1,900	0.771	1,465
3	2,500	0.678	1,695
4	2,700	0.594	1,604
			RM $1,081

NPV = 1,081/2.000 = £541k

Test your understanding 1 – Simple foreign NPV

Report

To: Finance Director
From: Financial Manager
Subject: Evaluation of investment in South America
Date: Today

Introduction

This report provides an evaluation of the proposed investment in South America. It contains the NPV calculations of the project, based on our estimated cash flows, and a recommendation.

Calculations of NPV and recommendation

	0 (now)	1	2	3
SA cashflows (SA currency m) (real)	(1,000)	250	350	450
SA cashflows (SA currency m) (nominal)	(1,000)	350	686	1,235
Exchange rates 1USD =... – multiply by 1.346 each year	30	40.38	54.35	73.16
Converted cashflows (USD 000) (nominal)	(33,333)	8,668	12,622	16,881
Extra USD cashflows (USD 000) (real)	(10,000)	(300)	(400)	(500)
Extra USD cashflows (USD 000) (nominal)	(10,000)	(312)	(433)	(562)
Total nominal USD cashflows (USD 000)	(43,333)	8,356	12,189	16,319
DF 20%	1	0.833	0.694	0.579
PV	(43,333)	6,961	8,459	9,449
NPV years 0–3	(18,464)			
PV years 4 onwards (16,319/0.20)×0.579	47,244			
Overall NPV	28,780			

On the basis of my calculations, I would recommend that we proceed with the investment.

However, the following reservations should be noted:

- Positive cash flows are not evident in the first 3 years of operations. An estimated discounted payback period would be 5 years.
- The length of the payback, the volatility of the currency and the political risks make this a very high risk venture.

Signed: Financial Manager

Test your understanding 2 – Complex foreign NPV

(a) RFmillion

		0	1	2	3	4	5
Sales (W2)	(RFm)	–	506	682	1123	1336	1556
Local costs (W3)	(RFm)	–	(352)	(484)	(610)	(747)	(896)
Royalty (W4)	(RFm)	–	(34)	(46)	(56)	(67)	(78)
Taxable Dep'n	(RFm)	–	(100)	(100)	(100)	(100)	–
Taxable Income	(RFm)	–	20	52	357	422	582
Tax @ 10%	(RFm)	–	(2)	(5)	(36)	(42)	(58)
Taxable Dep'n	(RFm)	–	100	100	100	100	–
Initial investment	(RFm)	(400)	–	–	–	–	–
Working capital	(RFm)	(250)	–	–	–	–	250
Remit to UK	(RFm)	(650)	118	147	421	480	774
Ex Rate (W1)		195.5	210.8	227.3	234.0	238.5	243.1
		£million					
Remit to UK	(£m)	(3.32)	0.56	0.65	1.80	2.01	3.18
Royalty (W4)	(£m)	–	0.16	0.20	0.24	0.28	0.32
UK tax on royalty	(W4)	–	(0.05)	(0.06)	(0.07)	(0.08)	(0.10)
Extra UK tax (W5)		–	(0.02)	(0.05)	(0.31)	(0.35)	(0.48)
Redundancy (note 1)		(0.02)	(0.02)				
Net flows	(£m)	(3.34)	0.63	0.74	1.66	1.86	2.92
DF@14%(W6)		1.0	0.877	0.769	0.675	0.592	0.519
PV	(£m)	(3.34)	0.55	0.57	1.12	1.10	1.52
NPV	£1.52m						

The NPV calculation shows a positive NPV of £1.52 million. On the basis of these figures, the project is viable and should be undertaken.

Note 1 : The £500,000 survey cost is not relevant as it is a sunk cost.

Workings

(W1) **Exchange rates**

using interest rate parity i.e. the future exchange rate = spot × (1+RF rate) / (1+ £ rate)

T0		**195.5**
T1	195.5 × 1.1/1.02	**210.8**
T2	210.8 × 1.1/1.02	**227.3**
T3	227.3 × 1.05/1.02	**234.0**
T4	234.0 × 1.05/1.03	**238.5**
T5	238.5 × 1.05/1.03	**243.1**

(W2) **Sales**

		1	*2*	*3*	*4*	*5*
Units		80,000	100,000	120,000	140,000	160,000
Price (£)		30	30	40	40	40
Revenue (£m)		2.4	3.0	4.8	5.6	6.4
Ex rate	(W1)	210.8	227.3	234.0	238.5	243.1
Revenue (RFm)		**506**	**682**	**1,123**	**1,336**	**1,556**

(W3) **Local costs**

		1	*2*	*3*	*4*	*5*
Units		80,000	100,000	120,000	140,000	160,000
Price (RF p.u.)	labour	2200	2420	2541	2668	2801
	Material	1100	1210	1270	1334	1400
	Other	1100	1210	1270	1334	1400
Total (RFm)		**352**	**484**	**610**	**747**	**896**

(W4) **Royalty**

	1	2	3	4	5
Units	80,000	100,000	120,000	140,000	160,000
Royalty p.u. (£)	2	2	2	2	2
Royalty (£m)	**0.16**	**0.20**	**0.24**	**0.28**	**0.32**
UK tax @ 30%	**(0.05)**	**(0.06)**	**(0.07)**	**(0.08)**	**(0.10)**
Ex Rate (W1)	210.8	227.3	234.0	238.5	243.1
Royalty (RFm)	**34**	**46**	**56**	**67**	**78**

(W5) **Extra UK tax**

	1	2	3	4	5
Taxable Repub Inc (RFm)	20	52	357	422	582
Extra tax @20% (30% - 10%)	(4.0)	(10.4)	(71.4)	(84.4)	(116.4)
Ex Rate (W1)	210.8	227.3	234.0	238.5	243.1
Extra tax £m	**(0.02)**	**(0.05)**	**(0.31)**	**(0.35)**	**(0.48)**

(W6) **Discount rate**

2 + (10 – 2)1.5 = 14%

(b) The agreement is heavily dependent on the current regime being in place for the length of the project. The government won with a small majority and hence there must be a risk that in three years they will be deposed. Allmodcoms needs assurances that the agreement would be honoured if this were the case. If the market is indeed much larger than the volumes in the agreement, it may be that the local regime is protecting its own industry to some extent. Subsequent regimes may take an even more aggressive approach and hence cut the agreement totally.

Even if the current regime does remain in place, it is unclear as to whether the inflation targets will be met. Although levels have decreased, historically they have been high and, if the new government seeks rapid economic growth, then simultaneously halving inflation may prove difficult.

The effect of high inflation will be to lower the value of the Republica Franc relative to the £, and hence lower the value of the projected £ cash flows. Allmodcoms does have some protection from these effects as the sales price and royalty are fixed in sterling. However, it is unclear what will happen to the sales price agreed if inflation targets are not met.

The favourable tax rate may also be revoked if there is a regime change. It would be helpful to know what the standard Republica tax rate is. If it is higher than the UK rate of 30%, it would lead to Allmodcoms paying extra tax overall.

The company also needs to build into the appraisal what will happen at the end of the five-year period. The project may give Allmodcoms a good base to expand further into the country having established itself as a major supplier. The danger, however, is that the Republica government may refuse to allow further production and instead would use Allmodcom's assets and intellectual property to further its own local producers.

It is unclear from the information presented what will happen to the fixed assets initially invested as they are not returned at the end of the project. This must be established before the project is undertaken.

There is also a degree of uncertainty regarding the local costs in the appraisal, and Allmodcoms should carry out sensitivity analysis to see how changes in these estimates would affect the NPV. Although the NPV is positive, it is only £1.52 million and this could easily be wiped out by inflation and cost increases.

chapter

12

Business Valuation

Chapter learning objectives

Lead	Component
C1: Evaluate investment choices.	(c) evaluate potential investments in organisations of different types and intangible assets.

Indicative syllabus content

- Valuation bases for assets (e.g. historic cost, replacement cost and realisable value), earnings (e.g. price/earnings multiples and earnings yield) and cash flows (e.g. discounted cash flow, dividend yield and the dividend growth model).
- The strengths and weaknesses of each valuation method and when each is most suitable, e.g. by reference to type of investee organisation (service, capital intensive etc).
- Forms of intangible asset (including intellectual property rights, brands etc). and methods of valuation.
- Application of the efficient market hypothesis to business valuations.
- Selection of an appropriate cost of capital for use in valuation.

1 Overview of Chapter

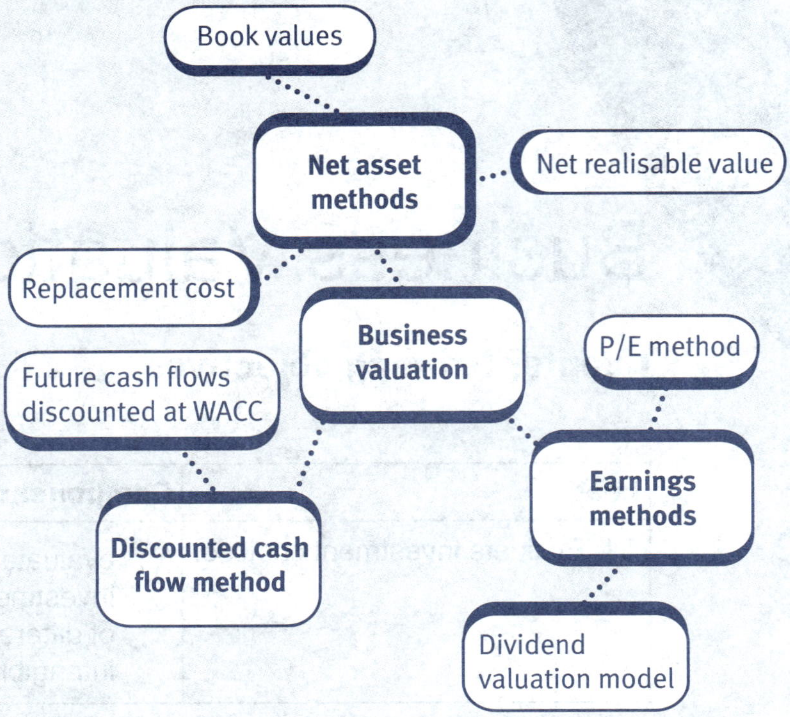

NEW

2 Introduction to business valuation

Business valuation is not a precise, scientific process. The value of a business is affected by:

- reported sales, profits and asset values
- forecast sales, profits and asset values
- type of industry
- level of competition
- range of products sold
- breadth of customer base
- perspective – the buyer and the seller will often have different expectations and hence may value the business differently.

The valuation methods covered in this Chapter give suggested values of a business.

The final value is then agreed between buyer and seller after a process of negotiation.

Valuation of listed and unlisted companies

Listed companies

A listed company will have a stock market value (or market capitalisation).

If small numbers of shares are being traded on the stock market, this share price will be used by traders.

However, if one company is attempting to take over another by acquiring the majority of the shares, the market capitalisation value will not necessarily give a suitable value for the transaction, since the shareholders will not have any incentive to sell their shares at the current market price.

In order to encourage the shareholders in the target company to sell their shares, a premium is normally offered on top of the current stock market share price.

In conclusion, when valuing a listed company, the current stock market share price should be used as a starting point for the calculations rather than as a definitive final figure.

Unlisted companies

An unlisted company has no stock market value, so the valuation process is more complex. Also, there is likely to be less published information available which might help a purchaser to assess the value of an unlisted company.

Therefore, when valuing an unlisted company, estimates often have to be made, based on available information taken from similar listed companies ("proxy" companies).

The valuation methods shown below often value unlisted companies using data derived from proxy listed companies e.g. cost of equity, beta, dividend yield, P/E ratio

In practice, it can be difficult to find a similar listed company.

The final answer may have to be discounted by 25% to 35% to account for:

- relative lack of marketability of unquoted shares - it is more difficult for investors to sell their shares if the company is not listed
- lower levels of scrutiny, therefore greater risk of poor quality financial information.
- higher risk of being a smaller, less well-regarded company with, possibly, a more volatile earnings record.

3 The different valuation methods

There are three basic ways of valuing a business:

Net asset based valuation method

The business's assets form the basis for the valuation. Net asset based valuation methods are difficult to apply to businesses with high levels of intangible assets, but this Chapter covers methods of valuing intangible as well as tangible assets.

Earnings based valuation method

The projected earnings for a business will give an indication of the value of that business. For example, a business with high forecasted earnings will be attractive to a potential purchaser, and hence will be valued highly. In this Chapter, we shall see how earnings and dividends (which are dependent on earnings) can be used in business valuation.

Discounted cashflow method

In theory, a business's value should be equal to the present value of its future cashflows, discounted at an appropriate cost of capital. This Chapter explains how to identify and forecast future cashflows, and how to choose an appropriate discount rate.

Exam approach

Frequently, the compulsory case study (Section A) question in the examination will give information on an entity and request the candidate to calculate a range of values for that entity.

Part of the test is not only to be able to use the various methods to calculate values but to understand the circumstances in which each is most appropriate.

For example asset-based valuations have very limited relevance for entities which are going concerns especially if they have substantial intangible assets.

In each of the following sections, the various valuation methods are explained together with the circumstances in which they might be most appropriate.

4 Net asset based valuation

In this method the company is viewed as being worth the sum of the value of its net assets.

Remember to deduct borrowings when arriving at a net asset value if just the equity is being acquired, but not if only the physical assets and related liabilities are being purchased without acquiring any liability for the borrowings.

A net assets based valuation is most useful when a company is being broken up, rather than purchased as a going concern. Since the method does not incorporate the valuation of intangible assets, it usually gives a low valuation figure, which helps the parties to set a minimum price in a takeover situation.

Asset valuations are therefore likely to be more useful for capital-intensive businesses, than for service businesses, where many of the assets are intangible.

Alternative asset valuation bases

The net asset valuation can be calculated in various ways:

Book value

This method suffers from being largely a function of depreciation policy, for example, some assets may be written down prematurely and others carried at values well above their real worth. Original costs may be of little use if assets are very old, or if asset replacement has been irregular over time.

Thus, this method is of little use in practice.

Replacement value

This method calculates the cost of replacing the business's assets, which may be relevant if the assets are going to be used on an on-going basis.

Break-up value / Net realisable value

Individual assets are valued at the best price obtainable, which will depend partly on the second-hand market and partly on the urgency of realising the asset.

This method can be used to set a minimum selling price for the vendors, as they could liquidate the business as an alternative to selling the shares.

The strengths and weaknesses of net asset based valuations

The main strengths of asset-based valuations are:

- the valuations are fairly readily available;
- they provide a minimum value of the entity.

The main weaknesses of asset-based valuations are:

- future profitability expectations are ignored;
- balance sheet valuations depend on accounting conventions, which may lead to valuations that are very different from market valuations;
- it is difficult to allow for the value of intangible assets such as intellectual property rights.

More detail on net asset based valuation

A net asset based valuation method for a listed company will usually give a value considerably lower than the market value of all the company's shares (the market capitalisation value).

So it should be obvious that shareholders/the market does not value the company on the basis of the balance sheet's net asset figure.

Shareholders are not buying the company for its assets but for the income those assets can produce.

This future income is generated from the use of the balance sheet assets together with the non-balance sheet assets (intangible assets) like highly skilled workforce, strong management team and competitive positioning of the company's products.

Thus assets in the crude sense of balance sheet values are only one dimension of a company's overall value (in a normal going concern situation).

Example 1

The summarised balance sheet (statement of financial position) of Owen at 31 December 20X7 is as follows:

Assets	$000
Non current assets	23,600
Current assets	8,400
	32,000
Equity and liabilities	
Capital and reserves	
$1 Ordinary shares	8,000
Retained earnings	11,200
	19,200
Non current liabilities	
6% Unsecured bond	8,000
Current liabilities	4,800
	32,000

Required:

Calculate the value of one ordinary share in Owen, using a net assets based valuation method.

Example 2

Fowler is wanting to make a bid for Owen (see details for Owen in the previous Example).

It has estimated that the replacement cost of Owen's non-current assets is $40 million.

Required:

Calculate the value of a share in Owen from Fowler's perspective.

Example 3

Ray plc, a UK listed manufacturing company, is considering a takeover bid for Ribbon Ltd, a smaller, unlisted company in the same industry.

Ribbon Ltd has been making losses in the last 2 years, so it is considered that an asset based method should be used to value the business.

Extracts from Ribbon Ltd's Statement of Financial Position

Assets	GBP000
Non current assets (Note 1)	1,207
Current assets (Note 2)	564
	1,771
Equity and liabilities	
Capital and reserves	
GBP1 Ordinary shares	100
Retained earnings	553
	653
Non current liabilities	
5% bonds	600
Current liabilities	518
	1,771

Note 1: The non current assets comprise specialised manufacturing equipment. To replace the equipment would cost GBP1.5m, but if Ribbon Ltd were to be closed down, the assets would sell for no more than GBP1m.

Note 2: Receivables contain an amount of GBP120,000 from a large customer which has just gone into liquidation. A contract for the same customer, included in work in progress (inventory) at a value of GBP30,000 will now have to be scrapped.

Required:

Calculate the expected valuation of Ribbon Ltd, from the perspective of Ray plc. Explain and justify your figures.

5 Valuation of intellectual capital / intangible assets

Definition of intellectual capital

The term 'intellectual capital' has many complex connotations and is often used synonymously with intellectual property, intellectual assets and knowledge assets.

Intellectual capital can be thought of as the total stock of capital or knowledge-based equity that the entity possesses. As such, intellectual capital can be both the end result of a knowledge transformation process or the knowledge itself that is transformed into intellectual property or intellectual assets of the firm.

Intellectual capital includes:

Human resources – The collective skills, experience and knowledge of employees

Intellectual assets – Knowledge which is defined and codified such as drawing, computer program or collection of data

Intellectual property – Intellectual assets which can be legally protected such as patents and copyrights.

Intellectual property is legally defined and assigns property rights to such things as patents, trademarks and copyrights.

These assets are the only form of intellectual capital that is regularly recognised for accounting purposes.

However, accounting conventions based upon historical costs often understate their value:

Valuation of intellectual capital / intangible assets

It is recognised that goodwill, brands and other intellectual capital (intangible assets) often have a significant value. Indeed often intellectual capital is the main contributor of value to an entity.

The net asset based methods covered above do not incorporate this value.

There are two ways of valuing the intangible assets of an entity:

(1) **Simple estimate:**

Value of intangibles =

Value of equity (either using a quoted market capitalisation or using one of the earnings based methods below i.e. DVM, P/E method, or PV of future cashflows)

minus

Value of the tangible assets (see Net Asset Valuation above)

(2) **Calculated Intangible Value (CIV) method:**

The CIV method examines the excess return earned by the entity over the return expected on its tangible assets (this excess is called the Value Spread). The discounted value of the post tax Value Spread is the CIV of the entity, and then:

Total value of equity = Value of tangible assets + CIV

Example 4

Chapman Co has just reported a pre tax profit of $24.29m, and the value of its tangible assets in the balance sheet is $128.66m.

The average return on assets for companies in the same industry is 10%.

The tax rate is 30% and Chapman Co's cost of capital is 16%.

Required:

Calculate the value of Chapman Co using the CIV approach.

6 Earnings based based valuation – the dividend valuation model

Dividend Valuation Model (DVM) Theory

The theory states that the value of the company / share is the present value of the expected future dividends, discounted at the shareholders' required rate of return.

This links to the NPV method covered earlier, where the discounted cashflows from a project represented the gain in wealth to shareholders if the project were undertaken - wealth (share value) is linked to discounted future cashflows.

DVM formula

Either: $Po = \frac{do}{k_e}$ $Po = \frac{do(1 + g)}{k_e - g}$

Assuming: a constant dividend **or** constant growth

Note that:

g = forecast future growth rate in dividends, and:

P_o = Value of company, when do = Total dividends

P_o = Value per share, when do = Dividends per share

Also, note that the simple formula (when assuming a constant dividend) is just a rearrangement of the standard dividend yield formula:

Dividend yield = (Dividend / Share price) × 100%

Example 5

Target has just paid a dividend of EUR250,000. It has 2 million shares in issue.

The current return to shareholders in the same industry as Target is 12%, although it is expected that an additional risk premium of 2% will be applicable to Target, being a smaller and unlisted company.

Required:

Calculate the expected valuation of Target, if

(a) **dividends are expected to be constant**

(b) **dividends are expected to grow at 4% per annum**

The strengths and weaknesses of dividend-based valuations

The strengths of dividend-based valuations are:

- value is based on the present value of the future dividend income stream, so the method has a sound theoretical basis;
- they are useful for valuing minority shareholdings where the shareholder only receives dividends from the entity (rather than a share of total assets or cashflows – factors which form the basis of the other valuation methods).

The main weaknesses of using dividend models include:

- investors tend to have very different expectations from each other, so it is difficult to estimate what dividends will be in the future (Modigliani and Miller's theories can hardly cope with the present-day wide difference in attitude between institutional and individual investors);
- most investors look for a return based on two components: dividend and capital appreciation leading to capital gain on sale of the shares - the DVM approach only looks at the dividend element;
- it is difficult to estimate a future growth rate;
- particularly for unlisted companies, it can be difficult to estimate the cost of equity (note that in the exam, if you are not given the cost of equity, you should use CAPM to derive it, or use proxy company information);
- dividend-based valuations are suitable for valuing small shareholdings rather than for valuing a controlling interest.

Uneven growth rates

The dividend valuation model formula cannot be used directly when the annual growth rate is expected to change.

In such cases, the entity's lifespan should be segmented into the periods for which the varying growth rates apply, and value each separately.

e.g

Illustration 1

Target has just paid a dividend of EUR250,000. It has 2 million shares in issue.

The current return to shareholders in the same industry as Target is 12%, although it is expected that an additional risk premium of 2% will be applicable to Target, being a smaller and unquoted company.

Required:

Calculate the expected valuation of Target, if dividends are expected to stay constant for 3 years, then grow at 4% per annum thereafter.

Solution:

Separate the future dividend stream into two parts: first, the constant dividends for 3 years, then the growing perpetuity thereafter.

First 3 years

Present value of expected dividends = 250,000 x AF $_{1\text{-}3}$ (14%) = EUR 0.580m

Perpetuity from year 4:

Use the given DVM formula, then adjust for the fact that the dividend stream starts in year 4, not year 1 as normal:

[(250,000x1.04) / 0.14–0.04)] x DF $_3$ (14%) = EUR 1.755m

Total value = 0.580m + 1.755m = EUR 2.335m

or 2.335 / 2 = EUR1.17 per share.

7 Earnings based valuation – the P/E method

The P/E valuation method is a very simple method which values a business by applying a suitable P/E ratio to the business's earnings (profit after tax).

P/E valuation method formula

Value of company = Total post-tax earnings× P/E ratio

Value per share = EPS × P/E ratio

Using the P/E valuation formula

The P/E ratio method is the simplest valuation method. It relies on just two figures (the post-tax earnings and the P/E ratio).

Post-tax earnings

The current post-tax earnings, or EPS, for a company can easily be found by looking at the most recent published accounts. However, these published figures will be historic, whereas the earnings figure needed for valuation purposes should be an expected, future earnings figure.

It is perfectly acceptable to use the published earnings figure as a starting point, but before performing the valuation, the historic earnings figure should be adjusted for factors such as:

- one-off items which will not recur in the coming year (e.g. debt write offs in the previous year);

- directors' salaries which might be adjusted after a takeover has been completed;
- any savings ("synergies") which might be made as part of a takeover.

P/E ratio

The P/E ratio for a listed company is a simple measure of the company's share price divided by its earnings per share.

The P/E indicates the market's perception of the company's current position and its future prospects. For example, if the P/E ratio is high, this indicates that the company has a relatively high share price compared to its current level of earnings, suggesting that the share price reflects good growth prospects of the company.

An unlisted company has no market share price, so has no readily available P/E ratio. Therefore, when valuing an unlisted company, a proxy P/E ratio from a similar listed company is often used.

Proxy P/E ratios

As explained above, an unlisted company will not have a market-driven P/E ratio, so an industry average P/E, or one for a similar company, will be used as a proxy.

However, proxy P/E ratios are also sometimes used when valuing a listed company – of course if a listed entity's own P/E ratio is applied to its own earnings figure, the calculation will just give the existing share price.

In particular, proxy P/E ratios are used in the context of bootstrapping, which is covered in the next Chapter.

Example 6

Molier is an unquoted entity with a recently reported after-tax earnings of $3,840,000. It has issued 1m ordinary shares. A similar listed entity has a P/E ratio of 9.

Required:

Calculate the value of one ordinary share in Molier using the P/E basis of valuation.

The strengths and weaknesses of earnings-based valuations

The main strengths of earnings-based valuations are:

- they are commonly used and are well understood;
- they are relevant for valuing a controlling interest in an entity.

The main weaknesses of earnings-based valuations are:

- they are based on accounting profits rather than cash flows;
- it is difficult to identify a suitable P/E ratio, particularly when valuing the shares of an unlisted entity;
- it is difficult to establish the relevant level of sustainable earnings.

Example 7

Company X is considering a bid for Company Y.

X has earnings of $3m per annum, and Y has earnings of $1.5m per annum. The P/E ratio of X is 12 and that of Y is 8.

If the takeover proceeds, it is expected that synergies of $0.5m per annum will be generated, and that the combined company will have a P/E ratio of 11.

Required:

Calculate the maximum price that X should pay for Y, and the minimum price that Y should accept.

Earnings yield method

In some questions, you may not be given the P/E ratio, but you may be given the Earnings Yield instead.

The earnings yield is the reciprocal of the P/E ratio i.e. Earnings Yield = 1/ (P/E ratio).

Hence,

Value of company = Total earnings / Earnings Yield

Value per share = EPS / Earnings Yield

Understanding and interpretation of Earnings Yield

Some deeper analysis is desirable, for example examining the trend of share price over a number of quarters in the light of any events such as profits warnings and acquisitions (or rumours thereof), and the likely effect that they have had on earnings.

The stability of Earnings Yield is often as important as its growth, bearing in mind that in a general way the market is absorbing new information to try to assess a sustainable level of EPS on which to base growth for the future. Clearly, effective growth is dependent on a stable base, and the trend of Earnings Yield over time is to an extent a reflection of this factor.

A prospective acquirer would, of course, be concerned to assess the worth of a prospective biddee on the basis of its becoming part of the acquiring entity, and the valuation will especially need to take into account the expectations of the biddee's shareholders.

A further point relates to the acquirer's intentions regarding the biddee. If, for example the latter entity is to be partially demerged, that is certain parts disposed of to other entities in which they would provide a better fit, then the share price valuation may well be greater than if the whole biddee entity was to be retained. Nevertheless, any such break-up considerations will need to take into account all the stakeholders, including employees, suppliers and customers of the biddee, as any serious demotivation will take away from the goodwill value of the acquisition and quite possibly damage that of the acquiring entity itself.

8 Discounted cash flow method

Overview of the method

Under the discounted cash flow (DCF) method, a value for the equity of the entity is derived by estimating the future annual after-tax cash flows of the entity, and discounting these cash flows at an appropriate cost of capital. This is theoretically the best way of valuing a business, since the discounted value of future cashflows represents the wealth of the shareholders (as seen in the earlier Chapter 'Investment Appraisal - basic techniques').

The cost of capital used to discount the cash flows should reflect the systematic risk of the cash flows.

Example 8

The expected after-tax cash flows of Thomas, an all equity financed company with 2 million shares in issue , will be as follows:

Year	GBP
1	120,000
2	100,000
3	140,000
4	50,000
5 onwards	130,000

A suitable cost of capital for evaluating Thomas is 12%.

Required:

Calculate the value of Thomas's equity (in total and per share) using the DCF basis of valuation.

More details on cashflows and cost of capital

The introductory paragraph above explained that "an appropriate cost of capital" should be used for discounting. In some exam questions, such as the Example above, you will be told directly which cost of capital to use. However, if you are not told specifically, it is important to understand the following relationships:

Use of WACC as a discount rate

WACC can be used to discount post-tax cashflows (BEFORE financing charges) when valuing a project or an entity (debt + equity value). To find the company's equity value, the value of debt would need to be deducted.

Use of cost of equity as a discount rate

The cost of equity can be used to discount the post-tax cashflows (AFTER financing charges) in order to value the equity in a company directly.

Use of proxy company information

The cost of capital used must reflect the risk of the entity's cashflows. If a cost of capital is not given, or if is difficult to derive one (perhaps because the entity is unlisted and therefore there is a lack of available information), a proxy cost of capital from a similar listed company could be used instead.

When using a proxy cost of capital, care must be taken to ensure that it reflects the entity's business risk and its capital structure. If necessary, a risk adjusted cost of capital could be used, as covered in the earlier Chapter on 'Capital Structure'.

e.g

Illustration 2

Eamon Co is forecast to generate a constant stream of post tax cashflows (after interest charges) of $10m per year.

The company is not listed, and no cost of equity has been calculated. However, a similar listed entity, Frank Co, which operates in the same business sector has a cost of equity of 10%.

Frank Co is all equity financed whereas Eamon Co has 20% debt and 80% equity by market values. The tax rate is 30%, and the yield on Eamon's debt is 4%.

Required:

Calculate the value of Eamon Co, using the discounted cashflow method.

Solution:

The given post tax and post interest cashflows need to be discounted using an appropriate cost of equity.

Although Frank Co operates in the same business sector, its gearing is different. Hence, a risk adjusted cost of equity (suitable to Eamon Co's circumstances) would be (using M + M's formula):

$k_{eg} = k_{eu} + (k_{eu} - k_d)(1 - t) V_D / V_E$

$= 10\% + (10\% - 4\%)(1 - 0.30) 20/80$

$= 11.05\%$

Therefore, the value of Eamon Co's equity is $10m / 0.1105 = $90.5m

Free cash flows

The post-tax cashflows (after financing charges) are often referred to as "free cash flows".

Free cash flows

The problem of lack of information

In a project appraisal, the cash flows generated from the project are easily identifiable, but in a business valuation they are not necessarily.

This is because there are so many of them, and because the necessary information does not usually exist in the public domain.

Therefore, for business valuation, we often have to estimate cash flows using the readily-available accounting information.

The concept of "free cash flows"

The cashflow available for distribution to investors after the entity has made all the investments in non-current assets and working capital necessary to sustain ongoing operations is referred to as "free cash flow".

Definition: (CIMA Official Terminology, 2005)

Free cash flow: Cash flow from operations after deducting interest, tax, preference dividends and ongoing capital expenditure, but excluding capital expenditure associated with strategic acquisitions and/or disposals and ordinary share dividends.

Use of free cash flows

The free cash flow for a company can be calculated by taking the readily available accounting profit figure and adjusting it.

The value of the shareholders' stake (equity) in an entity is then the sum of the future free cash flows discounted at the cost of equity.

Example of free cash flows

The recently published accounts of Carey show the following figures:

Operating profit (after deducting depreciation of USD3m) = USD32m
Interest paid = USD2m
Taxation = USD9m
Capital expenditure = USD4m

Required:

Calculate the free cash flow in the year.

Solution:

Free cash flow = 32m + 3m – 2m – 9m – 4m = USD 20m

Example 9

Chassagne Co is considering making a bid for Butler Co, a rival company.

The following information should be used to value Butler Co.

Income statement for the most recent accounting period

	GBP m
Revenue	285.1
Cost of sales	(120.9)
Gross profit	164.2
Operating expenses (inc depreciation GBP 12.3m)	(66.9)
Profit from operations	97.3
Finance costs	(10.0)
Profit before tax	87.3
Taxation	(21.6)
Profit after tax	65.7

Other information

- selling prices are expected to rise at 3% pa for the next 3 years and then stay constant thereafter.
- sales volumes are expected to rise at 5% pa for the next 3 years and then stay constant thereafter.
- assume that cost of sales is a completely variable cost, and that other operating expenses (including depreciation) are expected to stay constant.
- Butler Co invested £15m in non current assets and £2m in working capital last year. These annual amounts are expected to stay constant in future.

- Butler Co's financing costs are expected to stay constant each year in the future.
- the marginal rate of tax is 28%, payable in the year in which the liability arises.
- assume that book depreciation equals tax depreciation.
- Butler Co has 500 million shares in issue.
- the WACC of Butler Co is 9% and its cost of equity is 12%.

Required

Calculate the value of the equity in Butler Co (in total and per share) by forecasting future free cash flows and discounting them to present value.

The strengths and weaknesses of cash-based valuations

The strengths of this method of valuation are:

- theoretically this is the best method of valuation;
- it can be used to place a maximum value on the entity;
- it considers the time value of money.

The weaknesses of this method are:

- it is difficult to forecast cash flows accurately;
- it is difficult to determine an appropriate discount rate;
- what time period should we evaluate in detail and then how do you value the company's worth beyond this period? i.e. the realisable value at the end of the planning period;
- the NPV method does not evaluate further options that may exist;
- It assumes that the discount rate and tax rates are constant through the period.

The EMH and business valuation

Implications of the Efficient Market Hypothesis (EMH) in business valuation

The EMH was introduced in the earlier Chapter on 'Long Term Finance'.

The level of efficiency in the market is very important when considering the value of a business.

In a strongly efficient market, the share price of a listed company will reflect all factors which are known (both publicly and privately) about that company. Hence it is less likely that a premium will be paid (above the existing share price) in a takeover.

In a semi strongly efficient market, the existing share price will reflect all that is publicly known about a company. Therefore, if we can identify or predict other factors which are not currently in the public domain, this might justify a higher value and hence the payment of a premium on acquisition.

The company's intentions and prospects may well have to be communicated to the market (unless the market is strongly efficient) in order for a purchaser to make a proper assessment of the company's value. This will be particularly important when using earnings or cashflow based valuation methods, which rely on accurate forecasts of future information.

Summary of valuation methods – when should each be used?

This Chapter has covered the different valuation methods in turn, and has separately identified the strengths and weaknesses of each of the methods.

To conclude, we should consider the circumstances in which each valuation method is most useful.

Net asset based methods

The net asset based valuation methods are most appropriate when valuing capital intensive businesses with plenty of tangible assets.

For a service business, the net asset based approach is likely to significantly undervalue the business, unless some effort is also made to value the intangible assets of the business.

Note however that in times of uncertainty, the net asset based approach avoids the need to forecast future earnings or cashflows, so it may be favoured in these circumstances.

Dividend valuation model (DVM)

The DVM is a suitable valuation method when valuing a minority shareholding in a company, because if an investor purchases a minority stake, the dividends represent the forecast income from the investment, which will impact his wealth.

If the investor were to purchase a majority stake, it would be more relevant to consider overall company cashflows or net asset values as a basis for the valuation.

P/E method and discounted cashflow method

Both these methods are based on forecasts of the future, and often use proxy information from proxy companies. These factors may be difficult to identify in practice.

Providing that the forecasts are accurate, these methods value the business based on its future prospects, so automatically include a measure of the goodwill / intangible assets associated with a business.

For service businesses, these methods are generally preferred to the net asset based methods.

9 Exam style questions

Note: Several of the exam style questions at the end of the next Chapter ('Financial and Strategic Implications of Mergers and Acquisitions') also contain business valuation calculations.

Test your understanding 1 – Valuation methods

The board of directors of Predator plc, a UK company, is considering making an offer to purchase Target Ltd, a private limited company in the same industry. If Target Ltd is purchased it is proposed to continue operating the company as a going concern in the same line of business.

Summarised details from the most recent financial statements (statements of financial position and income statements) of Predator and Target are shown below:

	Predator plc as at 31 March		Target Ltd as at 31 March	
	£m	£m	£000	£000
Freehold property		33		460
Plant and equipment		58		1,310
Inventory	29		330	
Receivables	24		290	
Cash	3		20	
less current liabilities	(31)	25	(518)	122
		116		1,892
Financed by:Ordinary shares			35	160
Reserves			43	964
Shareholders funds			78	1,124
Medium term bank loans			38	768
			116	1,892

Predator plc, 50 pence ordinary shares, Target Ltd, 25 pence ordinary

Year	Predator plc PAT £m	Predator plc Dividend £m	Target Ltd PAT £000	Target Ltd Dividend £000
T5	14.30	9.01	143	85.0
T4	15.56	9.80	162	93.5
T3	16.93	10.67	151	93.5
T2	18.42	11.60	175	102.8
T1	20.04	12.62	183	113.1

N.B. T5 is five years ago and T1 is the most recent year.

Target's shares are owned by a small number of private individuals. Its managing director, who receives an annual salary of £120,000, dominates the company. This is £40,000 more than the average salary received by managing directors of similar companies. The managing director would be replaced if Predator purchases Target.

The freehold property has not been revalued for several years and is believed to have a market value of £800,000.

The value of plant and equipment in the statement of financial position is thought to reflect its replacement cost fairly, but its value if sold is not likely to exceed £800,000. Approximately £55,000 of inventory is obsolete and could only be sold as scrap for £5,000.

The ordinary shares of Predator are currently trading at 430 pence ex-div. A suitable cost of equity for Target has been estimated at 15%.

Both companies are subject to corporation tax at 33%.

Required:

Estimate the value of Target Ltd using the different methods of valuation and advise the board of Predator as to how much it should offer for Target's shares.

Test your understanding 2 – Valuation methods

AB is a telecommunications consultancy based in Europe that trades globally. It was established 15 years ago. The four founding shareholders own 25% of the issued share capital each and are also executive directors of the entity.

The shareholders are considering a flotation of AB on a European stock exchange and have started discussing the process and a value for the entity with financial advisors. The four founding shareholders, and many of the entity's employees, are technical experts in their field, but have little idea how entities such as theirs are valued.

Assume you are one of AB's financial advisors. You have been asked to estimate a value for the entity and explain your calculations and approach to the directors. You have obtained the following information.

Summary financial data for the past three years and forecast revenue and costs for the next two years is as follows:

Income Statements for the years ended 31 March

	20X4 (actual) EURm	**20X5 (actual) EURm**	**20X6 (actual) EURm**	**20X7 (forecast) EURm**	**20X8 (forecast) EURm**
Revenue	125.0	137.5	149.9	172.0	198.0
Cash operating costs	37.5	41.3	45.0	52.0	59.0
Depreciation	20.0	22.0	48.0	48.0	48.0
Pre tax earnings	67.5	74.2	56.9	72.0	91.0
Taxation	20.3	22.3	17.1	22.0	27.0

Statements of financial position at 31 March

	20X4	20X5	20X6
	EURm	EURm	EURm
Assets			
Non current assets			
Property, plant and equipment	150	175	201
Current assets	48	54	62
	198	229	263
Equity and liabilities			
Equity			
Share capital (EUR 1 shares)	30	30	30
Retained earnings	148	179	203
	178	209	233
Current liabilities	20	20	30
	198	229	263

Note: The book valuations of non-current assets are considered to reflect current realisable values.

Other information/assumptions

- Growth in after tax cash flows for 20X9 and beyond (assume indefinitely) is expected to be 3% per annum. Cash operating costs can be assumed to remain at the same percentage of revenue as in previous years. Depreciation will fluctuate but, for purposes of evaluation, assume the 20X8 charge will continue indefinitely. Tax has been payable at 30% per annum for the last three years. This rate is expected to continue for the foreseeable future and tax will be payable in the year in which the liability arises.
- The average P/E ratio for telecommunication entities' shares quoted on European stock exchanges has been 12.5 over the past 12 months. However, there is a wide variation around this average and AB might be able to command a rating up to 30% higher than this;
- An estimated cost of equity capital for the industry is 10% after tax;
- The average pre-tax return on total assets for the industry over the past 3 years has been 15%.

Required:

(a) **Calculate a range of values for AB, in total and per share, using methods of valuation that you consider appropriate. Where relevant, include an estimate of value for intellectual capital.**

(12 marks)

(b) **Discuss the methods of valuation you have used, explaining the relevance of each method to an entity such as AB. Conclude with a recommendation of an approximate flotation value for AB, in total and per share.**

(13 marks)

(Total 25 marks)

A report format is not required for this question.

Test your understanding answers

Example 1

Assuming the balance sheet values are realistic, the valuation is:

	$000
Non current assets	23,600
Current assets	8,400
Less: 6% Unsecured bond	(8,000)
Less: Current liabilities	(4,800)
	19,200

So the value per share is $19,200,000 / 8,000,000 = $2.40

(Note that the net asset value of $19,200,000 is equal to the value of the ordinary share capital plus reserves.)

Example 2

Value per share = ($19,200,000 + $40,000,000 – $23,600,000) / 8,000,000

= $4.45

Example 3

GBP000		**Explanation / justification**
Non current assets	1,500	Ray plc is buying the business, so would have to buy the machinery from scratch if it decided on the alternative of organic growth. The realisable value will be a useful minimum value from Ribbon Ltd's perspective, but it is not relevant to Ray plc.
Current assets (564–120–30)	414	The inventory and receivables relating to the bankrupt customer will not be acquired by Ray plc. They are therefore excluded from the valuation.
Less: 5% bonds	(600)	
Less: Current liabilities	(518)	In order for Ray plc to takeover Ribbon Ltd, it needs to buy the equity of the business. After the takeover, Ray plc will be responsible for meeting these liabilities, so they should be included in the valuation of Ribbon Ltd.
	796	

Value per share = GBP 796,000 / 100,000 = GBP 7.96

Example 4

		$m
Current pre tax profit		24.29
Less: Industry ROA x Net assets	10% x 128.66m	(12.87)
Value Spread		11.42
Post Tax Value Spread	11.42m x (1–0.30)	7.99
CIV (assuming constant perpetuity)	7.99m x 1/0.16	49.94

Therefore, the total value of Chapman Co is estimated to be

128.66m + 49.94m = $178.60m

Example 5

(a) $Po = \frac{250,000}{0.14}$

= EUR 1.786 million, or 1.786/2 = EUR 0.893 per share.

(b) $Po = \frac{250,000 \times 1.04}{0.14 - 0.04}$

= EUR 2.6 million, or 2.6/2 = EUR 1.30 per share.

Example 6

EPS = 3,840,000 / 1,000,000 = $3.84

Value = P/E × EPS = 9 × 3.84 = $34.56

Example 7

The maximum that X should be prepared to pay for Y is the total increase in value generated by taking over Y, i.e.

Value of combined	= 11 × (3m +1.5m +0.5m)	= $55m
Less value of X	= 12 × 3m	= $36m
Max. price to pay		= $19m.

However, the shareholders of Y will value their company at 8 × 1.5m = $12m since they will not have enough information to enable them to value the expected synergies.

The price paid by X to take over Y is then likely to fall somewhere between these two valuations, depending upon the negotiating skills of the buyer and seller.

Example 8

Year	GBP	DF (12%)	PV
1	120,000	0.893	107,160
2	100,000	0.797	79,700
3	140,000	0.712	99,680
4	50,000	0.636	31,800
5 onwards	130,000	0.567	73,710
		NPV	392,050

However, this ignores cash flows after year 5. Assuming the year 5 cash flow continues to infinity, this has a present value of:

130,000 / 0.12 = GBP 1,083,333

This has a present value today of:

GBP 1,083,333 × 0.567 = GBP 614,250

This gives a total present value (value of equity) of:

614,250 + 392,050 = GBP 1,006,300

With 2 million shares, this is 1,006,300 / 2,000,000 = GBP 0.50 per share.

Example 9

GBPm	Year 1	Year 2	Year 3 etc
Sales (×1.03×1.05)	308.3	333.5	360.6
Cost of sales (×1.05)	(126.9)	(133.3)	(140.0)
Gross profit	181.4	200.2	220.6
Operating expenses	(66.9)	(66.9)	(66.9)
Financing costs	(10.0)	(10.0)	(10.0)
Forecast profit before tax	104.5	123.3	143.7
Less Taxation (28%)	(29.3)	(34.5)	(40.2)
Add back depreciation	12.3	12.3	12.3
Less Capital expenditure	(15.0)	(15.0)	(15.0)
Less Working capital investment	(2.0)	(2.0)	(2.0)
Forecast free cash flows	70.5	84.1	98.8
DF 12%	0.893	0.797	0.797/0.12
Present value	63.0	67.0	656.2

So the net present value = GBP786.2m

This is the total value of the equity in Butler Co.

With 500 million shares in issue, this corresponds to a value of

786.2 / 500 = GBP 1.57 per share.

Test your understanding 1 – Valuation methods

The approaches to use for valuation are:

(1) Net asset valuation

(2) Dividend valuation model

(3) P/E ratio / Earnings valuation.

(1) **Net asset valuation**

Target is being purchased as a going concern, so realisable values are irrelevant.

	£000
Net assets per accounts (1,892 – 768)	1,124
Adjustments to freehold property (800 – 460)	340
Adjustment to inventory	(50)
Valuation	**1,414**
	Say £1.4m

(2) **Dividend valuation model**

The average rate of growth in Target's dividends over the last four years is 7.4% on a compound basis.

Growth working: $(113.1/85.0)^{(1/4)} - 1 = 0.074$

The estimated value of Target using the dividend valuation model is therefore:

$$\textbf{Valuation} \quad \frac{£113{,}100 \times 1.074}{0.15 - 0.074} = \textbf{£1,598,281 Say £1.6m}$$

(3) **P/E ratio/Earnings valuation**

A suitable P/E ratio for Target will be based on the P/E ratio of Predator as both companies are in the same industry.

$$\text{P/E of Predator: } \frac{70\text{m} \times £4.30}{£20.04} = \text{ or } \frac{430}{28.63} = \mathbf{15}$$

Target's maintainable earnings are:

£183,000 + (£40,000 x 67%) = £209,800 after adjusting for the savings in the director's remuneration.

The estimated value is therefore £209,800 x 15 = £3,147,000, **say £3.1m.**

Advice to the board

On the basis of its tangible assets the value of Target is £1.4m, which excludes any value for intangibles.

The dividend valuation gives a value of around £1.6m.

The earnings based valuation indicates a value of around £3.1m, which is based on the assumption that not only will the current earnings be maintained, but that they will increase by the savings in the director's remuneration. It is also based on a proxy P/E ratio of 15 which was taken from a much larger listed company with a higher level of historic growth. Arguably this P/E ratio is too high for the circumstances of Target.

On the basis of these valuations an offer of around £2m would appear to be most suitable. The directors should, however, be prepared to increase the offer to:

Maximum price:

It is worth noting that the maximum price Predator should be prepared to offer is:

The NPV of the combined group after the acquisition	X
The NPV of the acquiring company before the acquisition	(X)
Maximum price	**X**

If **synergy** occurs this could justify a higher price than shown by the valuation methods illustrated.

The comment on the maximum price is particularly appropriate in this question as this an example of horizontal integration where considerable synergies normally exist.

Test your understanding 2 – Valuation methods

(a) **Calculations**

Methods that could be considered are:

- Asset value
- Market capitalisation
- Dividend/earnings valuation model
- NPV

Each method is calculated as follows:

Asset value

The balance sheet for 20X6 shows net assets of EUR233m (€233m). However, this entity clearly has substantial intellectual capital, which the value of tangible assets in the balance sheet does not reflect. An estimate of the value of an intangible asset can be attempted as follows.

This method involves taking the excess returns on tangible assets and uses this figure as a basis for determining the proportion of return attributable to intangible assets.

(1) Calculation of average pre-tax earnings for three years:

(€67.5m + €74.2m + €56.9m)/3 = €66.2m

(2) From the balance sheet the average year end tangible assets over the last three years is calculated as:

(€198m + €229m + €263m)/3 = €230m

(3) The return on assets is calculated by dividing earnings by average assets as follows:

(€66.2m/€230m) x 100 = 28.8%

(4) The industry's return on assets for this same three years is 15% (as per the scenario)

(5) Multiply the industry average pre-tax return on assets by the entity's average tangible assets to show what the average telecoms entity would earn from that amount of tangible assets:

€230m x 15% = €34.5m

Subtract this from the entity's pre-tax earnings:

€66.2m – €34.5m = €31.7m This figure shows how much more AB earns from its assets than the average telecommunications company.

(6) The after tax premium attributable to intangible assets is calculated as follows:

(i) Three-year average income tax rate = 30%

(ii) Excess return = €31.7m

(iii) Multiply (i) by (ii) = €9.5m

(iv) (ii)–(iii) = €22.2m

(7) The NPV of the premium is calculated by dividing the premium by the entity's cost of capital as follows:

€22.2m/0.08 = €277m

If the NPV of the estimated value of intellectual capital is added to the value of net tangible assets we get €263m + €277m = €540m, less current liabilities gives a net figure of €510m.

Tutorial Note: Candidates would have gained credit for any valid attempt to place a value on intellectual capital.

Market capitalisation / PE method

If we use the industry average P/E of 12.5 the potential value is €497.5m. If AB can command a rating up to 30% higher, this value rises to €646.7m.

Note: €497.5m is calculated as €56.9m (20X6 pre-tax earnings) less €17.1m (taxation) multiplied by 12.5 (industry average P/E)

Dividend/earnings model

There is insufficient information to use the DVM, although earnings could be used as a proxy. However, as the future growth rate is not constant the simplified model cannot be used. The NPV approach would give broadly similar results.

NPV

	20X7	**20X8**
	EURm	**EURm**
After tax profit	50	64
Add: Depreciation	48	48
Cash flow	98	112
DF 10%	0.909	0.826
PV	89	93

DCF of cash flows for 20X9 and beyond are

€112m x 1.03 x 0.826/(0.10 – 0.03) = €1.361m

NPV = €89m + €93m + €1,361m = €1,543m

Tutorial Note

The calculations here use the industry average cost of capital. An acceptable alternative would use 8%, the earnings yield (reciprocal of P/E ratio of 12.5). In this case the NPV would be €2,164m.

Summary of valuations

	Total	Per share
	EURm	**EUR**
Asset value	233	7.70
Asset value including intellectual capital	455	15.17
PE method	497–647	16.57–21.57
NPV	1,543	51.43

(b) **Discussion of methods and recommendation**

Asset value

Asset value has little relevance except in specific circumstances such as a liquidation or disposal of parts of a business. Asset value is of even more limited usefulness in an entity such as AB, which earns a substantial proportion of its income from intellectual capital that generally does not feature in the balance sheet.

Market capitalisation / PE method

The P/E basis of valuation has the advantage that it bases value on the future earnings of the entity. In a listed entity, the P/E ratio is used to describe the relationship between the share price (or market capitalisation) and earnings per share (or total earnings). It is calculated by dividing the price per share by the earnings per share. Market capitalisation is the share price multiplied by the number of shares in issue. Market capitalisation is not necessarily the true value of a entity as it can be affected by a variety of extraneous factors but for a listed entity it provides a benchmark that cannot be ignored in, say, a take-over situation.

In the case of an unlisted entity, a P/E ratio that is representative of similar quoted entities might be used as a starting point for arriving at an estimated market value, based upon the present earnings of the unlisted entity. The potential market capitalisation would be the entity's latest earnings multiplied by the benchmark P/E ratio.

AB is an unlisted entity so it does not have a market capitalisation or a quoted P/E ratio. Applying the industry average P/E provides a benchmark but not a very good one. As noted in the scenario, there is a wide variation around this average. Also, although not stated, the definition of the industry is likely to be very broad. A better approach might be to find an entity similar to AB and apply its P/E. Again, this is very rough and ready. As AB is unlisted there are arguments for both lowering and raising the P/E as compared with either a proxy entity or the industry average. The Financial Advisor's estimate is that AB could command a rating 30% higher than the industry average. It is not clear how this estimate was made, as an argument could be made for lowering the P/E ratio to reflect the higher risk and lower liquidity of such entities. It would be more appropriate to use the NPV method and adjust the discount rate – as discussed below.

NPV/Earnings method

Forecasting cash flows and discounting at a specific risk adjusted discount rate is the theoretically correct valuation method. The valuation here uses the industry average cost of equity. Using an industry average suffers from the problems noted above. Also, the cost of equity will include an element of return for financial risk if entities have debt in their capital structure. Many entities included in the industry average will have substantial debt finance.

What is needed here is an exercise to calculate a more accurate cost of capital. As with using the P/E ratio approach, discussed above, finding a proxy entity may be more reliable than using an industry average.

Recommendation

As shown in the summary table in part (a), the likely market value ranges from €233m (net tangible assets) to €1,543m (NPV). The NPV valuation is substantially higher than any of the others. While this method is theoretically correct, the reliability of the results does of course depend on the accuracy of the forecast cash flows and the discount rate used. Using growth in perpetuity (although a sensible simplification for examination purposes) is unrealistic.

None of the figures produced by this exercise is wholly reliable, neither is it expected to be, as this is simply an estimate based on incomplete information. The main recommendation must be to conduct a more detailed evaluation involving other advisors such as the entity that will be responsible for the flotation. It needs also to be established what percentage of their shareholding each director wishes to sell on flotation and how many new shares will need to be reissued. The calculations have been made on the current number of shares in issue to the directors/founding shareholders.

However, if a recommendation has to be made, a flotation value in the region of €600m or €20 per share would be conservative.

(Tutorial Note: Any sensible recommendation, or argument for not making one on the evidence available, would gain credit.)

A secondary recommendation would be to split the shares in readiness for a flotation. The share prices produced by all valuation methods, except asset value, are 'heavy' – that is buyers would not get many shares for their money. More shares would need to be in issue to allow a reasonably liquid market in them.

chapter

13

Financial and Strategic Implications of Mergers and Acquisitions

Chapter learning objectives

Lead	Component
C2: Evaluate opportunities for merger, acquisition and divestment.	(a) evaluate the financial and strategic implications of proposals for mergers and acquisitions. (b) evaluate the financial and strategic implications of demergers and divestments.

Indicative syllabus content

- Recognition of the interests of different stakeholder groups in mergers, acquisitions and company valuations.
- The reasons for merger or acquisitions (e.g. synergistic benefits).
- Forms of consideration and terms for acquisitions (e.g. cash, shares, convertibles and earn-out arrangements), and their financial effects.
- The post-merger or post-acquisition integration process (e.g. management transfer and merger of systems).
- The function/role of management buy-outs and venture capitalists.
- Types of exit strategy and their implications.
- The reasons for (e.g. strategic change, opportunity cost of investment) and mechanisms of demerger or divestment.
- The implications of regulation for business combinations. (Note: Detailed knowledge of the City Code and EU competition rules will not be tested).

1 Overview of Chapter

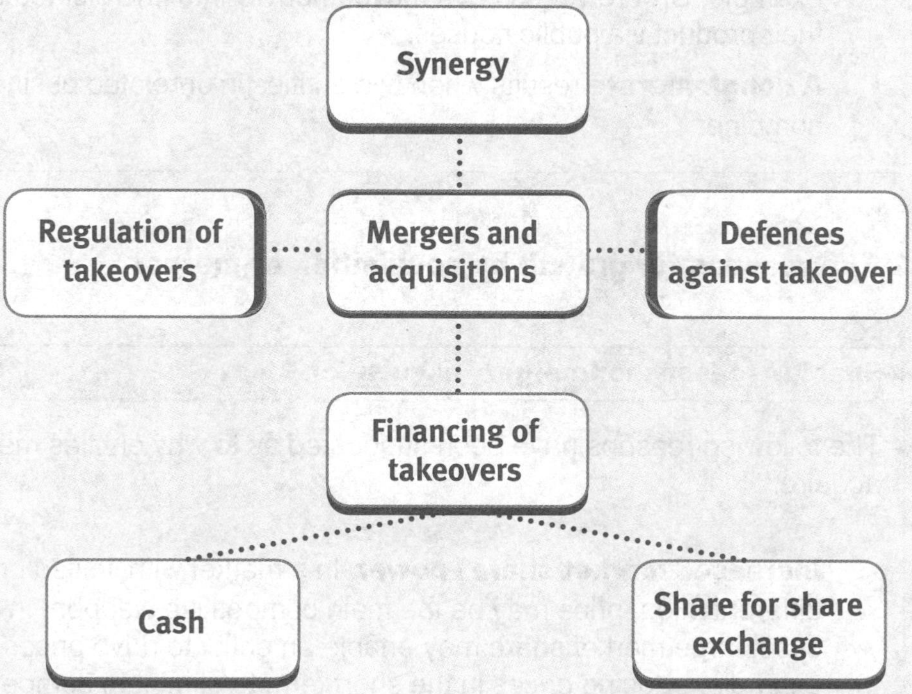

Terminology

The term 'merger' is usually used to describe the joining together of two or more entities.

Strictly, if one entity acquires a majority shareholding in another, the second is said to have been acquired (or 'taken over') by the first. If the two entities join together to submerge their separate identities into a new entity, the process is described as a merger.

In fact, the term 'merger' is often used even when an acquisition / takeover has actually occurred, because of the cultural impact on the acquired entity – the word merger makes the arrangement sound like a partnership between equals.

Types of merger / acquisition

Mergers and acquisitions can be classified to reflect the nature of the enlarged group:

- **Horizontal integration** results when two entities in the same line of business combine. For example, recent bank and building society mergers are a good example of this type of integration.

- **Vertical integration** results from the acquisition of one entity by another which is at a different level in the 'chain of supply' – as an example, UK breweries have moved heavily into the distribution of their product via public houses.
- **A conglomerate** results when two entities in unrelated businesses combine.

2 The reasons for growth by acquisition or merger

Specific reasons for merger / acquisition

The following reasons have been suggested as to why entities merge or acquire.

- **Increased market share / power**. In a market with limited product differentiation, price may be the main competitive weapon. In such a case, large market share may enable an entity to drive prices – for example reducing prices in the short term to eliminate competition before increasing prices later.
- **Economies of scale**. These result when expansion of the scale of productive capacity of an entity (or industry) causes total production costs to increase less than proportionately with output. It is clear that a merger which resulted in horizontal or vertical integration could give such economies since, at the very least, duplication would be avoided. But how could a conglomerate merger give economies? Possibly through central facilities such as offices, accounting departments and computer departments being rationalised. (Indeed, both sets of management are unlikely to be needed in their entirety.)
- **Combining complementary needs**. Many small entities have a unique product but lack the engineering and sales organisations necessary to produce and market it on a large scale. A natural course of action would be to merge with a larger entity. Both entities gain something – the small entity gets 'instant' engineering and marketing departments, and the large entity gains the revenue and other benefits which a unique product can bring. Also if, as is likely, the resources which each entity requires are complementary, the merger may well produce further opportunities that neither would see in isolation.
- **Improving efficiency**. A classic takeover target would be an entity operating in a potentially lucrative market but which, owing to poor management or inefficient operations, does not fully exploit its opportunities. Of course, being taken over would not be the only way of improving such a poor performer, but such an entity's managers may be unwilling to give themselves the sack.

- **A lack of profitable investment opportunities – surplus cash**. An entity may be generating a substantial volume of cash, but sees few profitable investment opportunities. If it does not wish to simply pay out the surplus cash as dividends (because of its long-term dividend policy, perhaps), it could use it to acquire other entities. A reason for doing so is that entities with excess cash are usually regarded as ideal targets for acquisition – a case of buy or be bought.
- **Tax relief**. An entity may be unable to claim tax relief because it does not generate sufficient profits. It may therefore wish to merge with another entity which does generate such profits.
- **Reduced competition**. It is often one benefit of merger activity – provided that it does not fall foul of the competition authorities.
- **Asset-stripping**. A predator acquires a target and sells the easily separable assets, perhaps closing down or disposing of some of its operations.

The following reasons are of questionable validity:

- **Diversification, to reduce risk**. While acquiring an entity in a different line of activity may diversify away risk for the entities involved, this is surely irrelevant to the shareholders. They could have performed exactly the same diversification simply by holding shares in both entities. The only real diversification produced is in the risk attaching to the managers' and employees' jobs, and this is likely to make them more complacent than before – to the detriment of shareholders' future returns.
- **Shares of the target entity are undervalued**. This may well be the case, although it would conflict with the efficient markets theory. However, the shareholders of the entity planning the takeover would derive as much benefit (at a lower administrative cost) from buying such undervalued shares themselves. This also assumes that the acquirer entity's management are better at valuing shares than professional investors in the market place.

Synergy

Definition

Synergy may be defined as two or more entities coming together to produce a result not independently obtainable.

For example, a merged entity will only need one marketing department, so there may be savings generated compared to two separate entities.

Importance of synergy in mergers and acquisitions

For a successful business combination we should be looking for a situation where:

MV of combined company (AB) > MV of A + MV of B

Note: MV means Market Value here.

If this situation occurs we have experienced synergy, where the whole is worth more than the sum of the parts. This is often expressed as 2 + 2 = 5.

It is important to note that synergy is not automatic. In an efficient stock market A and B will be correctly valued before the combination, and we need to ask how synergy will be achieved, i.e. why any increase in value should occur.

Sources of synergy

There are several reasons why synergistic gains arise. These break down into the following:

- **operating economies**, such as economies of scale and elimination of inefficiency,
- **financial synergy**, such as the reduced risk caused by diversification,
- **other synergistic effects**, such as market power.

Detailed examples of synergy

Synergy from operating economies

Economies of scale – Horizontal combinations (acquisitions of a company in a similar line of business) are often claimed to reduce costs and therefore increase profits due to economies of scale. These can occur in the production, marketing or finance areas. Note that these gains are not automatic and diseconomies of scale may also be experienced. These benefits are sometimes also claimed for conglomerate combinations (acquisition of companies in unrelated areas of business) in financial and marketing costs.

Economies of vertical integration – Some acquisitions involve buying out other companies in the same production chain, e.g. a manufacturer buying out a raw material supplier or a retailer. This can increase profits by 'cutting out the middle man'.

Complementary resources – It is sometimes argued that by combining the strengths of two companies a synergistic result can be obtained. For example, combining a company specialising in research and development with a company strong in the marketing area could lead to gains.

Elimination of inefficiency – If the victim company is badly managed, its performance and hence its value can be improved by the elimination of inefficiencies. Improvements could be obtained particularly in the areas of production, marketing and finance.

Financial synergy

Several financial arguments are proposed in this area.

Diversification – The argument goes that diversification normally reduces risk. If the earnings of the merged companies simply stay the same (i.e. no operating economies are obtained), there could still be an increase in value of the company due to the lower risk.

Diversification and financing – If the future cash flow streams of the two companies are not perfectly positively correlated (i.e. if they are forecast to fluctuate in different ways) then, by combining the two companies, the variability of their operating cash flow may be reduced. A more stable cash flow is more attractive to creditors and this could lead to cheaper financing.

The 'boot strap' or P/E game – It is sometimes argued that companies with high P/E ratios are in a good position to acquire other companies as they can impose their high P/E ratio on the victim firm and increase its value. An example of 'boot strapping' follows later in this Chapter.

Other synergistic effects

Surplus managerial talent – Companies with highly skilled managers can make use of this resource only if they have problems to solve. The acquisition of inefficient companies is sometimes the only way of fully utilising skilled managers.

Surplus cash – Companies with large amounts of surplus cash may see the acquisition of other companies as the only possible application for these funds. Of course, increased dividends could cure the problem of surplus cash, but this may be rejected for reasons of tax or dividend stability.

Market power – Horizontal combinations may enable the firm to obtain a degree of monopoly power that could increase its profitability. Removing competition from a market in this way could attract the attentions of the competition authorities, e.g. the Competition Commission in the UK, who could rule the acquisition unlawful.

Speed – Acquisition may be far faster than organic growth in obtaining a presence in a new and growing market.

By considering all the above sources of synergy, a company can work towards increasing the post-merger value of the newly formed joint company.

Example 1

Williams Inc is the manufacturer of cosmetics, soaps and shower gels. It also markets its products using its own highly successful sales and marketing department. It is seen as an employer of choice and as such has a talented and loyal workforce with a history of developing new and exciting products which have sold well. It is now considering extending its range, however it has currently a build up of unfulfilled orders due to a lack of capacity.

GSL is a well known herbal remedy for skin problems. GSL Co was founded by three brothers in the 1950s and until the death of the remaining brother in 2007 has performed well – however the new Chairman has limited experience and the company has not performed well over recent years. GSL has a dedicated team of herbalists who have developed products, which would find a ready market – however, there is insufficient funds and expertise to correctly market these products and market share is low.

Williams' products and GSL's products are made using similar production technologies and their financial and administrative systems are similar and it is hoped savings can be made here.

Required:

Identify any potential synergy gains that would emerge from a merger of Williams and GSL.

Reasons why mergers and acquisitions fail

Not all mergers and acquisitions are successful.

Synergy will not automatically arise. Unless the management of the two entities can work together effectively, there is a chance that any forecast benefits of the new arrangement might not be realised.

In many cases, the forecast synergy is not achieved, or is not as large as expected. It may be that the premium paid on acquisition by the acquirer was too high, so the shareholder value of the acquirer actually reduced as a result of the acquisition.

Detailed reasons why mergers / acquisitions fail

The fit/lack of fit syndrome

There may be a good fit of products or services, but a serious lack of fit in terms of management styles or corporate structure.

Lack of industrial or commercial fit

Failure can result from a horizontal or vertical takeover where the acquired entity turns out not to have the product range or industrial position that the acquirer anticipated. Usually in the case where a customer or supplier is acquired, the acquirer knows a lot about the acquired entity; even so, there may be aspects of the acquired entity's operations which may cause unexpected problems for the acquirer, such that, even in these cases, a prospective acquisition should be planned very carefully and not be based solely on experience gained from a direct relationship with the acquired entity.

Lack of goal congruence

This may apply not only to the acquired entity but, more dangerously, to the acquirer, whereby disputes over the treatment of the acquired entity might well take away the benefits of an otherwise excellent acquisition.

'Cheap' purchases

The 'turn around' costs of an acquisition purchased at what seems to be a bargain price may well turn out to be a high multiple of that price. In these situations, the amount of resources in terms of cash and management time could well also damage the acquirer's core business. In preparing a bid, a would-be acquirer should always take into account the likely total cost of an acquisition, including the input of its own resources, before deciding on making an offer or setting an offer price.

Paying too much

The fact that a high premium is paid for an acquisition does not necessarily mean that it will fail. Failure would result only if the price paid is beyond that which the acquirer considers acceptable to increase satisfactorily the long-term wealth of its shareholders.

Failure to integrate effectively

An acquirer needs to have a workable and clear plan of the extent to which the acquired company is to be integrated, and the amount of autonomy to be granted. At best, the plan should be negotiated with the acquired entity's management and staff, but its essential requirements should be fairly but firmly carried out. The plan must address such problems as differences in management styles, incompatibilities in data information systems, and continued opposition to the acquisition by some of the acquired entity's staff. Failure to plan can – and often does – lead to failure of an acquisition, as it leads to drift and demotivation, not only within the acquired entity but also within the acquirer itself.

Every aspect of a prospective acquisition, as it will affect the would-be acquirer, should be weighed up before embarking on a bid. Problems of integration have a much better chance of being resolved before bidding action is taken than they do after the event, when many more complications can ensue.

Even if a product fit is satisfactory, the would-be acquirer should be satisfied that the aspects of its own operation affected by the bid will be properly adaptable to the new activities. Running the rule carefully over one's own operations may yield vital information as to areas which may need adaptation before a bid can be contemplated, and provide vital clues to appropriate areas for search when a bid has actually been launched. One factor of special importance is a clear assessment of the flexibility of one's own information systems.

Inability to manage change

Several of the above points stress the need for an acquirer to plan effectively before and after an acquisition if failure is to be avoided. But this in itself calls for the ability to accept change – perhaps even radical change – from established routines and practices. Indeed, many acquisitions fail mainly because the acquirer is unable – or unwilling – reasonably to adjust its own activities to help ensure a smooth takeover. One such situation is where the acquired company has a demonstrably better data information system than the acquirer, which it might be greatly in the acquirer's interest to adopt.

3 Defences against hostile takeover bids

Any listed company needs to be aware that a bid might be received at any time.

The directors of a company subject to a hostile takeover bid should act in the best interests of their shareholders. However, in practice they will also consider the views of other stakeholders (such as employees, and themselves).

If the board of directors of a target company decides to fight a bid that appears to be financially attractive to their shareholders, then they should consider one of the following defences:

- Pre bid defences
  - Communicate effectively with shareholders
  - Revalue non-current assets
  - Poison pill
  - Change the Articles of Association (super majority)
- Post bid defences
  - Appeal to their own shareholders
  - Attack the bidder
  - White Knight
  - Counterbid ("Pacman")
  - Refer the bid to the Competition authorities

Details of takeover defences

Pre-bid defences

Communicate effectively with shareholders

This includes having a public relations officer specialising in financial matters liaising constantly with the entity's stockbrokers, keeping analysts fully informed, and speaking to journalists.

Revalue non-current assets

Non current assets are revalued to current values to ensure that shareholders are aware of true asset value per share.

Poison pill strategy

Here a target company takes steps before a bid has been made to make itself less attractive to a potential bidder. The most common method is for existing shareholders to be given rights to buy future bonds or preference shares. If a bid is made before the date of exercise of the rights, then the rights will automatically be converted into full ordinary shares.

Super majority

The Articles of Association are altered to require that a higher percentage (say 80%) of shareholders have to vote for the takeover.

Post-bid defences

Appeal to their own shareholders

For example, by declaring that the value placed on the target company's shares is too low in relation to the real value and earning power of the company's assets, or alternatively that the market price of the bidder's shares is unjustifiably high and is not sustainable.

A well-managed defensive campaign would include:

(i) Aggressive publicity on behalf of the company preferably before a bid is received. Investors may be told of any good research ideas within the company and of the management potential or merely be made more aware of the company's achievements.

(ii) Direct communication with the shareholders in writing stressing the financial and strategic reasons for remaining independent.

Note: Under the City Code in the UK, any forecasts must be examined and reported on by the auditors or consultant accountants.

Attack the bidder

Typically concentrating on the bidder's management style, overall strategy, methods of increasing earnings per share, dubious accounting policies and lack of capital investment.

White Knight strategy

This is where the directors of the target company offer themselves to a more friendly outside interest. This tactic should only be adopted in the last resort as it means that the company will lose its independence. This tactic is acceptable provided that any information given to a preferred bidder is also given to a hostile bidder. The alternative company's management will be considered to be sympathetic to the target company's management.

Counterbid (Pacman defence)

Where the bidding company is itself the subject of a takeover bid by the target company.

Competition authorities

The target entity could seek government intervention by bringing in the Competition authorities. For this to be effective it would have to be proved that the takeover was against the public interest.

NEW

4 The form of consideration for a takeover

Introduction

When one firm acquires another, two questions must be addressed regarding the form of consideration for the takeover:

(1) what form of consideration should be offered? Cash offer, or share exchange, or earnout are the three main choices.

(2) if a cash offer is to be made, how should the cash be raised? The choice is generally debt finance or a rights issue to generate the cash (if the entity does not have enough cash already).

The key considerations regarding these two questions are outlined below.

Form of consideration

Cash

In a cash offer, the target company shareholders are offered a fixed cash sum per share.

This method is likely to be suitable only for relatively small acquisitions, unless the bidding entity has an accumulation of cash.

Advantages:

- When the bidder has sufficient cash the takeover can be achieved quickly and at low cost.
- Target company shareholders have certainty about the bid's value i.e. there is less risk compared to accepting shares in the bidding company.
- There is increased liquidity to target company shareholders, i.e. accepting cash in a takeover, is a good way of realising an investment.
- The acceptable consideration is likely to be less than with a share exchange, as there is less risk to target company shareholders. This reduces the overall cost of the bid to the bidding company.

Disadvantages:

- With larger acquisitions the bidder must often borrow in the capital markets or issue new shares in order to raise the cash. This may have an adverse effect on gearing, and also cost of capital due to the increased financial risk.
- For target company shareholders, in some jurisdictions a taxable chargeable gain will arise if shares are sold for cash, but the gain may not be immediately chargeable to tax under a share exchange.
- Target company shareholders may be unhappy with a cash offer, since they are "bought out" and do not participate in the new group. Of course, this could be seen as an advantage of a cash offer by the bidding company shareholders if they want to keep full control of the bidding company.

Share exchange

In a share exchange, the bidding company issues some new shares and then exchanges them with the target company shareholders. The target company shareholders therefore end up with shares in the bidding company, and the target company's shares all end up in the possession of the bidding company.

Large acquisitions almost always involve an exchange of shares, in whole or in part.

Advantages:

- The bidding company does not have to raise cash to make the payment.
- The bidding company can 'boot strap' earnings per share if it has a higher P/E ratio than the acquired entity (terminology explained later in this Chapter).
- Shareholder capital is increased – and gearing similarly improved – as the shareholders of the acquired company become shareholders in the post acquisition company.
- A share exchange can be used to finance very large acquisitions.

Disadvantages:

- The bidding company's shareholders have to share future gains with the acquired entity, and the current shareholders will have a lower proportionate control and share in profits of the combined entity than before.
- Price risk – there is a risk that the market price of the bidding company's shares will fall during the bidding process, which may result in the bid failing. For example, if a 1 for 2 share exchange is offered based on the fact that the bidding company's shares are worth approximately double the value of the target company's shares, the bid might fail if the value of the bidding company's shares falls before the acceptance date.

Earn-out

Definition of an earn-out arrangement: A procedure whereby owners/managers selling an entity receive a portion of their consideration linked to the financial performance of the business during a specified period after the sale. The arrangement gives a measure of security to the new owners, who pass some of the financial risk associated with the purchase of a new entity to the sellers.

(CIMA Official Terminology, 2005)

The purchase consideration is sometimes structured so that there is an initial amount paid at the time of acquisition, and the balance deferred.

Some of the deferred balance will usually only become payable if the target entity achieves specified performance targets.

Summary of the key issues relating to forms of consideration

Considerations of different stakeholders

In order to evaluate which form of consideration is appropriate in a particular case, it is important to assess the positions of both the target company's shareholders, and the bidding company and its shareholders.

Position of the target company's shareholders

The target company's shareholders may want to retain an interest in the business, in which case a cash offer would not be welcomed. However, there is a greater certainty of value with a cash offer (share prices fluctuate, so in a share exchange the target company's shareholders cannot be completely sure whether they are receiving an appropriate valuation for their shares).

Position of the bidding company and its shareholders

The bidding company will have to issue new shares if it is to undertake a share exchange. This may require the consent of shareholders in a general meeting. The shareholders may be concerned in a share exchange that their control of the bidding company will be diluted by the issue and exchange of shares.

Another key consideration is the impact of the takeover on the bidding company's financial statements. An issue of new shares could reduce the level of earnings per share (a measure which is often used as a key performance measure by market analysts). However, if a cash offer is made, the raising of the necessary cash could have a significant impact on the gearing of the bidding company – see below for details.

Methods of financing a cash offer

If the bidding company has a large cash surplus, it might be able to make a cash offer without raising any new finance.

However, in most cases, this will not be the case, so various financing options will have to be considered by the bidding company. The main two options are debt or a rights issue.

Debt

The bidding company could borrow the required cash from the bank, or issue bonds in the market.

The advantage of using debt in this situation is the low cost of servicing the debt. However, raising new debt finance will increase the bidding company's gearing. This will increase the risk to the bidding company's shareholders, so might not be acceptable to the shareholders.

The disadvantage to the target company's shareholders is that debt might be infrequently traded, and this will affect their ability to liquidate the investment should they need to. Also, the lack of marketability might adversely affect the value of the securities.

Rights issue

If the bidding company shareholders do not want to suffer the increased risk which debt finance would bring, the alternative would be for the bidding company to offer a rights issue to its existing shareholders. In this case, the company's gearing is not affected, although its earnings per share will fall as new shares are issued.

From the shareholders' point of view, the problem with this financing option is that it is the shareholders themselves who have to find the money to invest.

Evaluating a share for share exchange

One popular question is to comment on the likely acceptance of a share for share offer. The procedure is as follows:

- Value the predator company as an independent entity and hence calculate the value of a share in that company.
- Repeat the procedure for the victim company.
- Calculate the value of the combined company post integration. This is calculated as:

Value of predator company as independent company	X
Value of victim company as independent company	X
Value of any synergy	X
Total value of combined company	X

- Calculate the number of shares post integration:

Number of shares originally in the predator company	X
Number of shares issued to victim company	X
Total shares post integration	X

- Calculate the value of a share in the combined company, and use this to assess the change in wealth of the shareholders after the takeover.

e.g

Illustration 1

Company A has 200m shares with a current market value of GBP4 per share. Company B has 90m shares with a current market value of GBP2 per share.

A makes an offer of 3 new shares for every 5 currently held in B. A has worked out that the present value of synergies will be GBP40m.

Required:

Calculate the expected value of a share in the combined company (assuming that the given share prices have not yet moved to anticipate the takeover), and advise the shareholders in company B whether the offer should be accepted.

Solution

MV of A = GBP800m

MV of B = GBP180m

PV of synergies = GBP40m

TOTAL = GBP1,020m

No. of new shares = 200m + (3/5) x 90m = 254m

New share price = 1,020m / 254m = GBP4.02

	Shares	*MV*	*Old wealth*	*Change*
A	200m	GBP804m	GBP800m	GBP4m
B	(3/5) x 90m = 54m	GBP216m	GBP180m	GBP36m

The wealth of the shareholders in company B will increase by GBP36m as a consequence of the takeover. This is a (36/180) 20% increase in wealth.

Company B's shareholders should be advised to accept the 3 for 5 share for share offer.

Further numerical illustration

Initial example – cash offer

Summary of information regarding Entity A and Entity B, two UK companies (currency GBP, or £):

	Entity A	Entity B
Market price per share (£)	75	15
Number of shares	100,000	60,000
Market value (£)	7,500,000	900,000

Required:

If A intends to pay £1.2m cash for B, what is the cost premium if:

(a) the share price does not anticipate the takeover;

(b) the share price of Entity B includes a 'speculation' element of £2 per share?

Solution:

(a) The share price accurately reflects the true value of the entity (in theory).

Therefore, the cost to the bidder is simply £1,200,000 – £900,000, that is, £300,000.

Entity A is paying £300,000 for the identified benefits of the takeover.

(b) The cost is £300,000 + (60,000 × £2), or £420,000.

The entity is therefore really worth only £13 × 60,000, or £780,000.

Follow up example – share exchange

Suppose A offers 16,000 shares (£1.2m / £75) instead of £1.2m cash. The cost appears to be £300,000 as before, but because B's shareholders will own part of A, they will benefit from any future gains of the combined entity. Their share will be (16,000/(16,000 + 100,000)), or 13.8%.

Further, suppose that the benefits of the combination have been identified by A to have a present value of £400,000 (i.e. A thinks that B is really worth £900,000 + £400,000, or £1.3m). Therefore, the combined entity of A and B is worth £7.5m + £1.3m, or £8.8m.

Required:

Calculate the true cost of the takeover to the acquirer's shareholders?

Solution:

Estimate of post-acquisition prices

	A	B
Proportion of ownership	86.2%	13.8%
Market value: £8.8m × proportion	£7.586m	£1.214m
Number of shares currently in issue	100,000	60,000
Price per share (£)	75.86	20.23

What we are attempting to do here is to value the shares in the entity before the takeover is completed, based on estimates of what the entity will be worth after the merger. The valuation of each entity also recognises the split of the expected benefits which will accrue to the combined form once the merger has taken place.

The true cost to A can now be calculated as follows:

	£
60,000 B shares at £20.23	1,213,800
Less: Current market value	(900,000)
Benefits being paid to B's shareholders	313,800

Example 2

Mavers Co and Power Co are listed on the Stock Exchange.

Relevant information is as follows:

	Mavers Co	Power Co
Share price today	$3.05	$6.80
Shares in issue	48 million	13 million

Mavers Co wants to acquire 100% of the shares of Power Co.

The directors are considering offering 2 new Mavers Co shares for every 1 Power Co share.

Required:

Evaluate whether the 2 for 1 share for share exchange will be likely to succeed.

If necessary, recommend revised terms for the offer which would be likely to succeed.

Bootstrapping and post acquisition values

In the previous examples, we were told specifically what the values of the separate companies were before the takeover, and the synergy generated by the takeover was also given.

Sometimes we might have to derive these figures, using the bootstrapping method as in the following illustration.

e.g

Illustration 2

	Post Tax Profit	P/E ratio	Pre-acquisition value
Company C	$10m	16	$160m
Company D	$1m	8	$8m

If Company C takes over Company D, the post acquisition value of the combined company can be estimated by applying Company C's P/E ratio to the combined post tax profit.

This is known as **bootstrapping,** and it is based on the assumption that the market will assume that the management of the larger company will be able to apply common approach to both companies after the takeover, thus improving the performance of the acquired company by using the methods that they have been using on their own company before the takeover.

Value of (C+D) post acquisition = 16 x ($10m + $1m) = $176m

Thus, the value of the synergy is this combined value, less the values of the individual companies pre acquisition, i.e.

$176m – $160m – $8m = $8m

5 The Regulation of Takeovers

Introduction to regulation

During a takeover, it is important that the companies comply with relevant legislation and regulations.

General principles of takeover regulation

The regulation of takeovers varies from country to country but focuses primarily on controlling the directors' behaviour and ensuring that the shareholders are treated fairly.

General principles include the following:

- At the most important time in the company's life – when it is subject to a takeover bid – its directors should act in the best interest of their shareholders, and should disregard their personal interests.
- All shareholders must be treated equally.
- Shareholders must be given all the relevant information to make an informed judgement.

- The board must not take action without the approval of shareholders, which could result in the offer being defeated.
- All information supplied to shareholders must be prepared to the highest with standards of care and accuracy.
- The assumptions on which profit forecasts are based and the accounting polices used should be examined and reported on by accountants.
- An independent valuer should support valuations of assets.

Examples of regulation

Although the exam questions will never test the details of any particular country's regulations, it might be useful to see how the general principles listed above are applied in the UK. Similar examples could be given for other countries.

The City Code (or Takeover Code)

The acquisition of quoted companies in the UK is regulated by the City Code on Takeovers and Mergers ('the City Code'), which is the responsibility of the Panel on Takeovers and Mergers.

This code does not have the force of law. It is enforced by the various City regulatory authorities, including the Stock Exchange (which has the power to suspend a company which does not comply), and specifically by the Panel on Takeovers and Mergers (the 'Takeover Panel').

Its basic principle is that of equity between one shareholder and another and it sets out rules for the conduct of acquisitions.

The Office of Fair Trading (OFT)

The Office of Fair Trading (OFT) regulates the monopoly aspects of bids.

Many bids, because of their size, will require review by the OFT, and a limited number will subsequently be referred to the Competition Commission under the Fair Trading Act if the OFT thinks that a merger might be against the public interest (i.e. constraining of competition).

The Competition Commission

As a rule of thumb the Competition Commission may investigate an acquisition if it will result in the combined entity acquiring 25% or more of market share.

Their investigations may take several months to complete during which time the merger is put on hold, thus giving the target company valuable time to organise its defence. The acquirer may abandon its bid as it may not wish to become involved in a time consuming Competition Commission investigation.

The Commission may simply accept or reject the proposals or accept them subject to certain conditions. In recent years, the Competition Commission has investigated the several UK banking mergers and also mergers in the UK airport industry. BAA was told by the Commission in 2009 that it had to sell off three of its existing airports in order to open up the market.

In addition, if the offer gives rises to a concentration (i.e. a potential monopoly) within the EC, the European Commission may initiate proceedings. This can result in considerable delay, and constitutes grounds for abandoning a bid.

6 The post-merger or post-acquisition integration process

Introduction to the post-merger or post-acquisition process

Mergers and acquisitions often fail to deliver the anticipated benefits as a result of failing to effectively integrate the newly acquired entity into the parent.

Poor planning and a lack of information to guide the integration plans ahead of the acquisition will lead to post-acquisition integration problems.

Druker's Golden Rules

P. F. Druker (1981) identified five Golden Rules to apply to post-acquisition integration.

(1) Ensure a 'common core of unity' is shared by the acquired entity and acquirer. Shared technologies or markets are an essential element.

(2) The acquirer should not just think 'What is in it for us?', but also 'What can we offer them?'.

(3) The acquirer must treat the products, markets and customers of the acquired entity with respect.

(4) Within 1 year, the acquirer should provide appropriately skilled top management for the acquired company.

(5) Within 1 year, the acquirer should make several cross-entity promotions of staff.

Post-acquisition value enhancing strategies

The following are key points to consider when determining strategy for the combined entity:

- The integration strategy must be in place before the acquisition is finalised.
- Review each of the business units for potential cost cuttings/synergies or potential asset disposals. It is possible there are outlets more valuable to another entity, but it is important they are in good shape before they are sold. However, more than this is needed for a full effective enhancement programme and a position audit could be carried out.
- Consider the effect on the workforce and determine how many, if any redundancies are likely and what the cost will be.
- Risk diversification may well lower the cost of capital and therefore increase the value of the entity.
- The entity's cost of capital should be re-evaluated.
- Make a positive effort to communicate the post-acquisition intentions within the entity to prevent de-motivation and avoid adverse post-acquisition effects on staff morale.
- There may be economies of scale to identify and evaluate.
- Undertake a review of assets, or resource audit, and consider selling non-core elements or redundant assets.
- There may well be a need to pursue a more aggressive marketing strategy.
- The risks of the acquisition need to be evaluated.
- There needs to be harmonisation of corporate objectives.

Impact on ratios or performance measures

Following the completion of an acquisition the purchaser will need to examine thoroughly the financial and management accounting records of each business unit of the acquired entity.

Thus, the directors of the acquirer will be particularly interested in the financial condition of those units which they might plan to dispose of.

From a strategic point of view these are likely to be of more use to another entity with whom they would form a better fit. However, it is still essential that financially and operationally they should be in as good shape as possible to ensure that a good price can be obtained for them.

e.g

Illustration 3

Hall Co has just acquired a subsidiary called Wodgits as part of a larger acquisition.

Hall Co has no other subsidiaries in the same business sector as Wodgits, so management are considering disposing of Wodgits.

A small listed company called Bigwodge, whose core business is similar to Wodgits, has been identified, and by using all published and any other information reasonably available, the following analysis has been prepared:

	Wodgits	**Bigwodge**
Return on Capital Employed (ROCE)	14.9%	25.0%
Asset turnover	1.3 times	1.8 times
Net profit margin	11.5%	13.9%
Current ratio	1.5 times	2.2 times
Inventory holding period	68 days	57 days
Receivables collection period	54 days	43 days
Payables payment period	49 days	37 days

Note: All these ratios were introduced in the earlier Chapters on 'Performance Measurement in Financial Strategy' and 'Short Term Finance – Working Capital Management'.

Other key information:

- Bigwodge has a P/E ratio of 18.
- Wodgits made an operating profit of $860,000 last year.
- Wodgits has total non current assets of $4.87m, out of which land and buildings comprise $2.5m. Its net assets at book value are $5.77m.
- The tax rate is 33%.

Required:

As the management accountant of Hall Co, prepare a report to the directors in which you analyse the performance of Wodgits compared with Bigwodge, and recommend a price which Hall Co ought to seek for the disposal of Wodgits.

Solution

Report to the directors of Hall Co

Return on capital employed (ROCE)

Wodgits' inadequate ROCE seems to be mainly due to a low rate of asset turnover, which we must carefully investigate.

We know that land and buildings account for £2.5m of Wodgits' fixed asset total of £4.87m and it is important to establish how much of this property value represents redundant assets. As to plant and machinery, it may be that this is substantially new or revalued, in which case the assets may be of good value and the faults may lie mainly in under-capacity working or production inefficiencies. Much more serious, however, would be a situation where the plant is old and requiring heavy maintenance, and would be hard put to cope with increased volume of throughput.

If the first of these plant scenarios is correct, then Wodgits may well fetch a reasonable price, as a bidder, possibly Bigwodge themselves, would be obtaining good assets to add to their own evidently successful performance in their sector. If the second scenario applies, then we might find it difficult to obtain net asset value for the assets remaining after sale of the redundant properties.

Current ratio

Wodgits' current ratio and inventory holding period are fairly good, but before we put the unit up for sale, we would improve our prospects for a reasonable price by taking early action in regard to both receivables and payables. Both are too high and we should aim to tighten up credit control and also bring payables down to the more acceptable level which Bigwodge's payables payment period indicates is appropriate for the industry sector.

Conclusions

Assuming that we can find that, say, $1.5m of land and buildings are redundant and can be separately sold, and that the plant scenario is favourable or can be made so, then it would not seem to be too difficult to make the remainder of Wodgits a saleable proposition.

Thus if we can assume no debt interest, and taxation of 33%, then after-tax profits could be $576,000 ($860,000 × 0.67), and as Bigwodge's current P/E is 18, we might achieve for Wodgits a P/E of 9 or 10 which suggests a price of between $5.2 and $5.8m, which is comfortably above an asset value of $4.3m ($5.8m – $1.5m assets sold).

The impact of an acquisition on the acquirer's post-acquisition share price

A very important aspect for an acquirer is the post-acquisition effect on its earnings per share (EPS), and the impact on the share price and P/E ratio arising from the market's perceived views on the acquisition.

Once again, detailed analysis of the accounts, and comparison to other companies in similar business sectors can help to assess whether the likely impact will be favourable.

Simple example of the impact on EPS

Assume that the new entity starts with a prospective EPS of 13.1 cents based on combined profits of acquirer and acquired of $8.4m, and 64m shares in issue, and if these earnings could be maintained in year 1 (post-acquisition) they would appear not to be diluted.

However, if the acquirer is expected from its previous performances to attain 10% per annum growth in normal (money) terms, then for year 1 EPS of 13.1 cents × 1.10 would be 14.4 cents, and arguably if this is not attained then dilution will seem to have taken place.

A serious threat to an acquirer's EPS is the 'getting to know you' costs and also the 'reverse synergy' effects of 2+2 = 3, which sadly seems to be the fate of numerous acquisitions.

A major question is whether the present value of the combined earnings, including assumed longer-term profit improvements, really takes into account all the downside costs of putting two different entities together, each with its own management style.

Illustration of strategic issues

You are acting as financial adviser to a public entity, H plc, in the hotel business. H plc is considering a takeover bid for the shares of G Limited. Information relating to G ltd is given in the table below.

G Limited operates in the gaming and betting industry.

The company was established 7 years ago, and the two founder directors still provide the necessary technical and marketing skills. They own 60% of the issued share capital, the balance plus the long-term loan capital having been subscribed by a firm of venture capitalists.

Extracts from the annual reports of G Limited are given below.

Required:

Discuss the extent to which each of the following six reasons might apply to the proposed acquisition of G Limited by H plc. Support your answers with appropriate analysis of the data provided.

(i) **Access to innovation**

(ii) **Growth in earnings per share**

(iii) **Achievement of operating economies**

(iv) **Reduction of risk through diversification**

(v) **Access to liquid funds**

(vi) **Improved asset backing for borrowing.**

Data relating to G Ltd – extracts from annual reports

Year to 30 June	**20X8**	**20X7**	**20X6**
	£000	£000	£000
Revenue	860	684	547
Operating profit	55	68	16
Loan interest	(20)	(14)	(12)
Taxation	(9)	(6)	–
Net profit	26	48	4

Year to 30 June	20X8	20X7	20X6
	£000	£000	£000
Tangible non current assets:			
Cost	224	174	133
Less depreciation	54	34	23
	170	140	110
Development costs			
Cost	254	189	129
Less written off	176	109	53
	78	80	76
Current assets			
Inventory	30	40	31
Receivables	109	72	57
Cash	1	14	5
	140	126	93
TOTAL ASSETS	388	346	279

Year to 30 June	20X8	20X7	20X6
	£000	£000	£000
Equity			
Share capital (25p shares)	100	100	100
Retained profit reserve	61	35	(13)
	161	135	87
Long term liabilities	160	160	160
Current liabilities	67	51	32
TOTAL EQUITY AND LIABILITIES	388	346	279

Solution

(i) **Access to innovation**

To comment upon this fully would require detailed income statement information. However, the development costs capitalised on the balance sheet give an indication of considerable increase in development as opposed to research expenditure which has been undertaken, assuming that this does not reflect changes in accounting policy.

Against this, the high rate of write-off suggests that the life of developed products may well be short.

As innovation depends on people, H plc should identify and take steps to retain key staff in the event of a takeover.

(ii) **Growth in earnings per share**

The impact of the acquisition on the earnings per share of H plc will depend upon the price paid and whether the price included shares of H plc.

The past profit performance of G Limited and forecast earnings are certainly erratic and lower in relation to revenue. This may be due to poor management, in which case the firm could be turned around and earnings improved or it could be uncontrollable factors in which case earnings might be low and volatile in the future.

The counter-view would be to suggest that if the rapid growth of the past 3 years can be maintained, then there must be opportunities for boosting earnings even if the profit forecasts do not reflect this.

(iii) **Achievement of operating economies**

The achievement of such economies depends upon integration of similar businesses. Given that hotels and gaming and betting are closely linked there may be scope for such economies if gambling operations already occur or are planned at the hotels of H plc.

(iv) **Reduction of risk through diversification**

G Limited has volatile earnings and is more likely to increase the risk profile of H plc than reduce it.

(v) **Access to liquid funds**

Although there is no ready cash in G Limited, the entity has had a satisfactory liquidity position for several years with current ratios of between 2.9 (20X6) and 2.1 (20X8).

However, it should be noted that the position has worsened slightly over recent years. It is probable that since the hotel industry typically has fairly low liquidity, acquiring G Limited will improve the liquidity position of the combined entity as compared with H plc.

(vi) **Improved asset backing for borrowings**

Tangible non current assets at cost less depreciation have increased dramatically during the period 20X6–20X8.

Obviously comments which can be made are limited due to a lack of categorisation of assets and detail of movements. However, the low depreciation charge suggests that there is land and buildings or long leasehold property among the assets.

Such assets provide good security for borrowing, and as assets are at cost the borrowing capacity may well be higher as it will reflect market values.

7 Divestment

So far in this Chapter, we have considered entities joining together in mergers and acquisitions. Now we turn our attention to the issue of divestment.

Definition

Divestment: Disposal of part of its activities by an entity.

(CIMA: Official Terminology, 2005).

Reasons for divestment

The reasons for divestment include:

The sum of the parts of the entity may be worth more than the whole

As identified earlier in this Chapter, businesses which combine will attempt to find areas where resources can be combined to generate synergy. However, it may be that a business with many disparate parts actually ends up suffering from the opposite effect. For example, the company could be spending a lot of money trying to integrate business units together where there are no apparent benefits.

In such situations, the divestment of part of the business should be considered.

Divesting unwanted or less profitable parts

If there is an underperforming business unit which fails to meet general company performance targets, divestment should be considered.

However, management should always consider the effect of the divestment on the other parts of the company. For example, if a division is sold off which previously performed some work for other business units within the company, disposing of that business unit will lead to the other parts of the business having to buy in goods and services from third parties.

To shift the strategic focus onto the core activities

A part of the business which operates in a different market sector from the rest of the group may be considered for divestment. Increased focus on the company's core activities should help to develop the expertise of management and staff, and the strength of the company's brand.

A response to crisis

In a crisis, when cash is needed quickly, a part of the business might be divested if an attractive offer is received.

The most common examples of divestments are sell offs (trade sales), spin offs and management buyouts.

More on divestment – sell-offs and spin-offs

Sell-off (or trade sale)

A sell-off is the sale of part of an entity to a third party, usually in return for cash.

The most common reasons for a sell-off are:

- to divest of a less profitable business unit if an acceptable offer is received – this could be through a management buyout – see below;
- to protect the rest of the business from takeover - a part of the business which is attractive to a purchaser may be sold off to avoid the whole company being taken over;
- to generate cash in a time of crisis.

A sell-off may disrupt the rest of the organisation if key staff or products from within the organisation are part of the business unit sold off.

Spin-off (or demerger)

In a spin-off (or demerger) a new entity is created, where the shares of that new entity are owned by the shareholders of the entity that made the transfer of assets into the new entity. There are now two entities, each owning some of the assets of the original single entity. The ownership has not changed, and in theory the value of the two individual entities should be the same as the value of the original single entity.

Reasons for spin-offs

Spin-offs may be justified as follows

- they allow investors to identify the true value of a business that was hidden within a large conglomerate;
- they should lead to a clearer management structure;
- they reduce the risk of a takeover bid for the core entity.

8 Management buyouts

Definition

Definition of a management buyout (MBO): Purchase of a business from its existing owners by members of the management team, generally in association with a financing institution.

(CIMA Official Terminology, 2005)

Overview of an MBO

In an MBO, the purchaser of the business is not another company (like in a sell-off / trade sale), but the existing management.

Usually the management provide some of the capital for the buyout, but the majority is provided by other financiers such as venture capitalists and financial institutions.

MBOs – considerations for the divesting company

Members of the buyout team may possess detailed and confidential knowledge of other parts of the vendor's business and the vendor will therefore require satisfactory warranties over such aspects which it will not be able to control.

More seriously, key members of the MBO team may have skills vital to the vendor's operation, especially in regard to information services and networking.

A vendor may be reluctant to allow key players to end their contracts of service to take part in an MBO, because losing vital operational skills can hardly be compensated by forms of warranty.

MBOs – considerations for the management team

Considerations before an MBO

MBOs are not dissimilar to other acquisitions and many of the factors to be considered will be the same.

- **Do the current owners wish to sell?** – The whole process will be much easier (and cheaper) if the current owners wish to sell. However, some MBOs have been concluded despite initial resistance from the current owners.
- **Potential of the business** – The management team engaged in the buyout will be making the switch from a relatively safe salaried position to a risky ownership position. They must, therefore, ensure that the victim business will be a long-run profit generator. This will involve analysing the performance of the business and drawing up a business plan (products, markets, required new investment, sources of finance, etc.) for future operations. Research shows that MBOs are less likely to fail than other types of new ventures, but several have collapsed, and managers must appreciate the risks they are taking and attempt to reduce them as far as possible.
- **Loss of head office support** – On becoming an independent firm many of the services that are taken for granted in a large organisation may be lost. The importance of these services varies from one industry to another but provision will have to be made for support in the areas of finance, computing, research and development, etc. Although head office fees might be saved, after the buyout these support services can involve considerable expense when purchased in the outside market.
- **Quality of the management team** – The success of any MBO will be greatly influenced by the quality of the management team. It is important to ensure that all functional areas (marketing, sales, production, finance) are represented and that all managers are prepared to take the required risks. A united approach is important in all negotiations and a clear responsibility structure should be established within the team.
- **The price** – As in any takeover situation the price paid will be crucial in determining the long-term success of the acquisition. The usual valuation techniques may be employed, often with more confidence as managers are likely to have a clearer idea of the future prospects of the firm. Care must be taken to ensure that all relevant aspects of the business are included in the package. For example, trademarks and patents may be as important as the physical assets of the firm. In a similar way, responsibilities for redundancy costs, etc. must be clearly defined.

Terminology – Leveraged buyout

A leveraged buyout occurs when an investor, typically a private equity firm, acquires a controlling interest in a company's equity and where a significant percentage of the purchase price is financed through leverage (borrowing).

Leveraged buyouts involve institutional investors and financial sponsors (like private equity firms) making large acquisitions without committing all the capital required for the acquisition.

Financing the MBO

In an MBO, unlike a corporate-backed takeover, the acquiring group usually lacks the financial resources to fund the acquisition.

For small buyouts the price may be within the capabilities of the management team, but it is unlikely that many managers could raise the large amounts involved in some buyouts.

Several institutions specialise in providing funds for MBOs. These include the following:

- venture capitalists;
- banks;
- private equity firms;
- other financial institutions.

The role of venture capitalists

Venture capitalists

Venture capitalists often provide their funds as a mix of equity and debt, in order to give themselves security (the debt) while allowing them to participate if things go well (the equity). Typically they will be prepared to advance funds for five to ten years, and will expect annual returns on their funds of 25% or more.

The types of finance and the conditions attached vary between the institutions. Points to be considered include the following.

The form of finance – Some institutions will provide equity funds. However, more commonly loan finance will be advanced. Equity funds will dilute the management team's ownership but, on the other hand, high gearing could put substantial strain on the firm's cash flow.

Exit strategy – The most important fact that any investing institution will want to know is how and when they will get their money back. The exit strategy is an important part of the agreement to advance money in the first place. Exit strategies are explained more fully later in this Chapter.

The involvement of the institution – Some institutions may require board representation as a condition of providing funds.

Ongoing support – The management team should also consider the institution's willingness to provide funds for later expansion plans. Some investors also offer other services such as management consultancy to their clients.

Details on financing MBOs

Financiers tend to favour established businesses with reliable cash flows (to pay down the debt) and a clear exit route.

They like definitive plans, but say they prefer them brief and to the point.

The emphasis should be on the competences of the team, and the market opportunity to be exploited, with detailed financial numbers (focussing on cash flow) put into an appendix. How services previously supplied by group departments, or fellow subsidiaries, will be replaced is likely to be a key item.

Managers will be required to invest some of their own money and this will take the form of shares with special features, for example a high proportion of any disposal value.

Suggested financial structure

Capital structures are inevitably complex, with several levels of risk/reward:

- **Secured loans** are usually obtained from a bank, with a first charge on the assets taken over by the venture.
- The provider of **senior debt** will require a first-ranking security over all the assets involved in the MBO venture and, usually, over the capital of the MBO as evidenced by shares in the new entity. Security will also involve undertakings from the MBO team regarding the provision of financial information and the setting of restrictions on the MBO's capacity to raise other debt finance and to dispose of assets.

- **Junior debt** is usually called mezzanine finance, which is an intermediate stage between senior debt and equity finance in relation to both risk and return. The return on mezzanine finance can comprise a mixture of debt interest and the ability to convert part of the debt into equity, perhaps by the conversion of warrants. By this means the lender can in time have a share in the premium resulting from eventual exit from the venture. The debt interest will carry a risk premium, as it is subordinate to the senior debt and with less security: it may even be unsecured.
- **Venture capital** is a form of equity provided mainly by institutional investors, whose reward will usually be in some form of dividends, probably preferential, combined with appreciation of their MBO equity holding which will build up a capital gain for when the investment is realised.
- The last link in the structural chain is the **equity holding granted to the MBO team** itself which, if their activities are successful, will provide a substantial capital gain when the venture is exited, either through flotation or by other means. Meanwhile, the MBO management will draw salaries or fees for their services.

MBOs – considerations for the financiers

Key points for investors – usually banks or other institutions – in deciding whether to support an MBO are as follows:

- What is actually for sale, and why? It may be a division or subsidiary of an entity which no longer fits that entity's strategy, or it may be separable assets such as a factory or group of retail outlets.
- Whether the activities are profitable and enjoy a satisfactory cash flow. The prospective returns must justify the operational and financial risks involved. Profits must be sustainable and cash flow adequate to sustain the level of activities proposed.
- Whether the management is sufficiently strong. This point is particularly significant if the MBO relates to loss-making activities, although sufficient allowance must be made for the possibility that its existing owners may be burdening it with excessive overheads. Financial competence and marketing skills in the MBO's sector are especially important.
- Whether the price is reasonable and a sufficient contribution is being made by the managers. The managers should have some financial involvement and the future prospects for the new entity should be demonstrable, especially in a 'turn-around' situation.

These points are important as the main risks associated with MBOs, and hence the reasons why they may fail are:

- the bid price offered by the MBO team might be too high;
- a lack of experience in key areas such as financial management;
- a loss of key staff who either perceive the buyout as too risky, or do not have capital to invest;
- a lack of finance;
- problems in convincing employees and fellow colleagues of the need to change working practices or to accept redundancy.

Investors, probably institutions, backing the MBO will initially hold a majority of the equity, with a relatively small minority of shares held by the managers.

Although the backers must be prepared to hold their investment for the long term, they and the managers will be looking to the entity growing successfully to the point where it can be launched on the stock exchange. At this stage, a market value can be obtained for the equity and, if desired, some portion of the investment can be realised.

Where the backers desire a lower-risk element in their investment, they can require that some part of it will be in the form of redeemable convertible preference shares. This can give them priority in obtaining income through a preference dividend and preferential rights of repayment if the entity should fail. There is also the prospect of redemption if the entity does not develop satisfactorily, or conversely, the convertible aspect will allow backers eventually to increase their equity holding if the entity should prove successful.

9 Exit strategies

Overview of exit strategies

The investors and financiers in an MBO will want to realise a profit from their investment in the medium term.

Debt finance will normally have a specified repayment date, so the debt providers will have a clear exit route (assuming the borrowing company has performed in line with expectations and can afford to repay the debt as planned).

Exit strategies for equity holders

For the providers of equity, the exit route is not as easy to identify.

The most common exit route for an equity investor is the sale of the shares to another investor. This could be through one of the following methods:

Trade sale

If the MBO company receives an offer for all its shares from another company, the financiers will be able to realise their investment. However, in a trade sale, all the shares are normally acquired by the bidding company, so the management would have to sell their shares in their own company too. They may not be happy to do this, because the appeal of an MBO to managers is that they will own their own company rather than have to report to other shareholders.

IPO (Initial Public Offering)

An IPO or flotation on the stock market was introduced in the earlier Chapter on 'Long Term Finance'.

An IPO gives the financiers who want to sell their shares the chance to do so on the stock market. If the managers want to keep hold of their shares, they will be able to do so.

The problem with an IPO is that the company will have to satisfy certain stringent criteria in order to join the stock exchange, and there will be significant costs associated with the listing.

After an IPO, the shares will be freely traded, which should increase their marketability and hence their value. On the other hand, the company becomes much more susceptible to takeover when its shares are listed.

Independent sale to another shareholder

The managers could try to increase their shareholdings in the company by 'buying out' the other financiers.

This would be expensive, but if the managers could afford it, it would prevent other external shareholders buying the shares and having a say in the running of the business.

10 Exam style questions

Test your understanding 1 – Practical problems of a takeover

Country Y

Country Y is a large industrialised country with strong motor vehicle and construction industries. The glass industry supplies glass to these industries as well as to specialist users of glass such as contact lens manufacturers. There are five major glass manufacturing entities, each with market coverage in Country Y of between 5% and 40%.

Entity Q

Entity Q is a quoted entity and a major player in the glass industry. It has a market share in Country Y of approximately 35%. It is an old, well-established entity with a number of factories used to manufacture glass both locally and abroad. It has a stable, but unexciting, growth rate of 3% per annum and is facing increasing competition from new glass manufacturing entities setting up in its key markets. However, Q's high earnings levels of earlier years have resulted in relatively low levels of debt.

The head office building of Q is in the far north of Country Y in a remote geographical area. It is a considerable distance from the capital city and major centres of population in the south of the country. The building is much larger than the entity requires and several floors are unoccupied.

The management team of Q is highly experienced; the majority of the senior managers have worked for Q for the whole of their working lives.

The computer systems of Q were written especially for the entity, but are in need of replacement in favour of something more flexible and adaptable to changing circumstances.

Entity Z

Entity Z, with a market share in Country Y of 10%, is a comparatively new and small, but fast growing unquoted family-owned entity. It specialises in certain niche markets for high security and extra heat-resistant glass. The patents for this specialist glass were developed by the founder owner who now acts as Managing Director. The development of the business has largely been funded by high levels of borrowings at rates of interest well above standard market rates. In addition, the directors have often been required to provide personal guarantees against personal assets.

The management team of Z works in the capital city of Country Y, which is in the more prosperous southern part of the country. Z has a manufacturing base on the outskirts of the capital city.

The management team of Z is enthusiastic to grow the business, but is continually frustrated by a lack of financial and human resources and marketing network that would enable Z to expand into international markets. Also, on a personal level, many of the senior managers own a substantial number of shares in Z and are keen to realise some of their capital gains and become financially more secure.

The computer systems of Z consist of a basic accounting package and an internal network of PCs. Spreadsheet packages are widely used for budgeting and other financial reporting.

Takeover bid

The directors of Q have approached the directors of Z with a view to making a takeover bid for Z. A condition of the bid would be the retention of the current management team of Z, who have vital knowledge of the specialist manufacturing techniques required to manufacture the product range of Z. The directors of Z have been initially quite positive about the bid.

Both parties are concerned that the deal may be referred to Country Y's Competition Directorate, which regulates the country's competition policy, for approval and that conditions may be imposed that could make the takeover less attractive.

Required:

(a) **Explain the role of competition authorities such as Country Y's Competition Directorate.**

(6 marks)

(b) **Advise the directors of Q and Z on the potential problems of merging the management structure and systems of the two entities and how these could be minimised.**

(9 marks)

(c) **Discuss whether the choice of capital structure for the new combined entity is likely to affect the overall value of the entity. Include references to Modigliani and Miller's (M & M's) theory of capital structure in your answer.**

(10 marks)

(Total 25 marks)

Test your understanding 2 – Valuation, share exchange

(a) One theoretical method of valuing a company's shares is to calculate the present value of future dividends using a discount rate that reflects the risk of the business. In respect of large, listed companies, current evidence suggests that this is far too simplistic a view of how company values and share prices are determined.

Required:

Comment on the reasons why share prices may be substantially different from the level suggested by theory. Include brief comments on the relevance of P/E ratios and net asset values in share price determination.

(7 marks)

(b) ML Co is an expanding clothes retailing company. It is all equity financed by ordinary share capital of $10 million in shares of 50 cents nominal. The company's results to the end of March 20X9 have just been announced. Pre-tax profits were $4.6 million. The chair's statement included a forecast that earnings might be expected to rise by 5% per annum in the coming year and for the foreseeable future.

CO, a children's clothes group, has an issued ordinary share capital of $33 million in $1 shares. Pre-tax profits for the year to 31 March 20X9 were $5.2 million. Because of a recent programme of reorganisation and rationalisation, no growth is forecast for the current year but subsequently constant growth in earnings of approximately 6% per annum is predicted. CO has had an erratic growth and earnings record in the past and has not always achieved its often ambitious forecasts.

ML Co has approached the shareholders of CO with a bid of two new shares in ML Co for every three CO shares. There is a cash alternative of 135 cents per share.

Following the announcement of the bid, the market price of ML Co shares fell while the price of shares in CO rose. Statistics for ML Co, CO and two other listed companies in the same industry immediately *prior* to the bid announcement are shown below. All share prices are in cents.

20X8		*Company*	*Dividend yield*	*P/E*
High	Low		%	
225	185	ML Co	3.4	15
145	115	CO	3.6	13
187	122	HR	6	12
230	159	SZ	2.4	17

Both ML Co and CO pay tax at 33%. ML Co's cost of capital is 12% per annum and CO's is 11% per annum.

Required:

Assume you are a financial analyst with a major fund manager. You have funds invested in both ML Co and CO.

- **Assess whether the proposed share for share offer is likely to be beneficial to the shareholders in ML Co and CO, and recommend an investment strategy based on your calculations.**
- **Comment on other information that would be useful in your assessment of the bid. Assume that the estimates of growth given above are achieved and that the new company plans no further issues of equity.**

State any assumptions that you make.

(18 marks)

(Total: 25 marks)

Test your understanding 3 – Post-acquisition share prices

Oscar Wills is the chief executive of OW plc, a UK listed company. The entity has been trading for 5 years. Oscar is ambitious and aims to make his entity market leader within 5 years.

He makes an offer to acquire Wilde plc, an older quoted entity of similar size to OW but with a profit record that has been erratic in recent years. Wills is of the opinion that Wilde lacks marketing strength and feels that he could make the entity much more profitable.

A summary of the financial data before the bid is as follows:

	OW	**Wilde**
Number of shares in issue	40m	44m
Earnings available to ordinary shareholders	£4m	£4.4m
P/E ratio	20	10

OW – estimated financial data post-acquisition

Estimated market capitalisation	£167.7m
Estimated share price	262 p
Estimated EPS	13.1 p
Estimated equivalent value of one old Wilde share	143 p

- The offer is six OW shares for eleven Wilde shares.
- The offer is not expected to result in any immediate savings or increases in operational cash flows, but in future, Oscar Wills expects the EPS to grow by 10% per annum..

Required:

(a) **Show how Oscar Wills calculated his estimate of post-acquisition values. Discuss the assumptions made by Oscar Wills, and calculate an alternative post-acquisition value for the company. State any assumptions that you make.**

(6 marks)

(b) **If Wilde's shareholders rejected the bid, calculate the maximum price OW could afford pay without reducing its shareholders' wealth (assuming Oscar Wills' estimate of post-bid market value is correct).**

(6 marks)

(c) **Explain why OW would wish to make the acquisition and comment on likely post-acquisition effects on the P/E ratio.**

(5 marks)

(d) **Discuss other post-acquisition impacts that the directors of OW plc should consider.**

(8 marks)

(Total: 25 marks)

Test your understanding answers

Example 1

- Operating efficiencies – the unused capacity at GSL can be used to produce Williams' products without adding to costs and capacity.
- Marketing synergies.
- If the cash flow streams of Williams and GSL are not perfectly positively correlated then by acquiring GSL – Williams may reduce the variability of their operating cash flow. This being more attractive to investors may lead to cheaper financing.
- The 'dedicated' herbalists of GSL and the R+D staff of Williams may be a complementary resource.
- Fixed operating and administrative costs savings.
- Consolidation of manufacturing capacity on fewer and larger sites.
- There may be bulk buying discounts.
- Possibility of joint advertising and distribution.
- GSL is badly managed – thus the elimination of inefficiency could allow for financial synergy.

Example 2

Calculations

Value of Mavers Co = $3.05 × 48m shares = $146.4m

Value of Power Co = $6.80 × 13m shares = $88.4m

Total value (assuming no synergistic gains) = 146.4 + 88.4 = $234.8m

Number of shares post-integration = 48 million + (2 × 13 million) = 74 million

So the post-integration share price will be:

$234.8m / 74 million = $3.173

	Shares	*MV*	*Old wealth*	*Change*
Mavers	48m	$152.3m	$146.4m	+$5.9m
Power	2 x 13m = 26m	$82.5m	$88.4m	–$5.9m

Advice

The Power Co shareholders will not accept a 2 for 1 share for share exchange since it causes their wealth to reduce.

Recommendation

In order for the Power Co shareholders to be encouraged to accept the offer, it must offer them a gain in wealth.

To make sure that Mavers Co is valuing Power Co at its current market value, the value of the offer needs to be ($6.80 x 13m shares) $88.4m in total.

Given the current Mavers Co share price of $3.05, this amounts to $88.4m / $3.05 = 28.98m shares in Mavers Co.

An exchange of 28.98m Mavers Co shares for the 13m Power Co shares represents a ratio of 28.98m to13m or 2.23 to 1.

However, if the terms of the offer were to be exactly 2.23 Mavers Co shares for every 1 share in Power Co, there would be no incentive for the Power Co shareholders to sell (financially, they'd be indifferent between keeping their existing shares and exchanging them for Mavers Co shares).

In order to encourage Power Co's shareholders to sell, a premium would have to be offered.

Hence, an offer of (say) 2.5 Mavers Co shares for every 1 share in Power Co would probably be needed to encourage the Power Co shareholders to sell.

Position of Mavers Co shareholders

In this situation, where no synergistic gains are included in the calculations, a gain to Power Co's shareholders will result in a corresponding loss to the Mavers Co shareholders. Clearly Mavers Co would not want to proceed with the takeover in these circumstances.

Unless some synergies can be generated, to improve the wealth of the overall company after the acquisition, there is no way of structuring the deal so that both sets of shareholders will be satisfied.

Test your understanding 1 – Practical problems of a takeover

(a) The Competition Directorate is a government-run or funded body which aims to protect competition within the local marketplace. Its brief will vary from country to country, but a Competition Directorate should consider the following issues:

- Whether a merger or acquisition is in the public interest. For example, there may be a policy to prevent all reservoirs being under one body for security reasons;
- Whether there would be substantial lessening of competition, leading to the risk of price setting and less competitive pricing so that the consumer is forced to pay an inflated price for goods or services;
- The ability to measure whether competition is still operating and prices set fairly after the merger has taken place. For example, for public utilities, there needs to be a sufficiently large number of utility entities to enable the regulator to compare prices with other entities in the same market.

(b) **Potential problems in merging the management structures and how to minimise them**

Potential problems that could be raised include the following:

- The importance of retaining the current management team. This is key to the success of the merger and plans to develop the business of Z;
- Different locations (opposing ends of the country);
- Spare capacity in the office building in the north of the country, but the management team of Z may well not be willing to move out of the capital. On the other hand, moving the management of Q down to the capital would result in an expensive empty office block in the north that may stand empty and, cost aside, there may not be a suitable office building to house the combined entity in or near to the capital city.

Possible solutions:

- Offer the current management team an attractive salary package;
- Obtain guarantees backed by financial incentives for management to stay with the business;
- Determine which key employees and managers are willing to relocate and which operations need to be centralised and then identifies the lowest cost solution.

Potential problems in merging the systems and how to minimise them

Potential problems include:

– Completely different type of systems at present: PC network for Z and bespoke system for Q. It is unlikely that Q could operate on a network of PCs and the transition would, in any case, be very problematic. On the other hand, it is unlikely that the different nature of the business of Z would fit well into the bespoke system that Q operates.

Possible solution:

– The management may need to agree to run the systems independently and build an effective interface.

(c) Under M & M, capital structure is irrelevant if you ignore taxes. However, if tax is included, debt becomes cheaper because of the tax shield and the value of the entity therefore increases as the proportion of debt increases. After a certain point, the entity reaches its debt capacity. That is, the level of debt at which there is a high risk of financial distress and both lenders and shareholders demand increased returns to compensate for the higher levels of risk.

From the information provided in the question, it would appear that Q is currently borrowing at levels well below its debt capacity and would therefore increase the value of the entity by taking on a higher proportion of debt.

Similarly, Z could well be borrowing in excess of its debt capacity and so its value would be enhanced by reducing the proportion of debt on its balance sheet.

It is therefore highly likely that both entities would benefit from the improved capital structure that would result from a merger or takeover if Q were to fund the takeover of Z using debt or were to acquire Z together with its high levels of debt.

Test your understanding 2 – Valuation, share exchange

(a) *Given the wording, you really need to explain why the dividend valuation model may break down, as it is the 'theory' specifically mentioned in the question. You probably have time only to mention a couple of drawbacks with each approach.*

A common way of valuing the ordinary shares in a company is discounting all future dividends anticipated from holding the shares. Although having a ring of truth, it often fails to give a price which corresponds to the current market price, due to its inherent flaws:

– It requires constant dividend growth, which in turn implies a constant retention ratio and return on re-invested funds. It is possible to cope with varying growth rates but the calculation is awkward.

– It requires a continuous supply of investment opportunities through time to justify retention.

– It can give nonsensical results e.g. zero current dividend generates zero value, thus ignoring the value of the firm's assets and/or its earnings stream.

– It is only suitable for valuing minority stakes in a firm because it ignores the opportunities for managers to restructure firms to improve earnings and cash flow. The key to value is not the portion of profit paid out to shareholders but the earning power of the business.

Price earnings (P/E) ratios

This is not a method of valuing shares of quoted firms – P/E ratios are the *product* of valuation. When the market sets a value, the resulting share price divided by the last reported earnings gives the P/E ratio. Generally, a high P/E ratio indicates that a company is expected to grow its earnings rapidly in the future.

The P/E ratio can be used to cross-check against the value of other companies – if their relative P/E ratios look out of line, it may suggest under- or overvaluation somewhere. P/E ratios can also be used when valuing the shares of unquoted companies, taking due care when interpreting the accounting data used.

Net Asset Value (NAV)

The NAV is the value per share of the firm's assets net of all liabilities i.e. the owners' stake in the firm. It has some merit for unlisted companies whose shares are not traded, but it is highly unreliable for many reasons:

- Based on IFRS, asset values in the Statement of Financial Position are primarily designed to satisfy the directors' duty to account for past performance.
- It can be distorted by accounting practices e.g. different depreciation policies.
- Revaluation of assets is not mandatory (except in the property sector) so asset values could seriously understate market values.
- It is only valid at one point in time, the Balance Sheet date.
- It (usually) ignores intangibles such as brands and market standing.
- It may exclude some liabilities – 'off-balance sheet' debts like operating lease obligations and warranty commitments.
- Inventory values quickly outdate in some industries, and some receivables / debtors may be doubtful.

The NAV provides merely a floor to equity value – usually, the market value is many times the NAV because the market is valuing future earnings capacity. A discounted cash flow approach is the most appropriate method of valuation.

(b) *The length of answer that you can offer will be limited. The bulk of your time will be spent on computation. The solution presented here gives a step-by-step guide that you would need to follow, rather than just a summary of the results.*

Basic information

	ML	*CO*	*Combined*
Profit after tax (PAT) for each firm is			
ML: (0.67 × $4.6m)	$3.082m	$3.484m	$6.566m
CO: (0.67 × $5.2m)			
Given respective P/E ratios, market values are:			
ML: (15 × $3.082)	$46.23m	$45.29m	$91.52m
CO: (13 × $3.484)			
Given the number of shares, share price is:			
ML: ($46.23m/20,000)	$2.31	$1.37	
CO: ($45.29m/33,000)			
EPS:			
ML: ($3.082/20,000)	15.41c	10.56c	
CO: ($3.484/33,000)			

Analysis

No. of shares post-bid: 20,000 + (2/3 × 33,000)	= 42,000
Expected market prices post-bid	= Total market value/no of shares
	= (91,520/42,000) = $2.18
Value of bid at post-issue price = (2 shares × $2.18)	= $4.36
Cash value of bid per 3 shares offered: ($1.35 × 3)	= $4.05

Assessment

Assuming no changes in the level of market prices, and no re-rating of the sector, ML share price would fall post-acquisition to $2.18. At this price, the value of the 2-for-3 share offer should attract CO shareholders. They would be getting shares worth (2 × 2.18) = $4.36 in exchange for shares currently worth (3 × 1.37) = $4.11.

The share-for-share offer is also worth more than the cash alternative: $4.36 vs $4.05.

This is a 'reverse takeover', where the shareholders of the target end up holding a majority stake in the expanded company – but who gains from this?

Former CO shareholders would hold (22,000/42,000) × 91.52m = $47.939m of the value of the expanded firm, a gain of (47.939m – 45.290m pre-bid value of CO) = $2.649m.

ML shareholders would lose $2.649m, making the share-financed deal distinctly unattractive to them.

Conversely, the cash offer would create wealth for ML shareholders i.e. they give $4.05 for something worth $4.11 pre-bid.

The advice to the fund manager is: 'accept the bid in respect of CO shares and sell ML shares in the market if you can achieve a price above $2.18'.

Other information required

The advice given hinges on the behaviour of ML's share price – it has already fallen on the announcement, but by how much? It may already be too late if the market is efficient, as it would already have digested the information contained in the announcement.

Also:

- What benefits are expected from the merger i.e. cost savings and synergies? To make sense of the bid, ML must be setting the PV of these benefits above $2.649m to yield a positive NPV for the acquisition.
- How quickly are these benefits likely to show through? Any delay in exploiting these lowers the NPV.

- It is feasible that the market might apply a higher P/E ratio to the expanded company – maybe not as high as ML's but possibly at the market average, currently 14.25, compared to the weighted average P/E ratio for ML/CO of 14.
- Is ML likely to sell part of CO's operations? And to whom? If ML has already lined up a buyer, it must expect to turn a profit on the deal.
- Is the bid likely to be defended by the target's managers, fearful for their jobs? If so, a higher bid might be expected.
- Is a White Knight likely to appear with a higher bid on more favourable terms?
- Are there competition implications likely to attract the interest of the authorities?

Test your understanding 3 – Post-acquisition share prices

(a)

	OW	**Wilde**	**OW+Wilde**
Earnings (£m)	4	4.4	8.4
Number of shares (m)	40	44	64
EPS (p)	10	10	13.1
P/E ratio	20	10	20
Share price (p)	200	100	262
MV (£m)	80	44	167.7 (estimate)

Post acquisition:

% of entity owned by OW (40 / 64)	62.5%	
% of entity owned by Wilde (24 / 64)		37.5%
Market value (% × £167.7m)	104.8	62.9
No. of shares pre-acquisition (m)	40	44
Post acquisition price per existing share (p)	262	143

Oscar Wills has applied his own pre-acquisition P/E ratio to the combined earnings of the new entity.

The difference between the combined market values pre-acquisition (£124m) and the estimated market value post-acquisition (£167.7m) is £43.7m.

This is Wilde's pre-acquisition earnings multiplied by the difference between the entity's pre-acquisition P/E and the combined post-acquisition P/E (20 – 10 = 10). EPS for Oscar Wills appears to have increased from 10 p to 13.1p because of this 'bootstrapping' effect.

In the absence of any immediate commercial benefits, or the disclosure of new information during the bid, there is no reason why the market value of the combined entity should be any different from the total of the two individual entities' market values – that is, £124m. This would suggest the following post-acquisition prices per existing share:

Wills: £124m × 62.5% = £77.5m or 194p per existing share compared with 200p per share now

Wilde: £124m × 37.5% = £46.5m or 106p per existing share compared with 100p per share now

There is a transfer of wealth from Wills' shareholders to Wilde's, because the terms of the offer are slightly more generous than the ratio of the old share prices.

The pre-acquisition prices suggest 1-for-2, not 6-for-11.

(b)

- Estimated value of combined firm (per OW) £168m
- Value of OW before merger £80m
- Maximum price £88m

This is £44m over the existing value of Wilde's shares. It can be reconciled by multiplying the historic earnings by the difference between Wilde's P/E and OW's P/E – that is £4.4m × (20 – 10).

(c) OW plc may have had the following among their reasons for making a bid for Wilde plc:

- Expectation of growth. OW is an ambitious entity and it sees in Wilde a means of growing faster and more cheaply than by internal expansion, especially as Wilde seems to be a 'slumbering heavyweight' relative to OW.

- Management and technical staff. Wilde's results may be erratic, but OW is aware that in terms of size and quality of main products Wilde is a significant player in its market sector. It is reasonable to assume therefore that Wilde may be suffering from poor administrative as well as marketing management, which could considerably undervalue the earning potential of its products. By means of more aggressive marketing and improved administration, OW believes that dramatic profit improvements are possible. Also Wilde may possess strong technical expertise which OW might find difficult and expensive to obtain by internal development.
- Market share. If Wilde is in the same industry sector as OW, this could well be a main reason for the bid, in which case OW's shareholders might have less reason to be concerned over the price. Thus if the acquisition led to OW's market share rising fairly quickly to make the new entity second or third in its sector, and not excessively far below the leader, it could begin to wield significantly greater influence in that sector.
- Synergy savings. Wilde may have a number of 'dogs' (Boston Consulting Group term for bad failure) among its business units, which OW may be much less prepared to pour resources into, even though some may be the Wilde chairman's 'pets'. However, if this aspect is known to the market, then the synergy savings may well attract a higher bidder.
- Risk reduction. From the comparative P/E ratios it seems evident that Wilde is regarded by the market as being much riskier than OW, and this could well be due to Wilde being an acquirer of struggling entities, bought at cheap prices, possibly even in sectors only remotely related to Wilde's core business. Such entities often turn out to be disasters, taking up disproportionate amounts of the acquirer's valuable management time. At OW, Mr Wills does not believe in keeping a 'kennelful of dogs'! and the profit improvement suggested is likely to come not only from more aggressive marketing but from a concentration of resources on key products, thereby reducing risk in the new entity.

Next, the acquirer needs to be concerned at the post-acquisition effects on its P/E ratio.

On the basis of the pre-acquisition estimates, Mr Wills looked to maintain OW's own P/E ratio of 20 (262p / 13.1p), but on the more realistic basis of assuming a value of 194 p per share – which assumes that OW inherits the greater risks of Wilde's current operations – then, as shown above, for the new entity the market capitalisations should be simply added together, making £124m and the P/E ratio becomes 194p / 13.1p = 14.8.

However, we must now consider the possibility of downside costs in year 1; thus even assuming that OW has taken several steps to improve Wilde's operations and perhaps made some significant asset sales, an upset to earnings caused by 'teething troubles' could do more than offset the effect of the improvements. Thus, EPS of, say, 13.5p for year 1 (instead of 14.4p, showing 10% expected growth), which one would expect to yield a P/E ratio of approximately 15.2 (13.5p /13.1p × 14.8), might well fall back to about 13, or even 12. Downside factors often seem to the market to be more significant than improvements.

Clearly then, at the time of making its bid, it would have been most unwise for OW to pay excessively for 'synergy savings' and not to give due regard to possible adverse post-acquisition impacts.

(d) **Further post-acquisition aspects**

Position audit

As an initial move, OW will need to do much more than analyse key financial factors of each of Wilde's units. OW's management will need to get a proper understanding of the main 'stakeholders' of each Wilde unit, for example, staff, customers and suppliers, and an appreciation of the products or services provided. In company planning, this wide-ranging survey is of the nature of a 'position audit', which should help considerably in speeding up the 'getting to know you' aspect which is so important if the full benefits of the acquisition are to be obtained.

Improving efficiency

It is better for OW to approach Wilde more as a management consultant rather than to demand immediate changes without adequate explanation. Administrative savings mainly involve people, and OW must try to ensure that the logic of its proposals is clearly explained to Wilde's management and staff, and as far as possible their cooperation gained.

Redundancies need to be worked out fairly but firmly with an emphasis on voluntary redundancy as far as possible; the main purpose must be to reduce the resentment of those who are losing their jobs and to provide as much help as possible by way of counselling or assistance in job-seeking. In these situations uncertainty should be avoided, as it tends to demotivate the entire workforce, and rumour is liable to feed greedily on rumour.

Even if Mr Wills is convinced that Wilde's marketing needs to be more aggressive, he should first of all make himself fully aware of the nature of Wilde's marketing policies and of their customers and competitors. If Wilde is substantially in the same market sector as OW, there may be certain valuable niches occupied by Wilde which OW would do well to retain.

Profit improvement

The financial analysis of Wilde's units suggested above will help to pinpoint the areas where profit improvements can be obtained, but it is essential that a comprehensive action plan is then prepared, as far as possible in co-operation with Wilde's management, and reasonable time allowed for the phasing-in of significant changes.

It is not helpful to go 'stomping around' offices and factories, thereby emphasising the perceived incompetencies of Wilde personnel. It may be that many faults, especially of inadequate systems, may already be recognised by Wilde staff and, faced with the necessity of correcting them, they may be quite willing to join in making appropriate changes. Sadly, it is often the case that obstinate managers may be standing in the way of improvement, and in this situation OW is in a good position to take quick but fair and firm action, possibly by grasping the nettle of making major changes in Wilde's organisation structure if this is seen to be necessary for a more profitable operation.

Asset sales

Here it is often the reluctance of top management to dispose of redundant assets and 'dog' units, even though it is recognised that keeping them represents a serious waste of management time and scarce resources. OW will need to make it quite clear as to which activities are to be retained, which merged with OW units and which disposed of, but in all cases the logic of each move should be clearly explained to the Wilde management and staff affected. This assumes, of course, that OW has thought through what it intends to do, which again is a good reason for first carrying out a position audit before taking action on Wilde's operations.

Effective communication

Finally, a qualitative factor of the utmost importance, as by effective communication we mean that OW must do all possible to ensure that Wilde is on the same 'wavelength' as itself. New reporting systems and procedures should only be introduced after proper consultation, in which OW will need to make clear their purposes and ensure that changes will not cause serious disruption to Wilde's operations. This is especially true in seeking computer system compatibility, which will call not only for careful planning but an acceptance by OW that in this, as with other system changes, a sufficient period of parallel running may be an essential procedure.

There should be reasonable opportunities for Wilde staff to have contact with those of OW and vice versa, especially through participation in training procedures and conferences; also Wilde staff should be encouraged to feel that promotional prospects throughout the new entity will be open to them.

All the points made in this section concerning redundancies, changes and reorganisation created by the acquisition of Wilde apply equally to the need for OW to keep its own staff properly informed, otherwise demotivation may also affect OW with consequent damage to its own profitability whatever happens with Wilde.

Perhaps, in the end, the most effective post-acquisition strategy that OW can apply to Wilde and itself is to provide an atmosphere in which both sides are able to talk freely with each other, seeking co-operation wherever possible, and even though some of OW's actions – improving profitability and making asset sales – may be very hurtful to Wilde, at least things can probably be made somewhat more acceptable if the justification for them is properly explained to all concerned, and that includes any of OW's own staff who may also be affected.

chapter

14

Implementation and Control Procedures

Chapter learning objectives

Lead	Component
C3: Evaluate procedures for investment projects.	(a) evaluate procedures for the implementation and control of investment projects.

Indicative syllabus content

- Project implementation and control in the conceptual stage, the development stage, the construction stage and initial manufacturing/operating stage.
- Post completion audit of investment projects.

1 Overview of Chapter

The investment cycle

The financial evaluation of projects (covered in several earlier Chapters) is only one part of the investment process. The full process is represented by the following diagram:

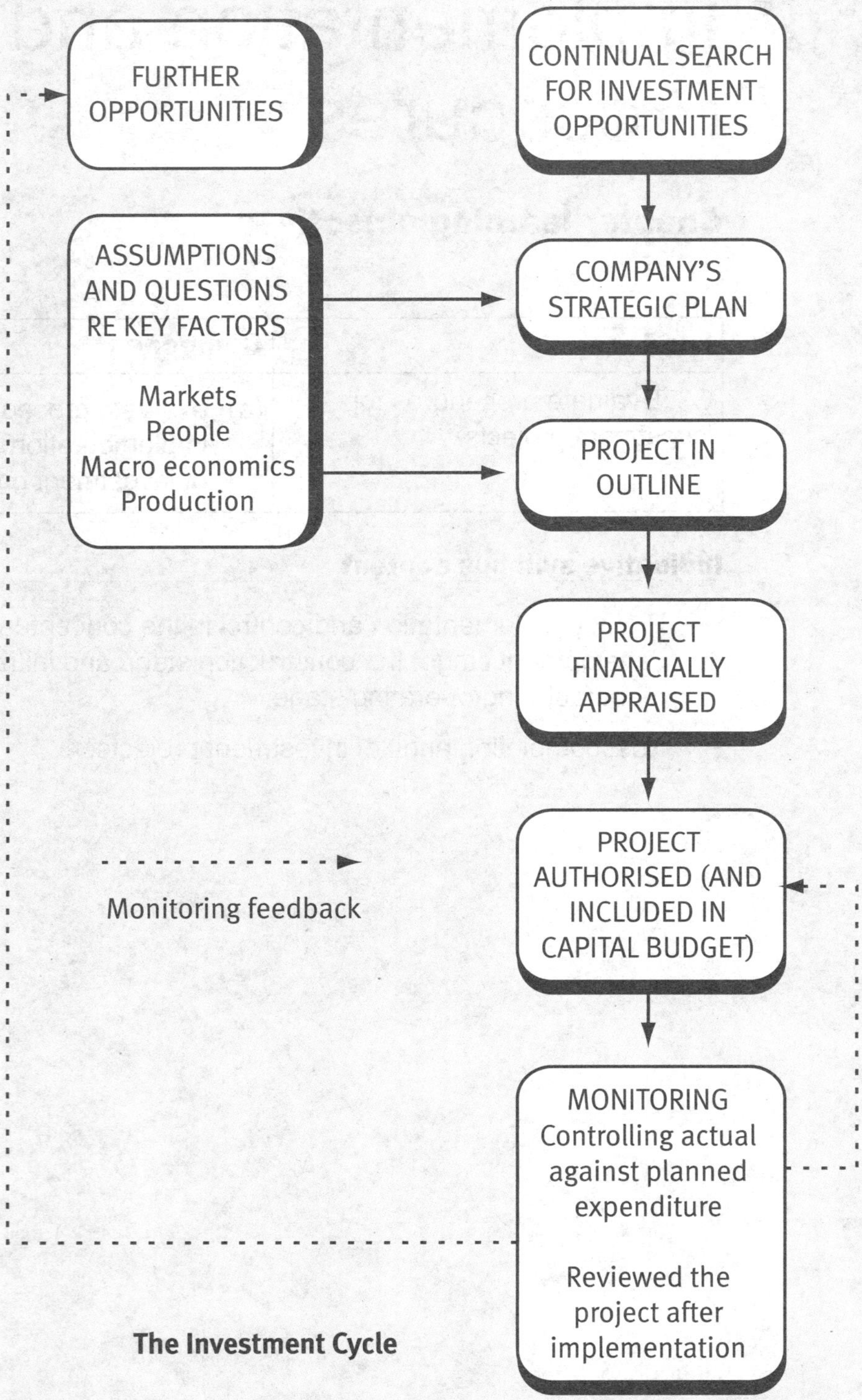

The Investment Cycle

More detail on the investment cycle diagram

The cycle can also be represented as follows:

Gather information

- collect historical costs
- gather external information
- assess opportunity costs
- consider strategic direction

Make predictions

- determine costs of project e.g. purchase and installation
- evaluate the expected benefits of the new system

Accept project

- compare predicted costs with benefits over a period of years, that is, investment appraisal
- consider all other aspects of decision

Implementation decision

- prepare a plan for implementation
- carry out implementation

Evaluate performance

- monitor events by collecting regular statistics
- carry out a post-completion audit

Use knowledge gained

- assess findings of post-completion audit
- implement improvements to system
- publicise findings for future benefits
- adjust or terminate project.

This shows that the investment process is a cycle, rather than a single discrete event.

The topics of capital budgeting and project appraisal have been covered in detail in the earlier Chapters 'Investment Appraisal – basic techniques' and 'Investment appraisal - further techniques'.

This Chapter first covers the various stages in implementing and controlling investment projects, and then considers the benefits of performing a post-completion audit.

2 Project implementation and control

Introduction to stages of project implementation and control

In order for a project to succeed, it will need to have a clearly defined objective, a competent project manager and sufficient resources allocated to it.

At each stage of the project implementation and control process, the project manager will have to satisfy himself that the project will achieve its own objective, and in turn help to achieve the overall objectives of the entity.

There are several stages in the project implementation and control process, starting with conceptual stage and running through to control.

Conceptual stage

The conceptual stage is the first stage in the implementation of a new project. It is where the project team is brought together, under the control of the project manager. The team members will be allocated specific roles and responsibilities depending on their skills.

The conceptual stage is where the new product, service or process which is the focus of the project is worked on specifically.

For example, management might commission some market research to assess the key design features which customers require. Then (if the project is to involve the introduction of a new product) a product design will be created, and a trial product produced.

The aim of the conceptual stage is to finalise the design of the new product, service or process before high costs are incurred in the development and construction stages.

Development stage

Once the concept of the product, service or process has been well defined, the development stage is where the project team needs to check that the concept meets customer requirements.

This can be achieved by trial product testing and subsequent consumer feedback.

Any problems noted at this stage of the process can be addressed and the design can once again be amended before further costs are incurred.

Construction and initial manufacturing / operating stage

When the product, service or process has been developed, and any design problems have been addressed, the next stage is where the new product, service or process is launched.

For a product, this stage will be where the large scale production begins, making items based on the designs which were finalised during the development stage.

For a service or process, this is where the new service or process is implemented.

In the initial manufacturing / operating stage of the project, it will be critical for the project team to control the new product, service or process by continual product testing and product refinement (for products) or test runs and parallel running (for services or processes).

Control stage

Control is exercised by the project team all the way through the project.

It is however important that control continues even after the initial manufacturing / operating stage has ended.

The project team should continue monitoring the project, and comparing the actual results against the original budget (time and cost). It will be the job of the project team at the control stage to keep considering whether the project is likely to achieve its original objectives.

Any cost or time over runs should be communicated to management, and to the workers involved in the project at regular intervals. This feedback will help to prevent the project from deviating too far from its original budget and objectives.

Control by capital expenditure committee

Strict control of large projects must be maintained and the accountant must submit periodic reports to top management on progress and cost. A typical report would include data such as the following:

- Budgeted cost of the project, date started and scheduled completion date.
- Cost and over or underexpenditure to date.
- Estimated cost to completion, and estimated final over or under expenditure.
- Estimated completion date and details of penalties, if any.

The capital expenditure committee will seek explanations for any overspending that may have arisen. Where projects are incomplete and actual expenditure exceeds the authorisation, additional authority must be sought to complete the project. In so doing, the committee must consider the value of the project as it then stands and the additional value that will be gained by completing it, compared with the additional expenditure to completion.

NEW

3 Post-completion audit of capital projects

Definition

A post-completion audit (PCA) can be defined as an "objective independent assessment of the success of a capital project in relation to a plan. It covers the whole life of a project and provides feedback to managers to aid the implementation and control of future projects."

(CIMA Official Terminology 2005)

Overview of a PCA

The PCA reviews the cashflows from the project after the project has finished, or sometimes during the life of the project. The aim is to identify any variances from the original budget and particularly to discover the causes of those variances.

A project's PCA provides the mechanism whereby experience of past projects can be fed into the entity's decision-making processes as an aid to the improvement of future projects.

Anecdotal evidence also suggests that the growing interest in PCA has arisen from a realisation that past investments have frequently failed to live up to expectations, and firms are keen to avoid repetition of the same mistakes.

Organisation of a PCA

Scope and purpose of a PCA

A PCA does not adopt a narrow accounting focus.

A good PCA report does not set out to identify the costs and benefits of a project in precise detail, but rather seeks to identify general lessons to be learned from a project. It is not a policing exercise, and, if it is to be effective, should not be seen as such. A PCA will nevertheless encourage honesty in facing problems at all levels of the organisation, as attempts to ignore or hide realities are unlikely to remain uncovered.

The task is often carried out by small teams, typically consisting of an accountant and an engineer who have had some involvement in the project. Surprising though it may seem, it is not common to find PCA as the responsibility of the internal audit section.

A PCA reviews all aspects of a completed project, to assess whether it lived up to initial expectations in terms of revenues and costs, and analyses the causes of deviations from planned results.

The key thing is that management will try to identify the causes of any variances from budget, and the lessons which can be learned to help with future project implementation.

Causes of variances could include poor management decisions, lack of controls over expenditure, poor application of the process, or problems with the process itself. For example, if it can be identified that there were insufficient controls over the costs at a particular stage of the project implementation, this will show management where resources should be targeted during the next project implementation.

Its main purpose is to enable the experiences – good or bad – gained during the life of one project to be made available for the benefit of future projects. The role of a PCA is thus essentially a forward-looking one; it seeks to establish lessons from the past for the future benefit of the organisation.

Communication of the PCA findings

The formal mechanism for transmitting the information to management is the final post-audit report, which provides a history of the project from inception to completion.

In the case of successful ventures, the reports will distinguish between projects which have a good outcome due to effective planning and management, and projects whose good outcome is the result of luck; in the case of unsuccessful ventures, the causes will be fully disclosed.

It is at the planning stage that project control is most important and effective, and past experience provides an invaluable input into the process.

Benefits and limitations of PCAs

Benefits of post-completion auditing

Six potential benefits from the operation of a PCA system have been identified, and these are listed below in the order in which they appear in Management Accounting Guide 9: Post Completion Auditing (CIMA, 1993):

(1) It improves the quality of decision-making by providing a mechanism whereby past experience can be made readily available to decision-makers.

(2) It encourages greater realism in project appraisal by providing a mechanism whereby past inaccuracies in forecasts are made public.

(3) It provides a means of improving control mechanisms by formally highlighting areas where weaknesses have caused problems.

(4) It enables speedy modification of under-performing/over-performing projects by identifying the reasons for the under- or over-performance.

(5) It increases the frequency of project termination for 'bad projects'.

(6) It highlights reasons for successful projects which may be important in achieving greater benefits from future projects.

Mills and Kennedy reclassified these benefits into three types:

- Type (a) – those which relate to the performance of the current project, i.e. the project under review.
- Type (b) – those which relate to the investment system itself.
- Type (c) – those which relate to the choice and performance of future projects.

Using this subdivision, the benefits listed in the Guide are grouped under the three categories, as follows:

Type	**Guide benefit**
(a)	4,5
(b)	3
(c)	1,2, 6

The authors reported that all the surveyed entities that had an operational PCA system at the time of their research gained type (b) benefits from their system, and almost 40% sought type (c) benefits. Only 20% of the entities sought type (a) benefits, which may be considered surprising.

However, it is pointed out that control of the current project during its life may be effectively gained through other procedures, such as routine project monitoring.

Limitations of post-completion auditing

The main limitations of post-completion auditing are;

- the process can be costly and time consuming;
- it requires good data collection systems to be in place;
- it is not a panacea for all the business's problems;
- it can be used to blame rather than learn from past mistakes.

4 Exam style question

Test your understanding 1 – Implementation and control

KAL is a large, listed entity based in a country in the eurozone. Its principal activity is the manufacture and distribution of electrical consumer goods. Manufacturing operations are located in the home country but goods are sold to wholesalers worldwide, priced in the customer's local currency. The group has experienced rapid growth in recent years and many of its IS/IT systems need upgrading to handle larger volumes and increased complexity.

Group treasury is centralised at the head office and its key responsibilities include arranging sufficient long-term and short-term liquidity resources for the group and hedging foreign exchange exposures.

One of the first projects is a replacement treasury management system (TMS) to provide an integrated IS/IT system. The new integrated TMS will record all treasury transactions and provide information for the management and control of the treasury operations. It replaces the current system which consists of a series of spreadsheets for each part of the treasury operations.

Required:

(a) **Evaluate the benefits that might result from the introduction of the new TMS. Include in your evaluation some reference to the control factors that need to be considered during the implementation stage.**

(7 marks)

(b) **Advise the Directors of KAL on the following:**

- **The main purpose of a post-completion audit (PCA):**
- **What should be covered in a PCA of the TMS project;**
- **The importance and limitations of a PCA to KAL in the context of the TMS project.**

(8 marks)

(Total 15 marks)

A report format is not required in this question.

Test your understanding answers

Test your understanding 1 – Implementation and control

(a) **Key points**

- The primary benefit is that one integrated system will replace a number of apparently disparate legacy systems. It is not clear if the new system will be an "off-the-shelf" system or will be bespoke for the entity. An off-the-shelf system may not match perfectly the requirements of the entity and may require changes to the capture and processing of data. On the other hand, a bespoke system may prove difficult to implement and maintain. Upgrades to the system may be more difficult to manage.
- Greater security of data should be achieved by having all the data in one system, rather than being copied from one spreadsheet to another.
- More flexibility of operations – information needs change and require different solutions. The new TMS system can be designed to include extra treasury functions which KAL might need in the future (for example interest rate hedging techniques).
- The new integrated system takes advantage of technological developments.
- May provide benefits that are cost-reducing or even income generating. For example, the move to a single integrated system should lead to operational efficiencies and potential staff savings. New management information may be available from the system that the existing systems are not able to provide. Maintenance costs for the new system should be lower than for the existing systems.
- Does the new system assist KAL meet its corporate objectives in any way? Have the objectives of introducing a new system been clearly defined? – if not, how can success be measured? (see further comments in part (b)).
- Can the system be adapted to decentralised function if KAL chooses to change its treasury policy on centralisation?

Control

In the implementation stage of the project, it will be critical for the project team to control the new product, service or process by test runs and parallel running.

The project team should continue monitoring the project, and comparing the actual results against the original budget (time and cost). They should keep considering whether the project is likely to achieve its original objectives.

Any cost or time over runs should be communicated to management, and to the workers involved in the project at regular intervals. This feedback will help to prevent the project from deviating too far from its original budget and objectives.

(b) **Key points**

Purpose

A PCA reviews the cashflows from a project after the project has finished, or sometimes during the life of the project. The aim is to identify any variances from the original budget and particularly to discover the causes of those variances.

A project's PCA provides the mechanism whereby experience of past projects can be fed into the entity's decision-making processes as an aid to the improvement of future projects.

What should be covered?

In a PCA of the TMS project, the following areas should be covered:

- analysis of costs incurred, compared to budget
- analysis of time spent on the project, compared to budget
- analysis of the results of TMS system tests and parallel runs
- discussions with users – to identify whether there are any training needs
- discussions with management – to identify whether the new TMS system is helping to provide better management and control information as expected.

The key factors of importance of a PCA to KAL

- It enables a check to be made on whether the performance of the TMS corresponds with the expected results. If this is not the case, the reasons should be sought. This could form the basis for improvements in development of the system.
- It generates information, which allows an appraisal to be made of the managers who took the decision to upgrade the system. Managers will therefore tend to arrive at more realistic estimates of the advantages and disadvantages of the proposed investments.
- It can provide for better project planning in the future. If, in the evaluation, it is found that the planning of the investment programme was poor, provision can be made to ensure that it is better for future acquisitions.

Limitations

Sufficient resources are often not allocated to the task of completing PCAs so often are not undertaken. They can be time consuming and costly to complete. They are sometimes seen as tools for apportioning blame, so even where undertaken the lessons are often not disseminated and are not then embedded in future projects. If undertaken by the managers of the project, they may claim credit for all that went well and blame external factors for everything that didn't.

chapter

15

How to prepare for the exam

Chapter learning objectives

HOW TO PREPARE FOR THE EXAM

Section A of the Financial Strategy exam accounts for 50% of the paper, and it relates to a pre-seen case study which is common to all 3 Strategic Level papers. It is vital that you study the pre-seen material carefully before the exam. This Chapter explains how you should prepare for the exam and what you should do with the pre-seen material.

1 Introduction

About two months before the May or November exam sittings for the strategic level, a pre-seen case study will be released by CIMA.

It will be background information regarding a particular company in an industry which should be reasonably familiar to everyone. The case study is typically about seven pages long and includes information that would be useful when answering a range of unknown questions on any of the three strategic level papers – E3, P3 and F3.

The case study question is for 50 marks (50% of the exam). Since the exam is 3 hours long with 20 minutes reading time, you should spend one and a half hours only on answering the case study question.

No questions will be asked at this stage. They will be disclosed on the day of the exam.

Preparing for the exam

This Chapter explains how to use the pre-seen information, starting from the moment you receive it and going through to the exam day. Towards the end of the Chapter, you will find the real CIMA pre-seen material for the May 2010 and September 2010 exams, some detailed analysis of it, and then a question and answer based on it.

The idea is that if you follow the process through right to the end of the Chapter, this should give you an invaluable practice run which you can repeat when the real pre-seen material is released.

2 Two months before the exam

Initial reading

You should start by reading the pre-seen case study several times to assimilate the large amount of information.

While reading, keep asking yourself the question

> "If I were the management accountant in this organisation, what would I be interested in?"

Further research

Students are expected to research the industry and gain a wider knowledge which they can demonstrate in an exam question. This can be achieved in several ways:

- Research on the internet – Try to think of a similar real world company and look on its website. In particular the financial statements will be useful.
- Swap ideas and information with friends who are also sitting the exam. You may be lucky enough to have someone in your peer group who works in that industry. (Don't worry that they might fare better than you in the exam. The examiners have commented that those who do work in the industry specified in the case study appear to fare no better than others.) Industries so far have included electronics and an airport.
- Speak to your colleagues and managers at work.
- Discuss with your training provider if you are enrolled on a course covering these exams.
- Watch the television and read quality newspapers which may cover the industry or a similar company in the months preceding the exam.

Objectives of your reading and research

While it is important to understand the organisation in the pre-seen, and the industry in which it operates, you shouldn't spend too long researching the industry. In previous exams, all the information needed to answer the question has been contained within the pre-seen and the unseen information received on the exam day.

Your key objectives at this stage of the process should be:

- to analyse the context of the case organisation – what industry is it in? (with DEF airport in Nov 10, several students seemed to think that DEF was an airline, rather than an airport – lack of awareness)
- to analyse the current position of the case organisation (perhaps using SWOT)
- to identify and analyse key issues facing the case organisation
- to identify key issues from the pre-seen and consider how they might be developed in the unseen and the requirement – consider each chapter of this Text and try to think how the examiner might fit that particular topic into the case study, and how it could be examined.

3 One month before the exam

Question practice

Students are expected to be able to answer a range of questions based on this scenario in all of the three strategic level papers. The only way to achieve this is to practise as many potential questions as possible.

Past questions and answers are available on the CIMA website for:

- The Specimen exam paper released when the case study question was launched;
- The May 2010/September 2010 real exam;
- The November 2010/ March 2011 real exam
- The May 2011 real exam.

Your training provider will also have produced several practice papers covering other areas of the syllabus which may be tested.

While attempting these practice questions, you should start to think about how best to tackle the exam paper in its entirety.

It has been found by the P3 examiner that students who fare best seem to be those who tackle the case study question first, and the section B questions second. However, in paper F3 students who attack the Section A case study first sometimes get bogged down in the detail of the calculations.

By practising a few mock papers you will find which order best suits you for each paper. The critical point in all papers is that you must allocate time carefully and strictly.

For any question you attempt, you should always write down (on the exam paper possibly) the time you should start and stop that question. You should further break this down into what time to finish each individual requirement so that you have covered the whole paper at the end of the three hours.

4 The night before the exam

Last minute preparation

On the night before the exam, you should re-read the case study scenario fully and try to separate in your mind the real CIMA material from the practice scenarios you may have attempted in the previous weeks - you must make sure that you don't get confused in the exam and bring in fictional scenarios which you have seen during your revision.

Then, get a good night's sleep to ensure you are alert and ready for the exam.

5 The day of the exam

Unseen material

On the day of the exam, further unseen material will be supplied by CIMA along with the question paper. The unseen material tends to be about two further pages of information. (You will also receive a clean copy of the case study pre-seen material in the exam.)

There are commonly 3 or 4 requirements on each exam paper, which may be further broken down into parts (i), (ii), etc.

The requirements are likely to cover a range of topics across the syllabus.

Time management

For each mark available you have 1.8 minutes available. So for a 10 mark requirement you should spend no longer than 18 minutes answering it.

Remember to write down your start and stop times for each question / requirement.

There is a law of diminishing returns when answering exam questions – you will probably score the first half of the available marks in the early minutes of your answer. The last few minutes will probably score far fewer as you may have gone off on a tangent or be waffling. Stop! Move on to the next requirement where you will start to score rapidly once again.

Planning

For E3 and P3 your answer will probably be predominantly written although some calculations may be required that you will then need to discuss. In F3 the split between calculations and discussion is more even.

Planning your answers is absolutely critical if the requirement is for a large number of marks.

Most students can write a coherent answer for a requirement of, say, 5 marks. But when the requirement is larger than this many students will ramble, or move away from the actual question asked.

It is recommended that in your answer booklet, possibly on the middle two pages (which you could pull out, but need to put back at the end of the exam) you should plan your answer to each requirement.

Try considering:

- Information from the pre-seen material;
- Information from the unseen material;
- Technical topics from your study text;
- Past exam questions you may have done which might just cover the same topic if you are lucky (but be careful if they are slightly different not to answer the question you had earlier rather than the one asked in the exam);
- Common sense.

Writing up your answer

Write up your answer once your plan is complete. Remember that your plan should be very brief, so that you don't waste time rewriting it out in full without adding very much.

As you use points on your plan tick them off. Do not obliterate them since if you fail to use all of them in the time allowed, markers are allowed to consider whether any further marks are available within them for a marginal candidate.

The layout of your answer needs to be professional. Use full English sentences and avoid notes. Never use the word etcetera. This indicates that you know more but that you can't be bothered to tell the examiner!

Other exam tips

- Leave plenty of space between each requirements answer (possibly start a fresh page for each) so that you can go back to add to your answer later if need be.
- You can answer the requirements in any order, however, you should clearly mark which is (a), (b), (c) or (d), or part (i), (ii) etc.
- Keep looking at your watch to ensure that you do not run over your allocated time. Stop when you are supposed to. Many students think 'just two more minutes' and the next time they look at their watch ten minutes have passed. This can mean that whole requirements are not attempted later which is a recipe for failure.
- It is unlikely, but you may have time at the end of the exam to review what you have written. You should really make time to do this, but few students do since they think it is better to keep writing. At the end of the day, there is no negative marking, and therefore the more you write the more possible marks you might get.

- As a rough guide, a student with average sized writing might score about 6 marks per page, so aim to write about 2 sides for a ten mark requirement. (This includes the use of headings, and spacing between each point made.)
- Underline your headings and any key words which you are sure will gain marks (but don't go wild underlining everything).
- Use a black or blue biro. Never use red or green biro or highlighter pens anywhere in your answer booklet. Pencil can be used for diagrams.
- Leave plenty of space between different requirements in the answer booklet, so that you can add to your answer later if necessary. This also makes your answer much tidier and more professional.

6 Practice exam – Pre-seen material

The pre-seen information below is the real CIMA pre-seen case study for the May 2010 and September 2010 exams. It describes an electronic components manufacturer called Aybe.

Follow the steps above in order to prepare yourself for a requirement based on this pre-seen material and the following unseen material.

Read the pre-seen material first, prepare some analysis of it and compare this with our analysis in the next section. Then, when you feel that you are ready to spend 90 minutes attempting the question, start to look at the unseen material.

Pre-seen material – Aybe

Background

Aybe, located in Country C, was formed by the merger of two companies in 2001. It is a listed company which manufactures, markets and distributes a large range of components throughout Europe and the United States of America. Aybe employs approximately 700 people at its three factories in Eastern Europe and supplies products to over 0.5 million customers in 20 countries. Aybe holds stocks of about 100,000 different electronic components.

Aybe is regarded within its industry as being a well-established business. Company Ay had operated successfully for nearly 17 years before its merger with Company Be. Company Ay can therefore trace its history back for 25 years which is a long time in the fast moving electronic component business.

The company is organised into three divisions, the Domestic Electronic Components division (DEC), the Industrial Electronic Components division (IEC) and the Specialist Components division (SC). The Domestic and Industrial Electronic Components divisions supply standard electronic components for domestic and industrial use whereas the Specialist Components division supplies components which are often unique and made to specific customer requirements. Each of the three divisions has its own factory in Country C.

Composition of the Board of Directors

The Board of Directors has three executive directors, the Company Secretary and five non-executive directors. The Chairman is one of the five independent non-executive directors. The executive directors are the Chief Executive, Finance Director and Director of Operations. There is also an Audit Committee, a Remuneration Committee and a Nominations Committee. All three committees are made up entirely of the non-executive directors.

Organisational structure

Aybe is organised along traditional functional/unitary lines. The Board considers continuity to be a very important value. The present structure was established by Company Ay in 1990 and continued after the merger with Company Be. Many of Aybe's competitors have carried out structural reorganisations since then. In 2008, Aybe commissioned a review of its organisational structure from a human resource consultancy. The consultants suggested alternative structures which they thought Aybe could employ to its advantage. However, Aybe's Board felt that continuity was more important and no change to the organisational structure took place.

Product and service delivery

Customers are increasingly seeking assistance from their component suppliers with the design of their products and the associated manufacturing and assembly processes. Aybe's Board views this as a growth area. The Board has recognised that Aybe needs to develop web-based services and tools which can be accessed by customers. The traditional method of listing the company's range of components in a catalogue is becoming less effective because customers are increasingly seeking specially designed custom made components as the electronics industry becomes more sophisticated.

Financial data

Aybe's historical financial record, denominated in C's currency of C$, over the last five years is shown below.

Year ended 31/12	**2009**	**2008**	**2007**	**2006**	**2005**
	C$m	C$m	C$m	C$m	C$m
Revenue	620	600	475	433	360
Operating profit	41	39	35	20	13
Profit for the year	23	21	16	9	5
Earnings per share (C$)	0.128	0.117	0.089	0.050	0.028
Dividend per share (C$)	0.064	0.058	0	0	0

Extracts from the 2009 financial statements are given at Appendix A. There are currently 180 million ordinary shares in issue with a nominal value of C$0.10 each. The share price at 31 December 2009 was C$0.64. No dividend was paid in the three years 2005 to 2007 due to losses sustained in the first few years after the merger in 2001.

Aybe's bank has imposed an overdraft limit of C$10 million and two covenants: (i) that its interest cover must not fall below 5 and (ii) its ratio of non-current liabilities to equity must not increase beyond 0.75:1. Aybe's Finance Director is comfortable with this overdraft limit and the two covenants.

The ordinary shareholding of Aybe is broken down as follows:

	% holding at 31/12/09
Institutional investors	55
Executive directors and company secretary	10
Employees	5
Individual investors	30

The Executive Directors, Company Secretary and other senior managers are entitled to take part in an Executive Share Option Scheme offered by Aybe.

Performance Review

Aybe's three divisions have been profitable throughout the last five years. The revenue and operating profit of the three divisions of Aybe for 2009 were as follows:

	DEC division	IEC division	SC division
	C$m	C$m	C$m
Revenue	212	284	124
Operating profit	14	15	11

Financial objectives of Aybe

The Board has generally taken a cautious approach to providing strategic direction for the company. Most board members feel that this has been appropriate because the company was unprofitable for the three year period after the merger and needed to be turned around. Also, most board members think a cautious approach has been justified given the constrained economic circumstances which have affected Aybe's markets since 2008. While shareholders have been disappointed with Aybe's performance over the last five years, they have remained loyal and supported the Board in its attempts to move the company into profit. The institutional shareholders however are now looking for increased growth and profitability.

The Board has set the following financial objectives which it considers reflect the caution for which Aybe is well known:

(i) Dividend payout to remain at 50% of profit for the year;

(ii) No further equity shares to be issued over the next five years in order to avoid diluting earnings per share.

Capital budget overspends

Aybe has an internal audit department. The Chief Internal Auditor, who leads this department, reports directly to the Finance Director. Investigation by the Internal Audit department has revealed that managers with responsibility for capital expenditure have often paid little attention to expenditure authorisation levels approved by the Board. They have justified overspending on the grounds that the original budgets were inadequate and in order not to jeopardise the capital projects, the overspends were necessary.

An example of this was the building of an extension to the main factory at the DEC division that was completed in 2009 at a final cost of nearly C$3 million which was almost 50% over budget. The capital budget for the extension was set at the outset and the capital investment appraisal showed a positive net present value. It subsequently became apparent that the site clearance costs and on-going construction expenditure were under-estimated. These estimates were provided by a qualified quantity surveyor who was a contractor to Aybe. The estimates supplied by the quantity surveyor were accurately included in Aybe's capital investment appraisal system which was performed on a spreadsheet. However, no regular checks were carried out to compare the phased budgeted expenditure with actual costs incurred. It came as a surprise to the Board when the Finance Director finally produced the capital expenditure project report which showed the cost of the extension was nearly 50% overspent.

Strategic development

Aybe applies a traditional rational model in carrying out its strategic planning process. This encompasses an annual exercise to review the previous plan, creation of a revenue and capital budget for the next five years and instruction to managers within Aybe to maintain their expenditure within the budget limits approved by the Board.

Debates have taken place within the Board regarding the strategic direction in which Aybe should move. Most board members are generally satisfied that Aybe has been turned around over the last five years and were pleased that the company increased its profit in 2009 even though the global economy slowed down. Aybe benefited from a number of long-term contractual arrangements with customers throughout 2009 which were agreed in previous years. However, many of these are not being renewed due to the current economic climate.

The Board stated in its annual report, published in March 2010, that the overall strategic aim of the company is to:

"Achieve growth and increase shareholder returns by continuing to produce and distribute high quality electronic components and develop our international presence through expansion into new overseas markets."

Aybe's Chief Executive said in the annual report that the strategic aim is clear and straightforward. He said "Aybe will strive to maintain its share of the electronic development, operational, maintenance and repair markets in which it is engaged. This is despite the global economic difficulties which Aybe, along with its competitors, has faced since 2008. Aybe will continue to apply the highest ethical standards in its business activities."

In order to facilitate the achievement of the strategic aim, Aybe's Board has established the following strategic goals:

(1) Enhance the provision of products and services which are demanded by customers;

(2) Invest in engineering and web-based support for customers;

(3) Maintain the search for environmentally friendly products;

(4) Pursue options for expansion into new overseas markets.

The Board has also stated that Aybe is a responsible corporate organisation and recognises the social and environmental effects of its operational activities.

Concern over the rate of growth

Aybe's recently appointed Director of Operations and one of its Non-Executive Directors have privately expressed their concern to the Chief Executive at what they perceive to be the very slow growth of the company. While they accept that shareholder expectations should not be raised too high, they feel that the Board is not providing sufficient impetus to move the company forward. They fear that the results for 2010 will be worse than for 2009. They think that Aybe should be much more ambitious and fear that the institutional shareholders in particular, will not remain patient if Aybe does not create stronger earnings growth than has previously been achieved.

Development approaches

The Board has discussed different ways of expanding overseas in order to meet the overall strategic aim. It has, in the past, been reluctant to move from the current approach of exporting components. However the Director of Operations has now begun preparing a plan for the IEC division to open up a trading company in Asia. The DEC division is also establishing a subsidiary in Africa.

APPENDIX A

Extracts of Aybe's Income Statement and Statement of Financial Position

Income statement for the year ended 31/12/09

	C$m
Revenue	620
Operating costs	(579)
Finance costs	(4)
Profit before tax	37
Income tax expense	(14)
Profit for the year	23

Statement of financial position at 31/12/09

	C$m
ASSETS	
Non current assets	111
Current assets:	
Inventories	40
Trade and other receivables	81
Cash and cash equivalents	3
	124
Total assets	235
EQUITY AND LIABILITIES	
Equity:	
Share capital	18
Share premium	9
Other reserves	8
Retained earnings	75
Total equity	110
Non current liabilities	
Bank loan (8% interest, repayable 2015)	40

Current liabilities	
Trade and other payables	73
Current tax payable	8
Bank overdraft	4
Total current liabilities	85
Total liabilities	125
Total equity and liabilities	235

End of pre-seen material

7 Analysis of the pre-seen material

Introduction

Now that you have had chance to read the pre-seen material, you should do some further research into the industry and try to pick out key themes which might form the basis of the exam questions.

You will find below:

- a SWOT analysis on Aybe
- stakeholder analysis
- quantitative analysis
- a consideration of potential examinable F3 topics.

Before reading this information, try to do your own analysis first and then compare your analysis to the information below.

The examiners have commented that students really need to do their own analysis. Simply copying analysis from your tutors or colleagues will not necessarily help you to understand the pre-seen properly.

Aybe pre-seen analysis – SWOT

Strengths

- Steady financials – growth in revenue and margins
- Seems to comply with Governance "best practice" (e.g. many NEDs although should have executive input to nominations committee)
- Share option plan should motivate directors

Weaknesses

- Board lacks ambition
- Aybe may have outgrown its functional structure
- Restrictive bank covenant limits financing opportunities
- Poor MIS (e.g. Board surprised about capex overspend)
- Poor budgetary control processes

Opportunities

- Expansion into Asian and /or African markets
- Enhance CRM – especially for specialist components division
- Develop website and e-business – especially for managing customer relationship
- Switch manufacturing to be closer to markets or to cheaper countries
- Improve information systems
- Sell a division

Threats

- Increasing competitive pressure
- Further loss of major customers
- High risk of takeover as shareholders may become dissatisfied
- Risk of breaching covenant
- Political risks – e.g. Eastern European country, African target
- Currency and interest rate risks.

Aybe pre-seen analysis – Stakeholders

Key stakeholders

- Institutional Shareholders (since privatisation) are becoming dissatisfied with current levels of growth and returns
- Major customers may threaten to move their business elsewhere

Aybe pre-seen analysis – Quantitative analysis

Divisions

- IEC contributes the most to both revenue and profit and SC the least
- Operating margins are DEC 6.6%, IEC 5.6% and SC 8.9%

Overall company

Profitability

- Fairly steady and unexciting
- Average revenue growth of 14.6% pa since 2005
- Operating margin has grown from 3.6% in 2005 to 6.6% (41/620) in 2009
- ROCE = 41/150 = 27.3% (no comparisons)

Liquidity

- Current ratio = 124 / 85 = 1.46
- Quick ratio = (81+3) / 85 = 0.99
- Receivables days = 81/620 × 365 = 48 days – seems high
- Payables days using operating costs = 73/579 × 365 = 46 days
- Inventory days using operating costs = 40/579 × 365 = 25 days
- Length of operating cycle = 25 + 48 – 46 = 27
- All fairly unexciting except Aybe has low cash reserves

Investor ratios

- Market capitalisation = 180m × 0.64 = C$115.2m
- Eps growth of 9.4% in 2009
- Dividend payout ratio set at 50% in 2008 and 2009
- Gearing based on book value of debt/equity = 40 / 110 = 36% which seems low enough. Slightly lower if use market values.

Aybe Case Study – Key examinable issues for paper F3

Note: It is important that in the real exam you fully incorporate the new unseen information into your answers and do not rely too much on your analysis of the preseen. However, based on the preseen the following potential issues can be identified.

Investment appraisal

Aybe has a number of different options as it targets its overall strategic aim of expansion; the firm needs to develop web based services and tools, the IEC division is planning to open up in Asia, and the DEC division is considering setting up a subsidiary in Africa.

If investment appraisal is tested, it is likely that it will involve foreign currency, and that you will be asked to calculate the NPV of given future cashflows.

Takeover or organic growth

Rather than expanding by organic growth, you might be given information regarding an existing company which Aybe can acquire.

Learn the pros and cons of organic growth v acquisition, and make sure you have revised the various methods of business valuation. Methods such as P/E method, PV of future cashflows, and asset valuation, have been tested many times in the exams.

Capital budgeting

The current capital budgeting procedures are inadequate. There have been overspends in the past, and managers pay little attention to expenditure authorisation levels.

You could be asked to set out a formal policy for the capital budgeting process, incorporating a post completion audit (PCA).

Financial objectives

The firm has two financial objectives, relating to dividend levels and equity finance / earnings per share.
Whatever future plans are to be appraised, it will be important to relate your investment appraisal back to these two financial objectives.

Financing and debt covenants

If the firm is to undertake a new venture, finance will be required (Aybe currently has very little cash in its Statement of Financial Position).

Given the constraint regarding the issue of equity (financial objective (ii)), it is likely that debt will have to be raised.

Make sure that you consider the impact of raising any new debt finance on the current covenants set by the bank. Before the exam, make sure you calculate and understand the current levels for the debt covenant ratios.(i.e. interest cover = 10.25, and ratio of non current liabilities to equity = 0.36:1)

Also, note that as a listed company, Aybe will have a broad range of debt options available (e.g. debentures), and that if the investment is denominated in foreign currency, it would be wise to source finance in the same currency.

Financing v Investment v Dividend policies

Aybe's two financial objectives predetermine what its dividend policy and its financing policy should be. This puts a great constraint on the potential investment options of the firm.

Be prepared to discuss alternative ways of setting objectives i.e. it is useful to be able to consider the interrelationships between dividends, financing and investments, rather than having two of the policies predetermined.

Financial analysis

We are given historical financial information and segmented information for the three divisions. Make sure you compute ratios before the exam to enable you to discuss growth patterns, profit margins, and split between divisions (of profit, margin and turnover).

8 Sample unseen material

Note: You should only read this unseen information and the associated question when you have already read and analysed the Aybe pre-seen material in detail. For maximum benefit (to simulate the time you will have in the real exam), you should aim to spend 10 minutes reading the unseen material and the requirement, and then 90 minutes preparing and writing up your answer.

Unseen material for the Aybe Case Study

In response to the concerns expressed by the Director of Operations and one of the Non-Executive directors, the Board has asked the Financial Director of Aybe to prepare some forecast financial statements for Aybe for the current financial year (year ended 31 December 2010). The forecast incorporates the current financial objectives of Aybe, and the best current forecasts for the existing divisions. At this stage, the Financial Director has not attempted to include the impact of any proposed new projects or expansion plans.

The forecast shows a small profit for the year and the following forecast statement of financial position:

Extracts from the forecast financial statements for Aybe at 31 December 2010, the end of the current financial year:

	C$m
ASSETS	280
Total assets	
EQUITY AND LIABILITIES	
Equity:	
Share capital	18
Share premium	9
Other reserves	8
Retained earnings	78
Total equity	113
Non current liabilities	
Bank loan (8% interest, repayable 2015)	40
Current liabilities	
Total current liabilities	127
Total equity and liabilities	280

A new project for the SC division

An opportunity has been identified which the directors hope will move Aybe towards achieving all of its strategic goals. This opportunity has not yet been reflected in the forecasts above.

The directors are considering building a new, environmentally-friendly component manufacturing plant in Quod, a country in South America whose currency is the Quod Peso (QP).

Quod's government is very encouraging towards foreign investors, and the abundance of local expertise and raw materials means that it should be possible for Aybe to build a high-technology factory which is carbon neutral and which will be able to design and manufacture products according to customers' specifications.

The directors feel that this new project will improve the sales and profitability of the SC division. They have asked you, the management accountant, to prepare an initial investment appraisal in preparation for the next Board meeting in two weeks' time.

Project details

The project under consideration is the development of a factory in Quod, which would be owned and operated by a new subsidiary entity. A suitable site, subject to planning permission, has been located.

Forecast operating cash flows for the project are as follows:

	Year(s)	QPm
Initial investment (inc working capital)	0	200
Residual value	4	50
Pre tax operating net cash flows	1–4	70

Other relevant data and assumptions:

- The initial investment is expected to be made on 30 November 2010 and cash flows will arise approximately evenly during the following years.
- However, in any net present value (NPV) exercise, all cash flows should be assumed to arise on 31 December of each year.
- The local tax rate in Quod is set at a preferential rate of 10% to encourage foreign investment in environmentally friendly projects, rather than the normal rate of 25%.
- Tax is payable in the year in which it arises.
- No tax depreciation allowances are available.
- No additional tax is payable in Country C under the terms of the double tax treaties with Quod.
- Net cash flows are to be paid to the Country C parent entity as dividends at the end of each year.

Uncertainties affecting the outcome of the project

Tax rate

There is some uncertainty over the Quod tax rate over the period of the project, because there is to be a general election in Quod in the next six months. The governing party has pledged to keep the preferential tax rate at 10% for at least the four year duration of the next government. However, the main opposition party has vowed to increase the tax rate to 25% with immediate effect, and then to leave it constant for the four year period of their government. The opposition party has been gaining lots of support in these recessionary times, as many Quod citizens have become disillusioned with the government's policy of lower tax rates for foreigners than for Quod citizens.

Exchange rate

Economic forecasters expect the value of the C$ to either stay constant against the value of the Quod Peso for the next four years or to strengthen by 7% per annum. Assume that there is an equal probability of each of these two different exchange rate forecasts.

Environmental concerns

There is also significant risk to the project from strong objections from local farmers in Quod who are concerned about the impact of acid water run-off from the cooling systems for the new technology component manufacturing system. In addition, there are a number of executive holiday homes nearby whose owners are objecting to the visual impact of the factory.

Investment criteria

Aybe evaluates foreign projects of this nature based on a Country C cost of capital of 12% which reflects the risk profile of the proposed investment.

Alternative financing methods

The following alternative methods are being considered by Aybe for financing the new investment:

- long-term borrowings denominated in C$
- long-term borrowings denominated in Quod Pesos.

Organisational structure

In the light of the recent report on capital budget overspends, Aybe's Board are also considering changing the organisational structure of the firm and setting up separate treasury and finance departments. It is hoped that the separation of responsibilities will contribute to better capital budgeting and spending procedures in future.

Sample requirement

Required:

(a) **Calculate the NPV of the cash flows for the proposed investment for each of the following four possible scenarios:**

- **constant exchange rate and a tax rate of 10%**
- **constant exchange rate and a tax rate of 25%**
- **the C$ to strengthen against the Quod Peso by 7% a year and a tax rate of 10%**
- **the C$ to strengthen against the Quod Peso by 7% a year and a tax rate of 25%.**

In each case, assume that the exchange rate at year 0 is C$/QP6.47 (that is to say that QP 6.47 = C$1.00).

(12 marks)

(b) **Prepare the forecast statement of financial position (balance sheet) of Aybe on 31 December 2010, incorporating the project under each of the two alternative financing structures and each of the following two exchange rate scenarios A and B:**

Date	**Exchange rate under scenario A**	**Exchange rate under scenario B**
30 November 2010 (date of the initial investment and arrangement of financing)	C$/QP6.47 (that is to say that QP 6.47 = C$1.00)	C$/QP6.47 (that is to say that QP 6.47 = C$1.00)
31 December 2010 (financial reporting/statement of financial position (balance sheet) date)	C$/QP6.47 (that is to say that QP 6.47 = C$1.00)	C$/QP8.24 (that is to say that QP 8.24 = C$1.00)

Assume that no other project cash flows occur until 2011.

(8 marks)

(c) **Write a report addressed to the Directors of Aybe in which you, as management accountant, address the following issues relating to the evaluation and implementation of the proposed project:**

(i) **Discuss the internal and external constraints affecting the investment decision and advise Aybe how to proceed. In your answer, include reference to your calculations in part (a) above.**

(10 marks)

(ii) **Discuss the comparative advantages of each of the two proposed alternative financing structures and advise Aybe which one to adopt. In your answer include reference to your results in part (b) above, and further analysis and discussion of the impact of each proposed financial structure on the company's financial statements.**

(10 marks)

(iii) **Discuss the differing roles and responsibilities of the proposed treasury department and finance department in evaluating and implementing the Quod project and the interaction of the two departments throughout the process.**

(10 marks)

Total: 50 marks

Test your understanding answers

Sample requirement

(a) (i) NPV – constant exchange rate and tax at 10%

	0	**1**	**2**	**3**	**4**
Op cash flows (QPm)		70	70	70	70
Tax at 10% (QPm)		(7)	(7)	(7)	(7)
Inv and residual (QPm)	(200)				50
Net cash flow (QPm)	(200)	63	63	63	113
Exchange rate (C$1 = QP...)	6.47	6.47	6.47	6.47	6.47
Net cash flow (C$m)	(30.91)	9.74	9.74	9.74	17.47
DF 12%	1	0.893	0.797	0.712	0.636
Present value	(30.91)	8.70	7.76	6.93	11.11
Net present value (C$m)	**3.59**				

(a) (ii) NPV – constant exchange rate and tax at 25%

	0	**1**	**2**	**3**	**4**
Op cash flows (QPm)		70	70	70	70
Tax at 10% (QPm)		(17.5)	(17.5)	(17.5)	(17.5)
Inv and residual (QPm)	(200)				50
Net cash flow (QPm)	(200)	52.5	52.5	52.5	102.5
Exchange rate (C$1 = QP...)	6.47	6.47	6.47	6.47	6.47
Net cash flow (C$m)	(30.91)	8.11	8.11	8.11	15.84
DF 12%	1	0.893	0.797	0.712	0.636
Present value	(30.91)	7.24	6.46	5.77	10.07
Net present value (C$m)	**(1.37)**				

(a) (iii) NPV – strengthening C$ and tax at 10%

	0	1	2	3	4
Op cash flows (QPm)		70	70	70	70
Tax at 10% (QPm)		(7)	(7)	(7)	(7)
Inv and residual (QPm)	(200)				50
Net cash flow (QPm)	(200)	63	63	63	113
Exchange rate (C$1 = QP...)	6.47	6.92	7.41	7.93	8.48
Net cash flow (C$m)	(30.91)	9.10	8.50	7.94	13.33
DF 12%	1	0.893	0.797	0.712	0.636
Present value	(30.91)	8.13	6.77	5.65	8.48
Net present value (C$m)	**(1.88)**				

(a) (iv) NPV – strengthening C$ and tax at 25%

	0	1	2	3	4
Op cash flows (QPm)		70	70	70	70
Tax at 10% (QPm)		(17.5)	(17.5)	(17.5)	(17.5)
Inv and residual (QPm)	(200)				50
Net cash flow (QPm)	(200)	52.5	52.5	52.5	102.5
Exchange rate (C$1 = QP...)	6.47	6.92	7.41	7.93	8.48
Net cash flow (C$m)	(30.91)	7.59	7.09	6.62	12.09
DF 12%	1	0.893	0.797	0.712	0.636
Present value	(30.91)	6.78	5.65	4.71	7.69
Net present value (C$m)	**(6.08)**				

(b) Forecast balance sheets at 31/12/10

	Scenario A	**Scenario A**	**Scenario B**	**Scenario B**
	C$1=QP6.47	**C$1=QP6.47**	**C$1=QP8.24**	**C$1=QP8.24**
	C$ loans	**QP loans**	**C$ loans**	**QP loans**
Assets:	C$m	C$m	C$m	C$m
Total assets (excl. new investment)	280	280	280	280
New investment (W1)	30.9	30.9	24.3	24.3
	310.9	310.9	304.3	304.3
Equity and liabilities:				
Per forecast	113	113	113	113
Translation loss on QP asset	–	–	(6.6)	(6.6)
Translation gain on QP loans	–	–	–	6.6
	113	113	106.4	113
Non current liabilities	70.9	70.9	70.9	64.3
Current liabilities	127	127	127	127
	310.9	310.9	304.3	304.3

(W1) **Investment and finance**

Aybe plans to invest QP200 million on 30 November 2010 and will need to raise this sum, either by borrowing QP200 million or C$30.9 million.

At 31/12/10 the investment and Quod Peso borrowings would be shown at:

- Scenario A: book value = 200 / 6.47 = C$30.9 million. No change on 30/11.
- Scenario B: book value = 200 / 8.24 = C$24.3 million. Fall of 6.6 from 30/11.

(c) **REPORT**

To: The Board of Directors, Aybe

From: Finance Director

Date: 27 May 2010

Subject: Proposed Quod project

Introduction

This report has been prepared at the request of the Board of Directors to examine the proposed Quod project with particular emphasis on evaluation, finance and implementation.

(i) **Evaluation of the new project, and discussion of constraints**

The main external constraint on the firm's actions is that shareholders have an expectation that Aybe will increase their wealth by looking for increased growth and profitability. The project NPV under different scenarios is as follows:

Exchange rate	Constant	Constant	Strengthening C$	Strengthening C$
Tax rate	10%	25%	10%	25%
NPV (C$m)	3.59	(1.37)	(1.88)	(6.08)

Details of these calculations are given in Appendix 1 (i.e. part (a) of this question).

The project only gives a positive NPV, and hence increases shareholder value, if exchange rates are expected to remain constant and Quod tax stays at 10%.

If either the C$ strengthens and/or the Quod tax rate is raised to 25%, then the project will reduce shareholder value rather than adding to it. The project should thus be considered high risk as both of these factors are outside of Aybe's control. Consequently, it is worth considering whether the discount rate of 12% which has been applied is high enough to reflect the high level of risk attached to the project.

It is recommended that the firm carries out further research to assess the likelihood of exchange rate movements by investigating forecasts for inflation, economic growth and government policy regarding interest rates.

Furthermore, the directors should consider allocating funds to lobby the government in Quod, and to help fund their election campaign (if that is legal), to put pressure on them to keep the tax rate at 10%.

It would also be advisable to consider delaying the project decision for six months (until after the general election) to see what the impact is on tax rates, given the significance of this factor.

A further constraint is that Aybe has a stated objective to search for environmentally friendly products. Thus, even given the possibility of losses as discussed above, the directors may feel that the project should be undertaken to enhance/protect Aybe's reputation in this matter. An internal constraint may be that directors do not wish to be seen to 'lose face' by a change of policy here.

Further analysis should also be carried out to assess the likely environmental impact of the investment and the actions of local farmers and residents in protesting against the plans. Adverse publicity could be very damaging to Aybe's reputation as a socially responsible firm.

The final constraint (which will be discussed more fully below) is that the bank has imposed two covenants relating to the raising of debt finance. It is critical that Aybe does not breach these covenants in raising finance to fund the new project.

Advice

The project is only financially beneficial if the Quod tax rate stays at 10% and if the exchange rate stays constant. Hence, Aybe needs to evaluate the probability of these two factors before a final decision is made. However, even if the project will show a small negative NPV, it may still be worth going ahead given that the project helps Aybe to achieve other, non financial, objectives.

(ii) **Finance**

Two financing methods have been proposed – long-term borrowings in Quod Pesos and long-term borrowings in C$s. Given Aybe's financial objective to raise no equity over the next five years, both these options seem to be initially acceptable.

The relative advantages of these two schemes are as follows:

Translation risk

The Quod Peso loan will facilitate hedging of translation risk between the loan and the Quod investment.

For example, if the exchange rate were to move to C$1=QP8.24 by 31 December 2010, then there would be a fall of C$6.6 million in the book value of the Quod investment. However, the book value of the outstanding borrowings at 31/12/10 would also fall by C$6.6 million, giving a translation gain to net off against the loss on the asset. The result is no change in shareholders' funds. Details of these calculations are given in Appendix 2 (i.e. part (b) of this question).

With the C$ borrowings there would still be the loss on the asset but no corresponding gain on the borrowings.On the other hand, should the Quod Peso strengthen against the C$, then the C$ borrowings would have a net gain on the asset, while the Quod Peso borrowings would still result in netting off.

However, the gains and losses mentioned here are book movements and unrealised, so are not very significant commercially.

Also, if the economic forecasters only expect the C$ to strengthen by 7% per annum against the Quod Peso (and with only a 50% chance) it is highly unlikely that the exchange rate will fluctuate by such a large amount before the end of 2010.

Impact on covenants

Whether or not the exchange rate changes, the ratio of non current liabilities to equity (using book values) will change significantly if the new project is undertaken. (See Appendix 3 below for supporting calculations.)

The most problematic combination of circumstances would be if Aybe used a C$ loan and also the exchange rate changed to C$1=QP8.24 on 31 December 2010. In this case, the ratio would be 0.67:1 (up from a current level of 0.36:1 (40/110) at 31 December 2009).

It is not clear what the exact likelihood is of this arising (although as mentioned above, the chances of the rate changing by such a large amount appear to be slim). However, it is pleasing to see that even in this worst case scenario, the bank's limit of 0.75:1 is still not exceeded.

With regard to the other covenant (interest cover must not fall below 5), we are not told the interest rate on the new loan, so it is difficult to assess the likely impact. However, note that the current interest cover is 10.25 times (=41/4) which is much higher than the bank's limit. Raising C$30.9 million of new finance will increase the loans from C$40 million to C$70.9 million (an increase of 77%). A very simplistic calculation of interest cover assuming a 77% rise in interest but no rise in profit would give a revised interest cover ratio of (41/ (4 x 1.77) =) 5.79, still well above the limit of 5.

It appears that whichever method of finance is chosen, Aybe is unlikely to breach either of the bank's two covenants.

Matching of cash flows

With Quod Peso borrowings the cash receipts from the investment can be used to meet the interest payments, thus reducing the need and volume of funds to be converted from Quod Pesos to C$s. This should result in lower transaction costs.

Taxation

Presumably Quod Peso borrowings will be taken out by the Quod subsidiary so the interest would reduce the profits taxable in Quod.

With C$ borrowings the board needs to decide whether the Quod subsidiary should take out the loan or whether Aybe could take out the borrowings in Country C, where presumably it can get better terms. Here interest can be used to reduce Country C tax, which will probably be at a higher level than in Quod.

Recommendation

On balance, the use of a Quod Peso loan is recommended to facilitate translation risk hedging and better matching of cash flows.

(iii) **The role of the treasury and finance departments**

Treasury is the function concerned with the provision and use of finance and thus handles the acquisition and custody of funds whereas the Finance Department has responsibility for accounting, reporting and control. The roles of the two departments in the proposed investment will be as follows:

Evaluation

- Treasury will quantify the cost of capital to be used in assessing the investment.
- The finance department will estimate the project cash flows.

Implementation

- Treasury will establish corporate financial objectives and will identify sources and types of finance which satisfy these objectives (and the bank covenants which Aybe faces).
- Treasury will also deal with currency management – dealing in foreign currencies and hedging currency risks – and taxation.
- The finance department will be involved with the preparation of budgets and budgetary control, the preparation of periodic financial statements and the management and administration of activities such as payroll and internal audit.

Interaction

The treasury department has main responsibility for setting corporate objectives and policy and the finance department has responsibility for implementing policy and ensuring the achievement of corporate objectives. This distinction is probably far too simplistic and, in reality, both departments will make contributions to both determination and achievement of objectives.

There is a circular relationship in that Treasurers quantify the cost of capital, which the Financial Controllers use as the criterion for the deployment of funds; Financial Controllers quantify projected cash flows which in turn trigger Treasurers' decisions to employ capital.

Appendix 1: Part (a) of the answer

Appendix 2: Part (b) of the answer

Appendix 3: Impact on Bank Covenants

Using the statements of financial position (balance sheets) produced in (b) above:

	Scenario A	**Scenario A**	**Scenario B**	**Scenario B**
	C$1=QP6.47	**C$1=QP6.47**	**C$1=QP8.24**	**C$1=QP8.24**
	C$ loans	**QP loans**	**C$ loans**	**QP loans**
	C$m	C$m	C$m	C$m
Equity	113	113	113	113
Non current liabilities	70.9	70.9	70.9	64.3
Ratio of non-current liabilities to equity	0.63:1	0.63:1	0.67:1	0.57:1

chapter

16

Questions and Answers

1 Introduction

Exam questions in this text

At the end of each Chapter in this text, you will find some sample Section B style questions.

In the previous Chapter ('How to prepare for the exam'), there was an example of a Section A question based on the real pre-seen material for the May 2010 and September 2010 exams.

The Section A questions will be broader in scope and will cover topics from various parts of the syllabus. Some more examples of Section A questions are presented below. You will first find the pre seen material, then the unseen material and the requirements.

Note on these questions

These questions are based on real past exam questions, but for now the pre-seen information has been kept deliberately brief. Thus, you should be able to practise attempting long questions covering several topic areas, without having to spend too long analysing pre-seen material first.

Also, the requirements have been split up to make them more manageable.

2 Section A Question KL Group

Pre seen material

Background to the company

KL Group plc ("KL") provides a range of waste disposal products and services for sale in the United Kingdom and overseas. Its shares are listed on the London Stock Exchange and are held by both private and institutional investors, with institutions holding the majority of shares.

Background to the industry

Domestic waste disposal in the UK has traditionally been carried out by local authorities, who also provide small scale services for industrial clients. Most large businesses in the UK outsource their waste disposal to independent companies, such as KL.

KL has a substantial share of the UK waste disposal industry, and a growing share of the US and European markets.

Governments in all the developed economies are reviewing the activities of the waste disposal industry carefully, as awareness of environmental issues becomes ever more important and linked to economic growth.

The UK government in particular is reviewing the environmental controls currently in operation for waste processing and it is possible that tougher regulations will be introduced. Industry spokesmen are attempting to argue that current controls are adequate, but the government is also aware of the political advantages of being seen to make tough decisions, since an election is due to be called in the UK within the next year.

Structure of the company and governance

KL is structured as a group of wholly-owned subsidiaries. Each subsidiary specialises in a particular product or service. Each subsidiary is run by a board of executive directors, and the overall company has a board comprising 6 executive and 4 non-executive directors.

KL has in place an audit committee, led by the Finance Director (executive) and including two of the non-executive directors. This committee has responsibility for acting as the primary liaison with the external auditors, as well as contributing to the review of internal controls and risk management.

KL also has a group remuneration committee of non-executive directors, led by the non-executive chairman. This committee meets twice a year to review directors' performance and their remuneration packages.

Financial data

Key data for the group for the most recent year (to 31 December 20X1) is as follows:

Turnover	£850 million
Earnings	£105 million
Shares in issue	250 million
Share price today (21 May 20X2)	331 pence
Weighted Average Cost of Capital for the group	14% (nominal post-tax rate)

Notes on the financial data:

- 75% of the turnover arises in the UK, with 12% in the US, 8% in Europe and the rest elsewhere in the world.
- Foreign sales are always invoiced to customers in their local currency. KL does not tend to hedge the currency risk on these sales for two reasons:
  - the customers generally pay within 30 days of the invoice date
  - the main currencies involved (£, US$ and €) are considered to be stable.
- the share price has fluctuated between 348 pence and 307 pence over the last year.

Company objectives

The company has two stated objectives:

- To increase operating cash flow and dividends per share year-on-year by at least 5%.
- To increase the wealth of our shareholders whilst respecting the interests of our employees, customers and other stakeholders and operating to the highest ethical standards.

End of pre seen material

Unseen case material

Future plans

The directors are considering establishing a new subsidiary company, KL15, to process industrial waste. The subsidiary will require a factory. The directors have identified that the factory used by a long-established subsidiary, KL3, is currently operating at only 50% capacity. This factory could be converted for use by the new subsidiary at a cost of £1.3 million. KL3's annual net (after tax) earnings are £1.5 million. This subsidiary's operations would cease immediately the decision to proceed with KL15 is taken as it will take some months to convert the factory.

The company is aware that the UK government may introduce tougher controls, so the directors of the KL Group plc wish to consider the situation should these tougher controls be introduced. Consequently, two alternative methods of equipping the new subsidiary have been proposed by the company's technical advisers.

The company has sufficient cash available from a recent disposal to finance the capital costs of the new subsidiary under either alternative.

Alternative 1

This alternative will equip the factory to process waste to the highest environmental standards that the government regulations might impose. This would require the purchase of very expensive, specialised machinery from the USA. This machinery would have to be ordered and delivery time is approximately six months, which would coincide with completion of the factory conversion. The cost of this machinery is currently US$12 million but the price of the equipment is likely to rise by 5% over the next six months. If an order is placed immediately (year 0), together with a 50% deposit, the supplier will hold today's price. The balance of the purchase price is payable six months after installation. The current exchange rate, US$ to £1 sterling, is 1.45. Inflation in the USA is forecast to be 4% over the next 12 months. In the UK it is forecast to be 2.5%.

The equipment is not likely to need replacement for at least eight years.

Forecast revenues for KL15 under this equipment alternative are as follows. The probabilities are based on forecasts of the economy in the UK and the main overseas trading areas where the KL Group plc hopes to sell its services.

	Year 1 (6 months of operating)			Year 2			Year 3		
Revenues (£m)	0.5	2.5	3.5	8.5	10.5	12.5	10.5	13.5	16.0
Probability	0.4	0.5	0.1	0.4	0.5	0.1	0.4	0.5	0.1
Expected revenues		1.8			9.9			12.55	

The probabilities of sales for year 2 or 3 and beyond are assumed to be independent of the achievement of the previous year's sales.

The costs are as follows:

- Cash operating costs are expected to have a fixed element of £1.5 million each year starting as soon as the factory starts work, plus a variable element of 30% of sales revenue. A full year's fixed costs will be charged to production in year 1.
- Redundancy payments of £1.2 million will be necessary for staff from the KL3 subsidiary. These would be payable immediately.
- The costs of the factory conversion will be incurred during the six months following the decision to proceed but, for simplicity, it can be assumed that these are paid at the end of year 1.
- The availability of capital allowances and other tax reliefs mean that no tax is likely to be payable until year 4. For year 4 onwards a rough estimate suggests 20% of annual net cash flows (revenue less cash operating costs) will be payable in tax.

Alternative 2

To plan for a continuation of, or modest improvement to, current regulations and produce accordingly. This alternative has greater flexibility as there is a much larger market, worldwide, for processing waste at a lower and therefore much cheaper specification. The capital cost to the KL Group plc would also be much lower at £2.5 million. Equipment for this alternative is readily available in the UK and can be bought when the factory conversion is completed. However, the equipment is likely to need to be replaced in six years' time from the date of purchase.

The revenues shown below are forecast using similar methods as used in Alternative 1. However, sales will be made to a wider range of customers, many in developing countries.

	Year 1 (6 months of operating)			Year 2			Year 3		
Revenues (£m)	3.5	4.5	5.5	4.5	6.5	7.5	8.5	9.5	11.5
Probability	0.2	0.6	0.2	0.2	0.6	0.2	0.2	0.6	0.2
Expected revenues		4.5			6.3			9.7	

Costs are as follows:

- Fixed cash operating costs will be £1.2 million each year; variable costs will be 15% of sales revenue.
- With this alternative, there will be fewer redundancies from KL3 and the associated costs will be only 20% of those for Alternative 1.
- Costs of factory conversion are as Alternative 1.
- Tax relief will be similar to Alternative 1, that is, no tax will be payable until year 4 when tax will become payable at 20% of annual net cash flow (revenue less cash operating costs).

Question 1 – KL Group part a

Calculate net present values for the new subsidiary (KL15) under the two alternatives, using whatever assumptions you think are appropriate. Include brief comments on your assumptions.

(15 marks)

Question 2 – KL Group part b

Assume you are the company's financial manager. Write a report to the directors that

(i) **Discusses how the new subsidiary and the two alternatives might contribute to the attainment of the Group's objectives. Refer to the figures you have calculated in answer to part (a) above where appropriate.**

(10 marks)

(ii) **Analyses and discusses the various types of risk and limitations involved in each alternative.**

(10 marks)

(iii) **Recommends which, if either, of the alternatives should be chosen. Your recommendation should take into account all aspects of your evaluation, as discussed in parts (i) and (ii) of this question.**

(5 marks)

Question 3 – KL Group part c

Option pricing theory was originally developed to apply to share prices. The theory can also be applied to capital investment options, sometimes known as 'real options'.

Discuss the option features involved in KL Group plc's decision and explain, briefly, the benefits of including such options in the investment appraisal process.

(10 marks)

(Total for the three parts of KL Group: 50 marks)

3 Section A Question ErOs

Pre seen material

Company's business and background

ErOs Limited is an unquoted company that specialises in corporate design products, including web page designs. It has been trading for four years and has obtained a reputation for being one of the most innovative and technologically advanced operators in this particular field.

The company was formed in 20W7 by Eric Dee and Oscar George. The company borrowed £50,000 from the bank, secured on the two shareholders' personal property. It is repayable in 20X7. Interest is paid at 10% each year.

When the company was launched, it operated from rented premises and leased much of its computing equipment. It has subsequently bought additional and replacement equipment and other assets such as furniture and fittings. It has also moved premises and has taken out a 25-year lease on office premises that are large enough to allow for significant expansion.

The company now employs 15 people and is planning to recruit additional designers and programmers to handle a large new contract it is hoping to obtain from a supermarket group. ErOs Limited 'outsources' most administrative and accounting functions.

Financial information

Past data

Turnover has grown from £50,000 in the first year of operations to £750,000 last year, the year to 31 March 20X1. However, the company sustained losses in the first three years of operations and made only a small operating profit last year. The apparent poor results are primarily because of high research costs relative to sales. These were written off during the year. Expenditure on research and development will continue but not at such high levels. Other financial data for the year to 31 March 20X1 is as follows:

Shares in issue (ordinary £1 shares)	10,000
Earnings per share	125 pence
Dividend per share	0
Net asset value	£385,000

Note: The net assets of ErOs Limited are the net book values of purchased and/or leased buildings, equipment and vehicles plus net working capital. The book valuations are considered to reflect current realisable values.

Competitor / industry information

This is a niche market and there are relatively few listed companies doing precisely what ErOs Limited does. However, if the definition of the industry is extended to include all companies involved in electronic design and associated products, the following figures are relevant.

P/E ratios:

Industry average	27
Range (individual companies)	12 to 82
Increase in market capitalisation over the past 24 months:	
Industry average	22%
Range (individual companies)	–10% to +2,000%
Cost of equity:	
Industry average (net of tax)	16%
Individual companies	Not available

Share price movements of competitor companies are extremely volatile. Recently, two similar companies, one listed in 20W9 and one unquoted, have gone into liquidation. These and other failures of internet-style companies have caused widespread concern. Calls for improved regulation of 'new economy' companies have been made, largely because of the huge potential debts involved in some cases and suspicions of trading irregularities. Tougher regulatory controls might address the composition of boards of directors and require more substantial trading history before flotation can be considered.

End of pre seen material

Unseen material

Future plans

The company's two owners/directors have been approached by the marketing department of an investment bank and asked whether they have considered using venture capital financing to expand the business. No detailed proposal has been made but the bank has implied that a venture capital company would require a substantial percentage of the equity in return for a large injection of capital. The venture capitalist would want to exit from the investment in four to five years' time.

Neither Eric nor Oscar is wholly convinced that such a large injection of capital is appropriate for the company at the present time. Their objective has been to obtain a stock market listing in two to three years' time if their most optimistic expectations are realised. This would allow them to get some money back on their investment by selling some of their shares at the same time as raising additional funds for the company's expansion. However, the two directors have little financial expertise and have decided to take some independent advice from their accountants before responding to the investment bank.

Assume you are employed by ErOs Limited's firm of accountants. You have been asked to advise Eric and Oscar about the company's current financial situation and the various financing alternatives available to maximise ErOs Limited's growth potential. You have been presented with the following forecast financial information.

Forecasts

The company's forecast sales turnover for the year to 31 March 20X2 is heavily dependent on whether or not the company obtains the new contract from the supermarket group. If it does, forecast sales turnover is £1.8 million for the year. The company's directors think they have a 50% chance of getting this contract. Although this contract will be prestigious for ErOs Limited and should lead to a long-term business relationship, the terms will prevent ErOs Limited from undertaking work for the supermarket's competitors, a number of whom have also shown interest in the company's designs. If ErOs Limited does not get this contract, it will bid for other work which is likely to be less profitable.

Sales turnover for the following year, to 31 March 20X3, is dependent to some extent on the outcome of the year to 31 March 20X2. Estimated turnover and probabilities are as follows:

Estimates for year to 31 March 20X2			*Estimates for year to 31 March 20X3*	
Probability	*Turnover*		*Probability*	*Turnover*
	£000			£000
0.5	1,800	(Outcome 1)	0.8	2,500
			0.2	3,000
0.3	1,200	(Outcome 2)	0.5	1,700
			0.5	1,400
0.2	800	(Outcome 3)	0.5	1000
			0.5	800

Operating costs, inclusive of depreciation, are expected to average 35% of turnover in the year to 31 March 20X2, reducing to 30% in the year to 31 March 20X3 as a result of economies of scale. Interest costs will remain at the present level for both years.

Tax is expected to be payable at 30%. Assume book depreciation equals capital allowances for tax purposes. Also assume that profit after interest and tax equals free cash flow.

Growth in earnings in each of the years to 31 March 20X4 and 20X5 is expected to be 40%, falling to 10% each year after that. This assumes that no new long-term capital is raised. If the firm is to grow at a faster rate, then new financing will be needed.

Question 4 – ErOs part a

Write a report to the directors of ErOs Limited that explains the various methods by which the company might be valued and the alternative types of financing available for expansion. You should include in your report:

(i) **Calculation of a range of values for the company that could be used in negotiation with a venture capitalist, using whatever information is currently available and relevant. Make and state whatever assumptions you think are necessary.**

(15 marks)

(ii) **Discussion of the methods of valuation you have used. Explain, briefly, the relevance of each method to a company such as ErOs Limited.**

(9 marks)

(iii) **Discussion of the advantages and disadvantages of using either venture capital financing to assist with expansion or alternatively a flotation on the stock market in two to three years' time. Include in your discussion likely exit routes for the venture capital company.**

(9 marks)

(iv) **Discussion of alternative types of financial support that could be used by ErOs Limited to assist the company to expand. Advise on the issues that the directors should consider before deciding on the most appropriate type of finance.**

(9 marks)

Question 5 – ErOs part b

Advise the company's directors on what actions / measures the company might take to protect itself against the risk of loss of key staff with technical expertise.

(8 marks)

(Total for the two parts of ErOs: 50 marks)

4 Section A Question Groots

Pre seen material

Business background

The Groots Group (Groots) is a retailer of clothing for women and children. The group started as a single store in France in the early 1900s. The business grew by acquisition of new premises and, occasionally, by buying out small competitors. Expansion outside France started in 1955 and the group now has stores in most European cities. The parent company obtained a listing in 1968, although at that time the founding family still owned the majority of the shares. It is no longer controlled by the family although the grandson of the founder is a board member and owns 2% of the share capital. The company's other directors and senior managers own a further 8% between them.

The style of clothing sold in the Group's stores has changed over the years and its main theme now might be described as 'ethnic'. Most of its goods are manufactured outside Europe, predominantly in India and other parts of Asia.

Corporate objectives

Groots has two financial objectives and one non-financial objective. These are:

- to increase earnings and dividends per share year on year by 5% per annum
- to maintain an optimal debt/equity ratio within the range 25–30%
- to adhere to ethical trading policies and recognise the interests of our various stakeholder groups in all our business activities.

Future strategic plans

The directors of Groots believe they have exhausted possibilities for further expansion in Europe unless they are to diversify into different products such as men's clothing or household goods. They have, therefore, been reviewing opportunities for investment further afield for the past year.

Summary of financial statements

Income statement for the year ended 31 March 20X5	*Groots Group* €millions
Revenue	1,051.5
Operating profit	241.5
Finance costs (including overdraft interest)	48.0
Profit before tax	193.5
Taxation	46.9

Statement of financial position as at 31 March 20X5	
Assets	
Non-current assets	
Property, plant and equipment	895.0
Current assets	
Trade receivables and inventories	275.0
Cash and cash equivalents	45.0
Total assets	1,215.0
Equity and liabilities	
Equity	
Share capital (Nominal value of €1)	245.0
Retained earnings	290.0
Total equity	535.0
Non-current liabilities	
Secured loan stock 7% repayable 20Y2	475.0
Current liabilities	
Trade and other payables	205.0
Total liabilities	680.0
Total equity and liabilities	1,215.0

Other financial information	€
Share price today (25 May 20X5)	6.85
Shares last traded on	19 May 20X5
High-Low share prices in past 12 months	9.25-6.25
Debt value (market) per €100	105.50
Debt last traded on	30 December 20X4

End of pre seen material

Unseen material

Proposed acquisition

The directors of Groots have identified a small group of clothing stores trading in the East Caribbean and parts of South America, Cocomos Limited (Cocomos).

Cocomos is a listed company whose shares trade on an East Caribbean Stock Exchange. It has 18 stores as outlets for its products. Twelve of them are operated by the company itself and six are operated by franchisees. The clothing is at the expensive end of the market and aimed mainly at tourists.

Cocomos has followed a policy of buying locally-made clothing from within the Caribbean, Cuba or Puerto Rico, mainly from small co-operative-type manufacturers. The advantage of this policy is that the cost base is low, allowing for a substantial mark-up to retail. The disadvantage is that the quality is variable. If the acquisition proceeds, Groots would aim to review the product sources to improve the quality and expand the range. One alternative would be to supply the stores from sources in India, which already supply some of the European stores.

The directors of Cocomos and their families own 51% of the shares. A further 15% of the shares are owned by a local pension fund. The remaining 34% are owned by a number of wealthy individual investors, including a few who live most of the time in Europe or Canada.

Cocomos' directors are believed to be interested in opening discussions about a bid from Groots, but the franchisees are likely to be hostile. Although the franchisees are not shareholders, they will use the 'stealing our national assets' argument to agitate the press, local politicians and, ultimately, the local population.

On the basis of published accounts, industry information and discussions with Cocomos' directors, the Groots' directors have forecast the following post-tax cash flows for Cocomos:

Year	*1*	*2*	*3*	*4*
Net cash flows (C$millions)	31.5	37.5	41.5	47.2

Post-tax cash flows beyond year 4 are estimated to grow at 2% per annum.

The cash flows are in real terms; that is they do not include inflation. Groots evaluates all its domestic investment decisions at a nominal, post-tax discount rate of 10%. Cocomos' directors estimate their company's cost of capital as 12%. However, Groots' directors think this rate of 12% does not adequately reflect the risk of Cocomos' cash flows.

Summary of financial statements

Income statement for the year ended 31 March 20X5	*Cocomos Limited Caribbean* $millions
Revenue	215.8
Operating profit	63.6
Finance costs (including overdraft interest)	15.0
Profit before tax	48.6
Taxation	11.5

Balance sheet as at 31 March 20X5

Assets	
Non-current assets	
Property, plant and equipment	245.0
Current assets	
Trade receivables and inventories	88.0
Cash and cash equivalents	12.0
Total assets	345.0
Equity and liabilities	
Equity	
Share capital (Nominal value of C$1)	55.0
Retained earnings	100.0
Total equity	155.0
Non-current liabilities	
Secured loan stock 10% repayable 20X8	135.0
Current liabilities	
Trade and other payables	55.0
Total liabilities	190.0
Total equity and liabilities	345.0

Other financial information	C$
Share price today (25 May 20X5)	6.95
Shares last traded on	31 January 20X5
High-Low share prices in past 12 months	7.50-5.50
Debt value (market) per €100	n/a
Debt last traded on	n/a

Notes:

Exchange rate, interest and inflation rates

The spot exchange rate is C$/€0.30 (that is C$1 = €0.30). Forecast economic data relevant to the Caribbean, the US and the European Common Currency Area (ECCA) are as follows:

	ECCA	*Caribbean*
Risk-free interest rate per annum	3.5%	6.5%
Inflation rate per annum	2.5%	4.5%

You should assume the theory of interest rate parity applies when forecasting exchange rates.

Taxation

Both companies will pay tax at an average of 25% from next year for the foreseeable future. Assume a double taxation treaty is in existence between France and the Caribbean country.

Debt agreement

There is a clause in Cocomos' debt agreement that says the whole of the C$135 million debt is repayable immediately in the event of a successful takeover bid.

Question 6 – Groots part a

(i) **Calculate the maximum price that Groots would be prepared to pay for Cocomos based on the present value in euros of the forecast cash flows. Using appropriate discount rates, you should calculate present value using both the recognised methods of evaluating international investments.**

(7 marks)

(ii) **Comment briefly on why, in theory, these two methods should give the same answer and why, in practice, the answers might be different.**

(3 marks)

(iii) **Calculate the number of shares Groots might need to issue if it offers its own shares in exchange for Cocomos using the higher of the values for the company you have calculated in (i). Comment briefly on your calculations and/or assumptions.**

(4 marks)

Question 7 – Groots part b

Assume you are a financial manager with Groots. Write a report to the directors of Groots which should include the following:

(i) **A recommendation of the maximum price to be offered to Cocomos. You should base your recommendation on the figures you calculated in part (a) above, and other suitable methods of company valuation.**

(ii) **Identify and discuss alternative methods of financing the acquisition and make a recommendation of the most appropriate method in the situation here.**

(iii) **An analysis of strategies for enhancing the value of the combined company following the acquisition.**

(iv) **Advice on the benefits and limitations of a post-completion audit and review in the context of the acquisition.**

(36 marks)

(Total for the two parts of Groots: 50 marks)

Test your understanding answers

Question 1 – KL Group part a

Assumptions:

(i) Timescale: an eight-year timescale will be used to appraise Alternative 1 and a six year timescale for Alternative 2. For simplicity, no cash flows are assumed to arise in six months' time. First year cash flows will be assumed to arise at either t1 or t2 (as stated in the question).

(ii) It is assumed the expected revenues arise for Year 3 will also apply to Year 4 through to 8 for Alternative 1, and Years 4 through to 6 for Alternative 2.

(iii) Any workings will be to the nearest £10,000.

Alternative 1 – Calculations of NPV

	t_0	t_1	t_2	t_3	$t_4 - t_8$
	£m	£m	£m	£m	£m
Expected revenue		1.80	9.90	12.55	12.55
UK operating costs		(2.04)	(4.47)	(5.27)	(5.27)
		(0.24)	5.43	7.28	7.28
Less: Tax (20%)					(1.46)
		(0.24)	5.43	7.28	5.82
Factory conversion		(1.30)			
Equipment (W1)	(4.14)	(4.08)			
Redundancy	(1.20)				
KL opportunity cost		(1.50)	(1.50)	(1.50)	(1.50)
Net after tax cash flow	(5.34)	(7.12)	3.93	5.78	4.32
14% discount factor (W2)	1	0.877	0.769	0.675	2.317
	(5.34)	(6.24)	3.02	3.90	10.00

Net present value = £5.34m

Alternative 2 – Calculations of NPV

	t_0	t_1	t_2	t_3	t_4 - t_6
	£m	£m	£m	£m	£m
Expected revenue		4.50	6.30	9.70	9.70
UK operating costs		(1.88)	(2.15)	(2.66)	(2.66)
		2.62	4.15	7.04	7.04
Less: Tax (20%)					(1.41)
		2.62	4.15	7.04	5.63
Factory conversion		(1.30)			
Equipment	(2.50)				
Redundancy	(0.24)				
KL opportunity cost		(1.50)	(1.50)	(1.50)	(1.50)
Net after tax cash flow	(2.74)	(0.18)	2.65	5.54	4.13
14% discount factor (W3)	1	0.877	0.769	0.675	1.567
	(2.74)	(0.16)	2.04	3.74	6.47

Net present value = £9.35m

Workings

(W1) \$6m / 1.45 = £4.14m
Expected exchange rate in 12 months time is 1.45\$/£ × (1.04/1.025) = 1.47
\$6m / 1.47 = £4.08m

(W2) 4.639 – 2.322 = 2.317 (8 year less 3 year factor)

(W3) 3.889 – 2.322 = 1.567 (6 year less 3 year factor)

Conclusion

Based on the information given in the question and the assumptions made, Alternative 2 appears preferable. Even though the expected time horizons are different, Alternative 2 (the shorter time horizon) has the higher NPV.

Question 2 – KL Group part b

Report to the directors of KL Group plc on the new KL15 subsidiary

This report:

- considers how the new subsidiary and the two alternatives might contribute to the attainment of the Group's objectives
- analyses and discusses the various types of risk and limitations involved in each
- recommends a preferred alternative.

(i) Attainment of group's objectives

Neither alternative will attain an increase in operating cash flow by anything approaching 5% in the early years of the project (Alternative 1 produces an increase in turnover in Year 1 of 1% and negative cash flows in Year 2). It is therefore unlikely that either will have an impact on the dividend.

Both alternatives produce small positive expected net present values, and therefore an increase in shareholder wealth is expected. However, this is very small in relation to the current value of the company (250m shares at £3.31) and the share price is unlikely to rise by more than just a few pence. Even this is based on the assumption that the alternatives will generate their expected NPV's. The probability distributions provided for revenues indicate significant downside risk, and there must be a high probability that neither alternative will generate a positive NPV.

However, compared with the continuation of KL3, it may be felt that they offer a greater likelihood of maintaining full employment and customer satisfaction.

(ii) Risks and limitations

Risks may be categorised as follows:

(1) Financial

- The use of the company's existing WACC may be inappropriate as it does not necessarily reflect the systematic risks involved in each alternative. It would be useful to investigate the possibility of using the CAPM to provide an alternative appraisal.

- There is an element of exchange rate risk with both Alternative 1 and 2, in the latter's case due to many customers in developing countries.
- The possible degree of dispersion around the expected revenues should be examined, with particular reference to the downside risk of both alternatives.

(2) Operational, Commercial and Political

- The equipment involved in Alternative 2 may become unusable due to changes in current regulations. Although Alternative 1 has the lower NPV, it may be considered to be the least risky option when considering worst case scenarios.
- With Alternative 1, however, there are fewer customers, although many with Alternative 2 are in developing countries and both foreign exchange and audit risk will need careful evaluation.
- Political risks are involved not only with Alternative 2 (customers in developing countries), but also with Alternative 1 regarding the political uncertainty of the regulatory issue.

(iii) Recommendations

Alternative 2 is expected to increase shareholder wealth by a greater amount, but is also (on balance) probably the more risky. It also involves making fewer staff redundant, although Alternative 1 contributes more to environmental issues.

Neither alternative provides outstanding contributions to the range of corporate objectives, and before a final decision is reached, further alternatives/possibilities should be sought.

Question 3 – KL Group part c

There are three possible capital investment (real) options that may be relevant to KL Group's decision regarding KL15.

(i) The abandonment option

Unlike shares, if a capital project does not produce the expected returns, the decision cannot be reversed, but it may be abandoned or truncated.

In the case of KL15, Alternative 2 is the more attractive in this respect as the equipment can be purchased at any time. With Alternative 1 the company can defer the second instalment, but if abandonment takes place would have incurred 50% of the outlay.

(ii) The timing option

This is the 'wait and see' option. This views the decision as a call option which is shortly to expire on the new plant's outlay. The option will be exercised if a positive NPV is expected.

In this case delaying the decision by a year until the outcome of the government's review of environmental issues is known provides a valuable option.

(iii) The strategic investment option

This mainly relates to the availability of follow-on-opportunities relating to the new investment in technology. Investments may offer significant 'spin-off' benefits, or greater flexibility.

Question 4 – ErOs part a

REPORT

To: The directors of ErOs Ltd

From: An Accountant

Date: X – X – XX

Subject: Valuation of the company and methods of financing the expansion

Introduction

As requested, this report discusses:

(i) possible methods for valuing the company

(ii) the relevance of each method

(iii) the use of either venture capital financing or a flotation to assist expansion

(iv) alternative types of finance that could be used to fund expansion.

Examination tip: Present your answer using the four sections required in the question, so it is clear what part you are answering.

(i) **Possible methods for valuing the company**

ErOs is an unquoted company so there is no current share price that can be looked at to determine the value of the whole company when negotiating with a venture capitalist who may be interested in buying a large stake in the company.

There are therefore three possible approaches to determining the current value of the company:

- net assets basis – this values the whole company at £385,000
- earnings basis – this values the whole company at £17.4m
- discounted cash flow basis – this values the whole company at nearly £22m.

An appendix to this report contains the detailed workings deriving these numbers.

(ii) The relevance of each method of valuation

The net assets basis is almost irrelevant to a company such as ErOs. ErOs specialises in corporate design, so its assets will be principally its skilled employees and its intellectual capital which are not included in a traditional historical cost balance sheet. If the company were about to be put into liquidation, then the realisable value of the identified assets would be of interest. However, ErOs appears to be a going concern so the net assets valuation of the company is of little relevance, although it might be considered to be the absolute minimum value that could be attributed to the company.

The earnings basis valuation is a bit of a 'stab in the dark', since it requires the combination of two uncertain figures, the typical annual earnings and the typical P/E ratio. In principle the P/E ratio encapsulates the prospects of growth, so we should select last year's earnings, adjusted for any one-off items included. However, the earnings of ErOs are expected to grow rapidly so, using last year's earnings and the sector average P/E produces a very low company valuation, less even than the net assets basis, so this approach cannot be valid.

The amended approach shown in the appendix combines next year's expected earnings with the sector average P/E ratio, producing a valuation of £17.4m which is more credible. However, using the sector average P/E ratio takes no account of the specific circumstances of the company with its attractive growth prospects.

A common valuation basis to use is the dividend valuation basis, where ownership of a company is valued at the present value of the dividends to be received from owning shares in the company. Since ErOs as a company does not pay dividends (as is usual for 'new economy' companies in their early years), such a basis cannot be used. Instead we can use the DCF basis which values the company at the present value of the net cash inflows that the company itself will generate.

The DCF basis values the company at nearly £22m. Although the calculations include some simplifying assumptions (e.g. that capital allowances equal book depreciation), it is probably the most accurate basis of the three considered. It takes into account the specific circumstances expected for ErOs in a way that the other two bases did not.

In the final analysis, the value of a company is the value agreed between the seller and the purchaser. Any estimate from any basis, such as the £22m above, can be input into the negotiations, but the value agreed after the negotiations could be very different from this, depending on the purchaser's enthusiasm to buy and the seller's enthusiasm to sell.

(iii) **The use of venture capital financing or a flotation**

The company is considering various methods to finance the future expansion in operations, particularly if the new contract with the supermarket group is won.

One option would be venture capital financing. The venture capital organisation would buy a substantial proportion of the company's shares and plan to sell out its investment in four to five years' time. The advantage of this approach is the flexibility of the arrangement; the company remains unquoted and so does not have to comply with the detailed ongoing rules required for listed companies by the Stock Exchange. The question suggests that tougher regulatory controls are likely to be introduced soon, which would further tie the hands of the directors. The disadvantages are the loss of control to the venture capital company and the high returns that the venture capital company would expect to withdraw from its investment.

After the four to five years holding period, the venture capital company would seek to exit from its investment. Possible exit routes are a flotation at that time (either by a placing or an offer for sale) or a trade sale of the company to another company (possibly another venture capital company). If the founders of the company are unhappy to lose long-term control of ErOs, they could arrange a call option for themselves so that they have first refusal to buy the company when the venture capitalists want to withdraw.

An alternative method of raising funds for expansion is flotation in two to three years' time. A market capitalisation of around £22m is a bit low for a listing on the main market, so the company should instead be seeking a quotation on the Alternative Investment Market (AIM). The advantage is that the current shareholders need not lose control of the company, since only 40%, say, of the company's shares could be sold to the market. A further advantage is that an objective share price at any time will be provided by the market, reducing the need for protracted negotiations on possible future sales of shares.

The disadvantages of a flotation are the upfront costs and the need to comply with the detailed stock exchange rules in the future. The stock exchange also manages the number and type of companies that can join the market. If there are many other similar design companies that wish to float, then ErOs may have to wait in a 'queue' before it is allowed to join.

(iv) **Alternative types of finance that could be used**

So far I have only discussed two possible financing methods: venture capital financing and a flotation in two to three years' time. There are several further alternatives that should be considered:

- Issue new shares to private investors. If the prospects for the company are as good as currently expected, private investors may be interested in buying small parcels of shares, without wanting to control the company. It may be necessary to start paying dividends to make the investment more attractive.
- Increase the bank loan. Since interest rates are currently very low, now may be a good time to increase the company's borrowings from the current modest total of £50,000. Perhaps at the same time the current loan could be refinanced at a rate less than 10%. Security could be offered on the company's tangible assets (valued at £385,000 net asset value) or possibly on an equity stake in the company.
- Carry out an immediate flotation on the AIM. Rather than wait two or three years, a flotation could be carried out as soon as possible. If sentiment in the market is currently positive towards this type of company, there is no reason to delay. The company could float now and embark on its expansion plans straight away.
- Research the market for new revenue streams. Many internet-based companies are short of cash currently, so are unwilling to buy services that require an immediate cash outlay. If ErOs were willing to accept payments for new web designs over a number of years rather than all upfront, it may win a lot of new work. These debts could then be factored to give ErOs immediate access to the cash.

When deciding on the most appropriate type of finance, you must first be clear in your own minds about the factors that are important to you. Is keeping control of the company in the long-term important? Would you mind having to comply with the regulatory rules of the stock exchange? Do you need cash personally in the short-term (in which case an immediate flotation would be advisable)?

Subject to these factors, you should consider:

- the costs of each type of finance
- the current state of market sentiment towards 'new economy' companies
- the details of the stricter regulations expected to be imposed on such companies.

Conclusion

This report has tried to value ErOs Ltd as a company operating as a going concern. Three common bases of valuation have reached values ranging from £385,000 to £22m. Since ErOs is a relatively new company which is growing fast, valuation at any particular point in time is difficult. The expansion path will require new sources of finance to be found, especially if the large contract with the supermarket group is won. A range of financing methods has been described in this report.

APPENDIX

Alternative methods of valuing the company

(i) **Net assets basis**

At 31 March 20X1 (the latest financial year-end), the total net asset value of the company was given as £385,000. Since the book values of the net assets reflect the realisable values, no adjustments are necessary to this total.

(ii) **Earnings basis**

Value of the company = Typical annual earnings × Appropriate P/E ratio

The latest annual earnings we have are for the year ended 31 March 20X1, when the earnings were 10,000 shares × £1.25 earnings per share = £12,500. We are not told about any unusual one-off items included in last year's accounts, so we can take our best estimate of the company's maintainable annual earnings to be £12,500.

Selecting an appropriate price-earnings ratio is more judgemental since individual companies in this sector are so diverse, so a range of possible P/E ratios can be considered:

Possible P/E ratio				*Company valuation*
				£
Lowest in sector	=	12	} × Earnings 12,500	150,000
Average in sector	=	27		337,500
Highest in sector	=	82		1,025,000

These valuations seem very modest compared to the net asset value which is normally well below the earnings valuation. Since this company is expected to grow rapidly in future years, the use of last year's earnings figure as the estimate of future earnings is perhaps invalid. It would be better to use an estimate of next year's earnings:

	£000
Estimated turnover next year	
(0.5 × 1,800) + (0.3 × 1,200) + (0.2 × 800)	1,420
Operating costs (35% × 1,420)	(497)
Interest (10% × £50,000)	(5)
Profit before tax	918
Tax (30% × 918)	(275)
Earnings	643

This is much higher than last year's earnings. Using the average P/E ratio for the sector, an earnings basis valuation for the whole company would be: £643,000 × 27 = £17.4m.

(iii) **Discounted cash flow (DCF) basis**

This method values the company at the present value of the net cash inflows that the company will generate. We have already calculated the expected inflow for next year as £643,000. We must now carry out similar calculations for the year to 31 March 20X3, 20X4 and 20X5, and for 20X6 to infinity.

For 20X3:

	£000
Expected turnover 0.5 [(0.8 × 2,500) + (0.2 × 3,000)] + 0.3 [(0.5 × 1,700) + (0.5 × 1,400)] + 0.2 [(0.5 × 1,000) + (0.5 × 800)]	1,945
Operating costs (30% × 1,945)	(584)
Interest (as before, 10% × 50)	(5)
Profit before tax	1,356
Tax (30% × 1,356)	(407)
	949

We can now carry out the DCF analysis using the discount rate provided of 16% (net of tax).

Time		*Cash flow*	*Discount factor*	*Present value*
		£000	*at 16%*	*£000*
1		643	0.862	554
2		949	0.743	705
3	949 × 1.4 =	1,329	0.641	852
4	1,329 × 1.4 =	1,861	0.552	1,027
5 to ∞	1,861 × 1.1 =	2,047	$\frac{1}{0.16 - 0.10} \times 0.552 = 9.2$	18,832
				21,970

The DCF basis values the company at £21.97m, i.e. very nearly £22m.

Tutorial note

The calculation of the discount factor for time 5 to infinity needs some careful thought. An annuity of £1 growing at 10% pa with a cost of capital of 16% has a present value of:

$$\frac{1}{k - g} = \frac{1}{0.16 - 0.10} = 16.667$$

Starting the annuity at time 5 rather than time 1 will decrease the present value by a factor of 0.552, the discount factor for time 4 given an interest rate of 16%.

Question 5 – ErOs part b

ErOs Ltd is a design company dependent on the skills of its employees to generate the revenues required. Such a company would be severely damaged if its key staff were to become unavailable, for example through sickness or death, or if they left to join a competitor company or to set up on their own in competition.

The following actions should be taken:

- Insurance can be bought to provide compensation if a key member of staff falls ill or dies. Such 'key person insurance' can be expensive and will necessitate medical inspections and tests which can be time consuming and involve the irreplaceable member of staff having to visit a doctor during working hours, when the whole point of the exercise is that that employee should be present at the company.
- The best way to retain employees is to pay them well and offer them good working conditions. Most people are perfectly happy to continue to work for an organisation that treats them well. Incentives such as future bonuses or share option schemes can help to tie in any waverers, but the basic rule remains: treat your employees well and they will continue to work happily for you.

- It is possible to try to bully employees by including terms in their contract of employment that they are not permitted to work in competition with the company if they leave, but:
  - such terms are often not enforceable by law, and
  - they go against the 'treat employees well' philosophy.

Better results will usually be achieved by the carrot (e.g. decent pay, share options, attractive perks) rather than the stick (e.g. threatening employees, restrictive covenants in contracts of employment).

Question 6 – Groots part a

(i) There are two possible methods of evaluating overseas investments:

- discount the foreign cash flows using the foreign cost of capital, then translate this into the home currency
- translate the foreign cash flows into the home currency, then discount these flows using the home cost of capital.

Both these methods are shown below.

Method 1

Year	*1*	*2*	*3*	*4*	5+
Real cash flow (C$m)	31.50	37.50	41.50	47.20	
Inflated at 4.5% p.a.	32.92	40.95	47.36	56.29	
Discount factor at 13% (see Note 1)	0.885	0.783	0.693	0.613	
Present value	29.13	32.06	32.82	34.51	481 (Note 2)

Total present value of cash flows = C$609.52m

Translated at spot value = 609.52 ×0.30 = 182.86m

Deduct debt that must be repaid immediately C$135 ×0.30 = €40.5m

∴ Maximum price to pay for equity = 182.86 – 40.5 = €142.36m

Notes

(1) Groots' directors believe that Cocomos' cost of capital is a bit higher than 12%, so a cost of capital of 13% has been used.

(2) Real cash flow in Year 5 = 47.2 × 1.02 = C$48.14m

Inflated at 4.5% = 48.14 × 1.045 = C$50.31 m

The annual cash flow will grow at 2% p.a. in real terms, and 1.02 × 1.045 = 6.59% p.a. in money terms, from Year 5.

(1) PV of this perpetuity

$$\text{PV of this perpetuity} = \frac{50.31 \times 0.631}{1.132 - 1.0659} = \text{C\$481m}$$

Method 2

Year	*1*	*2*	*3*	*4*	*5+*
Real cash flow (C$m)	31.50	37.50	41.50	47.20	
Inflated at 4.5% p.a.	32.92	40.95	47.36	56.29	
Exchange rate (Note 1)	0.292	0.283	0.275	0.268	
Cash flow (€m)	9.61	11.59	13.02	15.09	
Discount factor at 10%	0.909	0.826	0.751	0.683	
Present value	8.74	9.57	9.78	10.31	112 (Note 2)

Total present value of cash flows = €150.4m

Deduct debt that must be repaid immediately = €40.5m

∴ Maximum price to pay for equity = 150.4 – 40.5 = €109.9m

Notes

(1) We are told to use interest rate parity to forecast future exchange rates.

	C$1 = €
Spot rate	0.300
In one year	$0.300 \times \frac{1.035}{1.065} = 0.292$
In two years	$0.300 \times \left(\frac{1.035}{1.065}\right)^2 = 0.283$
In three years	$0.300 \times \left(\frac{1.035}{1.065}\right)^3 = 0.275$
In four years	$0.300 \times \left(\frac{1.035}{1.065}\right)^4 = 0.268$

(2) As above, money cash flow in Year 5 = C$50.31m

$$\text{Exchange rate in Year 5} = 0.268 \times \frac{1.035}{1.065} = 0.260$$

So, money cash flow in Year 5 = 0.26 × 50.31 = €13.08m.

The annual cash flow will grow at the 2% annual real rate, from Year 5.

$$\text{PV of this perpetuity} = \frac{13.08 \times 0.683}{1.1 - 1.03587} = €111.67\text{m, rounded say to } €112\text{ m.}$$

Tutorial note

This is an extremely complicated and time-consuming requirement. In the exam you should have dealt with the cash flows for years 1 to 4 first for both methods. This should have been enough to pass comfortably! Only if you had time leftover (very unlikely) should you have attempted years 5 onwards.

The above answer follows CIMA's official suggested approach to give you an idea of what was expected. However, this does not allow the two methods to reconcile as certain aspects have been simplified (!). To get the two approaches to agree requires an even more complicated approach:

Method 1:

- Instead of assuming a rate of 13%, you could adjust Groot's normal discount rate of 10% using interest rate parity: 1 + discount rate = 1.10 × (1.065/1.035) = 1.1319, giving a more accurate figure of 13.2%.
- This would give a revised total present value of cash flows of C$595m and a value for equity of **€138m.**

Method 2:

- The Euro cashflows for time 5 onwards need to incorporate three aspects of growth:
  - real growth at 2% pa
  - inflation at 4.5% pa
  - the exchange rate continuing to 'grow' by a factor (1.035)/(1.065).
- This gives an overall growth rate factor of 1.02 × 1.045 × 1.035/1.065 = 1.03587…and a growth rate of 3.59%.
- This gives a revised PV for years 5 onwards of €139m and a final value for equity of **€139m**.
- The difference is now due to rounding.

(ii) In theory, the two methods illustrated above should give the same answer, since they are both trying to calculate the same value – the present value of a series of foreign currency cash flows. In practice, inefficiencies and imperfections in the market will cause differences.

For example, we have used the interest rate parity theory to forecast future exchange rates. If we had used the purchasing power parity theory, we would have obtained a different (but similar) set of forecast exchange rates.

In Method 1 we have arbitrarily increased the 12% cost of capital believed to be valid by the Cocomos directors, and used 13% in the discounting exercise. We could have gone along with the 12% figure, or used a greater risk premium.

In method 2 we have used 10% as the appropriate discount rate, but this relates to **domestic** investment decisions that Groots makes, so may need to be adjusted to reflect an international investment project such as is being considered.

(ii) The higher of the two values calculated in part (i) is a maximum price of €142.36m to pay for the equity of Cocomos.

There are 55m shares of Cocomos in issue.

Therefore Groots should be prepared to pay up to $\frac{139}{55}$ = €2.59 per share of Cocomos,

offering 2.59 / 0.3 = C$8.63 per share in the local currency.

Groots' shares are currently trading at €6.85 each.
To offer a value of €142.36m,

Groots needs to issue a further $\frac{139}{6.85}$ = 20.8 million new shares.

This is a substantial number of new shares in comparison to the 245m shares of Groots currently in issue, and is likely to require shareholder approval before the issue can be made.

Question 7 – Groots part b

REPORT

To: The Board of Directors of the Groots Group

From: Financial Manager

Date: 25 May 20X5

Subject: Possible takeover of Cocomos

Introduction

The Group has identified Cocomos Ltd as a possible takeover target. This report considers four aspects of this possible acquisition process:

- the maximum price to be offered
- the methods of financing the acquisition
- enhancing the post-acquisition value of the Group
- the role of a post-completion audit and review.

These four aspects are dealt with in turn below.

(i) **The maximum price to be offered**

There are a number of different valuation methods that can be applied to Cocomos. Four possibilities are as follows:

	Company in total	*Per share*
	€m	€
Net asset value	46.5	0.85
Market value of equity	114.7	2.09
Earnings basis	127.4	2.32
Valuing future cash flows (from part (a))	142.4	2.59

The workings for these amounts are as below:

Net assets = C$155m

= 0.3 × 155m = €46.5m at the current spot rate

Market value of equity = 55m × C$6.95

= C$382.25m

= 0.3 × 382.25m = €114.675m

Applying the Groots P/E ratio to the Cocomos earnings, an earnings valuation

$$= \frac{6.85 \times 245}{193.5m - 46.9m} \times (48.6m - 11.5m) \times 0.30$$

= €127.4m

One would usually expect to have to offer a premium over the current market value when making an offer for shares. The current market price is €2.09 per share, but it must be noted that the shares appear illiquid since there have been no shares traded since January 2005. Thus there is less importance in offering a premium over the market price than if the shares were traded every day.

If a friendly agreed bid can be negotiated, then a bid of around 10% above the latest share price should be offered as an opening bid, say €2.30 per share. Some modest increase could be ultimately agreed, up to say €2.40 per share.

However, if the franchisees start agitating, then a hostile bid may have to be launched. In theoretical terms, the maximum price that we offer should be the net present value of the cash flows arising from the acquisition, around €2.60 per share. Any premium above this would have to be matched by synergistic savings in addition to those already identified. If the local pension fund or individual investors look likely to be influenced by the franchisees' campaigning, then we can always walk away from this deal and look again at expansion possibilities in Europe.

(ii) **Methods of financing the acquisition**

If an agreed bid for, say €129m is decided upon, then we must finance this deal. We must decide between issuing shares to the vendors, or paying cash, or some combination of the two.

If we issue shares, then $\frac{129m}{6.85}$ = 19m shares (approximately) would be required.

This would need shareholder approval. It would have the positive effect of reducing our balance sheet gearing ratio, but the negative effect of reducing the reported EPS in the short term, until the benefits of the acquisition are fully realised.

If we offer cash, this would have the effect of increasing our gearing ratio.

Current gearing ratio (at market values) $= \frac{\text{Debt}}{\text{Debt + Equity}}$

$$= \frac{475 \times 1.055}{(475 \times 1.055) + (245 \times 6.85)}$$

= 23%, which is not excessive.

After the acquisition, we would have used up our €45m cash balance in paying off the Cocomos loan stock, so would have to raise the entire €129m in new debt.

New gearing ratio $= \frac{\text{New debt}}{\text{New debt + New equity}}$

New debt = (475 × 1.055) + 129 = 630.1

New equity = (245 × 6.85) + NPV of the acquisition

= 1,678.25 + 142.4

= 1,820.65

∴ New gearing ratio $= \frac{630.1}{630.1 + 1{,}817.25}$

= 26%, which is still not excessive.

So it appears that we can afford to offer cash without significantly increasing our risk profile.

In practice, we can consider whether the current shareholders of Cocomos would prefer shares or cash. The local pensions fund is unlikely to want shares in a European company. Its liabilities are in Caribbean dollars, so it will aim to hold assets denominated in C$. The individual shareholders who live in Europe may be interested in shares in a European company, but on the whole the shareholders will prefer cash.

In conclusion, we should offer a share exchange with a cash alternative, and be prepared for a majority of the shareholders to elect for the cash alternative.

(iii) **Enhancing post-acquisition value**

There are a number of strategies that we could follow to enhance the value of the combined company following the acquisition:

– We should review each of the operating units run by Cocomos to identify whether they should be disposed of in full, whether they should be kept but with cost savings imposed, or whether surplus assets can be identified for disposal. If the franchisees are going to be continuing troublemakers, they should be sold at the earliest opportunity.

– Deciding to finance the acquisition by debt and diversifying our range of activities should reduce our weighted average cost of capital, which in itself should increase the value of the combined group.

– In accordance with the ideas of management theorists, we should closely communicate our plans and intentions for the group with all the Cocomos stakeholders. Pinning a memorandum to the office notice board is not enough. Many acquisitions fail because the acquired workforce does not feel valued by the acquiring management. The geographical distance involved in the Cocomos acquisition will add to this problem. To maintain high staff morale, there should be regular exchange of staff between Cocomos and Groots, so that each can learn from the other.

– We should ensure that Cocomos is happy with our corporate objectives. Objectives must be consistent across the group. In particular Cocomos must commit to the group belief in ethical trading policies.

– The problem of variable quality in the Caribbean output must be addressed. If the solution is to source more product from India, then so be it, but difficult decisions must be taken.

(iv) **Post-completion audit and review**

A post-completion audit (PCA) or post-completion review (PCR) can be defined as 'an objective and independent appraisal of the measure of success of a capital expenditure project in progressing the business as planned' (CIMA *Official Terminology*). The appraisal should cover the implementation of the project from authorisation to commissioning and its technical and commercial performance after commissioning. The information provided can also be used by management as feedback which aids the implementation and control of future projects.

Success can only be 'measured' if it can be judged in terms of criteria that are measurable. Thus, at the outset of a project, the objectives of the project should be stated in numerical amounts, and these plans should be compared with the actual amounts as part of the PCA.

The benefit of a PCA in the context of the planned Cocomos acquisition would be:

- It enables Groots management to monitor whether the actual post-acquisition results of Cocomos are as was planned. If results are worse than expected, management should take prompt action to remedy the problem. If results are unsatisfactory, and the causes cannot be remedied, then Groots should consider exiting from the investment.
- It assists managers of Groots in making future investment appraisals. Mistakes will always be made, but the sign of a good manager is that they learn from their mistakes. Experience gained in auditing previous investment decisions should lead to better decisions being made in the future.
- Knowing that a PCA will be carried out in due course will prevent the Groots managers from making over-optimistic assumptions in their evaluation of Cocomos. They know that they will be held to account for any decisions that they take.

The disadvantages of a PCA in the context of the planned Cocomos acquisition will be:

- The whole process can be expensive in terms of the management time involved.
- It requires accurate data to have been collected throughout the life of the investment project, a period of some years.
- Some managers may believe that a PCA is a method of pinning blame for poor decisions on particular individuals, rather than being a value-adding activity to learn from past mistakes and improve performance in the future.

Conclusion

This report has considered four aspects of the possible acquisition of Cocomos. An initial bid of around €125m should be made, offering shares in Groots but with a cash alternative. If the acquisition proceeds, then active steps should be taken to identify possible cost savings and to maximise the post-acquisition value of the group. A post-completion audit could usefully be carried out in due course to confirm that the benefits anticipated from the acquisition are being realised.

Signed: Financial Manager

CIMA

Pillar F

F3 – Financial Strategy

Specimen Examination Paper

Instructions to candidates

You are allowed three hours to answer this question paper.
You are allowed 20 minutes reading time **before the examination begins** during which you should read the question paper and, if you wish, highlight and/or make notes on the question paper. However, you will **not** be allowed, **under any circumstances**, to open the answer book and start writing or use your calculator during this reading time.
You are strongly advised to carefully read ALL the question requirements before attempting the question concerned (that is all parts and/or sub-questions). The requirements for all questions are contained in a dotted box.
ALL answers must be written in the answer book. Answers or notes written on the question paper will **not** be submitted for marking.
Answer ALL compulsory questions in Section A on page 9.
Answer TWO of the three questions in Section B on pages 10 to 16.
Maths Tables are provided on pages 17 to 21.
The list of verbs as published in the syllabus is given for reference on the inside back cover of this question paper.
Write your candidate number, the paper number and examination subject title in the spaces provided on the front of the answer book. Also write your contact ID and name in the space provided in the right hand margin and seal to close.
Tick the appropriate boxes on the front of the answer book to indicate which questions you have answered.

F3 – Financial Strategy

Power Utilities

Pre-seen Case Study

Background
Power Utilities (PU) is located in a democratic Asian country. Just over 12 months ago, the former nationalised Electricity Generating Corporation (EGC) was privatised and became PU. EGC was established as a nationalised industry many years ago. Its home government at that time had determined that the provision of the utility services of electricity generation production should be managed by boards that were accountable directly to Government. In theory, nationalised industries should be run efficiently, on behalf of the public, without the need to provide any form of risk related return to the funding providers. In other words, EGC, along with other nationalised industries was a non-profit making organisation. This, the Government claimed at the time, would enable prices charged to the final consumer to be kept low.

Privatisation of EGC
The Prime Minister first announced three years ago that the Government intended to pursue the privatisation of the nationalised industries within the country. The first priority was to be the privatisation of the power generating utilities and EGC was selected as the first nationalised industry to be privatised. The main purpose of this strategy was to encourage public subscription for share capital. In addition, the Government's intention was that PU should take a full and active part in commercial activities such as raising capital and earning higher revenue by increasing its share of the power generation and supply market by achieving growth either organically or through making acquisitions. This, of course, also meant that PU was exposed to commercial pressures itself, including satisfying the requirements of shareholders and becoming a potential target for take-over. The major shareholder, with a 51% share, would be the Government. However, the Minister of Energy has recently stated that the Government intends to reduce its shareholding in PU over time after the privatisation takes place.

Industry structure
PU operates 12 coal-fired power stations across the country and transmits electricity through an integrated national grid system which it manages and controls. It is organised into three regions, Northern, Eastern and Western. Each region generates electricity which is sold to 10 private sector electricity distribution companies which are PU's customers.

The three PU regions transmit the electricity they generate into the national grid system. A shortage of electricity generation in one region can be made up by taking from the national grid. This is particularly important when there is a national emergency, such as exceptional weather conditions.

The nationalised utility industries, including the former EGC, were set up in a monopolistic position. As such, no other providers of these particular services were permitted to enter the market within the country. Therefore, when EGC was privatised and became PU it remained the sole generator of electricity in the country. The electricity generating facilities, in the form of the 12 coal-fired power stations, were all built over 15 years ago and some date back to before EGC came into being.

The 10 private sector distribution companies are the suppliers of electricity to final users including households and industry within the country, and are not under the management or control of PU. They are completely independent companies owned by shareholders.

The 10 private sector distribution companies serve a variety of users of electricity. Some, such as AB, mainly serve domestic users whereas others, such as DP, only supply electricity to a few industrial clients. In fact, DP has a limited portfolio of industrial customers and 3 major clients, an industrial conglomerate, a local administrative authority and a supermarket chain. DP finds these clients costly to service.

Structure of PU
The structure of PU is that it has a Board of Directors headed by an independent Chairman and a separate Managing Director. The Chairman of PU was nominated by the Government at the time the announcement that EGC was to be privatised was made. His background is that he is a former Chairman of an industrial conglomerate within the country. There was no previous Chairman of EGC which was managed by a Management Board, headed by the Managing Director. The former EGC Managing Director retired on privatisation and a new Managing Director was appointed.

The structure of PU comprises a hierarchy of many levels of management authority. In addition to the Chairman and Managing Director, the Board consists of the Directors of each of the Northern, Eastern and Western regions, a Technical Director, the Company Secretary and the Finance Director. All of these except the Chairman are the Executive Directors of PU. The Government also appointed seven Non Executive Directors to PU's Board. With the exception of the Company Secretary and Finance Director, all the Executive Directors are qualified electrical engineers. The Chairman and Managing Director of PU have worked hard to overcome some of the inertia which was an attitude that some staff had developed within the former EGC. PU is now operating efficiently as a private sector company. There have been many staff changes at a middle management level within the organisation.

Within the structure of PU's headquarters, there are five support functions; engineering, finance (which includes PU's Internal Audit department), corporate treasury, human resource management (HRM) and administration, each with its own chief officers, apart from HRM. Two Senior HRM Officers and Chief Administrative Officer report to the Company Secretary. The Chief Accountant and Corporate Treasurer each report to the Finance Director. These functions, except Internal Audit, are replicated in each region, each with its own regional officers and support staff. Internal Audit is an organisation wide function and is based at PU headquarters.

Regional Directors of EGC
The Regional Directors all studied in the field of electrical engineering at the country's leading university and have worked together for a long time. Although they did not all attend the university at the same time, they have a strong belief in the quality of their education. After graduation from university, each of the Regional Directors started work at EGC in a junior capacity and then subsequently gained professional electrical engineering qualifications. They believe that the experience of working up through the ranks of EGC has enabled them to have a clear understanding of EGC's culture and the technical aspects of the industry as a whole. Each of the Regional Managers has recognised the changed environment that PU now operates within, compared with the former EGC, and they are now working hard to help PU achieve success as a private sector electricity generator. The Regional Directors are well regarded by both the Chairman and Managing Director, both in terms of their technical skill and managerial competence.

Governance of EGC
Previously, the Managing Director of the Management Board of EGC reported to senior civil servants in the Ministry of Energy. There were no shareholders and ownership of the Corporation rested entirely with the Government. That has now changed. The Government holds 51% of the shares in PU and the Board of Directors is responsible to the shareholders but, inevitably, the Chairman has close links directly with the Minister of Energy, who represents the major shareholder.

The Board meetings are held regularly, normally weekly, and are properly conducted with full minutes being taken. In addition, there is a Remuneration Committee, an Audit Committee and an Appointments Committee, all in accordance with best practice. The model which has been used is the Combined Code on Corporate Governance which applies to companies which have full listing status on the London Stock Exchange. Although PU is not listed on the London Stock Exchange, the principles of the Combined Code were considered by the Government to be appropriate to be applied with regard to the corporate governance of the company.

Currently, PU does not have an effective Executive Information System and this has recently been raised at a Board meeting by one of the non-executive directors because he believes this inhibits the function of the Board and consequently is disadvantageous to the governance of PU.

Remuneration of Executive Directors
In order to provide a financial incentive, the Remuneration Committee of PU has agreed that the Executive Directors be entitled to performance related pay, based on a bonus scheme, in addition to their fixed salary and health benefits.

Capital market
PU exists in a country which has a well developed capital market relating both to equity and loan stock funding. There are well established international institutions which are able to provide funds and corporate entities are free to issue their own loan stock in accordance with internationally recognised principles. PU is listed on the country's main stock exchange.

Strategic opportunity
The Board of PU is considering the possibility of vertical integration into electricity supply and has begun preliminary discussion with DP's Chairman with a view to making an offer for DP. PU's Board is attracted by DP's strong reputation for customer service but is aware, through press comment, that DP has received an increase in complaints regarding its service to customers over the last year. When the former EGC was a nationalised business, break-downs were categorised by the Government as "urgent", when there was a danger to life, and "non-urgent" which was all others. Both the former EGC and DP had a very high success rate in meeting the government's requirements that a service engineer should attend the urgent break-down within 60 minutes. DP's record over this last year in attending urgent break-downs has deteriorated seriously and if PU takes DP over, this situation would need to improve.

Energy consumption within the country and Government drive for increased efficiency and concern for the environment
Energy consumption has doubled in the country over the last 10 years. As PU continues to use coal-fired power stations, it now consumes most of the coal mined within the country.

The Minister of Energy has indicated to the Chairman of PU that the Government wishes to encourage more efficient methods of energy production. This includes the need to reduce production costs. The Government has limited resources for capital investment in energy production and wishes to be sure that future energy production facilities are more efficient and effective than at present.

The Minister of Energy has also expressed the Government's wish to see a reduction in harmful emissions from the country's power stations. (The term harmful emissions in this context, refers to pollution coming out of electricity generating power stations which damage the environment.)

One of PU's non-executive directors is aware that another Asian country is a market leader in coal gasification which is a fuel technology that could be used to replace coal for power generation. In the coal gasification process, coal is mixed with oxygen and water vapour under pressure, normally underground, and then pumped to the surface where the gas can be used in power stations. The process significantly reduces carbon dioxide emissions although it is not widely used at present and not on any significant commercial scale.

Another alternative to coal fired power stations being actively considered by PU's Board is the construction of a dam to generate hydro-electric power. The Board is mindful of the likely adverse response of the public living and working in the area where the dam would be built.

In response to the Government's wishes, PU has established environmental objectives relating to improved efficiency in energy production and reducing harmful emissions such as greenhouse gases. PU has also established an ethical code. Included within the code are sections relating to recycling and reduction in harmful emissions as well as to terms and conditions of employment.

Introduction of commercial accounting practices at EGC
The first financial statements have been produced for PU for 2008. Extracts from the Statement of Financial Position from this are shown in **Appendix A.** Within these financial statements, some of EGC's loans were "notionally" converted by the Government into ordinary shares. Interest is payable on the Government loans as shown in the statement of financial position. Reserves is a sum which was vested in EGC when it was first nationalised. This represents the initial capital stock valued on a historical cost basis from the former electricity generating organisations which became consolidated into EGC when it was first nationalised.

Being previously a nationalised industry and effectively this being the first "commercially based" financial statements, there are no retained earnings brought forward into 2008.

APPENDIX A

EXTRACTS FROM THE PRO FORMA FINANCIAL STATEMENTS OF THE ELECTRICITY GENERATING CORPORATION

Statement of financial position as at 31 December 2008

	P$ million
ASSETS	
Non-current assets	15,837
Current assets	
Inventories	1,529
Receivables	2,679
Cash and Cash equivalents	133
	4,341
Total assets	20,178
EQUITY AND LIABILITIES	
Equity	
Share capital	5,525
Reserves	1,231
Total equity	6,756
Non-current liabilities	
Government loans	9,560
Current liabilities	
Payables	3,862
Total liabilities	13,422
Total equity and liabilities	20,178

End of Pre-seen Material

SECTION A – 50 MARKS

[Note: The indicative time for answering this section is 90 minutes]

ANSWER THIS QUESTION

Question One

Unseen material for Case Study

Background

Assume today is 20 May 2009.

Power Utilities (PU) is located in an Asian country. It is planning to diversify its business activities by moving away from total reliance on coal fired power stations and building a hydroelectric power station to produce electricity using natural resources. A dam would need to be constructed to create a reservoir of water above the dam. Electricity would be generated by releasing water from the upper reservoir through the dam. Modern hydroelectric power stations can be very responsive to consumer demand and it is expected that the power station would be able to generate up to 100 megawatts of electricity within 60 seconds of the need arising.

Hydroelectric power stations do not directly produce harmful emissions such as carbon dioxide. However, some carbon dioxide will be produced during the construction phase. There is also a potential source of harmful greenhouse gases in the form of methane gas from decaying plant matter in flooded areas.

Public opinion on the project has been very mixed and there is a significant risk of opposition to the project from local people. Their housing and farming businesses will be seriously affected by the proposed development which will require flooding of local land to construct the dam.

Corporate objectives

Corporate objectives in line with a recent government drive include:

- Improved efficiency of energy production;
- Reduction in harmful emissions such as greenhouse gases.

Financial objectives include maintaining group gearing (debt:debt plus equity) below 40% based on market values.

Hydroelectric power station project

Initial research has shown that a major river in the south of the country may be suitable for use in this project.

Extensive engineering and environmental studies have already begun to assess the viability of the project. These are expected to cost US$15,000,000 in total, payable in three equal instalments at the end of the calendar years 2008, 2009 and 2010. The payment for 2008 has already been made. PU is committed to pay the 2009 instalment but a clause in the contract would enable it to cancel the payment due in 2010 if it decides to withdraw from the project and future viability studies before the end of 2009.

Construction costs will be payable in US$. Other project costs and all project revenue will be in PU's functional currency, P$.

Construction and operating cash flows for the project are as follows:

	Year(s)	US$ million	P$ million
Construction costs	3 and 4	60 payment each year	-
Pre-tax net operating cash flows	5 to 24	-	150 receipt each year

Additional information:

- Time 0 is 1 January 2010;
- Cash flows should be assumed to arise at the end of each year;
- Business tax is 30% and is payable a year in arrears; also note that the government has announced plans to reduce the tax rate to 10% from 1 January 2014 on "clean" energy schemes such as this one (and would therefore only affect the tax position of the operating cash flows); however, this still needs to be approved by parliament and there is a risk that approval will not be obtained;
- Tax depreciation allowances of 100% can be claimed on construction costs but no tax relief is available on the cost of the engineering and environmental studies;
- The assets of the project have no residual value;
- Exchange rate as at today, 20 May 2009, is US$/P$6.3958 (that is, US$1 = P$6.3958). Some economic forecasters expect this exchange rate to remain constant over the period of the project but other forecasts predict that the US$ will strengthen against the P$ by 5% each year;
- PU normally uses a cost of capital net of tax of 10% to assess investments of this type.

Financial information for PU

Extracts from the latest available financial statements for PU are provided in the pre-seen material. The ordinary share capital consists of P$1 shares and the current share price on 20 May 2009 is P$2.80. The long term government borrowings shown in the statement of financial position are floating rate loans and the amount borrowed is unchanged since 31 December 2008

Financing the project

Two alternative financing schemes are being considered which would each raise the equivalent of US$130 million on 1 January 2012. These are:

(i) A five-year P$ loan at a fixed interest rate of 5% per annum;

(ii) A subsidised loan denominated in US$ from an international organisation that promotes "clean energy" schemes. There would not be any interest payments but US$145 million would be repayable at the end of the five year term.

The requirement for Question One is on page 9

Required:

(a) Calculate the NPV of the project as at 1 January 2010 for each of the two different exchange rate forecasts and the two tax rates.

(14 marks)

(b) Write a report to the Directors of PU in which you, as Finance Director, address each of the following issues:

(i) Explain your results in part (a) and explain and evaluate other relevant factors that need to be taken into account when deciding whether or not to undertake the project. Conclude by advising PU how to proceed;

(15 marks)

(ii) Explain and evaluate the costs and risks arising from the use of foreign currency borrowings as proposed by financing scheme (ii) and advise PU on the most appropriate financing structure for the project. Up to 7 marks are available for calculations;

(11 marks)

In the event, the Board of Directors of PU decided to go ahead with the project and it has now been operational for six years. The Board has, however, now decided to dispose of the hydroelectric power station. To assist with these plans, a new entity, PP, has been formed and the plant and its operations have been transferred to PP.

(c) Discuss why PU might wish to dispose of the hydroelectric power station and advise the Directors of PU on alternative methods for achieving the divestment.

(10 marks)

(Total for Question One = 50 marks)

End of Section A

Section B starts on page 10

TURN OVER

SECTION B – 50 MARKS

[Note: The indicative time for answering this section is 90 minutes]

ANSWER *TWO* OF THE THREE QUESTIONS – 25 MARKS EACH

Question Two

AB is a large retailing organisation with revenue in the last financial year exceeding €1 billion. Its head office is in a country in the euro zone and its shares are listed on a major European stock exchange. Over the last few years AB has opened several new stores in a number of European capital cities, not all of them in the euro zone. AB is planning to allow all of its stores to accept the world's major currencies as cash payment for its goods and this will require a major upgrade of its points of sale (POS) system to handle multiple currencies and increased volumes of transactions

AB has already carried out a replacement investment appraisal exercise and has evaluated appropriate systems. It is now in the process of placing an order with a large information technology entity for the supply, installation and maintenance of a new POS system. The acquisition of the system will include the provision of hardware and software. Routine servicing and software upgrading will be arranged separately and does not affect the investment appraisal decision.

AB is considering the following alternative methods of acquiring and financing the new POS system:

Alternative I

- Pay the whole capital cost of €25 million on 1 January 2010, funded by bank borrowings. This cost includes the initial installation of the POS system.
- The system will have no resale value outside AB

Alternative 2

- Enter into a finance lease with the system supplier. AB will pay a fixed amount of €7.0 million each year in advance, commencing 1 January 2010, for four years.
- At the end of four years, ownership of the system will pass to AB without further payment.

Other information

- AB can borrow for a period of four years at a pre-tax fixed interest rate of 7% a year. The entity's cost of equity is currently 12%.
- AB is liable to corporate tax at a marginal rate of 30% which is settled at the end of the year in which it arises..
- AB accounts for depreciation on a straight-line basis at the end of each year
- Under Alternative 1, tax depreciation allowances on the full capital cost are available in equal instalments over the first four years of operation.
- Under Alternative 2, both the accounting depreciation and the interest element of the finance lease payments are tax deductible.
- Once a decision on the payment method has been made and the new system is installed, AB will commission a post completion audit (PCA).

The requirement for Question Two is on the opposite page

Required:

(a)

(i) Calculate which payment method is expected to be cheaper for AB and recommend which should be chosen based solely on the present value of the two alternatives as at 1 January 2010

(10 marks)

(ii) Explain the reasons for your choice of discount factor in the present value calculations.

(3 marks)

(iii) Discuss other factors that AB should consider before deciding on the method of financing the acquisition of the system

(3 marks)

(Total for part (a) 16 marks)

(b) Advise the Directors of AB on the following:

- The main purpose and content of a post completion audit (PCA).
- The limitations of a PCA to AB in the context of the POS system.

(9 marks)

(Total for Question Two = 25 marks)

NOTE: A REPORT FORMAT IS NOT REQUIRED IN THIS QUESTION

Section B continues over the page

TURN OVER

Question Three

CD is a privately-owned entity based in Country X, which is a popular holiday destination. Its principal business is the manufacture and sale of a wide variety of items for the tourist market, mainly souvenirs, gifts and beachwear. CD manufactures approximately 80% of the goods it sells. The remaining 20% is purchased from other countries in a number of different currencies. CD owns and operates 5 retail stores in Country X but also sells its products on a wholesale basis to other local retail outlets.

Although CD is privately owned, it has revenue and assets equivalent in amount to some entities that are listed on smaller stock markets (such as the UK's Alternative Investment Market (AIM)). It is controlled by family shareholders but also has a number of non-family shareholders, such as employees and trade associates. It has no intention of seeking a listing at the present time although some of the family shareholders have often expressed a wish to buy out the smaller investors.

CD has been largely unaffected by the recent world recession and has increased its sales volume and profits each year for the past 5 years. The directors think this is because it provides value for money; providing high quality goods that are competitively priced at the lower end of its market. Future growth is expected to be modest as the directors and shareholders do not wish to adopt strategies that they think might involve substantial increase in risks, for example by moving the manufacturing base to another country where labour rates are lower. Some of the smaller shareholders disagree with this strategy and would prefer higher growth even if it involves greater risk.

The entity is financed 80% by equity and 20% by debt (based on book values). The debt is a mixture of bonds secured on assets and unsecured overdraft. The interest rate on the secured bonds is fixed at 7% and the overdraft rate is currently 8%, which compares to a relatively recent historic rate as high as 13%. The bonds are due to be repaid in 5 years' time. Inflation in CD's country is near zero at the present time and interest rates are expected to fall.

CD's treasury department is centralised at the head office and its key responsibilities include arranging sufficient long and short term financing for the group and hedging foreign exchange exposures. The Treasurer is investigating the opportunities for and consequences of refinancing.

CD's sole financial objective is to increase dividends each year. It has no non-financial objective. This financial objective and the lack of non-financial objectives are shortly to be subject to review and discussion by the board. The new Finance Director believes maximisation of shareholder wealth should be the sole objective, but the other directors do not agree and think that new objectives should be considered, including target profit after tax and return on investment.

The requirement for Question Three is on the opposite page

Required:

(a) Discuss the role of the treasury department when determining financing or re-financing strategies in the context of the economic environment described in the scenario and explain how these might impact on the determination of corporate objectives.

(15 marks)

(b) Evaluate the appropriateness of CD's current objective and of the two new objectives being considered. Discuss alternative objectives that might be appropriate for CD and conclude with a recommendation.

(10 marks)

(Total 25 marks)

Section B continues over the page

TURN OVER

Question Four

EF is a distributor for branded beverages throughout the world. It is based in the UK but has offices throughout Europe, South America and the Caribbean. Its shares are listed on the UK's Alternative Investment Market (AIM) and are currently quoted at 180 pence per share

Extracts from EF's forecast financial statements are given below.

Extracts from the (forecast) income statement for the year ended 31 December 2009

	£'000
Revenue	45,000
Purchase costs and expenses	38,250
Interest on long term debt	450
Profit before tax	6,300
Income tax expense (at 28%)	1,764
Note: Dividends declared	1,814

EF - Statement of financial position as at 31 December 2009

	£'000
ASSETS	
Non-current assets	14,731
Current assets	
Inventories	5,250
Trade receivables	13,500
Cash and bank balances	348
	19,098
Total assets	33,829
EQUITY AND LIABILITIES	
Equity	
Share capital (ordinary shares of 25 pence)	4,204
Retained earnings	16,210
Total equity	20,414
Non-current liabilities	
(Secured bonds, 9% 2015)	5,000
Current liabilities	
Trade payables	8,415
Total liabilities	13,415
Total equity and liabilities	33,829

You have obtained the following additional information:

1. Revenue and purchases & expenses are expected to increase by an average of 4% each year for the financial years ending 31 December 2010 and 2011.

2. EF expects to continue to be liable for tax at the rate of 28 per cent. Assume tax is paid or refunded the year in which the liability arises.
3. The ratios of *trade receivables to sales* and *trade payables to purchase costs and expenses* will remain the same for the next two years. The value of inventories is likely to remain at 2009 levels for 2010 and 2011.
4. The non-current assets in the statement of financial position at 31 December 2009 are land and buildings, which are not depreciated in the company's books. Tax depreciation allowances on the buildings may be ignored. All other assets used by the company are currently procured on operating leases.
5. The company intends to purchase early in 2010 a fleet of vehicles (trucks and vans). These vehicles are additional to the vehicles currently operated by EF. The vehicles will be provided to all its UK and overseas bases but will be purchased in the UK. The cost of these vehicles will be £5,000,000. The cost will be depreciated on a straight line basis over 10 years. The company charges a full year's depreciation in the first year of purchase of its assets. Tax depreciation allowances are available at 25% reducing balance on this expenditure. Assume the vehicles have a zero residual value at the end of ten years.

6. Dividends will be increased by 5% each year on the 2009 base. Assume they are paid in the year they are declared.

EF plans to finance the purchase of the vehicles (identified in note 6) from its cash balances and an overdraft. The entity's agreed overdraft facility is currently £1 million.

The company's main financial objectives are to earn a post-tax return on the closing book value of shareholders' funds of 20% per annum and a year on year increase in earnings of 8%

Assumption regarding overdraft interest

It should be assumed that overdraft interest that might have been incurred during 2009 is included in expenses (that is, you are not expected to calculate overdraft interest for 2010 and 2011).

The requirement for Question Four is on the next page

TURN OVER

Required:

Assume you are a consultant working for EF

(a) Construct a forecast income statement, including dividends and retentions for the years ended 31 December 2010 and 2011.

(6 marks)

(b) Construct a cash flow forecast for each of the years 2010 and 2011. Discuss, briefly, how the company might finance any cash deficit.

(9 marks)

(c) Using your results in (a) and (b) above, evaluate whether EF is likely to meet its stated objectives. As part of your evaluation, discuss whether the assumption regarding overdraft interest is reasonable and explain how a more accurate calculation of overdraft interest could be obtained.

(10 marks)

(Total for Question Four = 25 marks)

End of Question Paper

Maths Tables and Formulae are on Pages 17 - 21

MATHS TABLES AND FORMULAE

Present value table

Present value of 1.00 unit of currency, that is $(1 + r)^{-n}$ where r = interest rate; n = number of periods until payment or receipt.

Periods	Interest rates (*r*)									
(*n*)	1%	2%	3%	4%	5%	6%	7%	8%	9%	10%
1	0.990	0.980	0.971	0.962	0.952	0.943	0.935	0.926	0.917	0.909
2	0.980	0.961	0.943	0.925	0.907	0.890	0.873	0.857	0.842	0.826
3	0.971	0.942	0.915	0.889	0.864	0.840	0.816	0.794	0.772	0.751
4	0.961	0.924	0.888	0.855	0.823	0.792	0.763	0.735	0.708	0.683
5	0.951	0.906	0.863	0.822	0.784	0.747	0.713	0.681	0.650	0.621
6	0.942	0.888	0.837	0.790	0.746	0.705	0.666	0.630	0.596	0.564
7	0.933	0.871	0.813	0.760	0.711	0.665	0.623	0.583	0.547	0.513
8	0.923	0.853	0.789	0.731	0.677	0.627	0.582	0.540	0.502	0.467
9	0.914	0.837	0.766	0.703	0.645	0.592	0.544	0.500	0.460	0.424
10	0.905	0.820	0.744	0.676	0.614	0.558	0.508	0.463	0.422	0.386
11	0.896	0.804	0.722	0.650	0.585	0.527	0.475	0.429	0.388	0.350
12	0.887	0.788	0.701	0.625	0.557	0.497	0.444	0.397	0.356	0.319
13	0.879	0.773	0.681	0.601	0.530	0.469	0.415	0.368	0.326	0.290
14	0.870	0.758	0.661	0.577	0.505	0.442	0.388	0.340	0.299	0.263
15	0.861	0.743	0.642	0.555	0.481	0.417	0.362	0.315	0.275	0.239
16	0.853	0.728	0.623	0.534	0.458	0.394	0.339	0.292	0.252	0.218
17	0.844	0.714	0.605	0.513	0.436	0.371	0.317	0.270	0.231	0.198
18	0.836	0.700	0.587	0.494	0.416	0.350	0.296	0.250	0.212	0.180
19	0.828	0.686	0.570	0.475	0.396	0.331	0.277	0.232	0.194	0.164
20	0.820	0.673	0.554	0.456	0.377	0.312	0.258	0.215	0.178	0.149

Periods	Interest rates (*r*)									
(*n*)	11%	12%	13%	14%	15%	16%	17%	18%	19%	20%
1	0.901	0.893	0.885	0.877	0.870	0.862	0.855	0.847	0.840	0.833
2	0.812	0.797	0.783	0.769	0.756	0.743	0.731	0.718	0.706	0.694
3	0.731	0.712	0.693	0.675	0.658	0.641	0.624	0.609	0.593	0.579
4	0.659	0.636	0.613	0.592	0.572	0.552	0.534	0.516	0.499	0.482
5	0.593	0.567	0.543	0.519	0.497	0.476	0.456	0.437	0.419	0.402
6	0.535	0.507	0.480	0.456	0.432	0.410	0.390	0.370	0.352	0.335
7	0.482	0.452	0.425	0.400	0.376	0.354	0.333	0.314	0.296	0.279
8	0.434	0.404	0.376	0.351	0.327	0.305	0.285	0.266	0.249	0.233
9	0.391	0.361	0.333	0.308	0.284	0.263	0.243	0.225	0.209	0.194
10	0.352	0.322	0.295	0.270	0.247	0.227	0.208	0.191	0.176	0.162
11	0.317	0.287	0.261	0.237	0.215	0.195	0.178	0.162	0.148	0.135
12	0.286	0.257	0.231	0.208	0.187	0.168	0.152	0.137	0.124	0.112
13	0.258	0.229	0.204	0.182	0.163	0.145	0.130	0.116	0.104	0.093
14	0.232	0.205	0.181	0.160	0.141	0.125	0.111	0.099	0.088	0.078
15	0.209	0.183	0.160	0.140	0.123	0.108	0.095	0.084	0.079	0.065
16	0.188	0.163	0.141	0.123	0.107	0.093	0.081	0.071	0.062	0.054
17	0.170	0.146	0.125	0.108	0.093	0.080	0.069	0.060	0.052	0.045
18	0.153	0.130	0.111	0.095	0.081	0.069	0.059	0.051	0.044	0.038
19	0.138	0.116	0.098	0.083	0.070	0.060	0.051	0.043	0.037	0.031
20	0.124	0.104	0.087	0.073	0.061	0.051	0.043	0.037	0.031	0.026

Cumulative present value of 1.00 unit of currency per annum

Receivable or Payable at the end of each year for *n* years $\left[\frac{1-(1+r)^{-n}}{r}\right]$

Periods	Interest rates (*r*)									
(*n*)	1%	2%	3%	4%	5%	6%	7%	8%	9%	10%
1	0.990	0.980	0.971	0.962	0.952	0.943	0.935	0.926	0.917	0.909
2	1.970	1.942	1.913	1.886	1.859	1.833	1.808	1.783	1.759	1.736
3	2.941	2.884	2.829	2.775	2.723	2.673	2.624	2.577	2.531	2.487
4	3.902	3.808	3.717	3.630	3.546	3.465	3.387	3.312	3.240	3.170
5	4.853	4.713	4.580	4.452	4.329	4.212	4.100	3.993	3.890	3.791
6	5.795	5.601	5.417	5.242	5.076	4.917	4.767	4.623	4.486	4.355
7	6.728	6.472	6.230	6.002	5.786	5.582	5.389	5.206	5.033	4.868
8	7.652	7.325	7.020	6.733	6.463	6.210	5.971	5.747	5.535	5.335
9	8.566	8.162	7.786	7.435	7.108	6.802	6.515	6.247	5.995	5.759
10	9.471	8.983	8.530	8.111	7.722	7.360	7.024	6.710	6.418	6.145
11	10.368	9.787	9.253	8.760	8.306	7.887	7.499	7.139	6.805	6.495
12	11.255	10.575	9.954	9.385	8.863	8.384	7.943	7.536	7.161	6.814
13	12.134	11.348	10.635	9.986	9.394	8.853	8.358	7.904	7.487	7.103
14	13.004	12.106	11.296	10.563	9.899	9.295	8.745	8.244	7.786	7.367
15	13.865	12.849	11.938	11.118	10.380	9.712	9.108	8.559	8.061	7.606
16	14.718	13.578	12.561	11.652	10.838	10.106	9.447	8.851	8.313	7.824
17	15.562	14.292	13.166	12.166	11.274	10.477	9.763	9.122	8.544	8.022
18	16.398	14.992	13.754	12.659	11.690	10.828	10.059	9.372	8.756	8.201
19	17.226	15.679	14.324	13.134	12.085	11.158	10.336	9.604	8.950	8.365
20	18.046	16.351	14.878	13.590	12.462	11.470	10.594	9.818	9.129	8.514

Periods	Interest rates (*r*)									
(*n*)	11%	12%	13%	14%	15%	16%	17%	18%	19%	20%
1	0.901	0.893	0.885	0.877	0.870	0.862	0.855	0.847	0.840	0.833
2	1.713	1.690	1.668	1.647	1.626	1.605	1.585	1.566	1.547	1.528
3	2.444	2.402	2.361	2.322	2.283	2.246	2.210	2.174	2.140	2.106
4	3.102	3.037	2.974	2.914	2.855	2.798	2.743	2.690	2.639	2.589
5	3.696	3.605	3.517	3.433	3.352	3.274	3.199	3.127	3.058	2.991
6	4.231	4.111	3.998	3.889	3.784	3.685	3.589	3.498	3.410	3.326
7	4.712	4.564	4.423	4.288	4.160	4.039	3.922	3.812	3.706	3.605
8	5.146	4.968	4.799	4.639	4.487	4.344	4.207	4.078	3.954	3.837
9	5.537	5.328	5.132	4.946	4.772	4.607	4.451	4.303	4.163	4.031
10	5.889	5.650	5.426	5.216	5.019	4.833	4.659	4.494	4.339	4.192
11	6.207	5.938	5.687	5.453	5.234	5.029	4.836	4.656	4.486	4.327
12	6.492	6.194	5.918	5.660	5.421	5.197	4.988	7.793	4.611	4.439
13	6.750	6.424	6.122	5.842	5.583	5.342	5.118	4.910	4.715	4.533
14	6.982	6.628	6.302	6.002	5.724	5.468	5.229	5.008	4.802	4.611
15	7.191	6.811	6.462	6.142	5.847	5.575	5.324	5.092	4.876	4.675
16	7.379	6.974	6.604	6.265	5.954	5.668	5.405	5.162	4.938	4.730
17	7.549	7.120	6.729	6.373	6.047	5.749	5.475	5.222	4.990	4.775
18	7.702	7.250	6.840	6.467	6.128	5.818	5.534	5.273	5.033	4.812
19	7.839	7.366	6.938	6.550	6.198	5.877	5.584	5.316	5.070	4.843
20	7.963	7.469	7.025	6.623	6.259	5.929	5.628	5.353	5.101	4.870

Formulae

Valuation models

(i) Irredeemable preference shares, paying a constant annual dividend, d, in perpetuity, where P_0 is the ex-div value:

$$P_0 = \frac{d}{k_{\text{pref}}}$$

(ii) Ordinary (equity) shares, paying a constant annual dividend, d, in perpetuity, where P_0 is the ex-div value:

$$P_0 = \frac{d}{k_e}$$

(iii) Ordinary (equity) shares, paying an annual dividend, d, growing in perpetuity at a constant rate, g, where P_0 is the ex-div value:

$$P_0 = \frac{d_1}{k_e - g} \quad \text{or} \quad P_0 = \frac{d_0[1+g]}{k_e - g}$$

(iv) Irredeemable bonds, paying annual after-tax interest, $i\,[1 - t]$, in perpetuity, where P_0 is the ex-interest value:

$$P_0 = \frac{i[1-t]}{k_{\text{dnet}}}$$

or, without tax:

$$P_0 = \frac{i}{k_d}$$

(v) Total value of the geared entity, V_g (based on MM):

$$V_g = V_u + TB$$

(vi) Future value of S, of a sum X, invested for n periods, compounded at r% interest:

$$S = X[1 + r]^n$$

(vii) Present value of 1·00 payable or receivable in n years, discounted at r% per annum:

$$PV = \frac{1}{[1+r]^n}$$

(viii) Present value of an annuity of 1·00 per annum, receivable or payable for n years, commencing in one year, discounted at r% per annum:

$$PV = \frac{1}{r}\left[1 - \frac{1}{[1+r]^n}\right]$$

(ix) Present value of 1·00 per annum, payable or receivable in perpetuity, commencing in one year, discounted at r% per annum:

$$PV = \frac{1}{r}$$

(x) Present value of 1·00 per annum, receivable or payable, commencing in one year, growing in perpetuity at a constant rate of g% per annum, discounted at r% per annum:

$$PV = \frac{1}{r - g}$$

Cost of capital

(i) Cost of irredeemable preference shares, paying an annual dividend, d, in perpetuity, and having a current ex-div price P_0:

$$k_{pref} = \frac{d}{P_0}$$

(ii) Cost of irredeemable bonds, paying annual net interest, $i\,[1 - t]$, and having a current ex-interest price P_0:

$$k_{d\,net} = \frac{i[1 - t]}{P_0}$$

(iii) Cost of ordinary (equity) shares, paying an annual dividend, d, in perpetuity, and having a current ex-div price P_0:

$$k_e = \frac{d}{P_0}$$

(iv) Cost of ordinary (equity) shares, having a current ex-div price, P_0, having just paid a dividend, d_0, with the dividend growing in perpetuity by a constant g% per annum:

$$k_e = \frac{d_1}{P_0} + g \quad \text{or} \quad k_e = \frac{d_0[1 + g]}{P_0} + g$$

(v) Cost of ordinary (equity) shares, using the CAPM:

$$k_e = R_f + [R_m - R_f]\beta$$

(vi) Cost of ordinary (equity) share capital in a geared entity :

$$k_{eg} = k_{eu} + [k_{eu} - k_d]\,\frac{V_D\,[1 - t]}{V_E}$$

(vii) Weighted average cost of capital, k_0 or WACC

$$WACC = k_e\left[\frac{V_E}{V_E + V_D}\right] + k_d\,[1 - t]\left[\frac{V_D}{V_E + V_D}\right]$$

(viii) Adjusted cost of capital (MM formula):

$$K_{adj} = k_{eu}\,[1 - tL] \quad \text{or} \quad r^* = r[1 - T^*L]$$

(ix) Ungear β:

$$\beta_u = \beta_g\left[\frac{V_E}{V_E + V_D[1 - t]}\right] + \beta_d\left[\frac{V_D\,[1 - t]}{V_E + V_D\,[1 - t]}\right]$$

(x) Regear β:

$$\beta_g = \beta_u + [\beta_u - \beta_d]\,\frac{V_D\,[1 - t]}{V_E}$$

(xi) Adjusted discount rate to use in international capital budgeting (International Fisher effect)

$$\frac{1 + \text{annual discount rate B\$}}{1 + \text{annual discount rate A\$}} = \frac{\text{Future spot rate A\$/B\$ in 12 months' time}}{\text{Spot rate A\$/B\$}}$$

where A$/B$ is the number of B$ to each A$

Other formulae

(i) Expectations theory:

$$\text{Future spot rate A\$/B\$} = \text{Spot rate A\$/B\$} \times \frac{1+\text{nominal country B interest rate}}{1+\text{nominal country A interest rate}}$$

where:

A$/B$ is the number of B$ to each A$, and
A$ is the currency of countryA and B$ is the currency of country B

(ii) Purchasing power parity (law of one price):

$$\text{Future spot rate A\$B\$} = \text{Spot rate A\$/B\$} \times \frac{1+\text{country B inflation rate}}{1+\text{country A inflation rate}}$$

(iii) Link between nominal (money) and real interest rates:

$$[1 + \text{nominal (money) rate}] = [1 + \text{real interest rate}][1 + \text{inflation rate}]$$

(iv) Equivalent annual cost:

$$\text{Equivalent annual cost} = \frac{PV \text{ of costs over } n \text{ years}}{n \text{ year annuity factor}}$$

(v) Theoretical ex-rights price:

$$\text{TERP} = \frac{1}{N+1}[(N \times \text{cum rights price}) + \text{issue price}]$$

(vi) Value of a right:

$$\frac{\text{Theoretical ex rights price} - \text{issue price}}{N}$$

where N = number of rights required to buy one share.

LIST OF VERBS USED IN THE QUESTION REQUIREMENTS

A list of the learning objectives and verbs that appear in the syllabus and in the question requirements for each question in this paper.

It is important that you answer the question according to the definition of the verb.

LEARNING OBJECTIVE	VERBS USED	DEFINITION
Level 1 - KNOWLEDGE What you are expected to know.	List	Make a list of
	State	Express, fully or clearly, the details of/facts
	Define	Give the exact meaning of
Level 2 - COMPREHENSION What you are expected to understand.	Describe	Communicate the key features
	Distinguish	Highlight the differences between
	Explain	Make clear or intelligible/State the meaning purpose of
	Identify	Recognise, establish or select after consideration
	Illustrate	Use an example to describe or explain something
Level 3 - APPLICATION How you are expected to apply your knowledge.	Apply	Put to practical use
	Calculate/compute	To ascertain or reckon mathematically
	Demonstrate	Prove with certainty or to exhibit by practical means
	Prepare	Make or get ready for use
	Reconcile	Make or prove consistent/compatible
	Solve	Find an answer to
	Tabulate	Arrange in a table
Level 4 - ANALYSIS How are you expected to analyse the detail of what you have learned.	Analyse	Examine in detail the structure of
	Categorise	Place into a defined class or division
	Compare and contrast	Show the similarities and/or differences between
	Construct	Build up or compile
	Discuss	Examine in detail by argument
	Interpret	Translate into intelligible or familiar terms
	Prioritise	Place in order of priority or sequence for ac
	Produce	Create or bring into existence
Level 5 - EVALUATION How are you expected to use your learning to evaluate, make decisions or recommendations.	Advise	Counsel, inform or notify
	Evaluate	Appraise or assess the value of
	Recommend	Propose a course of action

Financial Pillar

Strategic Level Paper

F3 – Financial Strategy

Specimen Paper

Thursday Morning Session

CIMA

The Examiner's Answers – Specimen Paper F3 - Financial Strategy

SECTION A

Answer to Question One

Requirement (a)

Appendix A

1. Assume constant exchange rate							
Project years		*1*	*3*	*4*	*5*	*5 to 24*	*6 to 25*
Calendar years (31 December)		*2010*	*2012*	*2013*	*2014*	*from 2014 for 20 years*	*from 2015 for 20 years*
		US$m	*US$m*	*US$m*	*US$m*	*US$m*	*US$m*
Final payment for engineering/environmental		(5.0)	-	-	-	-	-
Initial investment		-	(60.0)	(60.0)		-	-
US$ cashflows		(5.0)	(60.0)	(60.0)	-	-	-
FX rate (P$ per US$)		6.3958	6.3958	6.3958			
		P$m	*P$m*	*P$m*	*P$m*	*P$m*	*P$m*
P$ equivalent of US$ cashflows		(32.0)	(383.7)	(383.7)	-	-	-
Tax relief on initial investment				115.1 *W1*	115.1		
Operating net cash inflows in P$		-	-	-	-	150.0	-
Less tax at 30%		-	-	-	-	-	(45.0)
Net total cashflows expressed in P$		(32.0)	(383.7)	(268.6)	115.1	150.0	(45.0)
Discount factor at 10.0%		0.909	0.751	0.683	0.621	5.815 *W2*	5.287 *W3*
PV		(29.1)	(288.2)	(183.5)	71.5	872.3	(237.9)
Total NPV in P$ millions:	205.1						
W1: 115.1 = 383.7 x 30%							
W2: 5.815 = 8.514 x 0.683							
W3: 5.287 = 8.514 x 0.621							

2. Assume that the US$ will strengthen against the P$ by 5% each year							
		P$m	*P$m*	*P$m*	*P$m*	*P$m*	*P$m*
Project years		*1*	*3*	*4*	*5*	*5 to 24*	*6 to 25*
Calendar years (31 December)		*2010*	*2012*	*2013*	*2014*	*from 2014 for 20 years*	*from 2015 for 20 years*
P$ equivalent of US$ cashflows (above)		(5.0)	(60.0)	(60.0)	-	-	-
FX rate reflecting 5% increase in US$ value		6.9206	7.6300 *W4*	8.0115		-	-
Adjusted US$ cash flows expressed in P$		(34.6)	(457.8)	(480.7)	-	-	-
Tax relief on initial investment				137.3 *W5*	144.2		
P$ cash flows (from above)		-	-	-	-	150.0	(45.0)
Total cashflows expressed in P$		(34.6)	(457.8)	(343.4)	144.2	150.0	(45.0)
Discount factor at 10.0% (from above)		0.909	0.751	0.683	0.621	5.815	5.287
PV		(31.5)	(343.8)	(234.5)	89.5	872.3	(237.9)
Total NPV in P$ millions:	114.1						

In both cases:
Saving if tax rate dropped to 10% is P$ 158.6million where 158.6 = 237.9 x (30-10)/30
So result in 1 above becomes P$363.7m (= 205.1 + 158.6)
and result in 2 above becomes P$272.7m (= 114.1 + 158.6)

W4: Exchange rates
Assuming the US$ strengthens against the P$ by 5% a year, future rates are:

Date	Year	FX Rate	Workings				
01 January 2010	0	6.5911	6.3958	1.05^(225/365)	where 225 days is:		
31 December 2010	1	6.9206	6.5911	x 1.05		May	11
31 December 2011	2	7.2667	6.9206	x 1.05		Jun	30
31 December 2012	3	7.6300	7.2667	x 1.05		Jul	31
31 December 2013	4	8.0115	7.6300	x 1.05		Aug	31
31 December 2014	5	8.4121	8.0115	x 1.05		Sep	30
						Oct	31
						Nov	30
W5: 137.3 = 457.8 x 30% and 144.2 = 480.7 x 30%						Dec	31
							225

Requirement (b)

To: The Directors of PU
From: Finance Director
Date: Today's date

Subject: Hydroelectric power station project – project appraisal

Introduction

The purpose of this report is to present the findings of recent exercises to evaluate:

- the likely financial contribution of the proposed project and examine other relevant factors that might affect the decision on whether or not to undertake the project; and
- suitable financing structures to fund the project.

Investment appraisal

Financial appraisal based on project cash flows

A full financial appraisal has been undertaken based on the present value of future cash flows arising from the project. There are several important uncertainties surrounding the project. In particular:

- a large proportion of US$ costs are involved which could vary in P$ terms, and
- it is possible that the tax rate for such projects may fall from 30% to 10% from 2014

The investment appraisal model was therefore run for each combination of these base assumptions. Summary results are given below.

Summary of results - NPV as at 1 January 2010 of forecast project cash flows:

	Tax rate 30%	Tax rate 10%
Constant exchange rate	P$205.1 million	P$363.7 million
US$ strengthening by 5% per annum	P$114.1 million	P$272.7 million

Full results of the exercise are attached at Appendix A.

Other relevant factors to take into consideration

Impact of movement in exchange rate

If the US$ were to strengthen against the P$ by 5% a year, the NPV of the project would fall by approximately P$90 million under both tax rate scenarios. For example, assuming a tax rate of 30%, the NPV of the project falls to P$114.1million from P$205.1million once the strengthening of the US$ has been taken into account.

This is a very large exchange rate risk and could be hedged by the use of short-term hedging instruments such as forward contracts. These forward exchange rates can then be used in the investment appraisal of the project and a revised NPV result obtained based on the hedge cash flows.

Forward contracts cannot be cancelled, so they should only be entered into if and when a firm decision has been taken to proceed with the project.

Impact of tax rates

The results in part (a) show that a fall in the tax rate in 2014 from 30% to 10% would result in a large increase in the NPV of the project from P$205.1million to P$363.7million, assuming a constant US$/P$ exchange rate.

A real option open to PU is to delay the project until a decision has been made on the future tax rate. In the meantime, the entity should lobby the government to try and influence the decision in its favour.

Reliability of base data

The investment appraisal exercise has been based on best estimates. Changes to the estimates could occur as a result of changes in underlying data such as:

- construction costs;
- market demand/prices for electricity that would impact on operating revenues;
- accuracy of estimates of maintenance costs;
- possible delays due to local objection to the scheme and how that might impact on costs and viability of the project;
- accuracy of estimates of relocation costs for people who are living or working on land that will be flooded as a result of the construction of the dam.

Sensitivity analysis would be useful to examine the impact of changes in the underlying data on the financial appraisal.

Suitability of the discount rate

The discount rate should be reviewed to see if:

- it meets the underlying risk expectations of the project;
- it needs to be adjusted to reflect a change in capital structure of PU as a result of proceeding with the project.

The project is not large enough to change the capital structure of the entity and so this is not a relevant issue here.

However, the project is moving the entity into a completely new and untested area of business and the discount rate may therefore need to be adjusted upwards to reflect the higher risks arising from this project.

Results of the environmental studies exercise

The environmental studies investigation is still on-going. Although it is considered highly unlikely that the project will be cancelled at this stage, final approval to proceed can only be made once the full results of the studies are known.

Impact on corporate and financial objectives

Financial objective: Gearing

Gearing is currently 38% (based on market values at 20 May 2009) against a maximum gearing target of 40%.

The project is so small in size in relation to the entity as a whole that it would not be expected to have a major impact on gearing levels. However, the size of the borrowing is still sufficient to push the gearing level just above the maximum gearing target of 40%. The new gearing level is estimated as 40.4%, an increase of approximately 2% from the current level of 38.2%.

Workings:
Current Gearing:

Equity	*P$15,470million*	*(= 5,525million x P$2.80)*
Debt	*P$9,560million*	
So, current gearing is	*38.2%*	*(= 9,560/(9,560 + 15,470))*

New gearing after taking into account the project and the following additional assumptions:

- *tax rate of 30%;*
- *an increase of 5% a year in the value of the US$ against the P$;*
- *a share price that has already moved to reflect the increase in shareholder value as represented by the NPV of the project.*

So new figures for equity and debt are:

Equity P$15,584million (= 5,525million x P$2.80 + P$114.4million (the project NPV)
Debt P$10,552million (= P$9,560million + P$992 (see workings W1))

So the new gearing level is: 40.4% (= 10,552/(10,552 + 15,584))

W1: US$130million x 7.6300 = P$992million

Other corporate objectives

The new power station is unlikely to improve efficiency rates of energy production but it would make a major contribution to reducing harmful emissions such as greenhouse gases when generating electricity. It is inevitable that some harmful emissions will be emitted during the construction process and there may also be some carbon dioxide emitted from decomposing vegetable matter that is flooded as part of the project. Overall, however, the hydroelectric power station would be expected to generate only a very small proportion of the harmful emissions that would have been generated by a coal fired power station with a similar output.

Conclusion – whether or not to undertake the project

It is recommended that PU should:

- wait for the full results of the environmental studies exercise before reaching a decision;
- recalculate the investment appraisal using forward exchange rates;
- perform a sensitivity analysis to determine the results under a "worst case scenario" and determine the probability of the project showing a loss if some of the key assumptions are changed;

If a decision is taken to proceed with the project, all US$ cash flows should be hedged using forward contracts to fix the exchange rate on these cash flows.

Overall recommendation: Only proceed with the project if satisfactory outcomes are obtained from all the above research and if the revised figures for the project using forward exchange rates still show a profit, even under a "worst case" scenario.

Financing structure

A significant exchange rate risk would arise in respect of US$ borrowings as proposed in financing structure (ii). At a constant exchange rate, the US$ borrowings are very attractive and have a significantly lower cost than the P$ borrowings. However, if the US$ were to strengthen by 5% a year against the P$, the US$ borrowings becomes comparatively more expensive.

The cash flows arising under the US$ borrowings and the effective cost of the borrowings (on a yield to maturity basis) under each exchange rate scenario are shown below:

US$ loan assuming a constant exchange rate							
Year	Cash flow US$ million	Exchange rate	Cash flow Local $ million	DF @ 3%	PV @ 3%	DF @ 2%	PV @ 2%
0	-130.0	6.3958	-831.5	1	-831.5	1	-831.5
5	145.0	6.3958	927.4	0.863	800.3	0.906	840.2
					-31.2		8.7
YTM by interpolation:		2.2%	= 2% + 1% x 8.7/(8.7 + 31.2)				
US$ loan assuming the US$ strengthens against the local $ by 5% a year							
Year	Cash flow US$ million	Exchange rate	Cash flow Local $ million	DF @ 6%	PV @ 6%	DF @ 8%	PV @ 8%
0	-130.0	7.2667 *(W1)*	-944.7	1	-944.7	1	-944.7
5	145.0	9.2744 *(W2)*	1344.8	0.747	1004.6	0.681	915.8
					59.9		-28.9
YTM by interpolation:		7.3%	= 6% + 2% x 59.9/(59.9 + 28.9)				
Workings:							
W1	7.2667 is the exchange rate on 1 January 2012 (see workings W4 in part (a))						
W2	9.2744 = 7.2667 x 1.05^5						

Ignoring any investment income on funds that are not needed in the first year, and assuming exchange rates stay constant, the US$ borrowings have an effective cost of 2.2% but this rises to an effective cost of 7.3% if the US$ were to strengthen against the P$ by 5% a year. This compares with a known cost of 5% under alternative financing structure (i).

If such a high risk is unacceptable, US$ borrowings should only be considered if it is possible to guarantee the exchange rate for the interest and capital repayments used to service the borrowings. This may be possible to arrange by using hedging instruments such as forward contracts or a cross currency swap.

Note that there is no US$ income that could be used to set off against US$ payments to service the borrowings.

Recommendation

Exchange rate risk arising on the borrowings could be effectively eliminated if PU were to enter into a cross currency swap contract to fix the exchange rate on the US$ borrowings. Calculations should be performed of the cost of debt for the hedged borrowings and this should be compared to the cost of the P$ borrowings. The calculations should also be adjusted to take account of any investment income that could be earned before the funds are required in the project. The cheapest method should then be chosen.

Requirement (c)

Possible reasons for disposing of the hydroelectric power station.

There are a number of possible reasons why PU might wish to dispose of the hydroelectric power station.

The most likely reason is one of strategic planning:

- to refocus the business on coal fired power stations and concentrate on the main area of management expertise - the hydroelectric power station may not have proved to be a good fit of business alongside the coal fired power stations;
- to raise funds for use in moving into new business areas such as developing new power stations using alternative fuels;
- to lower cost of capital by disposing of a high risk business.

PU may also have encountered problems in running the hydroelectric power station such as a failure to manage it efficiently or realise its full profit potential. There may be a potential buyer who has the expertise to run the hydroelectric power station more efficiently.

PU itself may have suffered a fall in business and need to raise cash by selling the hydroelectric power station.

Methods for achieving the divestment

1. Sell-off

In a sell-off, PP would be sold to another entity, usually in return for cash. This is most likely to be achieved by setting up PP as a separate subsidiary entity and selling the entire entity as a going concern. Shares in the acquirer would be of no interest to PU if its objective is to move out of this area of business and use the cash raised for other purposes.

2. Spin-off

In a spin-off, PP would be constructed so that it is owned by the same shareholders as PU. This is normally known as a demerger. A spin-off can lead to a clearer management structure as management of PP can concentrate solely on that business without reference back to PU.

3. Management buyout

A management buyout is where the business is purchased by members of the management team, generally in association with a financing institution.

SECTION B

Answer to Question Two

Requirement (a)(i)

The discount rate to be used in this type of evaluation is the after-tax cost of debt, which is 7% x (1 - 0·3 = 4.9%) say 5%.

Alternative 1 – Evaluation of 'borrow and buy'

Year	**0** **€million**	**1 to 4** **€million**
Purchase cost	(25)	
Tax relief on tax depreciation allowances *(W1)*		1.875
DF @5%	1.000	3.546
DCF	(25)	6.649
Present value	(18.4)	

W1: €1.875 million = 30% x €25 million/4

Alternative 2 – Evaluation of the finance lease

Base data

	€million		
Lease payments in advance	7.0	pa	Total payments: 4 x 7 = €28 million
Cost of leased asset	25		but use £18m in the calculations because the first lease payment is made in advance and should be deducted from the cost
Finance charge	3		= 28 - 25
Number of interest periods	3		Ignore the final period as there is no interest element

Examiner's note: As the question does not specify which method to use to allocate implicit interest between years, either the actuarial method or the sum of digits method would be acceptable. Both are shown here as a guide to students.

Method 1 – Actuarial method

Firstly, calculate the implied interest rate using IRR:

The annuity factor for the interest can be found by dividing the cost of the asset by the annual lease payment.
We will use a net cost of €18million and 3 interest periods.
So three year annuity factor = 18/7.0 = 2.5714
This approximates to an interest rate of 8% (which has a three year annuity factor of 2.577).

Examiner's note: if there is no exact match, use interpolation to find the implied interest rate.

Actuarial method – interest allocation (and proof of interest allocation)

Accounting year	**1**	**2**	**3**
	€million	**€million**	**€million**
Opening balance	18.0	12.44	6.44
Interest (add)	1.44 (=8% x 18.0)	1.00 (=8% x 12.44)	0.52 (=8% x 6.44)
Repayment (lease rental)	(7.0)	(7.0)	(7.0)
Closing balance	12.44	6.44	(0.04)

Actuarial method – present value calculation of finance lease

Time	**0**	**1**	**2**	**3**	**4**
	€million	**€million**	**€million**	**€million**	**€million**
Calculation of tax shield based on accounting figures:					
Depreciation	0	(6.25)	(6.25)	(6.25)	(6.25)
Implicit interest	0	(1.44)	(1.00)	(0.52)	0
Total eligible for tax relief	0	(7.69)	(7.25)	(6.77)	(6.25)
Cash flows:					
Tax relief at 30%	0	2.31	2.18	2.03	1.87
Finance lease	(7.0)	(7.0)	(7.0)	(7.0)	0
Total cash flows	(7.0)	(4.69)	(4.82)	(4.97)	1.87
DF @5%	1.000	0.952	0.907	0.864	0.823
DCF	(7.0)	(4.46)	(4.37)	(4.29)	1.54
Present value	(18.6)				

Method 2 - Sum of digits

Base the sum of digits calculation on three interest periods as before.
The sum of digits is 6. *Workings: 6 = n (n+1)/2 = 3 x (3 + 1)/2*
So the interest in the first period is 3m x 3/6 and in the 2nd period is 3m x 2/6 etc.

Sum of digits – interest allocation (and proof of interest allocation)

Accounting Year	**1**	**2**	**3**
	€million	**€million**	**€million**
Opening balance	18.0	12.5	6.5
Interest (add)	1.5 (=3m x 3/6)	1.0 (=3m x 2/6)	0.5 (=3m x 1/6)
Repayment (lease rental)	(7.0)	(7.0)	(7.0)
Closing balance	12.5	6.5	0.0

Sum of digits – present value calculation of finance lease

Time	**0 €million**	**1 €million**	**2 €million**	**3 €million**	**4 €million**
Calculation of tax shield based on accounting figures:					
Depreciation	0	(6.25)	(6.25)	(6.25)	(6.25)
Implicit interest	0	(1.5)	(1.0)	(0.5)	0
Total eligible for tax relief	0	(7.75)	(7.25)	(6.75)	(6.25)
Cash flows:					
Tax relief at 30%	0	2.33	2.17	2.03	1.87
Finance lease	(7.0)	(7.0)	(7.0)	(7.0)	0
Total cash flows	(7.0)	(4.67)	(4.83)	(4.97)	1.87
DF @5%	1.000	0.952	0.907	0.864	0.823
DCF	(7.0)	(4.45)	(4.38)	(4.29)	1.54
Present value	(18.6)				

(Which gives the same result as that obtained using the actuarial method)

On the basis of the present value analysis, there is a marginal benefit from choosing alternative 1, giving a relatively small saving of approximately €200,000. However, this is small in relation to the size of the project and other factors may have a greater impact on the choice of financing structure.

Requirement (a)(ii)

The two main possible discount rates to consider are:

- The cost of capital to the entity (which has presumably been used to evaluate the decision to acquire the POS) or
- The cost of the next best alternative means of finance (here, bank borrowings).

The discount rate that should be used in financing decisions is the opportunity cost. Finance leases are considered a direct substitute for borrowing, the opportunity cost of leasing is the after-tax cost of borrowing.

Requirement (a)(iii)

- Consideration must be given as to how or when the borrowings are to be repaid if alternative 1 is chosen.
- Tax benefits appear to have a significant influence on the decision; a sensitivity analysis should be carried out to determine the impact on the decision if tax rates or regulations change.

Requirement (b)

The main purpose of a PCA:

A post-completion audit (PCA) can be defined as "an objective and independent appraisal of all phases of the capital expenditure process as it relates to a specific project". The main purposes include: project control; improving the investment process; and assisting the assessment of performance of future projects.

A major requirement of a PCA is that the objectives of the investment project must be clear and an adequate investment proposal should have been prepared. The objectives should also be stated, wherever possible, in terms that are measurable. If these have not been done before the POS system was acquired then a PCA is not possible.

The PCA should provide a source of information that will help future management decision making and should include an assessment of the reasons for any variance from the expected performance, cost and time outcomes. This should improve project control and governance and enable changes to be introduced to put the project back on track in a timely manner.

The key factors of importance of a PCA to AB:

- It enables a check to be made on whether the performance of the system corresponds with the expected results. If this is not the case, the reasons should be sought. This could form the basis for improvements in development of the system.
- It generates information, which allows an appraisal to be made of the managers who took the decision to upgrade the system. Managers will therefore tend to arrive at more realistic estimates of the advantages and disadvantages of the proposed investments.
- It can provide for better project planning in the future. If, in the evaluation, it is found that the planning of the investment programme was poor, provision can be made to ensure that it is better for future acquisitions.

The limitations of a PCA to AB in the context of the POS system:

- Sufficient resources are often not allocated to the task of completing PCAs so often are not undertaken.
- They can be time consuming and costly to complete.
- They are sometimes seen as tools for apportioning blame, so even where undertaken the lessons are often not disseminated and are not then embedded in future projects. If undertaken by the managers of the project, they may claim credit for all that went well and blame external factors for everything that did not.

Answer to Question Three

Requirement (a)

The scenario in this question concerns a privately owned entity based in a holiday destination. Inflation is near zero and interest rates are expected to fall. The treasury department needs to decide how to deal with the challenges and opportunities the specific set of circumstances provide and evaluate the impact on the entity's capital structure.

Finance theory suggests that entities should use a certain amount of debt in their capital structure to lower the cost of capital. Debt is cheaper than equity because interest payments (usually) attract tax relief and expected returns are lower. This is because interest is (usually) secured and providers of debt do not participate in profits. Here we have a mixture of secured and unsecured debt, but the entity appears sound and of high credit worthiness so should be able to borrow at comparatively favourable rates.

This might even be an argument in favour of increasing gearing which will provide the ability to undertake a share buyback, as seems to be the desire of the major, family shareholders.

The opposite argument is that in a period of low and falling interest rates, fixed rate debt becomes a burden. Some of the reasons are as follows:

- The real value of debt is not being eroded when there is low or no inflation, so one of the benefits of debt disappears.
- If growth is expected to be modest, debt interest may have to be paid out of static (or even falling) profits, lowering returns to shareholders.
- Although nominal interest rates may fall, they never become negative, so the real cost of borrowing increases.

Raising equity is safer if profits are falling as dividends do not have to be paid and the shareholders do not get their money back in a liquidation. However, raising new equity in a private entity is more difficult than in a public entity and this method of raising new capital raises many additional issues such as whether to plan for a public listing or a rights issue and how to value the shares.

In theory (according to Modigliani and Miller), the mix of debt and equity does not affect the value of the entity, other than the value of the tax shield, but it does have an effect on the attribution of profits to three groups of stakeholders: lenders, government and owners (shareholders).

The main issue for the treasury department to decide is what combination of dividend policy and capital structure is likely to maximise the present value of cash flows to shareholders. This is where the financing strategies adopted contribute to the determination of the objectives of the entity.

The treasury department needs to specifically:

- Look at the terms of existing borrowing to see if refinancing at lower rates is feasible, recognising any possible penalties for early retirement of loans.
- Discuss with the major shareholders the possibility (or even probability) that returns are likely to be lower; the lower the rate of interest, the lower the cost of capital and therefore the lower the returns that can be expected.

Requirement (b)

Theory supports the Finance Director, suggesting that maximisation of shareholder wealth is the only true objective of the entity but this is now considered an extreme view. Many entities now establish objectives that aim to maximise shareholder wealth while recognising constraints, legally enforceable or voluntary, imposed by society. A major problem with this objective in the circumstances of CD is that this is a private entity that does not have a quoted share price. Shareholder wealth, as traditionally valued, is difficult to determine.

In addition, although dividend levels may have no direct impact on shareholder wealth, there may well be private family shareholders who rely on a steady and predictable dividend stream from entity CD.

Looking only at dividends as an objective has its limitations, for example dividends could increase while earnings fall. The dividend ratio therefore needs to be considered alongside dividend payout. Other objectives mentioned such as profitability as measured by returns after tax and return on investment have some advantages. For example they are well understood measures and recognised guidelines are available in the form of International Accounting Standards. Also, shareholders expect and understand profitability.

Disadvantages of accounting-based measures include:

- They are historic and backward-looking;
- They can be subject to manipulation;
- A variety of accounting policies are available – even within Accounting Standards;
- Tax can be affected by factors outside the control of managers;
- They do not take account of non-financial objectives.

Recommendation

Maximisation of shareholder wealth, using the theoretical definition, is difficult to apply in the circumstances of CD. However, it would be worth introducing an objective that incorporates earnings growth as well as dividend growth.

A range of objectives could be considered, such as risk-related returns to investors, but again this is more difficult with a private entity than one with a share listing.

The entity needs to consult its shareholders and, possibly, consider using a balanced scorecard approach to determine a range of objectives appropriate for an entity such as CD.

Answer to Question Four

Requirement (a)

Forecast income statements for the years ended 31 December

	2009	2010	2011
	£000	*£000*	*£000*
Revenue	*45,000*	46,800	48,672
Purchase costs and expenses	*(38,250)*	(39,780)	(41,371)
Depreciation	*0*	(500)	(500)
Profit before finance costs	*6,750*	6,520	6,801
Less: Interest on long term debt	*(450)*	(450)	(450)
Profit before tax	*6,300*	6,070	6,351
Tax @ 28% (see note)	*(1,764)*	(1,490)	(1,656)
Profit after tax (earnings)	*4,536*	4,580	4,695
Dividends declared and paid	*(1,814)*	(1,905)	(2,000)
Retained earnings for year	*2,722*	2,675	2,695

Examiner's Note: the question did not require candidates to show the figures for 2009, they are shown here in italics for convenience.

Tax depreciation allowances:

Cost of vehicles	5,000
2010 WDA @ 25%	(1,250)
Written Down Value	3,750
2011 WDA @ 25%	(938)
Written Down Value	2,812

Note: Tax is calculated on profit before tax and depreciation less capital allowances:

2010	(6,070 + 500 - 1,250) x 28%	=	1,490
2011	(6,351 + 500 - 938) x 28%	=	1,656

Examiner's note: it was not intended that candidates should consider the impact of deferred taxation in their answer here. Credit was available for those who did so.

Requirement (b)

Cash flow forecasts for 2010 and 2011

Calculations of cash receivable and cash payable:

	2010	2011
	£000	*£000*
Revenue	46,800	48,672
O/B trade receivables	13,500	14,040
C/B trade receivables at 30% (13,500/45,000 x 100)	(14,040)	(14,602)
Cash receivable	46,260	48,110
Costs and expenses	39,780	41,371
O/B trade payables	8,415	8,752
C/B trade payables (at 22% of costs and expenses = 8,415/38,250 x 100)	(8,752)	(9,102)
Cash payable	39,443	41,021

Cash flow forecasts

	2010 *£000*		*2011* *£000*	
Cash received from sales		46,260		48,110
Costs and expenses	39,443		41,021	
Vehicles	5,000		0	
Tax	1,490		1,656	
Dividends	1,905		2,000	
Interest	450		450	
Total outflows		(48,288)		(45,127)
Net cash flows		(2,028)		2,983
Opening cash balance		348		(1,680)
Closing cash balance		(1,680)		1,303

An alternative, equally acceptable, approach to presenting the cash flow forecasts is as follows. Note that IAS7 allows for some discretion in the presentation format of cash flow statements. The question here required a forecast rather than a published statement and any sensible format gained credit.

	2010 *£000*	*2011* *£000*
Operations		
Profit before financing costs	6,520	6,801
Add back depreciation	500	500
Change in receivables	(540)	(562)
Change in payables	337	350
Subtotal	6,817	7,089
Interest paid	(450)	(450)
Taxation	(1,490)	(1,656)
Net cash flows from operations	4,877	4,983
Investments		
New vehicles	(5,000)	0
Financing		
Dividends paid	(1,905)	(2,000)
Total net cash flows	(2,028)	2,983
Opening cash balance	348	(1,680)
Closing cash balance	(1,680)	1,303

There is need to finance a cash shortfall of £1,680,000 by the end of 2010. Of course, if the vehicles are bought early in 2010, there may well be a requirement to finance a much greater cash shortfall earlier in the year. There is insufficient information in the question to comment further on this. By the end of 2011 there is a positive cash balance of £1,303,000 by just over half way through the year (if cash flows are spread more or less evenly throughout the year). If sales increase as forecast the cash balance is likely to become positive earlier.

As the shortfall is caused by the purchase of new assets, there should be no problem increasing the overdraft limit given the size of the entity and the relatively short period of time this facility is needed. Other possibilities include supplier credit or short-term leasing.

It could be argued that as these are long term assets they should be funded by long-term finance but the amount is relatively small compared to the value of the entity.

A problem that needs to be addressed is the disparity between the ratio of trade receivables to sales and trade payable to purchase costs & expenses. The former is 30% and the latter 22%. However a breakdown between cost of sales and operating expenses is necessary to analyse the problem further.

Requirement (c)

Key aspects and implications

Preliminary calculations:

	2009	*2010*	*2011*
	£000	£000	£000
Total equity:			
Share capital	4,204	4,204	4,204
Retained earnings	16,210	18,885	21,580
Total equity	20,414	23,089	25,784
Return on shareholders' funds	22.2%	19.8%	18.2%
EPS – pence	27.0	27.2	27.9
% increase	-	0.7	2.6
DPS – pence	10.8	11.3	11.9

Return on shareholders' funds:

EF met this objective in 2009 but narrowly falls short in 2010 and the ratio declines even further in 2011. The new assets might begin to contribute to an improvement but they are clearly replacement assets for an existing facility and as such are unlikely to have a significant impact.

The management of working capital needs to be addressed as noted above.

Investment and financing:

No investment appraisal appears to have been carried out for the purchase of the new assets. This should be done before the investment is made, even though the entity appears more than capable of funding the purchase.

Increase in earnings:

The increase in earnings is well below EF's target for 2010 and 2011 but is moving in the right direction. The main impact in 2010 was the sudden increase in depreciation (although there was a tax benefit as tax depreciation allowances were higher than book depreciation). EF needs to examine its costs and expenses as these are increasing in line with sales. There might be scope for reducing costs by reviewing its suppliers and/or terms of trade, and possible elimination of some expenses.

Dividends:

DPS are growing at 5% as per the scenario. If earnings increase in the future at the target rate of 8% then this implies EF will build up its retained earnings for future investment (assuming finance is available). The entity should perhaps review its dividend policy in the light of investment opportunities.

Key assumption regarding overdraft interest:

The removal of the simplifying assumption regarding overdraft interest can be expected to have a significant effect on forecast cash flows after tax. Indeed, the increase in earnings that is observed above is so small that an increase in overdraft interest in 2010 could reduce earnings to the point at which earnings actually decline in 2010 from 2009 levels.

I would advise the compilation of a more accurate calculation of overdraft interest (or deposit interest if there is a positive cash balance) and the associated tax benefit (or tax expense). This would involve identifying the timing of large items such as tax and dividend cash flows in order to calculate an average cash balance for each year. An estimate of overdraft interest or deposit interest could then be calculated based on that average cash balance and an assumed average overdraft or deposit rate. Note that any overdraft or deposit interest and associated tax cash flows will affect the closing cash balance for the year and therefore also impact on average cash balance and interest and tax cash flows in the following year.

Index

Index

Index